Law and Consent

Consent is used in many different social and legal contexts with the pervasive understanding that it is, and has always been, about autonomy – but has it?

Beginning with an overview of consent's role in law today, this book investigates the doctrine's inseparable association with personal autonomy and its effect in producing both idealised and demonised forms of personhood and agency. This prompts a search for alternative understandings of consent. Through an exploration of sexual offences in Antiquity, medical practice in the Middle Ages, and the regulation of bodily harm on the present-day sports field, this book demonstrates that, in contrast to its common sense story of autonomy, consent more often operates as an act of submission than as a form of personal freedom or agency. The book explores the implications of this counter-narrative for the law's contemporary uses of consent, arguing that the kind of freedom consent is meant to enact might be foreclosed by the very frame in which we think about autonomy itself.

This book will be of interest to scholars of many aspects of law, history, and feminism as well as students of criminal law, bioethics, and political theory.

Karla M. O'Regan is an Associate Professor of Criminology and Criminal Justice at St. Thomas University, Canada.

Law and Consent

Contesting the Common Sense

Karla M. O'Regan

Routledge
Taylor & Francis Group
LONDON AND NEW YORK

First published 2020 by Routledge

2 Park Square, Milton Park, Abingdon, Oxon, OX14 4RN
605 Third Avenue, New York, NY 10017

Routledge is an imprint of the Taylor & Francis Group, an informa business

First issued in paperback 2020

British Library Cataloguing-in-Publication Data
A catalogue record for this book is available from the British Library

Library of Congress Cataloging-in-Publication Data
Names: O'Regan, M. Karla, author.
Title: Law and consent: contesting the common sense /
Karla M. O'Regan.
Description: New York, NY : Routledge, 2019. | Includes index.
Identifiers: LCCN 2019013333 (print) | LCCN 2019013388 (ebook) |
ISBN 9780429465017 (ebk) | ISBN 9781138612501 (hbk)
Subjects: LCSH: Consent (Law)
Classification: LCC K5087.C6 (ebook) |
LCC K5087.C6 O74 2019 (print) | DDC 346.01—dc23
LC record available at https://lccn.loc.gov/2019013333

ISBN: 978-1-138-61250-1 (hbk)
ISBN: 978-0-367-78563-5 (pbk)

Typeset in Galliard
by codeMantra

For JR

Contents

Acknowledgements

This book is based on my doctoral dissertation at the London School of Economics, which would not have been possible without research funding from the School's Law Department and the 'reckless confidence' of my doctoral supervisor, Susan Marks. I am grateful for the kind and insightful direction she offered this project. Many others supported this project in its early stages, in particular Nicola Lacey and Jill Peay. I am also indebted to Emily Jackson and Alain Pottage, who were charitable readers at a time when the work was far from clear, and to Linda Mulcahy and Lindsay Farmer, whose generous and careful work as examiners enriched my reflections on what this book could be.

I owe a great deal of thanks to my home institution, St. Thomas University, which granted me a leave of absence to pursue my doctoral work and a sabbatical to write the book. My departmental colleagues have been a constant source of encouragement, in particular Claire Goggin, Susan Reid, Michael Boudreau, and Dawne Clarke. I am also thankful for my students, who keep me curious about law and its possibilities, and grateful for the 'Jenns' (Gorham and Richard) of the Fredericton Sexual Assault Centre, whose graceful tenacity keeps me hopeful for change.

A number of scholars were very generous with their work, including Clare Morgana Gillis, Hilary Young, Annette Houlihan, and Michael Thomson. I am also grateful to the editorial and production teams at Routledge, who have both supported and improved this work in its preparation for publication, particularly Colin Perrin, Nicola Sharpe, and Nazrine Azeez and her team at codeMantra. I also owe a great debt to Elizabeth Matheson, for her excellent work assembling the book's index, and to St. Thomas University's Senate Research Committee for funds to support her Research Assistantship.

Many friends, neighbours, and colleagues have been instrumental in getting me to the finish line, some by reading drafts or simply asking for progress reports, others by offering their homes, baked goods, senses of humour, or hockey expertise. Many others are wonderfully adept at brewing tea and lifting pints (and spirits). For this and much more, I am grateful for Roxana and Zach Atkinson, Rachel and Clarence Bennett, Tania Breen, Helen Brown Coverdale, Kathy and Gus Chan, Mary Coady, Tanya Duffy and Greg Webber, Fred and Lois Horsley, Russ and Anne Hunt, Moon Joyce, Heather Kelly, Rob Knox,

Martha Kolls and Mark Schram, Brad Lemon, Katie MacDonald, Patrick and Sylvia Malcolmson, Karolyn Martin, Ewan McGaughey, George McIntyre, Tricia Morris, Thom Parkhill and Pat Sikes, Eric and Sherry Price, Christa and Darren Priest, Matt Richardson, AJ Ripley and Jess Webster, the Belching Lasses, CBC Radio, and Nice Guy Graeme Walker. My family has been a constant source of support and encouragement. For this and a great deal else, I thank and love you: Mom, Dad, Stephen, Joan, Emily, Jamie, Bailey, Rylan, Hope, Bill, Mark, and Devon.

And to the pack: I write this amidst the snores of two very old cats and one very new puppy, while JR keeps a dinner he made for us warm on the stove. He is owed the greatest of my gratitude, for his warmth and tireless patience, unflappable kindness, and stellar mix tapes. He flew across the world with me (and back again) so I could write this, never once doubting that I would. It is to him that this book is dedicated. Stuff and nonsense, my love, and a road without end.

List of abbreviations

Acc Bus Finan Hist	Accounting, Business, and Financial History
AJPhil	American Journal of Philology
Akron LR	Akron Law Review
Alt LJ	Alternative Law Journal
Am Behav Sci	American Behavioral Scientist
Am Crim L Rev	American Criminal Law Review
Am Econ Rev	American Economic Review
Am Hist Rev	American Historical Review
Am J Bioeth	American Journal of Bioethics
Am J Econ & Soc	American Journal of Economics & Sociology
Am J Soc	American Journal of Sociology
Am Studies J	American Studies Journal
Ann R Coll Surg Engl	Annals of the Royal College of Surgeons of England
Ariz St LJ	Arizona State Law Journal
BCL Rev	Boston College Law Review
Book Psychoanal	Book of Psychoanalysis
BMJ	British Medical Journal
Body Soc	Body & Society
Bull Hist Med	Bulletin of the History of Medicine
Bull NY Acad Med	Bulletin of the New York Academy of Medicine
Cancer Pract	Cancer Practice
CCC	Canadian Criminal Cases
CCLR	Canadian Criminal Law Review
Can J L & Soc	Canadian Journal of Law & Society
Cdn J Phil	Canadian Journal of Philosophy
CJWL	Canadian Journal of Women & the Law
Clin Eth	Clinical Ethics
CLJ	Cambridge Law Journal
CLP	Current Legal Problems
CLQ	Criminal Law Quarterly
CMAJ	Canadian Medical Association Journal
Colum J Gen & L	Columbia Journal of Gender & Law

Colum J Transnat'l L	Columbia Journal of Transnational Law
Colum L Rev	Columbia Law Review
Comm Q	Communication Quarterly
Conn L Rev	Connecticut Law Review
CPhil	Classical Philology
CQ	Classical Quarterly
CR	Criminal Reports
Crim Law	Criminal Lawyer
Crim LR	Criminal Law Review
Crit Inq	Critical Inquiry
Crit Stud Mass Comm	Critical Studies in Mass Communication
Cult Health & Sex	Culture, Health & Sexuality
CUP	Cambridge University Press
CWS	Canadian Woman Studies
D&S	Discourse & Society
Econ & Soc	Economy & Society
EJPR	European Journal for Philosophy of Religion
Eth Med & Pub H	Ethics, Medicine & Public Health
Fem & Psych	Feminism & Psychology
Fouc Stud	Foucault Studies
G & R	Greece & Rome
Geo Wash L Rev	George Washington Law Review
GH Psych	General Hospital Psychiatry
Harv Educ Rev	Harvard Educational Review
Harv Health Pol Rev	Harvard Health Policy Review
Harv J Law & Gen	Harvard Journal of Law & Gender
Harv LR	Harvard Law Review
Hastings WLJ	Hastings Women's Law Journal
Health LJ	Health Law Journal
Health Soc Care Comm	Health & Social Care in the Community
HIV/AIDS Pol Law Rev	HIV/AIDS Policy & Law Review
Hous LR	Houston Law Review
HUP	Harvard University Press
Ind LJ	Indiana Law Journal
Int CLR	International Criminal Law Review
Int Rev Soci Sport	International Review for the Sociology of Sport
Iowa Orthop J	Iowa Orthopedic Journal
IRB: Eth Hum Res	IRB: Ethics and Human Research
Irish J Med Sci	Irish Journal of Medical Science
JAMA	Journal of the American Medical Association
J Amer Folk	Journal of American Folklore
JCL	Journal of Criminal Law
J Doc	Journal of Documentation
J Fem Sch	Journal of Feminist Scholarship
JHUP	Johns Hopkins University Press

J Hist Med	Journal of the History of Medicine
J Hist Med Allied Sci	Journal of the History of Medicine and Allied Sciences
JISHIM	Journal of the International Society for the History of Islamic Medicine
JL & Health	Journal of Law & Health
JLM&E	Journal of Law, Medicine & Ethics
J Med Eth	Journal of Medical Ethics
J Med & Phil	Journal of Medicine & Philosophy
J Moral Phil	Journal of Moral Philosophy
J Phil	Journal of Philology
JPHS	Journal of Psychology & Human Sexuality
J Pol	Journal of Politics
J Pol Phil	Journal of Political Philosophy
J Pos Sex	Journal of Positive Sexuality
J Rel Eth	Journal of Religious Ethics
J Sex Res	Journal of Sex Research
J Soc	Journal of Sociology
J Sport Soc Iss	Journal of Sport and Social Issues
JSWFL	Journal of Social Welfare & Family Law
Jur Rev	Juridical Review
JWCI	Journal of the Warburg & Courtauld Institutes
LEG	Legal Theory
Man LJ	Manitoba Law Journal
Med Hist	Medical History
Med LR	Medical Law Review
Me L Rev	Maine Law Review
Mich LR	Michigan Law Review
Miss Sports LR	Mississippi Sports Law Review
MJLH	McGill Journal of Law & Health
MLR	Modern Law Review
MULR	Melbourne University Law Review
NCLR	New Criminal Law Review
NE J Med	New England Journal of Medicine
New Left Rev	New Left Review
NLJ	New Law Journal
Oxford Stud Ancient Philos	Oxford Studies in Ancient Philosophy
OUP	Oxford University Press
P&P	Past & Present
PELJ	Potchefstroom Electronic Law Journal
Phil Persp	Philosophical Perspectives
Pol Theory	Political Theory
Proc Aristotelian Soc	Proceedings of the Aristotelian Society
Pun & Soc	Punishment & Society
Psychol Sci	Psychological Science

PUP	Princeton University Press
Qual Inq	Qualitative Inquiry
Read Mediev Stud	Reading Medieval Studies
S & LS	Social & Legal Studies
SA Med J	South African Medical Journal
SCR	Supreme Court Reports
Seton Hall J S&EL	Seton Hall Journal of Sports & Entertainment Law
Sex & RT	Sexual & Relationship Therapy
Sex Res & Soc Pol	Sexuality Research & Social Policy
Soc Anth	Social Anthropology
Soc Health & Illness	Sociology of Health & Illness
Soc Hist Med	Social History of Medicine
Soc Sci Info	Social Science Information
Soc Sci Med	Social Science & Medicine
Sport Educ Soc	Sport, Education, and Society
St John's J Legal Comm	St. John's Journal of Legal Commentary
SUP	Stanford University Press
Theo Crim	Theoretical Criminology
Theo Med	Theoretical Medicine
Theory Soc	Theory & Society
Trans Am Philos Soc	Transactions of the American Philosophical Society
Tul LR	Tulane Law Review
UBC L Rev	University of British Columbia Law Review
UCalP	University of California Press
UCHIP	University of Chicago Press
U Ill L Rev	University of Illinois Law Review
U Miami L Rev	University of Miami Law Review
U Pa L Rev	University of Pennsylvania Law Review
UTMJ	University of Toronto Medical Journal
VAW	Violence Against Women
Waikato LR	Waikato Law Review
Wm & Mary Bill Rts J	William & Mary Bill of Rights Journal
World J Surg	World Journal of Surgery
Yale J L & Fem	Yale Journal of Law & Feminism

Introduction

Everyone is talking about consent. Public discourse surrounding the high-profile sexual assault trial of Bill Cosby (or Jian Ghomeshi, or Harvey Weinstein, or far too many others) has brought words like 'rape culture' and 'slut shaming' to dinner tables and locker rooms alike. Never before has there been such public awareness and widespread condemnation of the harmful myths and stereotypes that have long plagued victims of sexual violence. Within an era of an increasing number of #MeToo sexual harassment stories, many have questioned whether this is a 'watershed moment' for feminism,[1] if not a shift in the 'common sense'.

But what is the new common sense of consent? Rates of sexual assault on university and college campuses have reached historic highs.[2] Crimes of sexual violence remain the highest under-reported offences *everywhere* (and by a wide margin). The 2017 release of the *Globe & Mail*'s 20-month long investigative report on Canadian police forces revealed that officers disbelieve one in every five reports of sexual assault – an unfounded rate more than *ten times* that of any other offence.[3] News headlines and academic articles alike have asked 'how drunk is too drunk to consent?',[4] while videos featuring the rapes of unconscious

1 Lara Bazelon, 'Is 2016 a Watershed Moment for Women?' *Politico Magazine* (13 October 2016). <www.politico.com/magazine/story/2016/10/2016-sexual-assault-allegations-watershed-moment-for-women-214355> accessed 31 January 2019. See also Sarah Barmak, 'What Consent Means in the Age of #MeToo' (2018) 15(2) *The Walrus* 30.

2 Sara Carrigan Wooten and Roland W Mitchell (eds), *The Crisis of Campus Sexual Violence: Critical Perspectives on Prevention and Response* (Routledge 2016).

3 Robyn Doolittle, 'Unfounded: Why Police Dismiss 1 in 5 Sexual Assault Claims as Baseless' *Globe & Mail* (Toronto, 3 February 2017) F2.

4 Anna Carline, Clare Gunby and Stuart Taylor, 'Too Drunk to Consent? Exploring the Contestations and Disruptions in Male-focused Sexual Violence Prevention Interventions' (2017) 20(10) *S & LS* 1. See also Claire Brownell, 'How Drunk Is Too Drunk to Consent? Legally, There's No Clear Answer' *Windsor Star* (Windsor, 6 June 2013) <https://windsorstar.com/news/sexual-assaultintoxication-feature> accessed 6 December 2018; and Mallika Viegas, 'Capacity for Consent: Two Cases Renew the Debate Over When Someone Is Too Drunk to Consent' (*Vice News Canada*, 3 March 2017) <https://news.vice.com/story/when-is-someone-legally-too-drunk-to-consent> accessed 3 December 2018.

women regularly go viral.[5] The non-consensual sharing of intimate photographs by jilted ex-lovers has become so commonplace that the practice has earned itself a (troubling) new name: revenge porn. And for the first time in history, the televised debates for the 2016 U.S. presidential race (dubbed the 'sexual assault election' by the *New Yorker*)[6] featured questions about sexual consent. Weeks later, the world watched the inauguration of a man who had boasted on the campaign trail about sexually touching women without their permission.[7] If consent's common sense is shifting, just what is it shifting to?

This seems an important question, particularly when it comes to the cultural understandings and legal uses of consent – a concept that is not limited to the realm of sexual violence. Debates about the appropriate scope of a player's consent to injury have taken centre field as sports leagues have been accused of failing to adequately protect players from the physical effects of the game. Mounting medical evidence that in-game head injuries result in long-term brain disorders and player deaths has led to the largest class action settlement in sports history – a billion-dollar payout to National Football League (NFL) players suffering from game-induced concussions.[8] Many other class action suits remain outstanding, while professional sports leagues continue to argue that these injuries are simply part of a player's *choice* to play the game.

The scope of the freedom to choose has also been tested in medical circles. Informed consent has long been required for the delivery of services, but do doctors need it before withdrawing treatment? In 2013, the Supreme Court of Canada said 'yes', bringing both the ethical and legal obligations of physicians – particularly with patients in non-responsive states – under the microscope.[9] (How unconscious is too unconscious to consent?) The introduction of assisted dying legislation in a number of places around the world (including Canada, four European countries, and six American states)[10] has launched global discussions about whether the right to life includes the freedom to die. At the heart of these

5 Cressida J Heyes, 'Dead to the World: Rape, Unconsciousness, and Social Media' (2016) 41(2) *Signs* 361. See also Kelly Oliver, 'Rape as Spectator Sport and Creepshot Entertainment: Social Media and the Valorization of Lack of Consent' (2016) 10 *Am Studies J* 61.

6 Jeannie Suk Gersen, 'The Sexual-Assault Election' *The New Yorker* (6 November 2016). <www.newyorker.com/news/news-desk/the-sexual-assault-election> accessed 3 December 2018.

7 Tim Wallace and Alicia Parlapiano, 'Crowd Scientists Say Women's March in Washington Had 3 Times as Many People as Trump's Inauguration' *New York Times* (22 January 2017). <www.nytimes.com/interactive/2017/01/22/us/politics/womens-march-trump-crowd-estimates.html> accessed 31 January 2019.

8 Ken Belson, 'After NFL Concussion Settlement, Feeding Frenzy of Lawyers and Lenders' *New York Times* (New York, 16 July 2017) <www.nytimes.com/2017/07/16/sports/football/nfl-concussion-settlement-lawyers.html> accessed 31 January 2019. The NHL settled a similar class action with 300 retired players in 2018 for 18.9 million U.S. dollars.

9 *Cuthbertson v Rasouli* 2013 SCC 53.

10 Nataly Papadopoulou, 'Assisted-dying Laws are Progressing in Some Places – The UK Isn't One of Them' *Independent* (London, 15 April 2017) <www.independent.co.uk/news/health/assisted-dying-laws-are-progressing-in-some-places-the-uk-isn-t-one-of-them-a7679846.html> accessed 31 January 2019.

debates lies consent – poked and prodded by doctors, judges, moralists, philosophers, and economists. (Presumably there are some patients in there too, but it's hard to make them out in the crowd.)

Consent is everywhere. Moreover, it is tasked with doing some very significant things in both law and life. It determines when property has been equitably traded, bodily contact lawfully made, and levels of personal integrity and cognitive awareness adequately reached. It serves as a gatekeeper for privacy rights and a flak jacket for legal gunfire. Consent is a central factor in the regulation of relationships, the establishment of political communities, and the constitution of legal personhood. In socio-legal contexts, the boundaries of consent (to bodily harm, for instance) delimit what's 'normal'. For political theorists, it is the very foundation for legitimate state authority.

Despite these varied and consequential uses, there is very little precision in law about just what consent *is*. It is described as a doctrine, device, defence, excuse, justification, process, signifier, capacity, and even a form of 'moral magic',[11] and it is used in as vast an array of applications as the diversity of law allows, including contract, tort, criminal, medical, family, property, and constitutional and administrative law, among others. As Peter Westen, author of *The Logic of Consent*, has noted, 'consent is a protean concept that takes diverse and shifting shapes depending upon the context'.[12] In this way, consent operates in law with what H.L.A. Hart described as an 'open texture', akin to how one might be familiar enough with a town to have put its roads and routes to memory 'without being able to draw a map of it'.[13] Consent's 'familiarity' is often noted explicitly in legal scholarship, particularly in accounts of its content or meaning. As Westen states at the onset of *The Logic of Consent*: 'To be sure, we all have a general sense of what consent means [citing a dictionary definition]. Beyond that, however, we have only vague and conflicting notions of what we mean by consent'.[14] This 'call to the familiar' in the law's approach to defining consent establishes a 'common sense' about what it means, signifies, and does: no one knows what consent is because *everyone* knows what consent is. Considered alongside its definitional elusiveness, this grants consent a contradictory status in law. It has both a 'shifting content' and a straightforward, universal meaning.

This contradictory status allows consent to act as a 'joker card', serving fairly different purposes depending on the context and way in which it is used. Legal assessments of the capacity for consent, for example, have been affected by one's

11 Heidi Hurd, 'The Moral Magic of Consent' (1992) 2(2) *LEG* 121.

12 Peter Westen, *The Logic of Consent: The Diversity and Deceptiveness of Consent as a Defense to Criminal Conduct* (Routledge 2004) vii.

13 Herbert LA Hart, 'Analytical Jurisprudence in Mid-Twentieth Century: A Reply to Professor Bodenheimer' (1957) 105 *U Pa L Rev* 953, 956–957. Hart is not referring explicitly to consent in this piece but rather to a variety of legal concepts which he felt were approached with a certain ambiguity – something he suggests is a consequence of analytical jurisprudence itself.

14 Westen (n 12) 3.

sexual orientation,[15] marital status,[16] and religious affiliations or beliefs.[17] The decisions of bipolar patients (including one who claimed to speak regularly with extra-terrestrials) to discontinue treatment have been upheld by the same courts which have determined Jehovah's Witness patients to lack the capacity for consent (and thus treatment refusal) on the basis that their judgment was impaired by the 'undue influence' of their religious community.[18] Importantly, these unstated norms are concealed by consent's paradoxical status as integral, undefinable, and already known. The content of consent is left to presumptions about its 'common sense' meaning of personal autonomy and free action.[19] This book seeks to interrogate this claim of clarity. What is achieved when the meaning of consent is positioned as a matter of 'common sense'? What does this apparent transparency keep obscure?[20]

Law and consent: a tale of contradictions

Consent is conventionally approached in socio-legal scholarship in one of three ways. The first might be described as a standardisation project where a description of consent's internal 'logic' or a set of guiding principles about its operation in a given field is sought so as to determine when consent is 'found' and what circumstances might serve to vitiate it.[21] These analyses are often normatively driven, with aims of critiquing and reforming how consent operates in theory[22] or legal

15 See, for instance, the debates and literature surrounding Britain's equalisation of the age of consent for homosexual and heterosexual persons in the 2012 amendments to the Sexual Offences Act 2003.

16 See section 150.1(2.1)(b) of Canada's *Criminal Code*, RSC 1985, C-46.

17 *BH (Next friend of) v Alberta (Director of Child Welfare)* 2002 ABQB 371.

18 See *Starson v Swayze* [2003] 1 SCR 722 and *BH* (n 17), respectively.

19 That is, where academic treatments and uses of 'consent' offer an examination of its meaning – most don't. See, for example, Terry Humphreys and Ed Herold, 'Should Universities and Colleges Mandate Sexual Behavior? Student Perceptions of Antioch College's Consent Policy' (2003) 15 *J Psych & Hum Sex* 35; Catherine Elliott and Claire De Than, 'The Case for a Rational Reconstruction of Consent in Criminal Law' (2007) 70 *MLR* 225. Similar sources are also identified by Melanie A Beres, '"Spontaneous" Sexual Consent: An Analysis of Sexual Consent Literature' (2007) 17(1) *Fem & Psych* 93. Notable exceptions include Pamela Haag, *Consent: Sexual Rights and the Transformation of American Liberalism* (Cornell University Press 1999); Mark Cowling and Paul Reynolds (eds), *Making Sense of Sexual Consent* (Ashgate 2004).

20 These questions are versions of those asked by Judith Butler in her 1999 Preface to *Gender Trouble: Feminism and the Subversion of Identity*, where she suggests '[t]he demand for lucidity forgets the ruses that motor the ostensibly 'clear' view … What travels under the sign of 'clarity'? …Who devises the protocols of 'clarity' and whose interests do they serve?' (10th ann edn, Routledge 1999) xix.

21 See Westen (n 12) and Cowling and Reynolds (n 19).

22 Rosemary Hunter and Sharon Cowan (eds), *Choice and Consent: Feminist Engagements with Law and Subjectivity* (Routledge 2004); Don Herzog, *Happy Slaves: A Critique of Consent Theory* (UCHIP 1989).

and clinical practice.[23] Second, investigations of consent can take the form of a comparative analysis, where general surveys are conducted of how consent is defined or can be seen to function across diverse areas of its application, often with the similar aim of providing alternatives to these operations.[24] The third approach is the theoretical reconstruction of consent, involving historical accounts,[25] philosophical ontologies,[26] or what some have simply termed 'jurisprudential analysis'.[27]

This book shares some components with each of these three approaches, including the examination of consent as it is used in more than one sub-field of law and the exploration of alternative theoretical accounts of the concept's operations and effects within these fields. This analysis diverges from these investigatory camps, however, in its exploration of consent as an historical artefact rather than a concept with doctrinal, cognitive, or communicative certainty. Instead, this book treats consent as a product of human relations that, in particular historical contexts, has come to house pervasive, truth-telling meanings about human activity and personhood. The book thus moves away from traditional legal inquiries into what is *said* about/in order to consent and considers instead the work that consent itself *does*. Specifically, this investigation begins with three atypical contentions.

First, that a series of unspoken presumptions about what is 'normal' human behaviour, cognitive capacity, communication strategy, and even the core components of recognisable personhood operate within contemporary treatments of consent in all areas of its legal application. Articulations of consent's preconditions in both moral philosophy and law, for example, reflect a foundation in a certain understanding of reason, particularly in terms of which persons or mental states should be excluded from consenting capacity (namely children, the mentally 'impaired', or the 'coerced'). Where the desires, behaviours, or identities of those seeking to give or refuse consent venture too far off the beaten path, the law denies the capacity to consent. Thus the few legislative definitions of consent that exist prioritise certain determinations of capacity that are in alignment with the common sense of consent, that is, informed, voluntary, and rational action. The UK Sexual Offences Act 2003, for instance, defines consent as a matter of agreement by 'choice' where one 'has

23 Robin West, 'Legitimating the Illegitimate: A Comment on *Beyond Rape*' (1992) 93(6) *Colum L Rev* 1442; Peter H Schuck, 'Rethinking Informed Consent' (1994) 103 *Yale LJ* 899; Tom Beauchamp and James F Childress, *Principles of Bioethics* (6th edn, OUP 2008).

24 Karin van Marle, 'The Politics of Consent, Friendship, and Sovereignty' in Hunter and Cowan (n 22); Gideon Calder, 'The Language of Refusal: Sexual Consent and the Limits of Post-structuralism' in Cowling and Reynolds (n 19).

25 Haag (n 19).

26 Brent M Kious, 'The Evidentiary Account of Consent's Moral Significance' (PhD dissertation, University of California 2009).

27 Sharon Cowan, '"Freedom and Capacity to Make a Choice": A Feminist Analysis of Consent in the Criminal Law of Rape' in Vanessa Munro and Carl Stychin (ed) *Sexuality and the Law: Feminist Engagements* (Routledge 2007).

the freedom and capacity to make that choice'.[28] *Black's Law Dictionary* defines consent as an 'agreement, approval, or permission as to some act or purpose, especially given voluntarily by a competent person'.[29] And in their well-regarded delineation of the four basic principles of bioethics, Beauchamp and Childress identify autonomy as foremost, linking it with the Greek etymology of 'self-rule', and manifested as voluntary choice(s) made by a competent, informed, and rational individual.[30] Even where the courts have ruled against the defence on the basis of public policy concerns,[31] the availability of consent hinges on the 'reasonableness' of the defendant's conduct, where the would-be consenter's rationality can be vitiated by the unintelligibility of her actions (eg self-harm or sadomasochistic activities) or the 'unwritten rules of the game'.[32]

Second, this book argues that these unstated norms are both concealed and produced by consent's contradictory status as an undefinable concept that is integral to almost every sphere of human life. As Emily Sherwin has noted, '[i]t is in the nature of law that law can and must determine whether consent has occurred, even if no one is sure just what consent is'.[33] This problem is compounded by a focus within consent jurisprudence on what consent is *not* (eg coercion) rather than on what it *is*.[34] Take, for example, the backgrounders to the consent provisions in the UK Sexual Offences Act 2003, including the Home Office Report, *Setting the Boundaries*,[35] and the White Paper, *Protecting the Public*,[36] which established the government's 'blueprint for legislation'.[37] Despite a declaration that the aim of the statutory revisions was to make consent 'clear and unambiguous', the legislation delineated a set of (rebuttable)

28 Sexual Offences Act 2003 (UK), s 74.

29 Bryan A Garner (ed), *Black's Law Dictionary* (7th edn, West Group 1999) 300.

30 Tom L Beauchamp and James F Childress, *Principles of Biomedical Ethics* (5th edn, OUP 2001) 67.

31 See the English case, *R v Brown* [1993] 2 All ER 75, where the House of Lords did not permit the defence of consent in a case involving sadomasochism given the lack of 'good reason' for the injuries caused. Similar arguments have been accepted in the arena of sporting activities: see the Canadian cases *R v Cey* (1989) 48 CCC 3d 480 (Sask CA), *R v Cicarelli (1989)* 54 CCC 3d 121 (ON Dist Ct), *R v Leclerc* (1991) 67 CCC 3d 563 (ONCA), and the English case *R v Barnes* [2005] 1 Cr App Rep 507. These public policy arguments are subject to a longer discussion in Chapters 4 and 5.

32 See *Cey* (n 31); *Cicarelli* (n 31); *Leclerc* (n 31); and *R v McSorley* [2000] BCPC 117 (all cases arising from assaultive behaviour within the context of an ice hockey game).

33 Emily Sherwin, 'Infelicitious Sex' (1996) 2 *LEG* 209, 229.

34 For example, Pamela Haag suggests two means by which sexual consent is defined and interpreted. First, through an enumeration of the 'parameters, physical conditions, and events' of what constitutes violence; and second, with an emphasis on the self-evident utterances of "yes" or "no". See Haag (n 19). Paul Reynolds makes a marked departure from this approach in his chapter, 'The Quality of Consent' in Cowling and Reynolds (n 19).

35 Home Office, *Setting the Boundaries: Reforming the Law on Sex Offences* (HMSO July 2000).

36 Home Office, *Protecting the Public: Strengthening Protection against Sex Offenders and Reforming the Law on Sexual Offences* (White Paper, Cm 5668, 2002).

37 Jennifer Temkin and Andrew Ashworth, 'The Sexual Offences Act 2003: (1) Rape, Sexual Assaults, and the Problems of Consent' (2004) *Crim LR* 328, 333.

circumstances in which 'non-consent' would be presumed (while maintaining the defence's right to argue that consent still existed).[38] Further, much of the scholarship that does address the content of consent (rather than its negative) – in fields as diverse as neurobiology and philosophy – is concerned with the circumstantial aspects of consent (eg how it is conveyed) rather than its meaning.[39] The content of consent is left to presumptions about its heralded foundations in personal autonomy and free action.

These foundations are often described as the common sense meaning of consent and represent the *third* contention guiding this book: that where attempts to offer definitions of consent do appear, they emerge from and within a discourse which prioritises a certain kind of freedom enacted by or belonging to certain kinds of subjects. This is the basis for the book's central argument: consent's freedom fable is a narrative which forecloses certain forms of personhood or liberty in the name of others, all the while concealing this exclusivity through a pervasive narrative of the doctrine's universality and familiarity. Not only does the story of autonomy that is told about consent obscure the social realities of inequality, difference, and subordination that might threaten a notion of a homogenous citizenry (and thus, governmental action made in its name), but it also conceals the historically specific conditions of existence which have brought consent's common sense story of autonomy into being. In this way, consent's commitment to individualised agency is unassailable, even amidst clear inequality in its application. This constitutes what I describe as the 'consent-as-autonomy story' – a narrative that has gained such widespread adoption that alternative accounts of the meaning of consent are not simply unintelligible, but non-existent.

Consent's autonomy story

While the literature on consent encompasses a wide array of perspectives, the content and scope of consent are delineated using a grammar of rational agency and possessive individualism. In these accounts, consent is configured as autonomy itself or, in the more critical analyses, as an inefficient model for reaching this ideal of self-governance. In both instances, the self-determining individual is maintained (if only, in more critical approaches, with an aim of dismantling it).[40] This can be seen in even the most general summaries or treatments of consent,

38 As Temkin and Ashworth note, this approach required 'that, once the prosecution had established beyond reasonable doubt that one of the listed circumstances existed, the burden of proof would then lie on the defence to prove consent on the balance of probabilities', (n 37) 333. Therefore, in its attempt to make consent as 'clear and unambiguous' as possible, the Sexual Offences Act did not define consent (in any way beyond an 'agreement to make a choice') but instead listed a set of (rebuttable) circumstances in which non-consent could be presumed.

39 Cowling and Reynolds (n 19).

40 See, for instance, Hunter and Cowan's compilation which is organised around an understanding of 'choice and consent as defining attributes of the sovereign, self-interested, masculine, liberal subject' (n 22) 1.

where its substantive content is aligned with the notion of capacity – an ability which, to be recognisable, must be exercised in reasonable or prescribed ways (reminiscent of the 'freedom' of the social contract).

In his text, *The Law of Consent*, Peter W. Young suggests that most legal dictionary offerings on the term 'consent' encircle three central elements, emerging from Fonblanque's eighteenth-century *Treatise on Equality*[41] and delineated in Jowitt's Law Dictionary as 'a physical power, a mental power, and a free and serious use of them'.[42] For consent to be established, these elements are to be employed in 'an act of reason accompanied with deliberation, the mind weighing as in a balance the good or evil on either side'.[43] These components of competency, rational willing, and moral standing are summarised in David Archard's 'Principle of Consensuality', which states that 'a practice, P, is morally permissible if all those who are parties to P are competent to consent, give their valid consent, and the interests of no other parties are significantly harmed'.[44] While Archard notes the need to clarify certain phrases within this general principle (eg 'valid consent' or 'competent'), he does attempt to identify some general conditions about the doctrine which flow from its 'moral significance' and its scope. This moral characteristic within the case law and secondary literature often houses explications of the necessary conditions of transforming an illegitimate transaction or event into a legitimate one, a transformation evoked by Heidi Hurd with the term 'moral magic'.[45] Thus the mere presence of a party's 'willingness' to agree, assent,[46] or acquiesce[47] is insufficient to satisfy consent's normative requirement. This mental state must be enacted (or performed)[48] in contexts and ways which are recognised, at law, as demonstrating a certain form of capacity.

This capacity is presumed, at least in the first instance, to exist in all persons. As a guardian against tyrannical rule and arbitrary exercises of power, Locke envisioned this inalienable right to liberty of each person as both the rationale and the means of state legitimacy, subject to limitation so as to maximise human welfare and prevent (unjustifiable) injury. Law, for Locke, was thus a means of 'confin[ing] the liberty [all persons] had by the Law of Nature'.[49] Yet to ensure

41 Specifically, Book 1, Ch 2, s 1.

42 As cited in Peter W Young, *The Law of Consent* (Law Book Co 1986) 13.

43 Young (n 42) 13.

44 David Archard, *Sexual Consent* (Westview Press 1998) 2.

45 Hurd (n 11).

46 Archard distinguishes between 'consent' and 'assent' by suggesting the former is an agreement *to* a set of conditions whereas the latter is an agreement *with* (n 44) 5. This distinction rests on an understanding of consent as a mental state made manifest (often through action). Other scholars support this view, see Young (n 42) 24.

47 See, for example, West (n 23).

48 See Heid Malm, 'The Ontological Status of Consent and Its Implications for the Law of Rape' (1996) 2 *LEG* 147, where she argues that consent is a 'signifier'.

49 John Locke, *Two Treatises of Government* (first published 1689, Peter Laslett tr, CUP 1963) 2.129, as cited in Kirstie McClure, *Judging Rights: Lockean Politics and the Limits of Consent* (Cornell University Press 1996) 250.

acceptance of these confines and prevent their abuse, liberal understandings of state sovereignty suggest that these limitations must themselves be expressions of freedom, that is, the acts of autonomous subjects. Consent emerges in these treatments as a signification of this autonomy, a means of participating in self-governance, and, as some authors have suggested, a marker of the boundaries of state power.[50]

The subject who is thought to perform consent is the basis for many of the critiques of these accounts of consent-as-autonomy which take issue with the individualistic account of agency and its demand to be 'left alone'. With a view to the social character of human lives and decision-making processes, theories of 'relational' autonomy have emerged which emphasise the need to consider the circumstances and relationships in which choices are made.[51] The difficulty these relational theorists identify with conventional approaches to consent is the equation of autonomy with mere choice.[52] This view, while often associated with the writings of John Stuart Mill, doesn't capture the meaning of Mill's notion of individuality, which required 'persons to "own" or identify with certain desires, to cultivate certain feelings and impulses rather than others, thereby becoming well-developed human beings'.[53] The normative (and exclusive) consequences of this model are easily noted; freedom to choose is limited by the circumstances in which the consenting subject finds herself, a notion hinted at in Slavoj Žižek's critique of the social contract's 'corporatist fantasy' of a homogenous populace.[54] The vision of autonomy as freedom from state interference fails to account for disenfranchised members of a society who do not enjoy the minimal preconditions for political life and, according to some critics, serves to privatise inequality.[55] As Jackson and Sclater have noted, privacy is a sphere of life respected for the space it provides an individual to make choices and self-determine away from 'the critical gaze of others', to the benefit of the socio-economically privileged and the detriment of those that remain.[56] In these instances, some form of state interference is needed to create the conditions for autonomous

50 'It is this notion [of consent] that is usually advanced as the minimal ground for differentiating between a "legitimate" or "acceptable" polity and its tyrannical or despotic counterpart': McClure (n 49) 2. McClure attributes these terms to Martin Seliger in *The Liberal Politics of John Locke* (Frederick Praeger 1969) and John Dunn in *The Political Thought of John Locke: An Historical Account of the Argument of the 'Two Treatises of Government'* (CUP 1969).

51 Jennifer Nedelsky, 'Reconceiving Autonomy: Sources, Thoughts, and Possibilities' (1989) 1 *Yale J L & Fem* 7; Emily Jackson and Shelley Day-Sclater, 'Introduction: Autonomy and Private Life' in Shelley Day-Sclater and others (eds) *Regulating Autonomy: Sex, Reproduction, and Family* (Hart 2009).

52 Onora O'Neill, *Autonomy and Trust in Bioethics* (CUP 2002).

53 O'Neill (n 52) 30. O'Neill notes that Mill 'hardly ever uses the word *autonomy*' in his writing and never in relation to individuals (as opposed to state action, to which O'Neill notes Mill makes only a passing reference).

54 Slavoj Žižek, *The Sublime Object of Ideology* (Verso 1989) 126.

55 Carole Pateman, *The Sexual Contract* (Stanford University Press 1988).

56 Jackson and Sclater (n 51) 1.

action or, as Joseph Raz has argued, autonomy needs to be more than the simple power to choose, but 'an adequate range of choices'.[57]

Despite the persuasiveness of these critiques of autonomy, their application to considerations of consent has largely resulted in the reformulation (and expansion) of the procedural requirements of consent, thus leaving its foundations in autonomy intact. One example is O'Neill's observation of how critiques of the embedded hierarchical relationship between patients and physicians have established a preeminent status for patient autonomy. Yet this has not led to an elaborate logic of character-building choices and reflective decision-making (à la Mill) or to a more communitarian approach to doctor-patient conversations. Instead, the result has been the development of elaborate procedural requirements to establish informed consent which amount to little more than a series of checked boxes.[58] Further, patients' resistance to or interrogation of these technical requirements is subject to scrutiny on the basis of reasonableness – itself a standard informed by understandings of the self-interested individual.[59] In these instances, the foundationalist character of the consent-as-autonomy story is evident in that particular premises or categories are left unstated and unquestioned and indeed *are* unquestionable as a result of their presumed permanence and ahistoricity.[60] The result is the creation of a 'common ground' of analysis where the evaluative terms of reference must themselves serve to both 'authorize and legitimize analysis; indeed, analysis seems not to be able to proceed without them'.[61] In such a context, it is all but impossible to theorise about consent without invoking its story of autonomy. Many other (largely feminist) writers have sought a means to address questions of inequality and oppression outside these terms of reference, contending that a need exists for a 'postindividualist concept of freedom'.[62] Yet finding the means

57 Joseph Raz, *The Morality of Freedom* (Clarendon Press 1986) 373.

58 O'Neill (n 52).

59 As Lori Beaman has suggested within the context of religious freedom and the right to refuse medical treatment, the margins of the 'reasonable' patient are demarcated by articulations of risk and excess. The law's assessment of what behaviour might fall into excessive categories of risk is informed (often explicitly) by a presumed shared understanding or common sense about 'community standards'. See Lori Beaman, *Defining Harm: Religious Freedom and the Limits of the Law* (UBC Press 2008). Beaman's research focusses exclusively on court assessments of consenting capacity in cases involving religious objections to medical treatment; however, an example of the same practice at work in criminal law contexts can be found in the case *R v Butler* [1992] 1 SCR 452, a Canadian Supreme Court of Canada decision which defined obscenity on a national community 'standard of tolerance not taste', 477 citing *Towne Cinema Theatres Ltd v The Queen* [1985] 1 SCR 494, 508. This qualifier hints at the protection of the private sphere as a space free from state intervention unless justified under a threat to the public. This is the foundation of the social contract – the surrendering of certain inalienable rights for the 'common good'.

60 Joan Scott, 'The Evidence of Experience' (1991) 17 *Crit Inq* 773.

61 Scott (n 60) 780.

62 Chantal Mouffe, 'Hegemony and New Political Subjects: Toward a New Concept of Democracy' in Cary Nelson and Lawrence Grossberg (eds), *Marxism and the Interpretation of Culture* (University of Illinois Press 1988).

of approaching this without re-engaging with the discursive foundations of autonomy is challenging. Articulations of consent in non-autonomy terms are absent from legal and theoretical discourse.

As such, an understanding of consent as a 'homeland' for self-governance is awarded a commonplace status, if not religious observance in law. Moreover, there is a form of 'fetishism' to these rather opaque conceptualisations of consent in so far as these meanings are disconnected from the processes that brought them into being. They appear, to quote Marx, as 'figures endowed with a life of their own, which enter into relations with each other and with the human race'.[63] This book is thus interested in the *conditions of possibility* for consent's autonomy story. It seeks to approach consent in ways that do not engage this grammar of autonomy as readily. This task, however, is not without its challenges. Much of the scholarship on consent is limited by its own 'intellectual horizons'[64] where consent as an expression of free will is 'found' or prioritised in interpretations and evaluations of state-intrusive legislation.[65] The effect is to posit consent as ahistorical and pre-juridical. It takes on the quality of a 'foundationalist discourse' where the human subject and its agency are reified, presumed to have always existed, precluding questions about how selves are produced.[66] Further, such 'foundations' make interventions in contemporary debates about consent reiterative of these presumptions. As such, this project proposes to 'read against the grain' of dominant consent discourses which debate its application, its codification, and its inadequacies but leave alone the productive forces which have made its signification of autonomy intelligible (and incontestable). I propose two methods of doing this.

Methodology: a juridical genealogy of consent

Exploring consent's common sense story of autonomy necessitates a methodological approach which can 'render the familiar strange'.[67] As noted,

63 Karl Marx, *Capital: A critique of political economy, Vol 1* (first published 1867, Ben Fowkes tr, Penguin 1976) 165.

64 David M Halperin, *One Hundred Years of Homosexuality and other essays on Greek love* (Routledge 1990).

65 Take, for example, the offence of 'depriving one of her virginity' in section 31 of the Laws of Eshnunna (thought to pre-date the Code of Hammurabi by almost two thousand years), which reads, 'If a man deprives another man's slave-girl of her virginity, he shall pay one-third of a mina of silver; the slave-girl remains the property of her owner', as cited in James B Pritchard (ed), *Ancient Near Eastern Texts Relating to the Old Testament* (3rd edn, PUP 1969) 162. A common description of this section of the Eshnunna Code is that it represents a 'rape law', where rape is defined (contemporarily) as 'non-consensual sex'.

66 Scott (n 60) 26–27.

67 This is a paraphrase of Barry Smart's description of Michel Foucault's methodological approach of 'archaeology' through which Foucault sought to '"defamiliarize" the phenomena of man, society, and culture which have been rendered all too transparent by a century of study, interpretation, and conceptual over-determination'. See Barry Smart (ed), *Michel Foucault (1): Critical Assessments* (Routledge 2004) 50.

contemporary understandings of consent are indivisible from notions of autonomy, defined in contemporary contexts using a neoliberal grammar of self-ownership. Although consent operates in many legal fields, those laws which aim to regulate the body (ie access to it and use of it) provide the most concrete instances of consent's common sense story of autonomy. They demonstrate the role of consent in *constituting* the persons whose bodies are at issue. This presents the difficulty of examining the role of consent in these instances (most notably, criminal and medical law) without re-engaging with this narrative of autonomy.

This book navigates this challenge with the aid of Foucault's approach of genealogy. Characterised predominantly as a 'history of the present', the genealogical gaze is meant to shift one's view; to 'look awry', as Slavoj Žižek has suggested, as a means of seeing more in the distortion or skewed glance than is visible in the direct glare. In the present case, this has meant looking at the legal regulation of the body in contexts where the autonomy narrative is either absent or simply can't ring true given the particular social and political conditions that are at work. These contexts have been selected through two means.

The first is a historical point of entry. In the case of sexual consent, the book examines how sexual behaviours and identities were regulated in Classical Athens and Rome during the Augustan moral reform period at the turn of the first century. This historical context is one where both personal and socio-political autonomy were explicitly denied to women; however, contemporary scholars often write about 'female consent' and 'sexual consent' when examining the legal regulation of sex of the period.[68] There are also ample discussions of consent and its role in sexual relationships in both the period's historical documents and their surrounding scholarly commentary. This provides a context where consent played a key role in the regulation of the (sexual) body, but in a manner that differs from its contemporary autonomy narrative.

The book takes the same historical approach to its examination of consent within medical law. Bioethicists are fairly uniform in their view of informed consent as a modern-day invention, established against traditions of paternalism and power within doctor-patient relationships. Consent in the modern medical context is positioned as a simple matter of (informed) 'choice'. Rethinking informed consent within this frame means tweaking the circumstances in which this choice occurs (eg revisiting the requirements for physician disclosure), rather than examining how this conception of consent prefigures the frame in which it is revisited or whether alternative accounts of the doctrine and its function might exist. To hear a different story, this book examines the doctor-patient relationship within a period far removed from the discourses of autonomy operating in

68 Angeliki E Laiou (ed), *Consent and Coercion to Sex and Marriage in Ancient and Medieval Societies* (Dumbarton Oaks 1993); and in the same collection: Diana C Moses, 'Livy's Lucretia and the Validity of Coerced Consent in Roman Law'; and David Cohen, 'Consent and Sexual Relations in Classical Athens'. See also David Cohen, 'Sexuality, Violence and the Athenian Law of *Hubris*' (1991) 38 *G&R* 171.

contemporary bioethical scholarship – Europe's Middle Ages, dubbed the 'dark age' of medical ethics for its reputed absence of any notion of patient autonomy.[69] Yet, a great number of ethical codes for medical practice and physician conduct existed within the medieval era. Consent also figures prominently in many of the philosophical treatises of the period. Akin to the book's exploration of sexual consent in antiquity, the aim is not to track a 'history of consent' but rather to find sites that, because of their socio-political (or discursive) conditions, offer opportunities to hear something different from consent's modern autonomy story.

The book then proposes to apply these 'skewed glances' of consent to the contemporary contexts in which consent is put to work. Do these other stories of consent still resonate today? This approach can be likened to the work of Benjamin Constant who explored 'Ancient' and 'Modern' models of liberty with the aim of better understanding a present state of affairs.[70] In an effort to move past the discourses of autonomy that dominate consent's role in the legal regulation of sex and health, the book shifts its contemporary gaze to the law's oversight of bodily harm in the context of play, most specifically, the professional sport context. This site has two advantages. The first is that despite taking place against a backdrop of consent's common sense story, the jurisprudence in the area of sporting violence rarely engages (at least explicitly) with this autonomy discourse. Instead, the law uses constructions of the 'public interest' or 'social utility' as a delimiter of consent when it is applied to bodily harm. The effect is to construct certain forms of violence or harm as 'reasonable' (and others as unreasonable). This establishes not just what is acceptable (and valuable) on the playing field but also the norms of the surrounding social order itself. This is the second advantage of using the context of sport as a site of investigation – it provides immediate access to consent's disciplinary and normalising function, helping to reveal the contemporary conditions of consent's existence. In addition, discussions about the regulation of consensual bodily harm among professional athletes take place in an explicitly capitalist context, frequently invoking neoliberal values in the negotiation of (un)allowable harm. This offers a useful contrast with the medieval chapter's examination of consent in the early onset of a capitalist economy.

The alternative narratives of consent uncovered in these three investigatory sites are explored for their application to contemporary law's regulation of bodily harm in both criminal and medical law, expanding coverage to include a 'skewed glance' at other roles consent plays in corporeal regulation, including sadomasochistic activities and cases of HIV non-disclosure. This leads to a contemplation of the meaning of 'autonomy' in neoliberalism and a revised narrative of consent's common sense.

69 Loren C MacKinney, 'Medical Ethics and Etiquette in the Early Middle Ages: The Persistence of Hippocratic Ideals' (1952) 26(1) *Bull Hist Med* 1.

70 Benjamin Constant 'The Liberty of the Ancients Compared with that of the Moderns (1833)' in David Boaz (ed), *The Libertarian Reader* (Free Press 1997).

Charting the course: a chapter outline

The hunt for understandings of consent that might challenge or differ from the consent-as-autonomy story has meant travelling to some fairly unexpected places. The following chapters will ask the reader to consider sexual offences in antiquity, medical ethics in the Middle Ages, and bodily harm on the sports field of the present day. The book begins, however, with a detailed reconstruction of the consent-as-autonomy story. In Chapter 1, I examine what might be thought of as the 'contemporary canon' of consent law in the three legal areas that are of central focus in upcoming chapters, namely: consent to sex, informed consent to medical treatment, and the defence of consent in sport. This contemporary picture of consent aims to reveal the dominance of the autonomy story even among more critical and reformist approaches to consent (and autonomy itself). Key components to this portrait include voluntariness, rationality, and knowledge as 'preconditions' of consent, and the role of legal paternalism in establishing the doctrine's parameters. In addition, the contributions of classical liberal scholars (such as John Locke) to the establishment of consent's claim to 'common sense' and the productive power of this claim in contemporary understandings of consent (as autonomy) are discussed in Chapter 1.

Chapter 2 marks the first of three substantive investigations into the conditions of possibility for contemporary understandings of consent, exploring how sexual behaviours and identities were regulated during the Augustan moral reform period at the turn of the first century when personal and socio-political autonomy was explicitly restricted to certain members of the polis (free male citizens). The chapter begins with an examination of the offences of sexual violence and transgression (eg adultery and prostitution), which figure most prominently in the period's legal codes, Attic rhetoric, and Greek and Roman dramatic sources as well as contemporary Classics scholarship. The analysis is then organised around the functions which consent can be seen to perform in the context of early Athenian and Roman sexual life. This includes a role of proprietorship in relation to the political and patrilineage interests which sexual offence legislation of the period was meant to protect, and a role of political belonging, where consent served as a form of juridical and cultural recognition. In Chapter 2, I suggest that what is at issue, at least in this ancient story of consent, is not a certain quality of free action, personal integrity, or the capacity for self-control, but rather the protection of property and the constitution of the public domain. Further, through an examination of those who were excluded from the socio-political status necessary to enact consent (ie women, slaves, foreigners, and various 'sexual transgressors'), the ability of consent to prescribe normative ways of being and acting is revealed, speaking to consent's contemporary conditions of voluntariness and rationality (that must be enacted in specific ways to be recognisable).

Chapter 3 continues the search for alternative stories of consent, investigating the introduction of the 'knowledge' precondition of consent within the medical field. David Halperin has suggested that genealogy is a method which 'enables us to glimpse contingency where before we had seen only necessity; it thereby allows us to suspend, however briefly, the categories of thought and action within which we habitually conduct our lives'.[71] This positions this methodological approach as particularly apt for destabilising one of the more secured juridical discourses of consent-as-autonomy: the informed consent doctrine. Leading medical ethics commentators have gone so far as to suggest that autonomy should be considered 'the single most important moral value for informed consent'.[72] Discerning an account of medical consent uninformed by notions of self-determination and individualism requires an archaeological site far removed from the accepted twentieth-century origins of autonomy-based medical ethics. Chapter 3 takes up this challenge with an entry into medieval accounts of medicine and its ethics. Although most accounts of the 'history' of informed consent begin with the aftermath of human experimentation in the Second World War and the codes of practice emerging from the Nuremberg trials, there is evidence to suggest that consent was contemplated in physicians' codes of ethics in the Middle Ages.[73] Against a backdrop where health and illness are understood to be acts of divine intervention, Chapter 3 explores how consent figured in medieval understandings of the doctor-patient relationship. As part of this, I also examine other period uses of consent, including theological analyses of Christian conversion and marriage formation (where the dilemma of knowing the inner will of another was of central concern), and the medieval marketplace (where consent played a central role in the arena of trade and commerce). In each instance, an understanding of consent as a form of submission emerges, challenging the contemporary story of autonomy.

In Chapter 4, I examine constructions of consent as they appear in judicial determinations of bodily harm, with a particular focus on the criminal law's approach to violence which occurs within sporting contexts. Emphasis is placed on leading decisions in the United Kingdom and North America, highlighting how the courts have defined 'harm' on the basis of 'public utility' when determining the scope of consensual violence. Operating as a criminal defence, consent transforms an otherwise criminal act into a legal one and, in the case of sporting activity, a universally desirable aim. The result is the production of a normative framework for players where it is both rational and laudable to subject the body to violence and high-risk activity, (provided it is in pursuit of social, cultural, and economic capital). In this respect, consent's 'transformation magic' is also a productive power. It creates new normative understandings of legitimate action and the components of subjectivity it is said to harbour. How

71 Halperin, (n 64) 70.

72 Ruth Faden and Tom Beauchamp, *A History and Theory of Informed Consent* (OUP 1986) 18.

73 See, for instance, Loren MacKinney's translation and study of source documents from 400 to 1100 AD, which 'bear resemblances to passages from Hippocratic works' among other medical codes of practice (n 69). Similarly, a 2010 article in the *Journal of Medical Ethics* discusses the discovery of a 'written consent' form signed in 1539, see Salih Selek, 'A Written Consent Five Centuries Ago' (2010) 36 *J Med Ethics* 639.

these subjectivities might be gendered or otherwise normatively constructed is discussed in the conclusion to Chapter 4, where I argue that consent's 'common sense' is integrally connected to a neoliberal rationality that both prescribes and produces subjectivities in service to its basic tenets.

Chapter 5 delves into this neoliberal rationality, examining what might be thought of as the 'political economy' of consent. It builds on my argument in Chapter 4 that contemporary uses of consent function within a frame where the rational subject is one who employs (and suffers) violence for the sake of economic and cultural capital, offering a more detailed view of the consent-as-autonomy story from within this capitalist logic. The chapter asks what 'social utility' and the 'common good' might mean in a neoliberal world and consequently, how freedom and autonomy are understood when envisioned as dispositions of commodities. Contemporary cases from criminal law and medical law are reviewed for evidence of this neoliberal rationality at work. I conclude Chapter 5 with the contentions that the consent-as-autonomy narrative emerged as an ideological component of contemporary capitalism and that this has obscured the wider universe of consent's history and functions. Moreover, this autonomy story belies the ways in which these historical uses and understandings of consent continue to resonate in judicial treatments of consent in the present day.

The book concludes with a glance at the implications of a consent-as-autonomy story that is in service to neoliberal rationality. Likening this narrative to the new 'art of government' that Foucault examined in his own study of the emergence of neoliberalism, I argue that 'consent' is best understood as a means of producing and managing a certain *kind* of freedom. The law's consenting subject is 'free' to act as she wishes, provided she does so in ways that are in alignment with neoliberal understandings of the 'common good'. Consent is a concept that has been widely understood as illusory,[74] a 'placeholder' for ideals of freedom and equality that are valued as dearly as they are summarily dismissed as unrealisable. If, however, the ability to (withhold) consent belongs only to the 'good girl', 'good patient', and 'good player', there may be very little truth to the promise of autonomy within consent's common sense story.

Bibliography

Table of cases

BH (Next friend of) v Alberta (Director of Child Welfare) 2002 ABQB 371
Cuthbertson v. Rasouli 2013 SCC 53
R v Barnes [2005] 1 Cr App Rep 507
R v Brown [1993] 2 All ER 75
R v Butler [1992] 1 SCR 452
R v Cey (1989) 48 CCC 3d 480 (Sask CA)

74 See, for example, Daniel I. O'Neill, Mary Lyndon Shanley and Iris Marion Young, *Illusion of Consent: Engaging with Carole Pateman* (Penn State University Press 2008).

R v. Ciccarelli (1989) 54 CCC 3d 121 (Ont Dist Ct)
R v Leclerc (1991) 67 CCC 3d 563 (ONCA)
R v McSorley [2000] BCPC 117 (CanLII)
Starson v Swayze [2003] 1 SCR 722
Towne Cinema Theatres Ltd v The Queen [1985] 1 SCR 494

Table of legislation

Criminal Code, RSC 1985, C-46 (Canada)
Sexual Offences Act 2003 (UK)

Secondary sources

Archard D, *Sexual Consent* (Westview Press 1998)

Barmak S, 'What Consent Means in the Age of #MeToo' (2018) 15(2) *The Walrus* 30

Bazelon L, 'Is 2016 a Watershed Moment for Women?' *Politico Magazine* (13 October 2016) <www.politico.com/magazine/story/2016/10/2016-sexual-assault-allegations-watershed-moment-for-women-214355> accessed 30 January 2019

Beaman L, *Defining Harm: Religious Freedom and the Limits of the Law* (UBC Press 2008)

Beauchamp TL and Childress JF, *Principles of Biomedical Ethics* (5th edn, OUP 2001)

Belson K, 'After N.F.L. Concussion Settlement, Feeding Frenzy of Lawyers and Lenders' *New York Times* (New York, 16 July 2017) <www.nytimes.com/2017/07/16/sports/football/nfl-concussion-settlement-lawyers.html> accessed 31 January 2019

Beres MA, '"Spontaneous" Sexual Consent: An Analysis of Sexual Consent Literature' (2007) 17(1) *Fem & Psych* 93

Brownell C, 'How Drunk Is Too Drunk to Consent? Legally, There's No Clear Answer' *Windsor Star* (Windsor, 6 June 2013) <https://windsorstar.com/news/sexual-assaultintoxication-feature> accessed 30 April 2019

Butler J, *Gender Trouble: Feminism and the Subversion of Identity* (10th ann edn, Routledge 1999)

Carline A, Gunby C and Taylor S, 'Too Drunk to Consent? Exploring the Contestations and Disruptions in Male-focused Sexual Violence Prevention Interventions' (2017) 20(10) *S & LS* 1

Carr JL, 'The SlutWalk Movement: A Study in Transnational Feminist Activism' (2013) 4 *J Fem Sch* 24

Cohen D, 'Sexuality, Violence and the Athenian Law of *Hubris*' (1991) 38 *G&R* 171

———, 'Consent and Sexual Relations in Classical Athens' in AE Laiou (ed), *Consent and Coercion to Sex and Marriage in Ancient and Medieval Societies* (Dumbarton Oaks 1993)

Constant B, 'The Liberty of the Ancients Compared with that of the Moderns (1833)' in David Boaz (ed), *The Libertarian Reader* (Free Press 1997)

Cowan S, '"Freedom and Capacity to Make a Choice": A Feminist Analysis of Consent in the Criminal Law of Rape' in Vanessa E Munro and Carl F Stychin (eds), *Sexuality and the Law: Feminist Engagements* (Routledge 2007)

Cowling M and Reynolds P (eds), *Making Sense of Sexual Consent* (Routledge 2004)

Doolittle R, 'Unfounded: Why Police Dismiss 1 in 5 Sexual Assault Claims as Baseless' *Globe & Mail* (Toronto, 3 February 2017) F2

Dunn J, *The Political Thought of John Locke: An Historical Account of the Argument of the 'Two Treatises of Government'* (CUP 1969)

Elliott C and Than CD, 'The Case for a Rational Reconstruction of Consent in Criminal Law' (2007) 70 *MLR* 225

Faden RR and Beauchamp TL, *A History and Theory of Informed Consent* (OUP 1986)

Garner BA (ed), *Black's Law Dictionary* (7th edn, West Group 1999)

Gersen JS, 'The Sexual-Assault Election' *The New Yorker* (6 November 2016). <www.newyorker.com/news/news-desk/the-sexual-assault-election> accessed 3 December 2018

Haag P, *Consent: Sexual Rights and the Transformation of American Liberalism* (Cornell University Press 1999)

Halperin DM, *One Hundred Years of Homosexuality and other essays on Greek love* (Routledge 1990)

Hart HLA, 'Analytical Jurisprudence in Mid-Twentieth Century: A Reply to Professor Bodenheimer' (1957) 105 *U Pa L Rev* 953

Heyes CJ, 'Dead to the World: Rape, Unconsciousness, and Social Media' (2016) 41(2) *Signs* 361

Home Office, *Setting the Boundaries: Reforming the Law on Sex Offences* (HMSO 2000)

——, *Protecting the Public: Strengthening Protection against Sex Offenders and Reforming the Law on Sexual Offences* (White Paper, Cm 5668, 2002)

Humphreys T and Herold E, 'Should Universities and Colleges Mandate Sexual Behavior? Student Perceptions of Antioch College's Consent Policy' (2003) 15 *J Psych & Hum Sex* 35

Hunter R and Cowan S (eds), *Choice and Consent: Feminist Engagements with Law and Subjectivity* (Routledge 2004)

Hurd H, 'The Moral Magic of Consent' (1992) 2(2) *LEG* 121

Jackson E and Day-Sclater S, 'Introduction: Autonomy and Private Life' in Shelley Day-Sclater and others (eds) *Regulating Autonomy: Sex, Reproduction, and Family* (Hart 2009)

Kious BM, 'The Evidentiary Account of Consent's Moral Significance' (PhD dissertation, University of California 2009)

Laiou AE (ed), *Consent and Coercion to Sex and Marriage in Ancient and Medieval Societies* (Dumbarton Oaks 1993)

Locke J, *Two Treatises of Government* (first published 1689, Peter Laslett tr, CUP 1963)

MacKinney LC, 'Medical Ethics and Etiquette in the Early Middle Ages: The Persistence of Hippocratic Ideals' (1952) 26(1) *Bull Hist Med* 1

Malm H, 'The Ontological Status of Consent and Its Implications for the Law of Rape' (1996) 2 *LEG* 147

Marx K, *Capital: A Critique of Political Economy, Vol 1* (first published 1867, Ben Fowkes tr, Penguin 1976)

McClure K, *Judging Rights: Lockean Politics and the Limits of Consent* (Cornell University Press 1996)

Moses DC, 'Livy's Lucretia and the Validity of Coerced Consent in Roman Law' in AE Laiou (ed), *Consent and Coercion to Sex and Marriage in Ancient and Medieval Societies* (Dumbarton Oaks 1993)

Mouffe C, 'Hegemony and New Political Subjects: Toward a New Concept of Democracy' in C Nelson and L Grossberg (eds), *Marxism and the Interpretation of Culture* (University of Illinois Press 1988)

Nedelsky J, 'Reconceiving Autonomy: Sources, Thoughts, and Possibilities' (1989) 1 *Yale J L & Fem* 7

Oliver K, 'Rape as Spectator Sport and Creepshot Entertainment: Social Media and the Valorization of Lack of Consent' (2016) 10 *Am Studies J* 61
O'Neill DI, Shanley ML and Young IM, *Illusion of Consent: Engaging with Carole Pateman* (Penn State University Press 2008)
O'Neill O, *Autonomy and Trust in Bioethics* (CUP 2002)
Papadopoulou N, 'Assisted-dying Laws are Progressing in Some Places – the UK Isn't One of Them' *Independent* (London, 15 April 2017) <www.independent.co.uk/news/health/assisted-dying-laws-are-progressing-in-some-places-the-uk-isn-t-one-of-them-a7679846.html> 31 January 2019
Pateman C, *The Sexual Contract* (Stanford University Press 1988)
Pritchard JB (ed), *Ancient Near Eastern Texts Relating to the Old Testament* (3rd edn, PUP 1969)
Raz J, *The Morality of Freedom* (Clarendon Press 1986)
Reynolds P, 'The Quality of Consent' in M Cowling and P Reynolds (eds), *Making Sense of Sexual Consent* (Ashgate 2004)
Scott JW, 'The Evidence of Experience' (1991) 17 *Crit Inq* 773
Selek S, 'A Written Consent Five Centuries Ago' (2010) 36 *J Med Ethics* 639
Seliger M, *The Liberal Politics of John Locke* (Frederick Praeger 1969)
Sherwin E, 'Infelicitous Sex' (1996) 2 *LEG* 209
Smart B (ed), *Michel Foucault (1): Critical Assessments* (Routledge 2004)
Temkin J and Ashworth A, 'The Sexual Offences Act 2003: (1) Rape, Sexual Assaults, and the Problems of Consent' (2004) *Crim LR* 328
Van Marle K, 'The Politics of Consent, Friendship, and Sovereignty' in Rosemary Hunter and Sharon Cowan (eds), *Choice and Consent: Feminist Engagements with Law and Subjectivity* (Routledge 2004)
Viegas M, 'Capacity for Consent: Two Cases Renew the Debate Over When Someone is Too Drunk to Consent' *Vice News Canada* (3 March 2017) <https://news.vice.com/story/when-is-someone-legally-too-drunk-to-consent> 3 December 2018
Wallace T and Parlapiano A, 'Crowd Scientists Say Women's March in Washington Had 3 Times as Many People as Trump's Inauguration' *New York Times* (22 January 2017) <www.nytimes.com/interactive/2017/01/22/us/politics/womens-march-trump-crowd-estimates.html> 31 January 2019
West R, 'Legitimating the Illegitimate: A Comment on *Beyond Rape*' (1992) 93(6) *Colum L Rev* 1442
Westen P, *The Logic of Consent: The Diversity and Deceptiveness of Consent as a Defense to Criminal Conduct* (Routledge 2004)
Wooten SC and Mitchell RW (eds), *The Crisis of Campus Sexual Violence: Critical Perspectives on Prevention and Response* (Routledge 2016)
Young PW, *The Law of Consent* (Law Book Co 1986)
Žižek S, *The Sublime Object of Ideology* (Verso 1989)

1 The common sense of consent

The indivisible association of consent with autonomy is commonplace in legal and political scholarship. There, consent is understood as a core element of personhood. There are, however, preconditions to the freedom and subjectivity that consent signifies. One must first demonstrate a *capacity* to consent, and the acts to which one is consenting must not be irrational or unreasonable. Consent, to be valid, must be adequately informed and enacted voluntarily by clear-thinking (and recognisable) subjects, for socially valuable ends. Thus, despite its promise of universal self-rule and independence, consent is a rather selective and highly governed means of enacting freedom. Some subjects are excluded from its presumption of autonomy and marginalised from the scope of consent not simply because of non-conformity to hegemonic ideals of subjectivity and statehood, but by way of being unintelligible within them. There is, then, a paradox in the story of autonomy that is told about consent which forecloses certain forms of personhood or liberty in the name of others.

This chapter seeks to interrogate this paradox through a contextualisation of contemporary deployments of consent in each of the three legal areas examined in upcoming chapters, namely: consent to sex, informed consent to medical treatment, and the defence of consent in sport. This modern account of consent aims to reveal the pervasiveness with which consent is defined as a form of personal autonomy, even among the more critical approaches that recognise its internal contradictions and an inequity in its application. An examination of the law's three most prevalent 'preconditions' of consent (ie knowledge, voluntariness, and rationality) and their roots in liberal concerns with legal paternalism forms part of this analysis.

Second, this chapter explores how this narrative of autonomy gains such widespread adoption through an invocation of a 'common sense' that not only serves to 'naturalise' the conditions needed for liberal accounts of autonomy but also establishes the frames of intelligibility that exclude all other notions of what consent might be or do. Ultimately, this chapter maintains that to suggest that autonomy is central to understandings of consent is to understate the matter. Autonomy is not simply the most popular or widely accepted understanding of consent; it is the only story there is. How this narrative is employed to limit the content and scope of consent on the basis of conformity to particular forms of (liberal) subjectivity is explored in the chapter's conclusion, highlighting the need to uncover alternative understandings of consent – a task to which the book's ensuing chapters take aim.

Mediated magic: paternalism and its paradox

The understanding of the human will as serving to eradicate wrongdoing is ascribed a long history, often sourced in the Roman maxim *volenti non fit injuria* ('to the willing no injury is done')[1] and used by the courts to cement the principle that one should be able to consent to anything, even the impossible.[2] While seemingly a prima facie case for consent's ancient origins in autonomy, there is evidence that twentieth-century understandings of 'autonomy as independence' have little in common with these early roots.[3] Onora O'Neill, for instance, has noted that autonomy in the antiquity context was a reference to the self-governance of *states* rather than the actions of individuals.[4] Instead, the association of consent with inviolable individualism owes more to the work of early theorists of liberalism than it does to ancient maxims.[5] John Stuart Mill's text, *On Liberty*, positioned consent as a tool for balancing the competing interests of the state and its individuals.[6] O'Neill observes that contemporary understandings of autonomy stem from Mill's work and amount to a kind of 'self-legislation' which is not more (nor less) than the establishment of a set of principles that all persons can employ to both govern their own behaviour and judge that of others. Instrumentalism lies at the heart of this conception of autonomy where 'some ways of choosing are more likely than others to produce valuable choices'.[7] Consent, in this frame, acts as a value exchange: unconstrained

1 Some commentators have suggested the 'germ' of this maxim can be found even earlier. See NGL Child, 'Volenti Non Fit Injuria' (1905) 17 *Jur Rev* 43, who sources it in Aristotle's *Ethics* (Book V, section ix).

2 'The law will suffer a man of his own folly to bind himself to pay on a certain day if he does not make the Tower of London come to Westminster' claimed a fourteenth-century English court (as cited in Terence Ingman, 'A History of the Defence of *Non Volenti Non Fit Injuria*' (1981) 26 *Jur Rev* (ns) 1, 3).

3 Onora O'Neill, 'Autonomy: The Emperor's New Clothes' (Inaugural Address 2003) 77(1) *Proc Aristotelian Soc* 1 ('Emperor's New Clothes').

4 Chapter 2 examines sexual consent in Ancient Greece and Rome at the turn of the first century where the interests of the state were paramount in the functions consent was meant to perform.

5 Some scholars, such as Louise Campbell, have argued that 'the concept of autonomy received its first modern expression – and its first application to the individual – in the moral theory of Immanuel Kant'. See Louise Campbell, 'Kant, Autonomy and Bioethics' (2017) 3(3) *Eth Med & Pub H* 381, 381. Onora O'Neill, however, explicitly rejects this view, noting that contemporary autonomy's 'claims to Kantian ancestry are greatly exaggerated; see 'Emperor's New Clothes' (n 3) 1.

6 Albeit, as O'Neill informs us, without mentioning the word 'autonomy' in reference to individual action at all, see Onora O'Neill, *Autonomy and Trust in Bioethics* (CUP 2002) 30; see also O'Neill, 'Emperor's New Clothes' (n 3) 4.

7 O'Neill, 'Emperor's New Clothes' (n 3) 6.

liberty is surrendered for some other (more valuable) aim (eg freedom in the universal).[8]

This has had implications for how the scope of consent operates in law, bringing to the fore one of liberalism's underlying tensions between the sacred ideal of individual autonomy and the state's forays into legal paternalism. Ostensibly, this discord is mediated through a narrowly interpreted harm principle, often attributed to Mill,[9] where governments are permitted some coercive power over the citizenry so as to act in its 'best interest'. This necessarily places limits on the 'moral magic' of consent when some actions are deemed to be too harmful to be permitted merely on the basis of individual will. As Ashworth notes:

> [I]ndividual autonomy has both positive and negative aspects: on the one hand it argues for liberty from attack or interference, whereas on the other hand it argues for the liberty to do with one's body as one wishes ... If a person wishes to give up her or his physical integrity in certain circumstances or to risk it for the sake of sport or excitement, should the criminal law allow the consent to negative what would otherwise be a crime?[10]

Joel Feinberg has suggested that this conundrum results from a misreading of the *volenti* maxim so as to interpret it as saying something about 'harm' whereas it might be better understood to be directed towards 'legal wrongs'.[11] This re-reading results in a view of consent as vitiating a liability claim rather than a harm or injury, similar to a waiver of legal right(s). Based on this view, Feinberg argues a better reading of the *volenti* maxim might be: 'To one who freely consents to a thing no *wrong* is done, no matter how harmful to [her/]him the consequences may be'.[12] This suggests that the 'magic' of consent to transform wrong to right is constrained by the liberal understanding of autonomy as individualised agency, where legal paternalism is positioned as its greatest foe. Thus, any state intervention which impedes an individual's exercise of free will (even if to prevent self-inflicted harm) amounts to a coercion which is itself too harmful to allow.[13] This has the effect of exempting certain 'problematic' or even

8 The view of consent as an exchange of reciprocal rights and duties is prominent in bioethics. See Ruth R Faden and Tom L Beauchamp, *A History and Theory of Informed Consent* (OUP 1986); Richard T Hull, 'Informed Consent: Patient's Right or Patient's Duty?' (1985) 10(2) *J Med & Phil* 183.

9 See Joel Feinberg 'Legal Paternalism' (1971) 1(1) *Cdn J Phil* 105; David Dyzenhaus, 'John Stuart Mill and the Harm of Pornography' (1992) 102(3) *Ethics* 534. See also Richard Vernon 'John Stuart Mill and Pornography: Beyond the Harm Principle' (1996) 106(3) *Ethics* 621, for an alternative reading of Mill's *On Liberty* and the standard approach to the harm principle.

10 Andrew Ashworth, *Principles of Criminal Law* (5th edn, OUP 2006) 318.

11 Feinberg, 'Legal Paternalism' (n 9).

12 Feinberg, 'Legal Paternalism' (n 9) 107.

13 Feinberg, 'Legal Paternalism' (n 9) 108. Feinberg maintains that this should effectively exclude self-inflicted and consensual harm from the category of 'harm' altogether on the basis that to prevent such harm the state would need to act too coercively to be proportionately justifiable.

'unconscionable' interactions from the label of 'illegitimate' (and thus criminal and civil liability) on the basis that the (self-inflicted) harm they occasion is less than the harm that would be incurred by state interventions to prevent it.[14]

There are, however, many circumstances in which interference with another's liberty or autonomous action might be deemed necessary or advisable for a multitude of reasons ranging from a broad sense of social welfare or the 'common good' to an assessment of individual interests or self-protection.[15] Indeed, the classic tenets of liberalism first penned by the political theorists of the seventeenth and eighteenth centuries were composed with these restraints on autonomy in mind.[16] This represents what Kultgen has characterised as the dilemma created by absolutist positions on autonomy where 'if one defines autonomy so that it always deserves respect, no one is autonomous; and if one defines it so that everyone is autonomous, it does not always deserve respect'.[17] This has prompted many liberal theorists to propose varying degrees of justifiable (or 'valuable') paternalism. Feinberg distinguishes between cases of 'hard' and 'soft' paternalism as a way of rationalising the use of state intervention to

---

Moreover, Feinberg argues that 'individuals themselves ... can know their own true interests better than any outsiders can' and therefore 'outside coercion is almost certain to be self-defeating' 108.

14 One such example is the 'complex relationship', proposed by Donald Dripps, where within the context of an otherwise satisfying marriage, one partner (in Dripps's case, the wife) 'cooperates' with the other's sexual advances despite no desire to do so. Dripps suggests she does this for a myriad of reasons ('a sense of reciprocity, of doing a favor for her best friend; fear that he might seek satisfaction elsewhere, etc. ...') but that this circumstance cannot be deemed to be non-consensual – despite the presence of constraints – because these constraints do not leave either party without the capacity to bargain. Furthermore, 'so long as the complex relationship is accepted as legitimate, the fact that only one party to sex found it enjoyable does not establish illegitimacy, given compensation in some nonsexual form', Donald A Dripps, 'Beyond Rape: An Essay on the Difference Between the Presence of Force and the Absence of Consent' (1992) 92 *Colum L Rev* 1780, 1789, 1801–1802. For a critique of this position, see Robin West, 'Legitimating the Illegitimate: A Comment on *Beyond Rape*' (1992) 93(6) *Colum L Rev* 1442.

15 The distinctions among these various justifications for infringements of liberty are the source of the many divisions within liberalism itself, eg between 'old' and 'new' liberalisms, the latter perhaps best exemplified by the concerns with social justice motivating Rawls's 'difference principle' in his seminal text, *Theory of Justice* (HUP 1971). For a general discussion of these differences see Gerald Gaus and Shane D Courtland's definition of 'Liberalism' in *The Stanford Encyclopedia of Philosophy* (Spring edn, 2011) <http://plato.stanford.edu/archives/spr2011/entries/liberalism/> accessed 30 April 2019.

16 Certainly the original 'social contract' espouses this view, and the majority of political theories which endorse classical liberalism employ a utilitarianism or contractarianism which assumes some limitations on individual autonomy are necessary for a functional social order. These views are well canvassed in the first two chapters of Horatio Spector's *Autonomy and Rights: The Moral Foundations of Liberalism* (OUP 2008). Don Herzog also makes the argument that consent theory emerged in response to Hobbes's 'masterless man' and the dangers he was thought to pose to civil order. See *Happy Slaves: A Critique of Consent Theory* (University of Chicago Press 1989).

17 John Kultgen, *Autonomy and Intervention: Parentalism in the Caring Life* (OUP 1995) 89.

prevent harm in some cases while opposing it in others.[18] Hard paternalism is thus understood to be coercive state action (eg criminal legislation) which prohibits individuals (against their will) from engaging in conduct that is harmful to themselves and/or others. Soft paternalism, on the other hand, is a more qualified form of state coercion reserved for determinations of an individual's will, exemplified by Mill's now famous example of a man about to cross a damaged bridge.[19] While the hard paternalist would prevent the man from crossing irrespective of his own wishes, the soft paternalist would detain the man only long enough to determine whether he was aware of the bridge's state of disrepair and its dangers, leaving him to his own actions once the nature of his will had been settled.

The scope of, limits to, and justifications for the state's acts of soft paternalism are the subject of much debate in legal and moral philosophy, political theory, bioethics, criminal, and contract law. It is within these deliberations that most of the contemporary discussions of consent take place (be that in the name of enhancing the informed choices of patients or contractors, the physical integrity of sexual actors or sport participants, or in debating the proper boundaries of free-acting citizens). This literature is largely concerned with the necessary conditions, capacities, circumstances, and evidences of consent. How much harm can a free citizen consent to? What steps or procedures must be taken to ensure a choice is made knowledgeably? What individual acts, if allowed, will garner more widespread harm than the harm of state-imposed infringements on personal freedom? And so on.

There is a paradox in this treatment of consent, however, given that the problem of paternalism and how (or if) it should be addressed stems from the liberal commitment to autonomy. Therefore, even attempts to offer solutions to or critiques of the problem must engage with this same narrative of autonomy. Consent discussions are also confined to this box.[20] Take, for instance, Tom Beauchamp's defence of soft paternalism in the field of 'biobehavioral control'[21] on the basis that such acts do not interfere with patient autonomy, given that

18 Joel Feinberg, *Harm to Self* (OUP 1986).

19 Mill phrases the example as such: 'If either a public officer or anyone else saw a person attempting to cross a bridge which had been ascertained to be unsafe, and there were no time to warn him of his danger, they might seize him and turn him back without any real infringement of his liberty; for liberty consists in doing what one desires, and he does not desire to fall into the river'. *On Liberty* (first published 1859, Hackett 1978) 95.

20 Keith Hyams has remarked on this presumed inseparability, suggesting that disagreements about the necessary conditions of consent are '[c]entral to many of the most violent clashes fought on the battleground of consent' and that reaching an understanding 'of the limits to consent's capacity to legitimise is key to unravelling the foundations of liberal morality and its attendant conflicts'. See 'When Consent Doesn't Work: A Rights-Based Case for Limits to Consent's Capacity to Legitimise' (2011) 8(1) *J Moral Phil* 110, 110.

21 Tom Beauchamp, 'Paternalism and Biobehavioral Control' (1977) 60(1) *The Monist* 62. Beauchamp defines 'biobehavioral control' as covering a series of what he refers to as 'technological capacities': namely information control (consisting of psychotherapy and behavioural engineering); biopsychological control (consisting of electrical stimulation of the brain, psychosurgery,

the patient lacks the requisite characteristics of an autonomous actor when the consent that is offered has not been 'adequately informed'. Beauchamp explains:

> It is not a question of protecting a man *against himself* or of interfering with his *liberty of action*. He is not *acting* at all in regard to this danger. He needs protection from something which is precisely *not himself*, not his intended action, not in any remote sense of his own making.[22]

Feinberg makes a similar point, suggesting that we should not 'expect anti-paternalistic individualism to deny protection to a person from his own non-voluntary choices, for insofar as the choices are not voluntary they are just as alien to him as the choices of someone else'.[23] For Beauchamp, any number of factors can serve to 'constrain free choice' in this regard, 'such as inadequate reflection, transitory desires, inner psychological compulsions, family pressures', and so forth.[24] Thus, despite the prominence awarded to autonomy in the liberal account of consent, it is a liberty to self-govern that comes with prerequisites. Further, it is from this liberal story of consent-as-autonomy that contemporary law gleans a number of factors which serve to vitiate or negate consent on the basis of their impact on one or more of these preconditions (the presence of fraud, duress, coercion, false pretences, or mistake are common examples). Although both Feinberg and Beauchamp in the excerpts above allude to one of the more commonly cited 'prerequisites' of consent (ie voluntariness), these stipulations can take different forms depending on whether the commentator is a moral philosopher, contract lawyer, rights advocate, bioethicist, critical theorist, and so on.[25] These preconditions of consent also help to establish the characteristics of

---

and the use of psychotropic drugs); and biomedical control (consisting of life-sustaining and reproductive controls and genetic engineering).

22 Beauchamp, 'Paternalism' (n 21) 67–68 (emphasis in original). Beauchamp is even more explicit about the correlativity between consent and autonomy in a much later work which he introduces in the following way: 'I [have] the objective of determining the nature of consent and autonomy. I will also examine what constitutes a consent, what sort of consent is valid, who qualifies as autonomous, and what sort of autonomy merits respect. I will argue that moral notions – in particular, the obligation to obtain consent and the obligation to respect autonomy – should affect how we construct theories of consent, theories of autonomous action, and theories of the autonomous person'. See Tom Beauchamp, 'Autonomy and Consent' in Franklin G Miller and Alan Wertheimer (eds), *The Ethics of Consent: Theory and Practice* (OUP 2009) 56.

23 Feinberg, 'Legal Paternalism' (n 9) 112.

24 Beauchamp, 'Paternalism' (n 21) 70.

25 For instance, Larry Alexander suggests that consent requires the preconditions of capacity, information, and motivation, while Victor Tadros endorses a contemplation of the magnitude of the harm, the self-regarding vs. other-regarding duties that may face the individual, and principles of sanctity that might apply to the decision; see Larry Alexander, 'The Moral Magic of Consent (II)' (1996) 2 *LEG* 1352; Victor Tadros, 'Consent to Harm' (2011) 64 *CLP* 23. Tom Beauchamp, when discussing the informed consent doctrine, identifies the three elements of voluntariness, understanding, and consent (understood as a favourable decision and an authorisation) as the doctrine's key components; see 'Autonomy and Consent' (n 22) 57.

consenting 'capacity', thereby defining (and regulating) not simply what might be surrendered (eg liberty) but for whom this surrendering is possible.

The following section turns its focus to three of the more common preconditions of consent: voluntariness, knowledge, and rationality. In each instance, the law's conventional approach to the precondition is examined alongside a discussion of its critiques, demonstrating the integral role the consent-as-autonomy story plays for each. While discussed separately below, it should be noted that these preconditions are both correlative, insofar as they rely on one another for coherence, and cumulative, in terms of their role in establishing a 'valid' consent, ie one which is offered voluntarily, knowingly, and rationally. This interdependence (examined in greater detail below) is derivative of liberalism's theory of state legitimacy. It is predicated on the fiction of political consent and its resultant paradoxes of autonomous action. In other words, the need to limit both what kinds of persons may consent and what kinds of things they may consent to emerges from a theory of state legitimacy grounded in individual autonomy: if persons are free to choose, they may choose not to be governed (or at least not to be governed by the same principles that might best serve the state).[26] Thus, the preconditions of consent establish not simply that a person must know what she is consenting to prior to voluntarily and rationally consenting, but rather that there are allowable (and unallowable) ways of willing, knowing, and rationalising produced by these very preconditions themselves.

The parameters of consent: productive preconditions

Voluntariness

Broadly understood as a legal recognition of free or unrestrained choice, voluntariness is arguably the most common ground upon which consent's validity is contested. Within liberal political theories of the state, government is positioned as a 'voluntary association', and while certain coercive elements will be necessary parts of state functionality, it is the degree of approximation to this ideal of voluntariness which underlies state claims to legitimacy and, as we have seen, critiques of its paternalism.[27] A similar formula functions in both medical and criminal law's theorisations of consent. Informed consent in medical law has been identified as serving legal, moral, and clinical aims.[28] Alongside ideals of preserving a patient's right to self-determination and protecting physicians

26 Mark Kann refers to this as the 'dialectic of consent' where 'the government which promotes conscientiousness and reason simultaneously maximizes the potential for citizens to dissent. Therefore, the most legitimate government is the one which promotes and tolerates the greatest challenge to its own authority'; 'The Dialectic of Consent Theory' (1978) 40(2) *J Pol* 386, 388.

27 Ruth CA Higgins, *The Moral Limits of Law* (OUP 2004) 95–96.

28 Emily Jackson, *Medical Law: Text, Cases, and Materials* (OUP 2009) 217.

from legal sanctions against battery and assault, the voluntary participation or assent to treatment is thought to facilitate care and, ideally, improve patients' clinical experiences.[29] Stemming from the Nuremberg Code, voluntariness (in its association with autonomy) is 'the most frequently mentioned moral principle in the literature on informed consent'.[30] This is an interesting contention, given the prevailing view that medical treatment operates predominantly on the basis of tacit consent. Even where a consent form is signed, a patient's consent is conceptualised as ongoing, subject to revocation at any time. Emily Jackson identifies three factors which serve to vitiate consent in medical contexts: coercion, undue influence, and mistake.[31] Each of these is discursively linked in the case law to consent's precondition of voluntariness and positioned as an interference with the free-willed action of the patient. English Courts have been reluctant to find coercion to have vitiated consent to medical treatment unless a 'real' threat can be determined to have diminished the patient's free choice, even when the political or social context the patient is in might significantly alter this range of options (eg prison).[32] Tom Beauchamp has argued for a distinction between considerations of coercive factors that are *external* to the patient versus those that are *internal*.[33] (The latter, I would suggest, are more often addressed by the courts in terms of another precondition of consent, ie 'rationality', discussed at length below.)

The same practice can be found in criminal law contexts. To be valid, consent must be given voluntarily where the level of volition is assessed in conjunction with what a reasonable (ie rational) person can be considered to have done with the knowledge the victim had at the time. This is predominant in assaults which arise within the context of sporting activities or what courts have termed 'horseplay'. In these cases, participation in the activity serves as a form of tacit consent, provided the level of risk does not exceed what is deemed 'reasonable'. Although some of the difficulties associated with judicial reliance on standards of reasonableness are explored in the ensuing subsections examining the preconditions of knowledge and rationality, the requirement of voluntariness

29 Thomas F Hack and others, 'Promoting Consultation Recording Practice in Oncology: Identification of Critical Implementation Factors and Determination of Patient Benefit' (2013) 22 *Psycho-Oncology* 1273. See also Peter C Agre and others, 'Patient Satisfaction with an Informed Consent Process' (1997) 5(7) *Cancer Pract* 162. There are studies, however, which highlight the detrimental effects of giving patients *too much* information; see Rebecca Erwin Wells, 'To Tell the Truth, the Whole Truth, May Do Patients Harm: The Problem of the Nocebo Effect for Informed Consent' (2012) 12(3) *Am J Bioeth* 22.

30 Faden and Beauchamp (n 8) 7. Yet, in his 2009 explication of the doctrine, Beauchamp has suggested that 'voluntariness is almost certainly the most neglected dimension of consent in contexts of medical practice and research' on account of the over-emphasis on the 'information' component of informed consent. See Beauchamp, 'Autonomy and Consent' (n 22) 55.

31 Jackson, *Medical Law* (n 28).

32 *Freeman v Home Office (No. 2)* [1984] 1 All ER 1036.

33 Beauchamp, 'Autonomy and Consent' (n 22).

highlights one of the oldest 'dilemmas' of consent theory and its application. Kann states the problem in this way:

> If we are social beings, how can we consent 'voluntarily'? Do our desires and reasons reveal our 'true' selves or do they merely reflect social prejudices? Herbert Marcuse's challenge that consent procedures are vacuous if our desires and reasons are socially determined is a serious one.[34]

Although perhaps easy to dismiss as a merely esoteric philosophical inquiry, the difficulty in matching the ideal (if not hypothetical) consenter with the lived realities of the actual citizen has been a tangible challenge identified in much of the literature on consent, largely with respect to its precondition of voluntariness. Carole Pateman, for instance, has argued that consent theorists suffer a 'standard embarrassment' when 'attempt[ing] to show how and when citizens perform this act [of consent]' given that grand assertions of its universality and fundamental nature tend to 'gloss over the ambiguity ... about which individuals or groups are capable of consenting and so count as full members of the political order'.[35] For Pateman, among others, consent emerges from a 'voluntarist theory of society' rooted in early political liberalism which maintains that any interferences with a citizen's liberty must be freely undertaken. Yet as Pateman has observed, such formulations do not take into account the structural inequalities within society (and the organisation of its members) which prevent any form of pure voluntariness.[36] Instead, the 'bitterest fruit of the liberal deception' is when the most disadvantaged believe social inequity to be a result of misfortune rather than the organisation of the social order itself.[37] For some scholars this is attributable to the nature of the social contract, whereby protection is granted to citizens in exchange for obedience.[38] Consent, in this frame, is more an act of submission than voluntary agreement. '[I]t marks the presence of power, arrangements, and actions that one does not oneself create but to which one submits'.[39]

Aside from these broader based concerns with the amount of voluntary action that might be possible in an unequally ordered society, consent's precondition of voluntariness is evaluated in practice in exclusionary ways. This stems from

34 Kann (n 26) 389.

35 Carole Pateman, 'Women and Consent' (1980) 8(2) *Pol Theory* 149, 150.

36 Carole Pateman, *The Disorder of Women* (Polity Press 1989).

37 Jane Mansbridge, 'Carole Pateman: Radical Liberal?' in Daniel I O'Neill, Mary Lyndon Shanley and Iris Marion Young (eds), *Illusion of Consent: Engaging with Carole Pateman* (Penn State University Press 2008) 24.

38 Charles Mills, working from Carole Pateman's *The Sexual Contract*, suggests this entrenched social inequality creates a 'class contract' rather than a social contract. See C Mills, 'The Domination Contract' in O'Neill, Shanley and Young (n 37).

39 Wendy Brown, *States of Injury: Power and Freedom in Late Modernity* (PUP 1995) 162–163. This is akin to the medieval understanding of consent as a form of submission to God – something that is explored at length in Chapter 3. The difference, of course, is that in the medieval medical and canonical context, consent was not presented as a form of personal freedom as it is within liberal articulations.

the same measured approach to paternalism which Feinberg (and others) have advocated, given the paradox of autonomy that classical liberalism creates and maintains. Liberal notions of autonomy attempt to house both individual self-determination and individual well-being, where the latter can often fall into conflict with the former.[40] Feinberg's soft paternalism brings voluntariness to the fore, questioning how voluntary any act of self-harm can be. He suggests that '[w]hen there is a strong presumption that no *normal* person would voluntarily choose or consent to the kind of conduct in question, that should be a proper ground for detaining the person until the voluntary character of his choice can be established'.[41] This demonstrates that consent's precondition of voluntariness is often assessed alongside a consideration of the perceived reasonableness of either an act of self-harm or an assumption of risk. Further, Feinberg's own use of the term 'normal' points to a dominant (if not hegemonic) notion of reasonableness that is at work in these considerations, perhaps most poignantly when the courts have made determinations of consent on 'public policy' grounds.[42] As noted by the UK Law Commission in its 1994 *Report on Consent*:

> The law clearly reserves the right to say that some activities do not qualify for special exemption at all; just as it reserves the right to say that, within a lawful sport, public policy requires that injury caused by some of the sport's practices, even though accepted by the injured player, should be dealt with as criminal in nature.[43]

This reveals that in both the criminal and medical contexts, the would-be-consenter's voluntariness is not a stand-alone consideration but rather one linked (arguably inseparably) to both the level of information or knowledge the participant can be said to have had when expressing a voluntary will and an assessment of the reasonableness or rational acceptability of that volition. These two preconditions are examined in greater detail below.

Knowledge

The word 'consent' is derived from the Latin *consentire*, meaning 'to feel or sense with' – an origin which alludes to the cognitive and emotional requirements that make up another of consent's preconditions: knowledge. Alongside considerations of voluntariness and rationality, the law's assessment of the validity of consent relies on a judgment of what the would-be-consenter *knows*. Even the *capacity* to consent is defined in relation to a subject's ability to know

40 Dan W Brock, 'Paternalism and Autonomy: Review of Feinberg's *Harm to Self* and VanDeVeer's *Paternalistic Intervention*' (1988) 98(3) *Ethics* 550.

41 Feinberg, 'Legal Paternalism' (n 9) 114 (emphasis added).

42 See, for instance, the English cases of *Brown* [1993] 2 All ER 75 and *Wilson* [1996] 2 Cr App Rep 241.

43 Law Commission (UK), *Consent and Offences against the Person* (Law Com No. 134, 1994) 22–23.

and understand the relevant circumstances of a consent (or its waiver): a person is held to be competent to consent if they are deemed able to understand what they are consenting to.

The link between consent and knowledge is most explicitly recognised in the medico-legal doctrine of informed consent where a patient's ongoing understanding of the treatment process is viewed as central to the fiduciary relationship between physicians and their patients. The 1767 English case of *Slater v Baker and Stapleton*[44] is widely cited as the 'first informed consent case' and the beginning of a physician's legal duty to ensure that patients are adequately informed about the procedures awaiting them.[45] A view of the 'self-governing' patient, however, is attributed a twentieth-century origin, alongside the development of a 'partnership model' of decision-making between doctors and their patients.[46] This has led some medical legal scholars to describe informed consent as an ongoing 'process', given the continuing dialogue thought necessary to ensure that patients understand the nature and consequences of their condition and its treatment.[47] Consent's 'process model' entails a series of steps from an initial report of injury or illness through the documentation of a patient's history, diagnosis and/or designation of a care plan, disclosure of treatment options and risks, confirmation of a patient's understanding of available options and associated contingencies, and the patient's (ongoing) decisions with respect to treatment(s).[48]

The precondition of knowledge figures large in this process model and is perhaps most explicitly represented by the 'consent form', thought to signify a patient's clear understanding of the treatment in question (despite ample evidence to the contrary).[49] Where comprehension is an issue, some medical scholars have suggested that the solution lies in enhanced procedural requirements, such as a formal assessment of language and reading comprehension skills administered prior to the signing of a consent form,[50] whereas others have experimented with shortened consent forms as a means of improving patient understanding.[51] Still others have suggested that the problem of ascertaining whether a patient has sufficient knowledge of a treatment prior to granting consent lies in the unequal

44 (1767) 2 Wils KB 359, 95 ER 850.

45 Walter KG Leclercq and others, 'A Review of Surgical Informed Consent: Past, Present, and Future. A Quest to Help Patients Make Better Decisions' (2010) 34 *World J Surg* 1406; Kayvan Shokrollah, 'Request for Treatment: The Evolution of Consent' (2010) 92 *Ann R Coll Surg Engl* 93.

46 Jackson, *Medical Law* (n 28).

47 Lorne Elkin Rozovsky, *The Canadian Law of Consent to Treatment* (3rd edn, Butterworths 2003).

48 Rozovsky (n 47).

49 See, for instance, a 1993 study reported in the *British Medical Journal* that found 69% of patients admitted to not reading the consent form before signing it ($N = 265$); C Lavelle-Jones and others, 'Factors Affecting Quality of Informed Consent' (1993) 306 *BMJ* 885.

50 DW Fitzgerald and others, 'Comprehension during Informed Consent in a Less-Developed Country' (2002) 360(9342) *Lancet* 1301.

51 Traci Mann, 'Informed Consent for Psychological Research: Do Subjects Comprehend Consent Forms and Understand their Rights?' (1994) 5(3) *Psychol Sci* 140.

power relations between doctors and patients. In her consideration of tort law's treatment of medical malpractice cases, Emily Jackson argues that the doctrine of informed consent serves as a kind of 'shorthand for two distinct duties: the duty to obtain the patient's consent before treatment, and the duty to ensure that the patient has been properly informed about its risks and benefits'.[52] Jackson contends that in neither case does the law adequately protect patients' rights to make informed decisions nor provide remedies for when they have not done so. Instead, medical law's emphasis on consent (and its precondition of knowledge) creates a 'paternalistic model of medical decision making in which a doctor offers the patient one treatment option, which can then be accepted or declined'.[53]

These critiques of informed consent's ability to ward off the dangers of paternalism echo those raised by Feinberg, Dworkin, and others as they struggled with preserving liberalism's commitment to autonomy within socio-political contexts that constrain rather than foster free choice. It is in this way that the limits of consent can be defined by its preconditions such that an inadequate amount of information or a lack of reasonable alternatives will vitiate the 'moral magic' of consent and act as impediments to autonomous decision-making. Jackson alludes to these difficulties when rejecting the law of negligence as an appropriate avenue for the protection of patients' autonomous interests, given juridical determinations of the appropriate standard of care in non-disclosure cases. There, considerations of the 'reasonable doctor' and/or the 'prudent patient' are often not desirable, given their reliance on customary standards and hypothetical contexts.

Consent's knowledge requirement is also positioned within a sphere of normative standards in the criminal law context, particularly in assault cases that occur during sporting activities. A player's participation in a sport is understood to be a form of tacit consent to injury, provided the conduct is that which could be reasonably expected during the regular rules of play. Determining the parameters of what is 'reasonable' or 'normal', however, is a daunting task. Courts have often taken judicial notice of behaviour and attitudes that fall outside the official rulebooks, taking into account unwritten codes of playing culture and attitudes. When dismissing an assault charge against a rugby player who had stomped on the head of an opposing player during a match, a Newcastle judge asserted she was 'flabbergasted' the Crown had pursued the case at all, dismissing the injury as 'the sort that happens within the rough and tumble of a rugby match'.[54] This speaks to a number of the issues raised in Chapter 4's

52 Emily Jackson, 'Informed Consent and the Impotence of Tort' in Sheila McLean (ed), *First Do No Harm: Law, Ethics, and Healthcare* (Ashgate 2006) 273.

53 Jackson, 'Informed Consent' (n 52) 279. This is akin to Wendy Brown's argument that consent serves as a marker of 'legitimate subordination'. See Brown, *States of Injury* (n 39) 163 (discussed later in this chapter at text to n 103).

54 *R v Evans* (unreported) Crown Court (Newcastle), 14 June 2006; as cited in Paul Stokes, 'Judge Throws Out Assault Case Over Rugby Player's Small Bruise' *The Telegraph* (15 June 2006). The UK case law often employs the term 'on-the-ball' (rugby, football) or 'off-the-puck' (ice hockey) to describe incidents of violence which occur during the ordinary play of a game from those which exceed what could normally be expected among players. As Hartley (2009)

survey of the consent defence in sport and play contexts, where codes of hegemonic masculinity figure prominently. Players are expected to learn '"how things are done here" through unwritten rules/norms, expectations, shared values, role models, traditions, attitudes, reactions to incidents of violence, which they internalise from the moment they join that group'.[55] The player's knowledge of these codes is a key component in the law's assessment of whether an 'implied sporting consent' can be claimed.

This same discourse of 'unwritten rules' is employed in consent discussions of sexual assault law, even accompanied in some cases with explicit 'game playing' language.[56] While knowledge of and abidance with the often unstated 'codes' of (sexual) conduct are integral considerations of consent in sexual assault cases, in contrast to assaults which take place on a sporting field, in sexual contexts these codes speak to the reasonableness of the assailant's belief in consent rather than the validity of the consent itself. This distinction is often explained in the literature with reference to the mental elements of the offence. The requisite *mens rea* of sexual assault requires that the assailant knew the victim was not consenting or, in the event of an honest but mistaken belief in consent, the establishment that this mistaken belief was reasonable.[57] The difficulty arises when these standards of reasonableness are established within frameworks that both rely on and propagate harmful stereotypes about male and female sexuality.[58] This was explicitly recognised by the Supreme Court of Canada in the sexual assault case, *Seaboyer* (1991) in the dissenting judgment offered by L'Heureux-Dubé J:

> The woman who comes to the attention of the authorities has her victimization measured against the current rape mythologies, i.e. who she should be in order to be recognized as having been, in the eyes of the law, raped; who her attacker must be in order to be recognized, in the eyes of the law, as a potential rapist; and how injured she must be in order to be believed. If her victimization does not fit the myths, it is unlikely that an arrest will be made or a conviction obtained.[59]

---

observes, these on-the-ball incidents rarely come to trial and when they do, they can suffer critiques similar to the one offered by Judge Bolton in the *Evans* case: Hazel Hartley, *Sport, Physical Recreation, and the Law* (Routledge 2009) 109.

55 Hartley (n 54) 114.

56 David Archard, *Sexual Consent* (Westview Press 1998) 8.

57 *R v Ewanchuk* [1999] 1 SCR 330 (SCC). There is also an allowance in both the British and Canadian jurisprudence for considerations of recklessness or 'culpable indifference' where it can be established that the accused was either unsure as to whether the complainant was consenting or, based on all the circumstances, *ought* to have known she wasn't. See: *B (A Child) v DPP* [2000] 1 All ER 833; and *R v Sansregret* [1985] 1 SCR 570.

58 Anastasia Powell speaks to this when she argues that the law's treatment of sexual consent creates a circumstance where 'it is considered normal, even expected, that a woman would not be forthright in expressing sexual desire (so as not to appear unfeminine) and thus it is considered normal, even likely, that a man might misinterpret a woman's sexual signals'; *Sex, Power and Consent: Youth Culture and the Unwritten Rules* (CUP 2010) 87.

59 *R v Seaboyer* [1991] 2 SCR 577, 650–651.

The 'reasonableness' of an accused's belief in a sexual partner's consent is thus reliant on a set of unwritten rules about sexuality, communication, and gender codes, which privilege certain subjects and experiences while prejudicing others. This is perhaps best evidenced in the case law addressing the defence of an honest but mistaken belief in consent where both English (*DPP v Morgan*)[60] and Canadian (*Pappajohn*)[61] Courts have a history of upholding the mistake defence even where the accused's belief was explicitly recognised as not reasonable.[62] Elizabeth Sheehy speaks to the inherent bias of this standard:

> Men's stories can aspire to 'reasonableness' not only because the women assaulted have been silenced by sleep, alcohol, drugs or some combination, but also because these stories tap into phallocentric beliefs. Such beliefs condition our willingness to disregard women's accounts of rape and to instead accept that their bodies have betrayed them, and that honest men, bewildered by what Carol Smart calls the unknowability of women's sexual desires and consistent with male pornographic imagination, have been seduced by unconscious women.[63]

Studies within the field of conversation analysis suggest ways in which hegemonic norms about male and female sexuality inform both judicial treatments of consent within sexual assault law and feminist advocacy projects which emphasise 'just say no' strategies.[64] Using comparisons with other forms of refusals found in day-to-day conversation, Kitzinger and Frith found that 'it should not ... be necessary for a woman to say "no" for her to be understood as refusing sex'.[65] Instead, these policies serve to cement and proliferate assumptions about the

60 [1976] AC 182.

61 [1980] 2 SCR 120.

62 In Canada there have been some legislative attempts to remedy this (see section 273.2 of the Criminal Code), although even these reforms are not without their critics: see Elizabeth Sheehy (ed), *Sexual Assault in Canada: Law, Legal Practice & Women's Activism* (University of Ottawa Press 2012). Similarly, in the United Kingdom, the Sexual Offences Act suggests the reasonableness of the accused's belief should be assessed 'having regard to all the circumstances' (section 4(2)). The legal allowance for unreasonable (and mistaken) beliefs in consent can be found in other jurisdictions as well. For a comment on the relevant Australian jurisprudence, see Wendy Larcombe, '*Worsnop v The Queen:* Subjective Belief in Consent Prevails (Again) in Victoria's Rape Law' (2011) 35(2) *MULR* 697. For a review of the American case law and statutory regimes, see Michelle J Anderson, 'From Chastity Requirement to Sexuality License: Sexual Consent and a New Rape Shield Law' (2002) 70 *Geo Wash L Rev* 51.

63 Sheehy (n 62) 488, referencing Carol Smart, 'Law's Truth/Women's Experiences' in Regina Graycar (ed), *Dissenting Opinions: Feminist Explorations in Law and Society* (Allen & Unwin 1990). See also the 2011 Supreme Court of Canada case, *R v JA* [2011] 2 SCR 440, which overturned an appellate court's decision to issue an acquittal in a sexual assault case involving an unconscious complainant on the basis that she had previously consented to being choked into an unconscious state (as part of the couple's experimentation with erotic asphyxiation).

64 Celia Kitzinger and Hannah Frith, '"Just Say No?" The Use of Conversation Analysis in Developing a Feminist Perspective on Sexual Refusal' (1999) 10(3) *D&S* 293.

65 Kitzinger and Frith (n 64) 294.

inherent 'nature' of women's lack of assertiveness and submissive sexuality. As Kitzinger and Frith note:

> If there is an organized and normative way of doing indirect refusal which provides for culturally understood ways in which (for example) 'maybe later' means 'no', then men who claim not to have understood an indirect refusal (as in 'she didn't actually say no') are claiming to be cultural dopes, and playing rather disingenuously on how refusals are usually done and understood to be done. They are claiming not to understand perfectly normal conversational interaction, and to be ignorant of ways of expressing refusal which they themselves routinely use in other areas of their lives ... [T]he root of the problem is not that men do not understand sexual refusals, but that they do not like them.[66]

This suggests that approaches to consent which propose 'just say no' strategies do more to protect the rapist from criminal liability than they do to empower sexual agency or remedy the harm of sexual assault – a critique that has also been made of informed consent in medical law for protecting doctors from malpractice suits rather than increasing patient choice.[67] Further, these beliefs underlie the unwritten codes which inform both cultural and legal assessments of the reasonableness of an accused's mistaken belief in consent.[68]

This highlights an important aspect of consent's precondition of knowledge, ie the explicitness with which it demonstrates the epistemological hierarchy law employs when assessing the validity (or availability) of consent. Players, patients,

66 Kitzinger and Frith (n 64) 310.

67 See, for instance, Emily Jackson's critique of the use of tort law in cases involving arguably inadequately informed consent, 'Informed Consent' (n 52). In the area of criminal law, Matthew Weait identifies a legal tension in consent's role as the definitive element in the *actus reus* of sexual assault (ie to enhance or protect a person's bodily integrity) and its role as a defence to the assault (where it vitiates liability). He argues that where consent is used as a defence, 'the law protects a putative defendant from criminal liability not on the basis that no recognisable harm has been caused, but because of the context in which it has taken place. It follows that in such circumstances the law is not, at least *prima facie*, concerned with protecting, or indeed "enhancing" the autonomy of the person harmed, but rather with protecting the person who harms from the imposition of unjustified liability. Put simply, it is his autonomy (in the sense of his right to be free from unwarranted interference and condemnation by the state) that the law is concerned to protect'. Interestingly, Weait identifies this tension in relation to the types of autonomy consent serves in each instance (thus, even in complicating the consent-as-autonomy story, his critique maintains it): Matthew Weait, 'Knowledge, Autonomy, and Consent: *R v Konzani*' (2005) *Crim LR* 763, 768–769.

68 A 2009 study at Yale law school found that 'cultural cognition' (defined by the researcher as 'the tendency of individuals to conform their perceptions of legally consequential facts to their defining group commitments') had a significant impact on participants' understandings and applications of consent. 'Cultural predispositions', the study reported, 'exert such a powerful influence over perceptions of consent and other legally consequential facts that no change in the definition of rape is likely to affect results': Dan M Kahan, 'Culture, Cognition, and Consent: Who Perceives What, and Why, in Acquaintance-Rape Cases' (2010) 158 *U Pa L Rev* 729, 805.

and sex partners are required to know certain things in certain ways before their consent is legally recognised. A key delimiter of the 'right way' of knowing in consent configurations is a legal (and cultural) standard of reasonableness, grounded in the third precondition of consent: rationality.

Rationality

The law's aim of protecting the 'public interest' is a central engine in considerations of a consenter's rationality. Alluded to in the common law maxim *non consentit qui errat* (one who errs does not consent), consent is only valid if it is deemed to 'make sense'. Where one's choice is likened to a mistake or illogic, the law prohibits consent.[69] Amartya Sen has argued that this practice of public assessment is an integral component to reason, defining rationality as the 'discipline of subjecting one's choices – of actions as well as objectives, values, and priorities – to reasoned scrutiny'.[70] Although often articulated in a form consistent with liberal political theory, considerations of rationality found in judicial treatments of consent are not simply matters of reasoned self-interest or preservation. Sen, for instance, links rationality to freedom of thought, where rationality serves to recognise (and ideally) 'accommodate the diversity of reasons that may sensibly motivate choice'.[71] The law's interpretation of the meaning and scope of 'sensibly', however, creates a wide ambit from which many acts and desires are excluded.

In the criminal law context this is perhaps most explicit in cases involving sadomasochistic activity. In the English case of *Brown* (1993), the court rejected the defence of consent put forth by the defendants who had willingly participated in sadomasochistic (homosexual) activity over a period of ten years.[72] The defendants' voluntariness was not in question (nor their knowledge of the activities in which they willingly engaged), but the court denied the defence of consent because 'the infliction of bodily harm *without good reason* is unlawful'.[73] Determining the content of 'good reason' is largely a matter left to consent's precondition of rationality. Whereas the court in *Brown* was able to recognise the underlying rationale for such risk-associated and purposely harmful activities as tattooing, ritual circumcision, and violent sports, it viewed the sadomasochistic activity of the defendants as lacking in good reason and thus contrary to the 'public interest'.[74] Far less extreme cases exhibit the same approach. Judicial treatments

69 Cases involving refusals to medical treatment on religious grounds (eg Jehovah's Witness patients and blood transfusions) provide good examples of this; see Lori Beaman, *Defining Harm: Religious Freedom and the Limits of the Law* (UBC Press 2008).

70 Amartya Sen, *Rationality and Freedom* (HUP 2004) 4.

71 Sen (n 70) 5.

72 *Brown* (n 42).

73 *Brown* (n 42) 16 (emphasis added).

74 Interestingly, the court in *Brown* relied upon the judgment in *R v Donovan* [1934] 2 KB 498, where Lord Lane equated 'good reason' with the public interest. Marianne Giles in her commentary on the *Brown* case suggests this amounts to requiring 'a court to in effect ask

of consent in any case involving a form of voluntary self-harm have emphasised the 'general principle' that interference with autonomy is justified only where a strong reason to do so exists.[75] In these cases, language of the 'common good' or public interest is invoked to construct the content of this reason.

In the medical law field, the articulation of consent's requirement of rationality is, at first glance, treated quite separately from concerns about public policy. The evaluation of one's rational decision-making abilities often rests on an assessment of whether 'undue influence' has been exerted on the would-be consenter. Similar to the law's consideration of the external and internal aspects of voluntariness, the courts have sought to identify the leading influences on medical patients' consenting capacities. This has been articulated by the courts as an exercise in assessing the patient's 'strength of will' and the degrees to which it might be tempered by states of illness or pain or the presence of a 'persuasive' relationship.[76] This is an approach which echoes the court's attempts in *Brown* to negate the defendants' consent through renderings of the activity involved as coerced or involuntary as a result of drug/alcohol use and the 'undue influence' of older participants.[77] Similar negations of consent are found in cases involving religious objections to medical treatment, where the conflation of consent's preconditions of voluntariness and rationality can be seen (even amidst explicit statements to the contrary). See, for instance, the reasoning of Lord Donaldson in *Re T*,[78] a case involving an adult who was Jehovah's Witness and refused blood transfusions on religious grounds:

> Prima facie every adult has the right and capacity to decide whether or not he will accept medical treatment, even if a refusal may risk permanent injury to his health or even lead to premature death. Furthermore, *it matters not whether the reasons for the refusal were rational or irrational, unknown or even non-existent.* This is so notwithstanding the very strong public interest in preserving the life and health of all citizens.[79]

---

the same question twice', see Marianne Giles, '*R v Brown:* Consensual Harm and the Public Interest' (1994) 57(1) *MLR* 101, 104.

75 UK Commission Paper (n 43) 11. Interesting to note is the discursive similarity between judicial treatments of 'irrational' acts conducted under the guise of (infelicitous) consent with articulations of the 'public interest' at stake in security measures which infringe upon fundamental freedoms. See, for instance, Peter Ramsay's work on Anti-Social Behaviour Orders and the re-articulation of 'public policy' as a discretionary power of the state to determine the components of a 'good way of life' (Lord Justice Glidewell in *Hughes v. Holley* (1988) 86 Cr App R 130 at 139, as cited in Peter Ramsay, 'Vulnerability, Sovereignty, and Police Power in the ASBO' in Markus D Dubber and Mariana Valverde (eds), *Police and the Liberal State* (SUP 2008) 164.

76 See, for example, the discussion of the legal test for competence to consent to medical treatment in Cameron Stewart, Carmelle Peisah, and Brian Draper, 'A Test for Mental Capacity to Request Assisted Suicide' (2011) 37(1) *J Med Eth* 34.

77 Giles (n 74) 107.

78 *Re T (adult) (refusal of medical treatment)* [1992] 4 All ER 649.

79 *Re T* (n 78) 664 (emphasis added).

Lord Donaldson goes on to note that the presumption of consenting *capacity*, however, is a rebuttable one. Through an invocation of the 'public interest', the court is able to question the rationality of the patient's consent refusal under the rubric of 'undue influence', ultimately denying its validity:

> Persuasion based upon religious belief can also be much more compelling and the fact that arguments based upon religious beliefs are being deployed by someone in a very close relationship with the patient will give them added force and should alert the doctors to the possibility—no more—that the patient's capacity or will to decide has been overborne. In other words the patient may not mean what he says.[80]

Some scholars have suggested that distinctions can be drawn between patient wishes which are 'mere desires' and those which can be thought sufficiently rational to signify consent.[81] While this view has led some to argue for a more structured format for assessing consenting competency, others suggest that evaluations of a patient's capacity are 'often omitted if the patient's decision "makes sense"'.[82] Similar to the epistemological hierarchy enacted in consent's precondition of knowledge, the danger in these assessments of what constitutes a rational choice or action lies in their tendency to rely upon and further inscribe hegemonic belief systems. As Lori Beaman demonstrates in her examination of cases involving religious objections to medical treatment, the freedom to make decisions according to religious belief is restricted, in law, to 'those religions that look like mainstream Christianity or are most familiar to many Canadians. Those beliefs and practices that lie outside that hegemony are often constructed as harmful, or as potentially resulting in harm, and thus their limitation is justifiable'.[83] Thus, the law's assessment of what behaviour might fall into excessive categories of 'risk' is mediated by consent's precondition of rationality – itself constructed with shared understandings or common sense 'community standards'.[84] Beaman suggests this point is well illustrated in the

80 *Re T* (n 78) 662.

81 See Julian Savulescu, 'Rational Desires and the Limitation of Life-Sustaining Treatment' (1994) 8 *Bioethics* 191, where he argues the decisions of Jehovah's Witnesses to refuse blood transfusions are irrational on the basis that they are 'mere desires' rather than rational forms of will. See also Tom Beauchamp's (2009) commentary on Savulescu in 'Autonomy and Consent' (n 22) 62–63.

82 Andrew S Pomerantz and Alexander de Nesnera, 'Informed Consent, Competency, and the Illusion of Rationality' (1991) 13(2) *GH Psych* 138, 138.

83 Beaman (n 69) 67.

84 See *R v Butler* [1992] 1 SCR 452, a Canadian Supreme Court decision which decided the confines of obscenity on a national 'community standards test', described as a 'standard of *tolerance,* not taste' by (then) Chief Justice Dickson in the earlier case, *Towne Cinema Theatres Ltd v The Queen* [1985] 1 SCR 494. When describing the application of the test to a film challenged with obscenity, Dickson elaborated: 'What matters is not what Canadians think is right for themselves to see. What matters is what Canadians would not abide other Canadians seeing', 508–509, as cited in *Butler*, 477. The American '*Miller* test' (so named for its development

Canadian case, *BH*,[85] where the courts forced a 16-year-old Jehovah's Witness to undergo a blood transfusion, vitiating her consent (in part) on the basis of rationality. Provocatively, Beaman positions the court's reasoning as an articulation of the 'common sense' position that '[a]nyone who is willing to risk death for her religious beliefs cannot be thinking rationally. Clearly, she has been unduly influenced, duped, brainwashed'.[86]

Although many of the difficulties stemming from the law's use of public policy or 'community standards' arguments in legal assessments of the reasonableness of a consent to injury or refusal of medical treatment has been amply reviewed in the literature,[87] what is often left unexamined is the contribution the consent-as-autonomy story makes to this framework. As Ackerman has argued within the context of medical law's informed consent doctrine, autonomy is rooted in two fundamental beliefs about human behaviour and cognition which stem from classical political liberalism.[88] One of these is the principle of non-interference. Autonomy is often thought to be best preserved when persons are 'left alone' to make their own choices.[89] In the medical ethics field, this has manifested as a doctrine of 'non-interference' within the doctor-patient relationship where after sufficient disclosure, patients' choices and actions are their own. Ackerman's own position on this model of non-interference is akin to that taken by many contemporary bioethicists who suggest that aside from ample discussion about disclosure procedures, very little attention is paid to the myriad of factors which can influence one's ability to act autonomously, perhaps pre-eminently, illness.[90] Further, this principle assumes that patients are already autonomous in their decisions (when given the necessary conditions or opportunities) which pre-empts examinations of the ways that these decisions are made and the factors that can

in the obscenity case *Miller v* California, 413 US 15 (1973) contains a similar prong which examines the tolerance of 'the average person, applying contemporary community standards'. Chapter Three explores how a similar framework was employed during the medieval period where consent served as an indicator of how well human appetites and desires were 'balanced' or moderated so as to avoid sinful excess.

85 *BH (Next friend of) v Alberta (Director of Child Welfare)* 2002 ABQB 371.

86 Beaman (n 69) 91.

87 Nicola Padfield surveys some of the UK case law on this matter in her article 'Consent and the public interest' (1992) 142 *NLJ* 430. See also Chapter 4's discussion on the defence of consent in sport for a review of some of these critiques (and consequences) of the 'public policy' objections to consent.

88 Terrence F Ackerman, 'Medical Ethics and the Two Dogmas of Liberalism' (1982) 5 *Theo Med* 69.

89 This marks the distinction that some philosophers have made between 'autonomy' and 'freedom', where the former is limited to forms and capacities of self-governance and the latter is meant to represent unconstrained action. See, for instance, Gerald Dworkin, *The Theory and Practice of Autonomy* (CUP 1988); John Christman, 'Autonomy and Personal History' (1991) 21(1) *Cdn J of Phil* 1; and also Christman's 'Constructing the Inner Citadel: Recent Work on Autonomy' (1988) 99 *Ethics* 109.

90 There are, however, many legal and bioethics scholars who oppose the view that illness undermines one's ability to act autonomously. See Sheila McLean, *Autonomy, Consent, and the Law* (Routledge 2010) 55; and Miller and Wertheimer (n 22) as examples.

influence them. This has led many contemporary writers in the field to advocate for the 'process model' of obtaining consent, discussed earlier.[91]

A second tenet of classical liberalism that underlies dominant understandings of autonomy is that agentic or autonomous human behaviour is that which is governed by a plan or intended course of action which has itself been reached through a process of rational deliberation. For Ackerman, this deliberation entails an 'investigation of the factual circumstances affecting the choice of goals and the means for achieving them, as well as the setting of preferences based upon such investigation'.[92] For these deliberations to be considered 'rational', the investigation of the surrounding factual circumstances, the preferences an individual has within these circumstances, and the hierarchy or priority to which these preferences are assigned must conform in some meaningful way to dominant norms and preferences in similar circumstances. As Mele has argued, to be an autonomous agent one must be capable of *reliable* deliberation.[93] This reliability, then, is determined on the basis of whether the factors that have influenced a person's decision are familiar, common, or 'known' to those judging the deliberation. This requirement of familiarity or reliability – as the differently pleasured in *Brown* or the Jehovah's Witness in *BH* know already – is of central importance to the law, its notions of responsibility, and its limits. As Morse notes:

> The law's conception of the person as a practical reasoner is inevitable if one considers the nature of law. At base, law is a system of rules and standards expressed in language that are meant to guide human behaviour. The law therefore presupposes that people are capable of using rules and standards as premises in the practical syllogisms that guide action … The law's concept of responsibility follows from its view of the person and the nature of law itself. Unless human beings are rational creatures who can understand the applicable rules and standards, and can conform to those legal requirements through intentional action, the law would be powerless to affect human behavior. Legally responsible agents are therefore people who have the general capacity to grasp and be guided by good reason in particular legal contexts. They must be capable of rational practical reasoning.[94]

91 For Ackerman this would mean a reconceptualisation of patient autonomy from the 'ready-made ability' model to a 'process of personal growth … a re-direction of conduct'. This, he argues, helps to recognise the ways in which patients' autonomous choices are made in conjunction with (or as a result of) interactions they have had with a health care professional. However, Ackerman maintains that the application of liberalism's dogma of non-interference 'to the therapeutic relationship denies this insight. It suggests that maximal exercise of autonomous behavior by patients is to be secured by establishing recognition of "choice rights" which assure non-interference in their efforts to deal with the disruptive effects of illness … The only proviso is that disclosure through informed consent be undertaken to fill the usual information gap' (n 88) 72–73.

92 Ackerman (n 88) 70.

93 Mele also adds the requirements of a certain degree of mental stability and self-control to the recipe for autonomy: Alfred R Mele, 'Agency and Mental Action' (1997) 11 *Phil Persp* 231.

94 Stephen J Morse, 'Rationality and Responsibility' (2000) 74 *S Cal L Rev* 251, 252–253.

A key component, then, to the precondition of rationality is an evaluation of how well reasoned or deliberated a particular decision has been. Further, an assessment of this process of reasoning necessitates some knowledge and acceptance of the factors or 'rules and standards' used as 'premises in the practical syllogisms' that have guided one's decision (to employ Morse's terminology). For law and, in particular, its delineation of who can and cannot consent, this requires an invocation of the 'common sense'. It echoes notes of familiarity and reliability – key elements of liberalism's view of rational deliberation. This presents little difficulty to those subjects whose own beliefs and value systems (if not bodies and identities) fall squarely within the familiar; however, for those whose creeds and choices are deemed too 'strange', consent's precondition of rationality is not met.[95] To employ the language of the House of Lords in *Brown*, these nonconformists are left with 'no good reason'.

In some instances, being too far outside the realm of the 'common' renders a consideration of consent irrelevant from the onset, irrespective of whether it has met the necessary preconditions. This lends credence to MacLean's observation that 'for consent to have normative or justificatory force, it will have to be conceptually linked to other concepts, most importantly, to the concept of rationality'.[96] The promise of free will, liberty, and self-governance that consent is meant to signify and protect seems available for some people and practices but not others. Central to the production and maintenance of these governing norms of 'good reason' is the establishment of a 'common sense' – one that can privilege certain behaviours and subjectivities while obscuring alternative accounts of being and acting in the world. This relationship between consent and the 'sense we hold in common' warrants further exploration.

Conceptualising the common: tacit consent and intelligibility

While writing about penal reform during the late eighteenth and early nineteenth centuries, Alan Norrie notes that many of the central notions of the Enlightenment which influenced the reform movement, such as free individualism, are 'tempting simply to see … ahistorically, as part of the triumph of reason and progress in human affairs'.[97] In spite of a recognition that this ahistorical lens is the one most often employed by lawyers and legal theorists, Norrie maintains that historicising these concepts is an essential task for legal scholars, given the ways in which these doctrines have 'served important social interests

95 For a discussion of how this characterisation of 'strangeness' functions in Canadian case law addressing indecency, obscenity, sexual deviance, polygamy, and freedom of religion (among minority religions), see Jennifer Olijnyk, 'A Question of Strangeness' (LLM thesis, University of Toronto Faculty of Law 2010).

96 Douglas MacLean (ed), *Values at Risk* (Rowman & Littlefield 1986) 17.

97 Alan Norrie, *Crime, Reason and History: A Critical Introduction to Criminal Law* (3rd edn, CUP 2014) 24.

and embodied particular ideological stances and strategies'.[98] An appreciation for these social relations is of particular importance when, as some critical legal scholars have argued, the relations are both unequal and supported by embedded ideologies. In such circumstances, 'the liberal emphasis on free individuals makes the theory itself the bearer of subordination'.[99]

Carole Pateman articulates this very position in her 1988 text, *The Sexual Contract*, where she contends that the social contract theory of classical liberalism both creates and relies on a fiction of property in the person. Although Pateman's central concern throughout the text is with the civil subordination this fiction creates for women when control over their bodies is 'contracted out' to others via marriage, prostitution, and surrogacy agreements (among other social relationships governed by contract theory), her critique is equally applicable to other circumstances where the consent-as-autonomy story operates amidst conditions of social inequality. Although the power to contract is often heralded among liberal scholars as the ultimate symbol of freedom,[100] Pateman maintains that this is dependent on the social context in which a contract is made.[101] In this way, Pateman draws a distinction between contract and consent on the basis that the former can create new relationships whereas the latter merely operates within a given frame of existing social relations. Wendy Brown has made a similar observation, suggesting that the liberal understanding of consent constructs a state of subservience rather than autonomy wherein one submits to terms that are not one's own; one acquiesces to the circumstances set by another.[102] For Brown, this leaves consent to mark the boundaries of 'legitimate subordination'. Using the example of contemporary rape law, she elaborates:

> If in rape law, men are seen to *do* sex while women *consent* to it, if the measure of rape is not whether a woman sought or desired sex but whether she acceded to it or refused it when it was pressed upon her, then consent

98 Norrie (n 97) 24. Norrie's study is largely concerned with how these ideological positions become 'embedded in the law itself', thus gaining a somewhat unquestionable status. In her own historical study of the notion of criminal responsibility in English law, Nicola Lacey observes the same pervasive influence of classical liberalism, noting that 'the responsible subject of criminal law today is a certain kind of citizen, and a rational, self-determining moral agent' which owes its roots to 'a set of ideas about human being and a set of values which finds expression, variously, in the work of [Enlightenment] philosophers': Nicola Lacey, 'In Search of the Responsible Subject: History, Philosophy and Social Sciences in Criminal Law Theory' (2001) 64(3) *MLR* 350, 357.

99 Mansbridge (n 37) 27.

100 Take, for example, Robert Nozick's position that 'voluntary slavery' can be morally justifiable on the basis that it has been freely consented to: Robert Nozick, *Anarchy, State, and Utopia* (Basic Books 1974) 331; or Richard Posner's contention that 'consensual enslavement' is a 'wealth-maximizing, voluntary, and thus moral sale of labor': Robin West, 'Authority, Autonomy, and Choice: The Role of Consent in the Moral and Political Visions of Franz Kafka and Richard Posner' (1985) 99 *Harv LR* 384, 395; describing Richard A Posner, *The Economics of Justice* (HUP 1981).

101 Carole Pateman, 'Afterword' in O'Neill, Shanley and Young (n 37).

102 Brown, *States of Injury* (n 39).

> operates both as a sign of subordination and a means of its legitimation. Consent is thus a response to power – it adds or withdraws legitimacy – but is not a mode of enacting or sharing in power. Moreover, since consent is obtained or registered rather than enacted, consent is always mediated by authority … and is thus both constitutive of that authority and legitimated by it.[103]

Pateman makes a parallel contention within the context of employment contracts, where an employee's continued participation in the workplace is viewed as a form of agreement with its conditions, however unequal they might be. Pateman notes '[i]t might be argued that, rather than giving consent, the individual assents or acquiesces to the power structure, but this raises other equally familiar difficulties about tacit consent'.[104]

Although Pateman herself doesn't tackle these 'familiar difficulties', it seems safe to assume that at least one of them is tacit consent's necessary (and widely acknowledged) hypothetical character. As this chapter's earlier discussion of political theorists' battles with legal paternalism noted, consent's status as a political fiction is often attributed to a practical problem, ie the impossibility of obtaining actual consent in many cases. Yet, what this kind of account overlooks is the role of this fictional status in establishing and entrenching the consent-as-autonomy story. In the first instance, attributing a 'common sense' to a group can serve homogeneous ends within a collection of persons who are likely never to know one another. This is acknowledged explicitly in the work of Benedict Anderson, who argues that the sense of socio-political belonging that is produced through invocations of a hypothetical or tacit consent creates an 'imagined community', given that 'the members of even the smallest nation will never know most of their fellow members, meet them, or even hear of them, yet in the minds of each lives the image of their communion'.[105] For Anderson, this sense of belonging forms the crux of how nation states are understood and actions in their name are carried out. Echoing some of the observations made by Pateman and others, Anderson remarks that 'regardless of the actual inequality and exploitation that may prevail in each [community], the nation is always conceived as a deep, horizontal comradeship'.[106]

This is something addressed directly by John Locke, to whom the concept of 'tacit consent' is attributed.[107] Of particular importance to the current inquiry

103 Brown, *States of Injury* (n 39) 163.

104 Pateman, 'Afterword' (n 101) 238–239.

105 Benedict Anderson, *Imagined Communities: Reflections on the Origin and Spread of Nationalism* (rev edn, Verso 2006) 6.

106 Anderson (n 105) 7.

107 Locke is a useful figure to examine for a number of reasons, the first of which is the period in which he was writing and the influence his work has had on the development of both liberal theory and its concept of consent. Further, the critiques his work has garnered and the continued relevance his writings have had in the contemporary fields of law, politics, and consent theory situate Locke as a pivotal figure. Bruno Anili puts the point in the following way: 'While other thinkers, ranging from Hobbes to Montesquieu, from Adam Smith to the French

is the link Locke himself makes between 'common' or familiar understandings and tacit consent. Locke positions tacit consent as the means by which government gains legitimacy over the natural freedom all persons are presumed to have.[108] Akin to more contemporary scholars' struggles with legal paternalism explored at this chapter's outset, Locke notes the impossibility for this consent to be anything other than hypothetical, thus necessitating the presumptive or unspoken consent of all citizens. While most readers of Locke's work suggest that this tacit consent marks the formation of the social contract, others have reinterpreted Locke's notion of tacit consent in light of the empiricist views he expressed in *An Essay Concerning Human Understanding* (1690), wherein Locke pursues questions about how human beings come to know and understand the world around them.[109] This work provides insight into Locke's own epistemological stance, one deeply rooted in the Christian medieval world.[110] Regarding the human mind as a blank slate, Locke maintained that knowledge was gained through sensory and reflective experience.[111] Further, Locke viewed words as merely signifiers of these experiences[112] and these signifiers themselves as being, in the first instance, subjective. 'Words', Locke writes, 'in their primary or immediate signification, stand for nothing but the ideas in the mind of him who uses them, how imperfectly soever or carelessly those ideas are collected from the things which they are supposed to represent'.[113]

This relationship between words and their subjective meanings raises a problem for Locke, not unlike the one pursued by Thomas Aquinas with respect to the unknowable nature of another's internal will.[114] If words are merely the marker of ideas within the minds of individuals, how can anyone be assured

philosophes certainly participated in shaping the early phases of the complex political project that was to be called liberal, it may legitimately be argued that Locke's system of thinking is the central knot in that web of contributions'; Bruno Anili, 'Beyond Liberal Discourse: Meta-Ideological Hegemony and Narrative Alternatives' (PhD dissertation, University of Oregon 2010) 71.

108 This is an argument repeated even among contemporary critics of liberalism. The Wendy Brown excerpt cited above (n 103) imbues consent with the same magical power to 'add or withdraw legitimacy'.

109 Anili (n 107).

110 While somewhat anecdotal, Locke's own medical training and education (which were undertaken in the eve of the medieval period) suggest a further relevance of considering the influence of his work on contemporary understandings of consent, given the upcoming chapter on medieval medicine. For some discussion of Locke's personal history and circumstances and the (potential) impact they can be seen to have had on his written works, see David Walsh, 'Locke' in Kenneth L Deutsch and Joseph R Fornieri (eds), *An Invitation to Political Thought* (Thomson 2000).

111 'Though the qualities that affect our senses are, in the things themselves, so united and blended, that there is no separation, no distance between them; yet it is plain, the ideas they produce in the mind enter by the senses simple and unmixed'; John Locke, *Essay*, Book II, Chap II, §1: 'Uncompounded Appearances' as cited in Anili (n 107) 83.

112 Anili uses the example of the word 'hot' when used to signify the sensory experience of touching a heated object (n 107) 84.

113 *Essay*, Book III, Chap II, §2 (267 of Kay and Troutman edition) as cited by Anili (n 107) 84.

114 Aquinas's own struggles with consent and the difficulty of assessing its authenticity are examined in greater detail in Chapter 3.

that the same meanings have been ascribed to the same words in the minds of others?[115] Locke is clear that the ability to impose shared meanings is an epistemological (if not political) power that no individual, not even 'the great Augustus himself' possesses.[116] Instead, these shared meanings can be nothing more than approximations that are established as a familiarity with words and their associated meanings is gained among a community – a process that occurs, according to Locke, through common use. Moreover, this common use is granted an epistemological authority via tacit consent, for as Locke explains, as 'certain sounds to certain ideas' gain common appropriation, the 'signification of that sound' becomes limited such that 'unless a man applies it to the same idea, he does not speak properly: and let me add, that unless a man's words excite the same ideas in the hearer which he makes them stand for in speaking, he does not speak intelligibly'.[117] Anili characterises this use of tacit consent as a semiotic contract, given its role in producing the 'conditions for communication' – an operation which he likens to the social contract on the basis that each 'rests on the agreement of individuals, and on the power of community to enforce it'.[118] While this articulation relies heavily on the liberal story of consent (ie as an autonomous choice or agreement to the terms of political authority), Anili's characterisation of Lockean individualism as 'semiotic' is a useful insight. Locke himself identifies the role a shared language or system of signs plays in the construction and maintenance of schemes of intelligibility. He reminds us, in the passage quoted above, that one must use the words shared 'in common' to 'speak properly' in order to be understood. Further, the use of these words and their shared meanings marks one as a member of the community. Not unlike Hegel's notion of reciprocal recognition, to be an intelligible person, one must be seen or understood as such (by other recognisably intelligible persons). This requires the use of the common language, something which for Locke was understood as (tacit) consent – the mark of community membership.[119]

115 Locke presents the difficulty as two-fold: 'First, They suppose their words to be marks of the ideas in the minds also of other men, with whom they communicate: for else they should talk in vain, and could not be understood, if the sounds they applied to one idea were such as by the hearer were applied to another, which is to speak two languages … Secondly, Because men would not be thought to talk barely of their own imagination, but of things as really they are; therefore they often suppose the words to stand also for the reality of things' (*Essay*, Book III, Chap II, §4) as cited by Anili (n 107) 85.

116 'No one hath the power to make others have the same ideas in their minds that he has, when they use the same words that he does. And therefore the great Augustus himself, in the possession of that power which ruled the world, acknowledged he could not make a new Latin word: which was as much as to say, that he could not arbitrarily appoint what idea any sound should be a sign of, in the mouths and common language of his subjects' (*Essay*, Book III, Chap II, 'Of the Signification of Words' §8).

117 *Essay*, Book III, Chap II, 'Of the Signification of Words' §8.

118 Anili (n 107) 86.

119 This function of consent (to signify socio-cultural belonging) is evidenced in the legal regulation of sex in Ancient Greece and Rome, explored at length in Chapter 2.

This points to one of two ways in which the fictional status of consent serves to entrench the consent-as-autonomy story. Through invocations of a 'common sense' that prioritises autonomy, the frames of intelligibility of consent are established so as to prevent the possibility of thinking of it in any other way. Within the context of contemporary treatments of consent, these might be thought of as the 'unwritten codes' that establish the parameters of 'good reason' or the 'public interest'. If one steps too far off the beaten path, violating these normative codes, one's actions become unintelligible. They lack 'good reason' or demonstrate an inability to 'speak properly', as Locke might phrase it.[120] This demonstrates how these structures of normative grammar or frames of intelligibility contain a coercive element, compelling speakers or subjects to adopt dominant discursive practices as their own (or risk not being understood). Consent thus becomes the means by which a subject's intelligibility is both produced and enforced and must therefore be understood in conjunction with (rather than in opposition to) coercion.[121] The power to establish a 'common sense' or to set the frames of intelligibility is the power to establish and define communities and the subjects who live within them.[122]

This creates a conundrum of considerable social and political consequence when consent is the means by which members of certain groups are not merely excluded from intelligibility but are held to have agreed to the terms which make this exclusion compulsory. This speaks to the second way in which consent's hypothetical character serves to entrench the autonomy story. Tacit consent is often positioned as a substitute for an impossible experience; it is a fiction meant to stand in for an unlived reality. This is what Jeremy Webber has argued is the 'trope' of consent, where it is imputed to members of a political community on one of three bases: that it represents what citizens *could* consent to (thus examining the limits of what constitutes 'legitimate' state action); that it represents what citizens *should* consent to (thereby invoking the issue of rights and correlative duties); or that it represents what citizens *would* consent to (if only it were possible to ask them).[123] Consent

120 This unintelligible actor can be thought of as a Gramscian 'idiot' – a term he employs in reference to the Greek word, *idios*, meaning 'individual' or 'one's own' (ie idiosyncratic), in reference to speech patterns that are too individualistic, too much 'one's own' to be understood. See Antonio Gramsci, *Selections from Cultural Writings* (David Forgacs and Geoffrey Nowell Smith, eds, HUP 1985) 124.

121 This is what lies at the core of Gramsci's concept of hegemony, described as 'a theory of the organization of consent' by Peter Ives, *Language and Hegemony in Gramsci* (Fernwood 2004) 64.

122 In this way, consent can be understood to operate as an onto-epistemology (to employ a term coined by Karen Barad), where it sets the terms for what can be known, in what ways, and how this knowledge, in turn, constitutes how subjects are understood (both by themselves and others). See Karen Barad, *Meeting the Universe Halfway: Quantum Physics and the Entanglement of Matter and Meaning* (Duke University Press 2007).

123 Jeremy Webber, 'The Meanings of Consent' in Jeremy Webber and Colin M MacLeod (eds), *Between Consenting Peoples: Political Community and the Meaning of Consent* (UBC Press 2010) 9–10.

thus functions as an acceptable substitution only if its imaginary form contains the fiction of its realisability. In other words, consent – to be operable as an adherent of political community – must be unreal (ie hypothetical) while not being so unreal as to be unimaginable (and thus ineffective). This is particularly important when, as Anderson notes above, the imagined community consent is meant to produce and hold together is not homogenous but rather rife with inequality.

Difference, while prima facie threatening to the imagined homogeneity of the community, is an integral component of the community's constitution and is often the basis for differential or unequal treatment of its members.[124] This is not simply because of the role of the 'other' in constructing a shared (if imagined) identity – although this, too, is part of the work of consent's autonomy story. Rather, one might argue (as Judith Butler does with respect to pornography) that the fiction of consent 'depicts impossible and uninhabitable positions, compensatory fantasies that continually reproduce a rift between those positions and the ones that belong to the domain of social reality'.[125] This rift is a necessary one – not because of the inequality or subordination that it reveals, but because of the ideal of autonomy that it preserves, the vision that if we can only 'get it right', consent will deliver self-actualisation, self-determination, and bodily integrity. Provided that the autonomy that consent promises remains unrealisable, it can continue to hold sway. It is able to house a vision of what could be, even in the face of what we know isn't.[126]

This creates an imperative to move beyond the notion of consent as merely an illusion, to an understanding of it as something more operative. In its claim to 'common sense', the consent-as-autonomy story also invokes 'a nonhistorical "before" ... that guarantees a presocial ontology of persons who freely consent to be governed, and thereby, constitute the legitimacy of the social contract'.[127] The production of this presocial ontology is the key to understanding how consent has continued to play an integral role in the establishment of political community, state legitimacy, and corporeal governance despite explicit recognition of its fictional and paradoxical promise of autonomy.

124 This is in keeping with Arendt's argument that the nation state must produce an exilic population to beget and preserve the homogenous citizen. See Hannah Arendt, *Origins of Totalitarianism* (Harcourt & Brace 1979).

125 Judith Butler, *Excitable Speech: A Politics of the Performative* (Routledge 1997) 68.

126 This is well evidenced by the practice among some scholars to employ what I think of as a 'retroactive reading' of consent, positioning it as a form of autonomy even within socio-political contexts that don't allow for this contemporary understanding. See, for instance, the discussion in Chapter 2 where twentieth-century scholars have remarked on the presence of 'female consent' (as autonomy) in the context of sexual relationships in Antiquity, despite women lacking the necessary socio-political status at the time for agentic acts of self-governance or freedom to be possible.

127 Judith Butler, *Gender Trouble: Feminism and the Subversion of Identity* (10th ann edn, Routledge 1999) 5.

Conclusion

This chapter has surveyed what might be thought of as the 'canon' of contemporary consent law. Despite performing a multitude of functions across diverse areas of law, there is a common underlying story of autonomy that is told about consent. Moreover, this story is awarded a 'common sense' status in consent theorising, to the exclusion of all other narratives. This represents something of a paradox in how consent is understood both in legal theory and practice. Although claims of its 'shifting content' or ambiguous meaning are commonplace, legal treatments of consent in both medical law and criminal contexts take place against a backdrop of this common sense story. Understanding consent as an enactment of personal autonomy or means of self-governance is what 'everybody knows' consent means. A review of how courts in North America, the United Kingdom, and other parts of the Commonwealth assess the availability of consent reveals that it is a 'freedom' that has prerequisites, each of which serves to allow consent in some contexts (and for some subjects) while prohibiting it in and for others. Moreover, these preconditions of voluntariness, knowledge, and rationality are defined in accordance with this common sense story of autonomy. Where subjects attempt to consent in contexts that don't conform to this narrative, the law does not recognise the consent as valid (or autonomous). Instead, these acts and subjects are rendered 'irrational', lacking in 'good reason', or under 'undue influence' for their failure to conform.

This lends an unquestionable status to the consent-as-autonomy story, creating a need to 'unhook' consent from this common sense narrative in order to understand the social, cultural, and political conditions which have made this view of consent possible and, indeed, necessary in contemporary determinations of the limits of self-rule. This book aims to address this imperative by treating consent as a human artefact, steeped in historically located ideologies, with significant implications for subjectivity. As Pamela Haag has argued:

> We don't know what consent *would* look like because 'it' hasn't existed in ideal form and therefore hasn't existed at all. But consent *has* looked like and *does* look like what it has been socially interpreted and conceived to be … [C]onsent is always an interpreted idea, not an idealised abstraction. To be sure, contemporary interpretations of consent often do not define heterosexuality in empowering, just, or consistent ways for women … but casting consent as a nonexistent ideal (what *would* it look like?) because it has yet to be developed according to feminist values seems to erase the rich and perhaps illustrative history of the idea as a social and not a philosophical artifact.[128]

The following chapters attempt to track consent as it travels through historical and cultural locations where its autonomy narrative is either absent or simply

128 Pamela Haag, *Consent: Sexual Rights and the Transformation of American Liberalism* (Cornell University Press 1999) xv.

can't ring true given the socio-political (or discursive) conditions that are at work. The hope is that we will uncover uses and functions of consent that both differ from and challenge its common sense story. This journey to unfamiliar territory begins with the following chapter's look at the social and legal regulation of sex in Ancient Greece.

Bibliography

Table of cases

B (A Child) v DPP [2000] 1 All ER 833
BH (Next friend of) v Alberta (Director of Child Welfare) 2002 ABQB 371
DPP v Morgan [1976] AC 182
Freeman v Home Office (No. 2) [1984] 1 All ER 1036
Hughes v. Holley (1988) 86 Cr App R 130
Miller v California, 413 US 15 (1973)
R v Brown [1993] 2 All ER 75
R v Butler [1992] 1 SCR 452
R v Donovan [1934] 2 KB 498
R v Evans (unreported) Crown Court (Newcastle), 14 June 2006
R v Ewanchuk [1999] 1 SCR 330
R v JA [2011] 2 SCR 440
R v Pappajohn [1980] 2 SCR 120
R v Sansregret [1985] 1 SCR 570
R v Seaboyer [1991] 2 SCR 577
Re T (adult) (refusal of medical treatment) [1992] 4 All ER 649
R v Wilson [1996] 2 Cr App Rep 241
Slater v Baker and Stapleton (1767) 2 Wils KB 359, 95 ER 850
Towne Cinema Theatres Ltd v The Queen [1985] 1 SCR 494

Table of legislation

Criminal Code, RSC 1985, C-46 (Canada)
Sexual Offences Act 2003 (UK)

Secondary sources

Ackerman TF, 'Medical Ethics and the Two Dogmas of Liberalism' (1982) 5 *Theo Med* 69
Agre PC and others, 'Patient Satisfaction with an Informed Consent Process' (1997) 5(7) *Cancer Pract* 162
Alexander L, 'The Moral Magic of Consent (II)' (1996) 2 *LEG* 1352
Anderson B, *Imagined Communities: Reflections on the Origin and Spread of Nationalism* (rev edn, Verso 2006)
Anderson MJ, 'From Chastity Requirement to Sexuality License: Sexual Consent and a New Rape Shield Law' (2002) 70 *Geo Wash L Rev* 51
Anili B, 'Beyond Liberal Discourse: Meta-Ideological Hegemony and Narrative Alternatives' (PhD dissertation, University of Oregon 2010)
Archard D, *Sexual Consent* (Westview Press 1998)
Arendt H, *Origins of Totalitarianism* (Harcourt & Brace 1979)

Ashworth A, *Principles of Criminal Law* (5th edn, OUP 2006)

Barad K, *Meeting the Universe Halfway: Quantum Physics and the Entanglement of Matter and Meaning* (Duke University Press 2007)

Beaman L, *Defining Harm: Religious Freedom and the Limits of the Law* (UBC Press 2008)

Beauchamp T, 'Paternalism and Biobehavioral Control' (1977) 60(1) *The Monist* 62

———, 'Autonomy and Consent' in Franklin G Miller and Alan Wertheimer (eds), *The Ethics of Consent: Theory and Practice* (OUP 2009)

Brock DW, 'Paternalism and Autonomy: Review of Feinberg's *Harm to Self* and VanDeVeer's *Paternalistic Intervention*' (1988) 98(3) *Ethics* 550

Brown W, *States of Injury: Power and Freedom in Late Modernity* (PUP 1995)

Butler J, *Excitable Speech: A Politics of the Performative* (Routledge 1997)

———, *Gender Trouble: Feminism and the Subversion of Identity* (10th ann edn, Routledge 1999)

Campbell L, 'Kant, Autonomy and Bioethics' (2017) 3(3) *Eth Med & Pub H* 381

Child NGL, 'Volenti Non Fit Injuria' (1905) 17 *Jur Rev* 43

Christman J, 'Constructing the Inner Citadel: Recent Work on Autonomy' (1988) 99 *Ethics* 109

———, 'Autonomy and Personal History' (1991) 21(1) *Cdn J Phil* 1

Dripps DA, 'Beyond Rape: An Essay on the Difference between the Presence of Force and the Absence of Consent' (1992) 92 *Colum L Rev* 1780

Dworkin G, *The Theory and Practice of Autonomy* (CUP 1988)

Dyzenhaus D, 'John Stuart Mill and the Harm of Pornography' (1992) 102(3) *Ethics* 534

Faden RR and Beauchamp TL, *A History and Theory of Informed Consent* (OUP 1986)

Feinberg J, 'Legal Paternalism' (1971) 1(1) *Cdn J Phil* 105

———, *Harm to Self* (OUP 1986)

Fitzgerald DW and others, 'Comprehension during Informed Consent in a Less-Developed Country' (2002) 360(9342) *Lancet* 1301

Gaus G and Courtland SD, 'Liberalism', *The Stanford Encyclopedia of Philosophy* (Spring edn, 2011) <http://plato.stanford.edu/archives/spr2011/entries/liberalism/> accessed 30 April 2019

Giles M, '*R v Brown:* Consensual Harm and the Public Interest' (1994) 57(1) *MLR* 101

Gramsci A, *Selections from Cultural Writings* (David Forgacs and Geoffrey Nowell Smith eds, HUP 1985)

Haag P, *Consent: Sexual Rights and the Transformation of American Liberalism* (Cornell University Press 1999)

Hack TF and others, 'Promoting Consultation Recording Practice in Oncology: Identification of Critical Implementation Factors and Determination of Patient Benefit' (2013) 22 *Psycho-Oncology* 1273

Hartley H, *Sport, Physical Recreation, and the Law* (Routledge 2009)

Herzog D, *Happy Slaves: A Critique of Consent Theory* (University of Chicago Press 1989)

Higgins RCA, *The Moral Limits of Law* (OUP 2004)

Hull RT, 'Informed Consent: Patient's Right or Patient's Duty?' (1985) 10(2) *J Med & Phil* 183

Hyams K, 'When Consent Doesn't Work: A Rights-Based Case for Limits to Consent's Capacity to Legitimise' (2011) 8(1) *J Moral Phil* 110

Ingman T, 'A History of the Defence of *Non Volenti Non Fit Injuria*' (1981) 26 *Jur Rev* (ns) 1

Ives P, *Language and Hegemony in Gramsci* (Fernwood 2004)
Jackson E, 'Informed Consent and the Impotence of Tort' in Sheila McLean (ed), *First Do No Harm: Law, Ethics, and Healthcare* (Ashgate 2006)
——, *Medical Law: Text, Cases, and Materials* (OUP 2009)
Kahan DM, 'Culture, Cognition, and Consent: Who Perceives What, and Why, in Acquaintance-Rape Cases' (2010) 158 *U Pa L Rev* 729
Kann M, 'The Dialectic of Consent Theory' (1978) 40(2) *J Pol* 386
Kitzinger C and Frith H, '"Just Say No?" The Use of Conversation Analysis in Developing a Feminist Perspective on Sexual Refusal' (1999) 10(3) *D&S* 293
Kultgen J, *Autonomy and Intervention: Parentalism in the Caring Life* (OUP 1995)
Lacey N, 'In Search of the Responsible Subject: History, Philosophy and Social Sciences in Criminal Law Theory' (2001) 64(3) *MLR* 350
Larcombe W, '*Worsnop v The Queen:* Subjective Belief in Consent Prevails (Again) in Victoria's Rape Law' (2011) 35(2) *MULR* 697
Lavelle-Jones C and others, 'Factors Affecting Quality of Informed Consent' (1993) 306 *BMJ* 885
Law Commission (UK), *Consent and Offences against the Person* (Law Com No. 134, 1994)
Leclercq WKG and others, 'A Review of Surgical Informed Consent: Past, Present, and Future. A Quest to Help Patients Make Better Decisions' (2010) 34 *World J Surg* 1406
Locke J, *An Essay Concerning Human Understanding and A Treatise on the Conduct of the Understanding* (first published 1690, Kay and Troutman, 1846)
MacLean D (ed), *Values at Risk* (Rowman & Littlefield 1986)
Mann T, 'Informed Consent for Psychological Research: Do Subjects Comprehend Consent Forms and Understand their Rights?' (1994) 5(3) *Psychol Sci* 140
Mansbridge J, 'Carole Pateman: Radical Liberal?' in Daniel I O'Neill, Mary Lyndon Shanley and Iris Marion Young (eds), *Illusion of Consent: Engaging with Carole Pateman* (Penn State University Press 2008)
McLean SAM, *Autonomy, Consent, and the Law* (Routledge 2010)
Mele AR, 'Agency and Mental Action' (1997) 11 *Phil Persp* 231
Miles SH, *The Hippocratic Oath and the Ethics of Medicine* (OUP 2005)
Mill JS, *On Liberty* (first published 1859, Hackett 1978)
Mills C, 'The Domination Contract' in Daniel I O'Neill, Mary Lyndon Shanley and Iris Marion Young (eds), *Illusion of Consent: Engaging with Carole Pateman* (Penn State University Press 2008)
Morse SJ, 'Rationality and Responsibility' (2000) 74 *S Cal L Rev* 251
Norrie A, *Crime, Reason and History: A Critical Introduction to Criminal Law* (3rd edn, CUP 2014)
Nozick R, *Anarchy, State, and Utopia* (Basic Books 1974)
Olijnyk J, 'A Question of Strangeness' (LLM thesis, University of Toronto Faculty of Law 2010)
O'Neill O, *Autonomy and Trust in Bioethics* (CUP 2002)
——, 'Autonomy: The Emperor's New Clothes' (Inaugural Address 2003) 77(1) *Proc Aristotelian Soc* 1
Padfield N, 'Consent and the Public Interest' (1992) 142 *NLJ* 430
Pateman C, 'Women and Consent' (1980) 8(2) *Pol Theory* 149
——, *The Disorder of Women* (Polity Press 1989)
——, 'Afterword' in Daniel I O'Neill, Mary L Shanley and Iris M Young (eds), *Illusion of Consent: Engaging with Carole Pateman* (Penn State University Press 2008)

Pomerantz AS and de Nesnera A, 'Informed Consent, Competency, and the Illusion of Rationality' (1991) 13(2) *GH Psych* 138

Posner RA, *The Economics of Justice* (HUP 1981)

Powell A, *Sex, Power and Consent: Youth Culture and the Unwritten Rules* (CUP 2010)

Ramsay P, 'Vulnerability, Sovereignty, and Police Power in the ASBO' in Markus D Dubber and Mariana Valverde (eds), *Police and the Liberal State* (SUP 2008)

Rozovsky LE, *The Canadian Law of Consent to Treatment* (3rd edn, Butterworths 2003)

Savulescu J, 'Rational Desires and the Limitation of Life-Sustaining Treatment' (1994) 8 *Bioethics* 191

Sen A, *Rationality and Freedom* (HUP 2004)

Sheehy E (ed), *Sexual Assault in Canada: Law, Legal Practice & Women's Activism* (University of Ottawa Press 2012)

Shokrollah K, 'Request for Treatment: The Evolution of Consent' (2010) 92 *Ann R Coll Surg Engl* 93

Smart C, 'Law's Truth/Women's Experiences' in Regina Graycar (ed), *Dissenting Opinions: Feminist Explorations in Law and Society* (Allen & Unwin 1990)

Spector H, *Autonomy and Rights: The Moral Foundations of Liberalism* (OUP 2008)

Stewart C, Peisah C and Draper B, 'A Test for Mental Capacity to Request Assisted Suicide' (2011) 37(1) *J Med Eth* 34

Stokes P, 'Judge Throws Out Assault Case Over Rugby Player's Small Bruise' *The Telegraph* (London, 15 June 2006)

Tadros V, 'Consent to Harm' (2011) 64 *CLP* 23

Vernon R 'John Stuart Mill and Pornography: Beyond the Harm Principle' (1996) 106(3) *Ethics* 621

Walsh D, 'Locke' in Kenneth L Deutsch and Joseph R Fornieri (eds), *An Invitation to Political Thought* (Thomson 2000)

Weait M, 'Knowledge, Autonomy, and Consent: *R v Konzani*' (2005) *Crim LR* 763

Webber J, 'The Meanings of Consent' in Jeremy Webber and Colin M MacLeod (eds), *Between Consenting Peoples: Political Community and the Meaning of Consent* (UBC Press 2010)

Wells RE, 'To Tell the Truth, the Whole Truth, May Do Patients Harm: The Problem of the Nocebo Effect for Informed Consent' (2012) 12(3) *Am J Bioeth* 22

West R, 'Authority, Autonomy, and Choice: The Role of Consent in the Moral and Political Visions of Franz Kafka and Richard Posner' (1985) 99 *Harv LR* 384

———, 'Legitimating the Illegitimate: A Comment on *Beyond Rape*' (1992) 93(6) *Colum L Rev* 1442

2 Ancient sex

The study of the legal regulation of sex has been inextricably bound to the concept of consent. Certainly much legal scholarship would lend itself to the assumption that consent has pre-existed rape. Its absence marks the presence of sexual violence. This chapter will approach sexual consent differently, positioning it as an historical artefact rather than a concept with a priori status. Further, in an attempt to move beyond discursive patterns in consent jurisprudence which foreground, if not privilege, the story of autonomy, this chapter examines sexual offence legislation in a context far removed from the contemporary one: ancient Greece. This is for several reasons.

Aside from examining the ancient period for an account of consent that differs from the autonomy story, this chapter is aimed at understanding how contemporary uses of consent in legal treatments of sexuality both rely upon and call to presumptions of this history. It is meant to be, to employ Foucault's term, a 'history of the present' to determine how what is 'known' about sexual consent and its origins has been necessitated by the circumstances in which these knowledges were produced.[1] What are the 'conditions of possibility' of what we know about sexual consent? How did the social and political context of ancient Greece and Rome frame (and place limits upon) this knowledge? And how might these early constructions help to illuminate modern debates among theorists of consent and their critics? As David Halperin has remarked:

> [T]he Greeks are hardly alien or lost to us. They are, on the contrary, all about us – not because we are (allegedly) their inheritors, not because we may expect to find vestiges of them buried within ourselves, faintly discernible beneath layers of historical encrustation, transformation, and displacement. Rather, the Greeks are all about us insofar as they represent one of the codes in which we transact our own cultural business: we use our 'truths' about the Greeks to explain ourselves to ourselves and to construct our own experiences, including our sexual experiences.[2]

1 Michel Foucault, *Discipline & Punish: The Birth of the Prison* (Alan Sheridan tr, Pantheon Book 1977) 31.

2 David M Halperin, *One Hundred Years of Homosexuality and other essays on Greek love* (Routledge 1990) 70.

Indeed, the influence of both ancient Athenian and Roman law within Continental Europe and North America has been well documented.[3] While the contemporary relevance of this early jurisprudence is sometimes questioned, given the scarcity of sources, contentious (mis)representations of rhetoric, and the difficulties associated with interpretation and translation, others have argued that the 'problem' of, in particular, Athenian *nomos* – the wide assemblage of statutes, ordinances, and customs that are thought to make up early Greek 'law' – is, in fact, its greatest attribute.[4] This case is arguably made stronger when a genealogical approach to law is taken. Given the primacy which Athenian legal discussions and rhetoric placed on social attitudes and political contexts, this wide jurisprudential field can only aid an examination of a matter as socially and politically charged as the legal regulation of sex.[5] Further, the challenge of destabilising the foundations of sexual consent discourse is perhaps lessened amidst a narrative of socio-sexual relations in which notions of female agency do not figure in familiar forms.

The influence of Roman law on contemporary understandings of political life, culture, and subjectivity is also of importance.[6] While much Roman legislation reflects the Athenian approach to sexual offences, some divergences (later influenced by the development of Christian thought) exist. The first of three substantive sections of this chapter will attempt to reflect this pattern, beginning with an examination of the core Athenian practices which informed the notion of consent. Roman adaptations of and divergences from the Greek tradition are incorporated into later subsections that review both Athenian and Roman approaches to offences of (sexual) violence and adultery. This first section's delineation of early attempts to codify social norms about sexual behaviour (seen most starkly in the legislation of Augustan's moral reform in Rome at the turn of the first century) will focus on the proprietary and patrilineal interests sexual offence legislation was meant to protect. The role of sexual consent in protecting these interests is a construction I refer to as 'consent-as-proprietorship', and highlights the function consent played in both signifying political status and protecting its parameters.

The chapter's second section examines an alternative story about consent as enacted among the 'outlaws' of early Athenian and Roman societies, ie those who were excluded from socio-political status: namely women, slaves, foreigners, and various 'sexual transgressors'. While it is tempting to characterise the actions

3 See Paul Cartledge, Paul Millett and Stephen Todd (eds), *Nomos: Essays in Athenian Law, Politics, and Society* (CUP 1990), particularly Chapter #1, 'Law, society and Athens'.

4 Cartledge, Millett and Todd (n 3).

5 Although, the manner in which the ancients may have legally regulated their sexual relations is not the primary matter under examination, but rather the role that consent can be seen to have played in this context.

6 Lewis and Ibbetson, for instance, suggest that the 'intellectual methodology' of the Romans (itself a remnant of the analytic modes of Greece's Classical jurists) was the foundational component to Rome's legal tradition and its continuing influence on contemporary forms of analytic jurisprudence, see David John Ibbetson and Andrew DE Lewis, *The Roman Law Tradition* (CUP 1994).

among this outlaw group as 'autonomous' (in keeping with modern articulations of consent), when viewed within the context of the Classical period, these acts are not intelligible either as enactments of agency or of consent. Rather, what the sexual behaviours of this group of ancient outcasts reveal is not a story of consent-as-autonomy but an account of the way in which the availability and deployment of consent is restricted and governed by dominant norms of intelligibility. This snapshot of early Athenian and Roman law reveals that consent was available only to certain subjects who were willing to act in certain ways. How this ancient story of consent might inform the doctrine's contemporary uses is explored in this chapter's third section.

In this way, this chapter might be seen to echo the theoretical approach of Benjamin Constant where 'Ancient' and 'Modern' models of liberty were explored with the aim of better understanding a present state of affairs.[7] My own exploration of ancient and modern forms of consent is rooted in a contention that both the 'consent of the ancients' and the 'consent of the moderns' invoke particular models of ownership, whether of others (in the case of the ancients) or of the self (in the case of the moderns). Yet in contrast to Constant, I have approached these models as artefacts, viewing consent (as autonomy) as a relatively modern construction which is 'found' by scholars in their investigations of earlier eras.[8] These discoveries thus engage in a liberal grammar of self-governance and possessive individualism characteristic of modern conceptions of consent-as-autonomy. Reading these constructions within a historical context which explicitly denied notions of self-rule on the basis of political status provides an opportunity to destabilise this foundational discourse and contemplate an untold story of consent.

Regulating sex among the ancients

Issues of consent figure most prominently in Athenian law in the designation and prohibition of 'illicit' or transgressive sexual behaviour. Sexual offences were addressed under three primary categories, namely: (i) *hubris*, (ii) *bia*, and

7 Benjamin Constant 'The Liberty of the Ancients Compared with that of the Moderns (1833)' in David Boaz (ed), *The Libertarian Reader* (Free Press 1997).

8 Take, for instance, the work of David Cohen, Diana Moses, and Angeliki Laiou, featured in Angeliki E Laiou (ed), *Consent and Coercion to Sex and Marriage in Ancient and Medieval Societies* (Dumbarton Oaks 1993), each of whom discuss the notion of 'female consent' to sex or marriage in Athens, Rome, and Byzantium (respectively) as a form of agency, despite explicitly noting women's lack of social, political, and legal status in each era. See David Cohen 1993; Diana C Moses 1993; and Angeliki E Laiou 1993. See also David Cohen, 'Sexuality, Violence and the Athenian Law of *Hubris*' (1991) 38 *G&R* 171. The disjuncture between persons exhibiting autonomy in socio-political contexts which did not recognise their personhood but rather treated them as property to be exchanged is left unexamined by these authors. The work of Rosanna Omitowoju stands as an exemplary exception to this pattern. See Rosanna Omitowoju, *Rape and the Politics of Consent in Classical Athens* (CUP 2002).

(iii) *moicheia*, each of which is examined in further detail below.[9] Roman legal developments in this area were largely subsumed under the single category of *stuprum*, understood to refer to 'illicit sexual intercourse in any form'.[10] While largely understood to refer to adulterous behaviour, *stuprum* was also used to identify instances of forcible sex. At times, this was made explicit in the language, for instance when combined with the term *raptus* (understood to mean 'forcible abduction'); however, *stuprum* was also used on its own to refer to violent sexual behaviour as well as consensual sex. As such, the Roman treatment of sexual consent is addressed in the second and third subsections below where the greatest overlap in the two jurisdictions' treatment of sexual offences occurs.

In each of these legal classifications, consent was a power limited to those members of the polis who enjoyed full rights of citizenship (ie free, Athenian-born men), and its enactment was a signifier of this status of political membership. In particular, consent served to represent a model of patriarchal rule and was employed as a means of protecting patrilineal interests and proprietary control over female sexuality. Where consent appears in circumstances that challenge this paradigm, it is treated as an aggravating factor to the sexual offence (rather than a means of vitiating a wrong, as in the contemporary context). Moreover, in such instances, consent did not establish a subject's autonomy, but rather served to remove the political status upon which such rights to self-rule were found. The following subsections explore this in further depth within each of the three forms of sexual offences of the period.

Offences of hubris

Perhaps indicative of the 'extra legal' character of Athenian juridical practice, the offence of *hubris* has been noted by some scholars of ancient history to represent something of a paradox.[11] Despite the prominence the concept is thought to have had in daily Athenian life, there are few recorded cases of *hubris* having been brought to the courts. One explanation for this may lie in the nature of the offence itself. Loosely interpreted to mean 'shame', the text of the law as existent in the fourth century reads:

> If anyone commits *hubris* against another, whether child or woman or man, whether free or slave, or if he does anything outrageous (*paranomon*) against any of these, let any one who wishes (*ho boulomenos*), of those Athenians who are entitled, bring an indictment (*graphē*) before the judges (*thesmothetai*).[12]

9 I am indebted to Omitowoju (n 8) for the delineation of these categories.

10 Moses (n 8), citing Charleton T Lewis, *A Latin Dictionary* (Charles Stewart ed, OUP 1879).

11 Nicolas Ralph Edmund Fisher, *Hybris: A Study in the Values of Honour and Shame in Ancient Greece* (Aris & Phillips 1992).

12 Demosthenes 21.47, as cited in Fisher (n 11) 123.

Understood to be an act of power used to shame another for pleasure,[13] the party bringing the charge or *graphē* has allegedly suffered some dishonour from the perpetrator's act and might presumably wish to avoid the publicity of a formal trial.[14] The offence of *hubris* also pertained to 'degrading acts' which were thought to bring shame upon the citizenry as a whole.[15] This was particularly the case in charges of *hubris* involving a sexual act, although the *graphē hubris* could encompass a wide array of actions, including verbal assault, and need not involve an element of violence.[16] Instead, the central component of the offence was a subjective one: did the perpetrator intend to shame? Often, the coercive element of the offence could be implied by the respective social positions of the parties.[17] David Cohen has noted a number of examples in the work of Xenophon, including the story of Hiero (a ruler) who desires the affections of Dailochus (a young male).[18] Xenophon relays Hiero's description of the 'tyrant's dilemma':

> I desire to get from him not what I may have for the asking, but that which a despot should be the last to take ... But what I long to get, I very strongly desire to obtain by his goodwill, and with his consent ... For to take from an enemy against his will is the greatest of all pleasures, but favors from a loved one are very pleasant only when he consents.[19]

13 Fisher, in what is considered by many to be the authoritative text on *hubris*, defines the offence as 'deliberate activity [with] the typical motive for such infliction of dishonour [being] the pleasure of expressing a sense of superiority, rather than compulsion, need or desire for wealth' (n 11) 1.

14 Omitowoju (n 8).

15 This is similar to contemporary judicial treatments of cases involving sadomasochism or obscenity offences, where a 'community standards test' is employed as a means of ascertaining the parameters of acceptable conduct. See, for example, the Canadian case *R v Butler* [1992] 1 SCR 452; and the English case *R v Brown* [1993] 2 All ER 75, as well as footnote 84 in Chapter 1 of this book.

16 See Galen O Rowe, 'The Many Facets of Hybris in Demosthenes' *Against Meidias*' (1993) 114(3) *AJPhil* 397 for a detailed analysis of the various meanings of *hubris* that are present in Demosthenes' text. Specifically, Rowe identifies four different aspects or 'facets' of the offence (at 399): (1) a violation of human or divine law (described as 'wrong', 'licentious', and 'dishonourable'); or indicative of (2) the character of the perpetrator (as 'shameless', 'savage'); (3) the quality of the offence ('base', 'disgusting'); or (4) the use of violence (*bia*).

17 The same presumption is made explicit in most contemporary sexual assault law definitions of consent where an offender's position of trust or authority will vitiate the possibility of the victim's consent. See, for example, section 273.1(2)(c) of Canada's *Criminal Code* and section 16(2) of the UK's *Sexual Offences Act*, 2003. According to 2017 data from the Rape, Abuse, & Incest National Network (RAINN), similar provisions can be found in 25 American states. (In 24 others, this ground for negating consent is limited to certain classes of persons (eg inmates and enforcement officers). See RAINN, 'Consent Laws' (*RAINN.org*, December 2017) <https://apps.rainn.org/policy/compare/consent-laws.cfm> accessed 30 April 2019.

18 Cohen also cites Aristotle's, *Politics* 1315a 15-28, Isocrates, *Nicocles* 36.5, and Demosthenes 17.4 as making the same claim with respect to a ruler's sexual abuse of children (without the consent of their *kurios*). See Cohen 1993 (n 8) 8.

19 Xenophon, *Hiero*, as translated by Cohen 1993 (n 8) 10.

Hiero knows that to seek favour from Dailochus would be to endanger a charge of *hubris*, given the shame in his implicit power to compel obedience (for his own pleasure).

Arguably, consent can be seen to play a key role in the charge of *hubris*, given that its absence would suggest domination over another's free will, thus causing dishonour.[20] Within the context of sexual assault, however, the *graphē hubris* was available to the 'outraged fathers, husbands or brothers' whose consent had not been sought before sexual access to the women in their care was obtained.[21] Coupled with the acknowledgment that a charge of *hubris* need not involve physical violence, some scholars have suggested that adultery would also have fallen within the offence's scope. As Fisher notes, 'it is clearly a deliberate act, involving pleasure for the agent, shame for the various victims, and consequently contempt for the laws and the values of a community'.[22] Cohen cites Lysias' *On the Murder of Eratosthenes* as evidence of this when Euphiletus raises the defence of justifiable homicide on the basis of *hubris* for having murdered Eratosthenes following his (consensual) seduction and sexual relations with Euphiletus' wife.[23] Rather than being immaterial, the evidence of the wife's consent serves to establish the grounds for a charge of *hubris*, given the dishonour the act brings to Euphiletus' house and children. In this way, consent does not vitiate the harm of a sexual offence but rather establishes it. The shame of the offence is made out through the consent of Euphiletus' wife, echoing a concern with familial lineage rather than physical integrity or female autonomy. Consensual extra-marital sex could result in uncertainty about a child's legitimate rights to inheritance and social status; thus its very invocation brought the property rights and obligations of the 'injured' male citizen to the fore.

The offence of *hubris* could also be employed to enforce attitudes about appropriate age requirements for sexual behaviour. While some remnants of what cultural anthropologists have suggested was a 'familial' or 'tribal' approach to linking sexual age with puberty are evident in so-called Athenian 'age of consent' mores, this was largely limited to female citizens and based on concerns

20 This is certainly Cohen's view and one endorsed by other sources which reference his scholarship.

21 Fisher (n 11) 41. The inclusion of *ho boulomenos* or 'anyone who wishes' within the *hubris* statute suggests that other members of the Athenian public could bring the charge, provided they had legal standing – which women, children, and slaves did not. Gardner notes that for Roman women, the consent of a tutor (similar to the Greek role of kurios) was required for obtaining standing for bringing a lawsuit, given the effects it would have on the family if the suit was unsuccessful. See Jane F Gardner, *Being a Roman Citizen* (Routledge 1993) 100.

22 Fisher (n 11) 104.

23 Lysias suggests that Euphiletus relies upon a law 'from the pillar on the Areopagus' which is thought to be the same as the law on justifiable homicide found in Demosthenes 23.53, allowing a husband to kill a man he found committing adultery with his wife: Cohen 1991 (n 8). Omitowoju offers an alternative analysis of this claim which effectively counters much of the accepted scholarship on this point (n 8), Chapter 3, in particular. A similar law is also found in Plato, *Laws*, Book 9, s 874c in Robert Gregg Bury (tr), *Plato in Twelve Volumes* (HUP 1968).

of (successful) reproduction.[24] In this respect, age of consent parameters might better be described as 'age of marriage' or 'age of access' norms as it was the consent of the woman's father, husband, or *kurios* (ie legal guardian) which determined a man's access to her in both Athens and Rome (rather than some level of sexual independence that reaching a certain age might bring).[25]

Where age and consent met more substantively in Athens was in the practice of paederasty, a homoerotic mentoring relationship between older Greek men and boys between the ages of 12 and 18 (or earlier if signs of 'manhood', eg beard growth, emerged).[26] While often represented in contemporary analyses as examples of accepted homosexuality, the relations between adult Greek men and their adolescent citizens-in-training were subject to a number of limitations that differentiate them from contemporary understandings and forms of homosexual love.[27] The paederastic relationship was understood to be one of 'friendship, virtue, and pedagogy' and did not extend beyond the youth's adolescence.[28] Paederastic practices are a good site for exploring alternative conceptions of consent, given that sex was not understood to be a reciprocal transaction in classical Greece but rather an act that was done *by* one *to* another, creating active and passive roles.[29] The Greek sexual 'actor' was regarded as having a penetrative and dominant role, necessitating a passive and recipient role for the other party. As such, sex had both hierarchical and polarising functions in Greek society, where free, full rights-bearing Greek (male) citizens could only engage in sexual activity with a person of inferior status.[30]

Sexual consent was thus understood to be a signifier of this lower, passive state. This is evidenced by the Greek perception that a boy's participation in paederastic relations was not indicative of any sexual desire, at least not in the reciprocally erotic fashion reserved among the Greeks for relations between free, adult citizens.[31] Instead, any enthusiasm the boy might display for his older lover was interpreted as 'co-operation' out of a sense of gratitude and affection rather than desire, thus avoiding the perception of any willed passivity, a state thought to emulate femininity and thus a lower status. Xenophon makes this point rather explicitly when he suggests that 'using men as women is to commit *hubris*

24 Vern L Bullough, 'Age of Consent' (2005) 16(2) *JPHS* 25.

25 Laiou 1993 (n 8).

26 Halperin (n 2).

27 Halperin (n 2) does recognise that the practice may have differed from the ethos in some cases.

28 Michel Foucault, 'The Hermeneutic of the Subject' in Paul Rabinow (ed) *Ethics: Subjectivity and Truth, Essential Works of Foucault 1954–1984* (Penguin 1994) 92.

29 Halperin (n 2). This view is not endorsed by all Classicists, however. Thomas Hubbard, for instance, disputes the frame of domination/submission that Halperin and others employ when examining sexual relations of the period; see Thomas Kent Hubbard, 'Popular Perceptions of Elite Homosexuality in Classical Athens' (1998) 6(1) *Arion* 48.

30 Halperin (n 2).

31 David M Halperin, 'Sexual Ethics and Technologies of the Self in Classical Greece' (1986) 107 *J Phil* 274.

against them'.[32] This serves as the basis for Timarchus's crime of committing *hubris* against himself by consenting to sexual intercourse and thus 'adopting the submissive sexual role of a woman'.[33] This view of consent as a delimiter of social roles and the rights pertaining thereto is also evident in the regulation of other forms of transgressive sexual behaviour within both Athens and Rome, such as the offences of *bia* and *raptus*.

Offences of bia/raptus

Unlike the term *hubris*, which can have no positive connotations, the use of *bia* (and its cognates) in the legal rhetoric of classical Athens could denote actions or characteristics deemed beneficial or admirable, depending on the circumstances.[34] Most often translated as 'force' or 'violence', the use of *bia* indicated offences involving the use of strength, but this need not involve a physical element, such as the compulsion of another's will.[35] While sometimes found to be associated with *hubris*,[36] the term *bia* is not thought to be as politicised a term as *hubris*, and its meaning is more dependent on the context in which it is used. When employed as a conjunctive with sexual language, *bia* can be interpreted to most closely resemble a modern definition of 'rape',[37] referenced by many scholars as *dike biaion*, where *dike* denotes a 'private suit' which had to have been brought by the offended party, as opposed to *graphē*, which was a public suit to which any (free) person had standing.[38]

The text most identified with the association between *dike biaion* and rape is Lysias' *On the Murder of Eratosthenes* (discussed in the previous section in

32 Xenophon, *Memorabilia* 2.1.30, as cited in Cohen 1993 (n 8) 13.

33 Cohen 1993 (n 8), citing Plato, *Phaedrus* 250e5. In his examination of the 'reference speeches' of the *Symposium* and the *Phaedrus*, Foucault notes the inquiry each speech addresses with respect to whom and under what circumstances a young boy should 'yield' to an older man. Foucault notes a 'common thematics' including 'that of dishonorable relations that place the boy under the domination of the lover; compromise him in the eyes of everyone, and alienate him from his family or from honorable relations ... that of the feminine role the boy is led to assume'. See Michel Foucault, *The History of Sexuality, Vol 2: The Use of Pleasure* (Robert Hurley tr, Vintage Books 1990) 231.

34 Omitowoju (n 8).

35 Some scholars have suggested *bia* is representative of an 'uncivilised' form of *peitho* or 'persuasion'. See, for example, Richard G Buxton, *Persuasion in Greek Tragedy: A Study of Peitho* (CUP 1982).

36 Omitowoju cites Demosthenes (21.58.5) and Herodotus (6.137.19) as examples (n 8) 53.

37 Plato, for instance, uses *bia* in conjunction with *hubris* to refer to the 'forcible violation' of women. See *Laws*, Book 9, s 874c in Bury (n 23).

38 Omitowoju cites Fisher (n 11), Alick Robin Walsham Harrison, *The Law of Athens, Vol. 1* (OUP 1968), and Stephen C Todd, *The Shape of Athenian Law* (OUP 1993) among others, as examples of those who adopt the understanding of *dike biaion* as representative of a rape offence (n 8) 55.

relation to its commentary on *hubris*).[39] In this text, Lysias makes reference to the law's treatment of sexual violence in a passage which many scholars employ as evidence of a legal distinction between consensual and non-consensual sex.[40] Omitowoju translates the text as follows:

> Hear, gentlemen, that he [the lawgiver] orders that if someone shames by force a free person or child he shall owe double damages: if a woman, from those for whom it is possible to kill, he is included in the same provisions. Thus, gentlemen, he thought that those who use *bia* deserve a lesser penalty than those who use persuasion.[41]

In this passage, Euphiletus's reference to persuasion or *peitho* is designed to denote the act as one of seduction or adultery rather than of rape, where the former was punished more severely than the latter. Many scholars interpret this punitive distinction as suggesting an act of *bia* against the woman's body (ie rape) was not thought as serious as an act of force against her soul (in the case of persuasion), thus reinforcing a legal significance to the woman's consent.[42] This reading seems misleading for two reasons. First, the concern with seduction seems more likely to have been about the dangers which sexual infidelity posed to patrilineal legitimacy than the violation of a woman's soul. Omitowoju has argued that the language used by Euphiletus is telling, given that *bia*, while a possible descriptor of forced sex, is accompanied with the verb *aischunein* meaning 'to shame', suggesting that it is more likely a description of the shameful behaviour which Eratosthenes has shown in entering Euphiletus's home without (its owner's) permission.[43] Second, to position Euphiletus's wife's consent as the factor which designates this offence as one of *bia* or rape is to grant women a status they did not have in Athenian society. Instead, it is the consent of her *kurios* that matters; thus the crime lies in Eratosthenes's theft of Euphiletus's property (or a 'forcing of his will' with respect to it).[44] To establish a category of female consent which is somehow left independent or unmediated by the

39 A second text, Plutarch's *Life of Solon* (23.1–2) is also frequently cited as evidence of a sexual assault provision. See Harrison (n 38) and Susan Guettel Cole, 'Greek Sanctions against Sexual Assault' (1984) 79 *CPhil* 97.

40 See Edwin Carawan, *Rhetoric and the Law of Draco* (OUP 1998) 290; James P Sickinger, 'Rhetoric and the Law' in Ian Worthington (ed), *A Companion to Greek Rhetoric* (Wiley Blackwell 2010). Cole makes the point explicitly with respect to the Plutarch passage, suggesting it 'encouraged a distinction between rape as an act of violence and *moicheia* as an act of choice' (n 39) 103.

41 Lysias I.32.1-5; as cited by Omitowoju (n 8) 63–64.

42 Cole (n 39) and Harrison (n 38).

43 Omitowoju (n 8) 64.

44 Sawyer confirms this view, noting a woman's lack of autonomy during the Hellenistic period is evidenced by the 'value' allotted to her virginity: '[I]n this society she was numbered among the household's possessions. To damage her would be an act of vandalism or, in taking her as a wife without her father's consent, an act of theft'; Deborah F Sawyer, *Women and Religion in the First Christian Century* (Routledge 1996) 38.

consent of her *kurios* would be to insert an anomaly in Athenian legal society and women's place within it. At best, a notion of female sexual consent is 'only ever a tangential issue in respect to the legal treatment of a crime' and the degree to which its *hubristic* consequences might impact upon male parties.[45] The legal consideration of the use of force in these ancient contexts demonstrates the proprietary interest consent represented (when exercised by a male citizen) as well as the connotations of passivity and lower status it signified within a sexual context.

A similar interpretation is made of the Roman term *raptus*, widely understood to refer to forcible abduction and associated with a proprietary theft (of another man's female dependent(s)).[46] While the term does not strictly include a sexual connotation, it is thought to have been presumed by the Classical period.[47] The offence remained one subject to private suit until the rule of Constantine when it was made a public crime punishable by death.[48] Forcible abductions were a common (and ritualised) component to nuptial and other religious ceremonies where brides (and boys in some paederastic rites of passage) were 'taken off' with the assumption that sexual activity would ensue.[49] However, in such instances the sexual act had to remain an apparent or 'public' one so as to differentiate it from 'actual violence [which was] equally condemned by public opinion and by the law'.[50] Even in these circumstances, the victim's consent was an irrelevant concept within social and legal framings of permissible sexual activity.

These understandings of *raptus* may have influenced the development of the concept in Roman law of 'coerced consent' where the presence of force was often insufficient to negate a finding of free choice. Diana Moses suggests that Roman law during the period between the end of the Republic and the beginning of the Principate struggled with the limits of acceptable use of force, resulting in a conceptual and temporal 'middle ground' where exceptions were carved out, including times of war[51] and elopements (where the father's consent had not

45 Omitowoju (n 8) 69. See also Craig Cooper, 'Forensic Oratory' in Worthington (n 40), whose translation of the Lysias passage highlights how the real danger of the 'persuasive' adulterer was his threat to other male interests, even when positioned as female independence or self-interest: '[T]hose who get their way by force are hated by those violated, while those who use persuasion corrupt women's minds *in such a way that make other men's wives more loyal to themselves than to their own husbands*' (emphasis added) 213.

46 Moses (n 8) cites the Latin Sexual Vocabulary entry for 'rapio' which reads, 'to drag off into captivity'. See JN Adams, *Latin Sexual Vocabulary* (JHUP 1990) 175.

47 This inclusion was continued into the medieval period and is the source of the contemporary use of the term 'rape'; see Kathryn Gravdal, *Ravishing Maidens: Writing Rape in Medieval French Literature and Law* (University of Pennsylvania Press 1991).

48 Gravdal (n 47).

49 Hans Licht, *Sexual Life in Ancient Greece* (Routledge 1932). See also Bishop C Thirlwall, *A History of Greece, Vol. 1* (Longman Rees 1835) 175–176 for commentary on this.

50 Licht (n 49) 134–135.

51 A similar exception was made in Athenian law for the sexual exploitation of women which occurred by an enemy in war. Such acts were excluded from the category of *moicheia*.

been sought).[52] The continued influence of the Greek notion of *peitho* can also be seen in early Roman treatments of *coacta voluit* (as termed in the *Corpus Juris Civilis*)[53] where coercion did not vitiate an understanding of preference or persuasion: 'although she was forced she willed it'.[54] Thus, the Roman understanding of coercion did not act to negate one's will but rather was thought to redirect it. In the case of women and transgressive sex, this redirection was often to a more illicit end. Similar to the role assigned to the will of Euphiletus's wife in Lysias's account of the murder of Eratosthenes, a determination of whether a woman had been persuaded (by force) into illicit sexual activity informed *her* culpability rather than that of her perpetrator. In Roman terms, this would have elevated the offence to one of adultery or *stuprum*, given the shame it brought upon her husband or guardian and the danger it brought upon her household (and heirs) with respect to legitimate claims to citizenship. The following section examines these offences of adultery in both ancient Athens (*moicheia*) and Rome (*stuprum*) to further explore this proprietary-informed role of sexual consent.

Offences of moicheia/stuprum

Contrary to modern classifications of rape as the most severe of sexual crimes, ancient Athenian society reserved this place for the offence of adultery.[55] As such, the role of consent in the early Greek period contrasts significantly with the 'morally transformative' power current scholarship designates the concept as having in its demarcation of 'good' and 'bad' sex.[56] In both Athens and Rome in the Classical era, women's sexual consent was immaterial but for circumstances of seduction or adultery where its 'transformative' power was to further criminalise or shame the behaviour at issue. In this way, where female consent to sexual activity can be seen to take form in these early juridical treatments, 'it does so only by reference to specific male concerns', often serving to aggravate the nature of an offence (rather than legitimise it).[57] More importantly, the concept enters the discourse only in retroactive readings of Classical orations and

52 Canon law referred to such circumstances as *raptus*, reinforcing the argument made by Omitowoju (n 8) that the woman's consent was immaterial to legal and political determinations of an act's validity. See also Gravdal (n 47) 7.

53 Moses (n 8) 40.

54 Moses (n 8) 40. See also Stafford's examination of Plutarch's text, 'Advice to the Bride and Groom', where the role of persuasion or *peitho* is positioned as existing in a 'long tradition ... against *bia* (force)': Emma J Stafford, 'Plutarch on Persuasion' in Sarah B Pomeroy (ed), *Plutarch's 'Advice to the Bride and Groom' and 'A Consolation to His Wife': English Translations, Commentary, Interpretive Essays, and Bibliography* (OUP 1999) 162.

55 For an alternative view, see Edward M Harris, 'Did the Athenians Regard Seduction as a Worse Crime than Rape?' (1990) 40(2) *CQ* 370. (Harris answers his title question in the negative.) For a rebuttal of Harris's position, see Chris Carey, 'Rape and Adultery in Athenian Law' (1995) 45(2) *CQ* 407.

56 See Heidi Hurd, 'The Moral Magic of Consent' (1992) 2(2) LEG 121; David Archard, *Sexual Consent* (Westview Press, 1998); Alan Wertheimer, *Consent to Sexual Relations* (CUP 2003).

57 Omitowoju (n 8) 72.

laws. While modern notions of consent are understood to imply autonomy, there is evidence to suggest that the concept was a signifier of other values within the polis, most particularly social status and property interests.

This is perhaps best seen in the Athenian category of *moicheia*. Although some scholars (most notably Cohen)[58] have argued that the Athenian offence of *moicheia* is limited to adultery (defined as a 'voluntary violation of the marital bond'),[59] I am persuaded by the arguments of others who suggest that the offence is more akin to the Roman term *stuprum*, which encompassed a more general grouping of transgressive sexual behaviours.[60] Archaic uses of *stuprum* are thought to have meant 'pollution', and certainly, as the offence was adapted over time (and codified during the Augustan era), an understanding of it as an act of shaming or dishonouring was maintained. As such, considerations of consent on the part of a victim of *stuprum* were largely irrelevant given that the word was used rather neutrally with respect to whether the sex that had occurred was forced or not. Instead, the act was shameful on account of the victim having been *used* (and one's consent to such use could not undo the damage done – although it could certainly aggravate it).[61] In this way, the offence of *stuprum* is better understood as protecting the property and patrilineal interests of male citizens in early Roman society than as sheltering sexual agency.[62] Certainly, this argument can be made for the Greek offence of *moicheia*, which could be brought as a *graphē* and thus would fall within the category of offences 'with political rather than purely personal resonance'.[63] *Moicheia* is thus best understood as a means by which the polis regulated not simply the limits of acceptable sexual behaviour but also matters of a greater political interest (such as legitimate familial lineage and the boundaries of rightful citizenship).[64]

The Augustan moral reform at the turn of the first millennium is thought among many scholars to have been an attempt to regulate these boundaries of citizenship, given its focus on rewarding procreation within marriage and penalising childless and unmarried unions.[65] As a result of Augustus's *leges Juliae*, acts of *stuprum* became punishable under public law and were widely viewed as

58 Cohen (n 8).

59 As cited in Omitowoju (n 8) 73.

60 Omitowoju goes to great lengths to refute Cohen's position, see (n 8) 73–91. See also Moses (n 8) for a discussion of the wider application of *stuprum*.

61 Unless, of course, the consent at issue had been offered by a *kurios* and thus represented a legitimate contract for the sexual availability of the woman involved.

62 Hunter H Gardner argues that there is evidence in the discourse of New Comedy to raise 'the possibility that Athenians could conceptualize sexual assault as a traumatic bodily experience rather than (or as well as) an act of *hubris* whose chief victims were a rape victim's male kin'. See Gardner's article 'Ventriloquizing Rape in Menander's *Epitrepontes*' (2012) 39(2) *Helios* 121.

63 Omitowoju (n 8) 86.

64 Stephen Todd, for instance, notes, 'the *graphe moikheias* is used against anyone attempting to pass off his suppositious child as the son of a citizen' (n 38) 111, as cited in Omitowoju (n 8) 95.

65 Richard A Bauman, *Women and Politics in Ancient Rome* (Routledge 1992). Bauman also suggests that the reformation project was a response to the scandal that arose from Augustus's daughter Julia's alleged promiscuous and adulterous conduct; see Chapter 9.

accusations against the victim's (usually a woman's) moral virtue.[66] Further, the invocation of the criminal law to enforce regulations on sexual behaviour (as in Augustus' *lex Julia de adulteriis*) allowed for further specification of instances where force was used in committing the act, (eg *per vim stuprum*, or *raptus ad stuprum*), leading some writers to postulate whether this development began to direct Roman jurisprudence towards a contemplation of the subjective state of mind of the victim. Diana Moses explores this issue, concluding that the distinction between acts accomplished by force and those that took place consensually was not an articulation which 'fit easily into Roman legal thinking and categories'.[67] Rather, in most sexual offences of the time, the sexual act itself was sufficient to warrant guilt irrespective of how it had occurred.[68]

This, of course, changes dramatically when the consent at issue is that of a male citizen, where the will of the *kurios* (or its absence) is a definitive component to establishing the commission of a sexual offence. At issue in both accounts is a violation of male proprietary rights to access and regulate female sexuality. In this way, consent does not operate as a form of agency but instead a juridical product of value, exchanged among men of sufficient political status. Women were, after all, the 'legal transmitters of the rights of inheritance and political participation'; thus the regulation of their sexual relationships was a key component to ensuring the stability of male property and their family lines.[69] The legal and social recognition, and instatement of consent was essential to maintaining this system.

Consent in this ancient context presumes male ownership of female sexuality and its value operates as a means of exchanging and recognising male property. This is akin to Luce Irigaray's argument about the 'market' of women's sexuality where the exchange value of a woman's body is intelligible only from the vantage point of a 'speculating third party' (ie male desire).[70] Early Athenian and Roman societies did value the female body for 'the work it could do', but the provision of access to these labours (via *kurios* consent) was a product of value in

66 Moses (n 8).

67 Moses (n 8) 50.

68 This is seen in Roman considerations of 'coerced consent', discussed earlier, where the presence of force or duress serves merely to show how the will of the victim was directed or by what means 'persuasion of the will' can be said to have occurred. Similarly, the Athenian concept of *moicheia* does not appear to contemplate female consent in its definition. Omitowoju presents a segment from Xenophon's *Hiero* (3.3) where the offence is made out when sex has occurred both through the woman's 'own fault' and her 'misfortune' (n 8) 93–94.

69 Omitowoju (n 8) 115.

70 Luce Irigaray, *The Sex Which Is Not One* (Catherine Porter tr, Cornell University Press 1985). Irigaray's work provides some insightful avenues for thinking through the politics of sex and its legal regulation within the Antiquity context given her study of Antigone. According to Judith Butler, Irigaray contends that Antigone signified the 'transition from the rule of law based on maternity … to a rule of law based on paternity' – an observation that aligns (partially) with my own view of the role of consent in preserving patrilineal interests and patriarchal control of female sexuality. See Judith Butler, *Antigone's Claim: Kinship between Life and Death* (Columbia University Press 2000) 4.

its own right, asserting male proprietary rights, ensuring patrilineal legitimacy, and policing these boundaries of status and kinship through the invocation of shame.[71] Further, this function of consent-as-proprietorship served to alienate women from mastering their own bodies and subjectivities apart from the frame of male ownership and desire.[72] Any relationships or actions on the part of women (or other non-persons) which did not fit this frame took place outside the polis.

Ancient outlaws: unintelligible acts

Judith Butler has suggested two dimensions to the law's disciplinary power, the first being a regulation (of what it permits) through acts of prohibition or limitation and the second, an effective production of subjects, gestures, and practices it is unable to contain.[73] Early Athenian and Roman approaches to regulating sexual conduct were certainly exclusionary in terms of being applicable only to free citizens of the state. Foreigners, women without a *kurios*, prostitutes, slaves, and persons of questionable social status were not subjects of the law. These persons could neither bring a charge of sexual misconduct (as articulated in any of the aforementioned offences) nor be subject to one.[74] This necessarily created an ambit of sexual acts and actors which were excluded from the period's regulatory scheme due to being unintelligible within it.

The case of Apollodorus's prosecution of Neaera provides a good example.[75] Neaera was a foreign woman living 'as if in marriage' with Stephanus, an Athenian. The union would not have been recognised as valid because of her lack of citizenship, and laws were in place to prohibit any children of the relationship from claiming Athenian citizenship.[76] A daughter was born to the couple, and following the Peloponnesian War, legal reform resulted in such unions being criminalised (with a penalty of slavery for the woman and a fine for the Athenian man). In Apollodorus's prosecution of Neaera, he provides the court

71 I take this phrase from Pamela Haag's chapter 'Chastity is Only Good for the Work It Can Do' in her book, *Consent: Sexual Rights and the Transformation of American Liberalism* (Cornell University Press 1999). Her use of it is a reference to Caroline Dall's publication, *The College, the Market, and the Court: Women's Relation to Education, Labor and Law* (Lee & Shepard 1867) in which Dall states: 'In the eye of the law, female chastity is only valuable for the work it can do' 293. This is an old story indeed.

72 Judith Butler, in conversation with Gayle Rubin, has also suggested that these systems which prioritise kinship relations are in service to heteronormativity. See 'Sexual traffic' (1994) 6.2+3 *differences* 62.

73 Judith Butler, 'Co-habitation, Universality and Remembrance: Further Reflections on Israel/Palestine' (Lecture, Department of Psychosocial Studies, Birkbeck University of London, 24 May 2010).

74 Unless, of course, their conduct implicated or endangered the status of a respectable free citizen, as was the case with Neaera, see (n 75) and accompanying text.

75 Demosthenes 59, *Against Neaera* in Augustus Taber Murray (tr), *Demosthenes with an English translation* (HUP 1939).

76 Omitowoju cites the Periklean citizenship law of 451–450 BCE as an example (n 8) 42.

with a brief description of her life, so as to establish her foreign status.[77] This history includes child prostitution and several acts of illicit sexual behaviour with Athenian men; however, as Omitowoju notes, Apollodorus is careful not to use *hubris* to describe any of these acts. To do so would be to introduce the possibility of Neaera having a status she is not entitled to have. 'There is no indication that what happens to Neaera ... could ever form the basis of a *graphē hubris* ... because Neaera does not have the status to maintain it'.[78] Consent in Neaera's case is elided. To mention it would be to call upon a *kurios* Neaera did not have, giving juridical recognition to her independence and her (transgressive) union with Stephanus.

The power of consent in Neaera's context is to create juridical or socio-political status for the 'wrong' person. There were also 'wrong' *ways* to consent, and where a subject was already recognised as having status, an improper or unintelligible use of consent could act to remove it. Cohen notes a passage from Demosthenes which describes Androtion, a male prostitute, as having suffered *hubris* at the hands of those 'men who had no love for him but could pay his price'.[79] These relationships would have fallen outside the ambit of paederastic mentorship, and as such, Androtion has lost his status by 'consent[ing] to conduct to which any honourable free man should never consent'.[80]

It is tempting to characterise these uses of 'outlaw consent' as producing a kind of autonomy for those whose sexual behaviour or identities fell outside the scope of state law or civic interests. The character of Glykera in Menander's play, *Perikeiromene*, presents an interesting example.[81] At the beginning of the play, Glykera is a *pallake* (non-citizen) because she was a child of unknown origin. She is living with Polemon, a mercenary soldier, 'as a concubine' and is assaulted by him in a jealous rage when he witnesses her embracing a male neighbour.[82] Polemon cuts off Glykera's hair (she is the 'shorn girl' of the play's title) and leaves her. When he later discovers the man Glykera embraced was her brother, he is repentant, but she refuses to forgive him, even when pressed to do so by others. Before the play ends, Glykera is discovered to be the daughter of Pataiko, a Corinthian citizen. When Polemon learns of this, the two reconcile, and Pataiko grants his consent (as *kurios*) for the two to be married.

Glykera is often described as 'a proud and independent woman' who enjoyed an uncommon autonomy for Greek women of the period, particularly

77 Her offence was likely *graphē xenias* (the unlawful exercise of citizenship rights). See Omitowoju (n 8) 125.

78 Omitowoju (n 8) 47.

79 Demosthenes 22.58, *Against Androtion*, as cited in Murray (n 75).

80 Cohen 1993 (n 8) 13.

81 Omitowoju (n 8) 81–82. See also David Konstan, 'Between Courtesan and Wife: Menander's *Perikeiromene*' (1987) 41(2) *Phoenix* 122.

82 Although Glykera is frequently described as a 'concubine', Polemon was unmarried, and so, she is a 'mistress' because she is living with Polemon without being his lawful wife. Of course, her lack of citizenship would have prevented her from being *any* man's wife. For further discussion, see Konstan (n 81) 128–129.

those without citizenship status.[83] She is recognised in the play as being 'her own mistress' who has no *kurios* whose consent is required to authorise her sexual availability, and her refusal to reconcile with Polemon is validated when she is allowed to know her own mind, replying 'that she best knows her own concerns'.[84] It would be misleading, however, to understand Glykera (in her concubine status) as enjoying sexual agency or autonomy via consent. As David Konstan has put it, in describing Glykera as 'her own mistress', Pataikos,

> does not mean to suggest she has the legal rights or status that pertain to an Athenian who is, in the Roman phrase, *in sua potestate* ... There is no question here of her having given herself to Polemon with full legal authority, which would have meant, among other things (and *per impossibile*), that she would have been able to transfer power over herself to Polemon ... Pataikos' expression, striking as it is, means simply that Glykera is independent, without a [*kurios*] at all.[85]

Glykera's 'independence' is a result of her exclusion from citizenship, from socio-political recognition. Her consent is only made possible when she *loses* this power to self-govern and becomes a female citizen.[86] Her new status is what renders her consent recognisable (as that of her *kurios*). Any notion of a 'female consent'[87] among Athenian concubines, non-citizens, and other 'independents' would have been unintelligible.

Consent among this group of Athenian outcasts is therefore a transgressive act in terms of the engagement it signifies with sexual activities and unions unsanctioned by the state but also in terms of the agency it is assigned (in retroactive readings) among a group not granted this proprietary (nor subjective) right. Similar to the oxymoronic designation of Victorian prostitutes as 'public women' who were assigned to the public domain without any of its state-sanctioned rights, the 'outlaws' of ancient Greek and Roman societies were neither owned nor substantively capable of being self-owners.[88] This problematises the association of individualism with self-ownership that is so prevalent in the consent-as-autonomy model, but it also highlights how status and consent are 'mutually constitutive' and the role of Greek myth 'in insisting that women establish their

83 Konstan (n 81) 127.

84 See Konstan's translation (n 81) 132.

85 Konstan (n 81) 129.

86 Glykera's new status would have come with expectations, including 'a silence that is the sign of dutiful obedience', as Konstan puts it (n 81) 134. As one scholar wrote of Athenian marriage, 'Once they have crossed the threshold of marriage, the husband becomes the provider and the wife earns the right to be quiet': Nicole Loraux, *Les enfants d'Athéna* (Maspero 1984) 177 as cited in Konstan (n 81) 134.

87 James Robson, *Sex and Sexuality in Classical Athens* (Edinburgh University Press 2013); Nancy Sorkin Rabinowitz, 'Greek Tragedy: A Rape Culture?' (2011) 1 *Eugesta* 1.

88 Patricia Williams makes a similar claim in her text *The Alchemy of Race and Rights: Diary of a Law Professor* (HUP 1991) between states of being 'owned' and 'unowned'.

respectability before they can be rape-able, that is, able to make a claim of rape'.[89] Two other observations about how consent can be seen to operate within this ancient outlaw sphere deserve mention.

First, the autonomy of the ancient outcast is possible only because these acts of (transgressive) sexual expression occur outside of the state and thus do not threaten its concerns with policing citizenship and property rights. As such, the outlaw's consent is only autonomous in its lack of socio-political consequence or recognition. While the liberal subject is autonomous in its self-owning, proprietary rights-bearing capacity, the outcast of the ancient society exercises agency in a non-public arena, challenging the possessive individualism at the heart of dominant modern discourses of consent. This stands in stark contrast to the autonomy which modern accounts have argued is made most manifest in consent. With a desire to preserve a dichotomy between the public and private spheres of human activity, liberal political theories argue for minimal government intervention, most notably within 'private' matters. Defining liberty as the freedom to be 'let alone', these theories contend that the secret of this independence lies in private property rights and a controlled role for state governance of economic affairs. In such models, consent is the means by which a citizen's 'natural' right to non-interference is recognised and exchanged for security. While contemporary scholars will often read consent-as-autonomy in accounts of early Greek and Roman treatments of sexual offence regulation, a conception of the individual most free from state intervention and self-determinative of private relations is more evident among those deemed *ineligible* to consent within state borders. Further, some aspects to modern liberalism's push for a more positive notion of liberty (ie a freedom *to* act rather than a freedom *from* (state) action) are better exemplified along these 'outer limits' to the polis.[90]

Second, the status of the outlaw is produced through at least a partial adherence to the normative categories of subjectivity found within the polis. These 'others' are socially intelligible in their physical form (ie as 'women' or 'men') but not in the attributes or behaviours they participate in, leaving their identities as 'homosexual men' or 'sexually autonomous women' incoherent. The myth of Caeneus, found in Ovid's *Metamorphoses*, provides a good example of this implicit code of intelligibility at work in the context of an outlaw's consent. Caeneus was a king's daughter who had rejected all of her suitors before being coerced into sex by Poseidon, who agreed to grant her

89 Rabinowitz (n 87) 7, 12.

90 I employ 'outer limits' in reference to Gayle Rubin's conception of the 'charmed circle' of good, normal, state-sanctioned (and in Rubin's argument, heterosexual) forms of sexuality. See Gayle S Rubin, 'Thinking Sex: Notes for a Radical Theory of the Politics of Sexuality' in Henry Abelove, Michèle Aina Barale, and David M Halperin (eds), *Lesbian and Gay Studies Reader* (Routledge 1993). Hannah Arendt's notion of the 'shadowy realm' and Judith Butler's use of it as a context which 'haunts the public sphere, which is precluded from the public constitution of the human, but which is human in an apparently catachrestic sense of that term', would also apply. See Hannah Arendt, *The Human Condition* (University of Chicago 1969) Pt 1, as cited by Butler (n 70) 81.

any wish she desired in return for her submission. Her wish was never to have to consent again, so Poseidon gave Caeneus an 'impenetrable' body – that of a man.[91] A woman with the authority (or sufficient 'self-ownership') to refuse consent was an unintelligible subject within the polis, demonstrated by Caeneus's wish manifesting itself in a new body – the only one empowered to refuse consent.[92]

A similar circumstance can be seen in the story of Antigone, as told by Sophocles. Antigone lacks the socio-political status of a legal subject both because of her gender and the fact that she was the daughter of an incestuous union. Her brother is declared a traitor of the state by Creon, her uncle and the newly crowned king of Thebes, and is denied a proper burial. Antigone violates these orders and buries her brother's body. When she is called before Creon to speak to her crimes, her transgressions against the state become two-fold: first, in her initial act of disobeying Creon's orders and second, in her act of appearing before the state to speak to her crimes. The latter act would have been one reserved for male citizens; thus, in asking Antigone to respond to her initial act of disobedience, Creon imparts a status to Antigone that she is not entitled to. This is explicitly acknowledged in the play when Antigone is called 'manly' by the chorus and when Creon accuses his son, Haemon (who is engaged to be married to Antigone), of being 'inferior to a woman' for his attempts to support her.[93] Here, Antigone's autonomy – her act of independence and, arguably, self-rule (as opposed to obedience to state sovereignty) – is unintelligible. Moreover, as Butler has suggested, '[h]er act is never fully her act'.[94] Rather, the autonomy Antigone exercises is not hers but that of a man; thus, it exists only in her transgression of the norms of intelligibility that serve to delegitimise her identity as an autonomous subject. As Butler notes:

> [Antigone] asserts herself through appropriating the voice of the other, the one to whom she is opposed; thus her autonomy is gained through the appropriation of the authoritative voice of the one she resists, an appropriation that has within it traces of a simultaneous refusal and assimilation of that very authority.[95]

91 Book XII, 525–532 as cited in Luc Brisson, *Sexual Ambivalence: Androgyny and Hermaphroditism in Graeco-Roman Antiquity* (Janet Lloyd tr, University of California Press 2002) 62.

92 This calls to mind Demosthenes's account of the prosecution of Androtion for *hubris* (see note 79 and accompanying text) and the status consequences for 'improper' uses of consent (including as a form of submission when used as such by male, status-holding citizens). Cohen cites Xenophon's remark that 'using men as women is to commit *hubris* against them' (Mem 2.1.30), noting that 'the description of the act as *hubris* arises from the view that a man is always dishonored by adopting the submissive sexual role of a woman'. See Cohen 1993 (n 8) 13–14.

93 Butler (n 70) 8.

94 Butler (n 70) 10.

95 Butler (n 70) 11.

This is akin to the paradox (discussed in Chapter 1) that is housed within contemporary understandings of consent. The autonomy that consent is meant to embody must ultimately be unrealisable so as to continue to hold the promise of universal applicability. This is particularly evident when this claim to autonomy (via consent) is made by those whose very status or subjectivity challenges the norms of intelligibility upon which the consent-as-autonomy story is built. Antigone, Caeneus, Glykera, and other transgressors of these rules of the ancients may be seen to act autonomously, but in so doing, they move out of the frame of intelligibility and thus out of the scope of consent. Through consent, they are made (to employ Butler's language), 'stateless within the state'.

> These spectral humans, deprived of ontological weight and failing the tests of social intelligibility required for minimal recognition include those whose age, gender, race, nationality, and labor status not only disqualify them for citizenship but actively "qualify" them for statelessness. This last notion may well be significant, since the stateless are not just stripped of status but accorded a status and prepared for their dispossession and displacement; they become stateless precisely through complying with certain normative categories.[96]

While this lack of coherence in the consent-as-autonomy story may be more visible when examined in a historical context where the rules of exclusion from socio-political recognition are more starkly or explicitly stratified, the question remains as to whether consent and its contemporary preconditions function all that differently today. In the Canadian Supreme Court case of *Mara,* for example (where charges of obscenity were laid against a tavern when its dancers allowed patrons to touch and kiss them during performances), the court dismissed the issue of consent on the grounds that the acts in question fell too far outside the realm of common decency. Writing for the court, Sopinka J stated:

> It is unacceptably degrading to women to permit such uses of their bodies in the context of a public performance in a tavern. Insofar as the activities were consensual, as the appellants stressed, this does not alter their degrading character. Moreover, as I stated in *Butler*, at p 479, '[s]ometimes the very appearance of consent makes the depicted acts even more degrading or dehumanizing'.[97]

In this case, the autonomy that consent is meant to signify is denied on the basis that it was enacted in ways that did not conform to dominant understandings of women and female sexuality. Akin to the effect a woman's consent

96 Judith Butler and Gayatri Chakravorty Spivak, *Who Sings the Nation State?: Language, Politics, Belonging* (Seagull 2007) 15–16.

97 [1997] 2 SCR 630, [35].

could be seen to have on an offence of *hubris* in the Classical context, 'the very appearance of consent' in the *Mara* case serves as an aggravating factor to the alleged harm (rather than a mitigating one). Moreover, this case demonstrates that the 'freedom' to consent is one that must be enacted in compliance with prescribed ways of being and acting in order to be recognisable, suggesting that the denial of autonomy experienced by Antigone is a more familiar experience for non-conforming subjects in the present day than the consent-as-autonomy story would lead one to believe.

(Post)modern reflections

This chapter's survey of how early Greek and Roman societies addressed sexual consent has demonstrated that consent has performed functions and housed meanings that run contrary to the foundationalist story of autonomy. In contrast to contemporary views of consent as a signifier of an ethical or equitable transaction, there have been both circumstances and subjects for whom consent aggravates rather than mitigates inequality. This is a concern raised by many of the left-leaning critiques, examined in the previous chapter, which strive to remove a distinction between the individual and her society. Rather than positing individuals as autonomous agents, these critiques suggest that subjects are tied to the communities in which they act, thus limiting and influencing the parameters of their choices. Subjects of any given socio-legal structure are not 'free' from the constraints of these systems. Rather, legal rights are correlative to others' vulnerabilities. Thus, even critical reformulations of the liberal account of consent are subject to the criticism that they do not adequately account for the relationship between juridical rights and socio-economic and cultural restraints.[98]

Wendy Brown, in her examination of 'constitutive dualisms' in liberal discourse, suggests that women are situated (ontologically within and through consent) as submitting, assenting to terms that they do not participate in framing.[99] Consent and its various ontological roles are not, then, power neutral, yet liberal theories of consent and their critiques seem ill-equipped to address how consent functions as a license not to property rights or sexual access but to cultural recognition.[100] Explorations of Athenian rape laws and attitudes involve

98 Critiques offered by Robert Paul Wolff and Susan Moller Okin on John Rawls's *A Theory of Justice* (HUP 1971) are good additional examples of these left-leaning perspectives. See Robert Paul Wolff, *Understanding Rawls* (PUP 1977) and Susan Moller Okin, *Justice, Gender, and the Family* (Basic Books 1989).

99 Wendy Brown, *States of Injury: Power and Freedom in Late Modernity* (PUP 1995).

100 Both classic and modern forms of liberalism, while demonstrating a shift in terms of rights of privacy and spheres of acceptable government intervention, construct the 'self' along a continuum of property-as-freedom, where consent figures against coercion. While critiquing this liberal notion of the self, more communitarian and socialist analyses are unable to escape the juxtaposition of this dichotomy, reinforcing a discourse founded in an (autonomously) acting subject.

'examining not just the sorts of behaviour they regulated, but the sorts of people whose behaviour they seemed to problematise or the sorts of people whom they sought to protect'.[101] I would contend that the same should be said for investigations into consent today. While Omitowoju describes female consent in Classical Athens as 'illegitimate' in that it performed different functions than contemporary theories of consent would anticipate (eg aggravating or altering the offence as seen in the case of *hubris*), I would argue that consent in the ancient context reveals more a story of intelligibility than of legitimacy, given its role in determining what subjects are *recognisable* (rather than what actions might be justifiable).

This is perhaps best illustrated by the population of ancient 'outlaws' examined in the previous section. Rather than simply representing various incarnations of 'illegitimate' or incomplete forms of consent, the Athenian polis employed consent to not only regulate this population of outlaws but, in the first instance, to produce it. The outcast represents the 'necessary other' for the creation and control of the ideal citizen, the latter made visible only through the transgressions of the former.[102] My examination of sexual consent in early Athens and Rome reveals a legal concept that is applied selectively and differentially on the bases of gender, social status, age, and sexual practice (discretions that are arguably as evident in contemporary articulations of consent). Some might suggest that this shows consent to be a right or privilege only available to certain subjects, be those men or free citizens or married, heterosexual couples. This might lead reformists to suggest that the problems with consent and its application can be remedied by simply expanding the category of persons to whom this right or privilege is available. The foundation for making discernments about this expansion project would vary depending on which theoretical camp critiques of consent were coming from, yet these analyses and their reform projects presume a fixed quality to consent. It is merely a tool that needs to be picked up and redirected in the 'right' way. The dominant narrative of consent as a form of freedom, whether to contract or to self-determine, is maintained.[103]

101 Omitowoju (n 8) 116.

102 This follows Foucault's understanding of law's productive power in demarcating particular populations as both marginal and in need of control. Take, for example, his comments on the 'success' of the prison system in his seminal work, *Discipline and Punish*: 'For the observation that prison fails to eliminate crime, one should perhaps substitute the hypothesis that prison has succeeded extremely well in introducing delinquency … in producing delinquents, in an apparently marginal, but in fact centrally supervised milieu; in producing the delinquent as a pathologised subject' (n 1) 277.

103 See, for instance, the critique of radical feminist approaches to sexual consent offered by Allison Moore and Paul Reynolds in 'Feminist Approaches to Sexual Consent: A Critical Assessment' in Mark Cowling (ed), *Making Sense of Sexual Consent* (Routledge 2016). While recognising the difficulty presented by a context where women have only a 'partial engagement in an unequal sexual contract' and sexual consent is 'the ideological misrepresentation of hetero-patriarchal sexual ownership, control and abuse', Moore and Reynolds maintain a commitment to this dominant narrative of consent-as-autonomy. They state: 'A concept of sexual consent that cannot appreciate the meaning of women's agency and autonomy, even under conditions

Further, while some commentators might argue that the outcasts of ancient Athens and Rome represent an explicit example of socio-economic inequity where the law services the interests of the wealthy and privileged, these analyses fall short of explaining how these exclusions contribute to rather than contest this 'natural' story of consent as a freedom pre-existing the subject who enacts it. I would suggest that what is at issue in contemporary applications of consent is not the quality of free action, property protection, or the capacity for reasonable self-control but rather the constitution of the public domain. Law has the power to give expression to imagined boundaries and spatialisations, and to define the parameters for who might inhabit these spaces.[104] Further, although many critical legal theories might frame the outcast population as a 'failed approximation' of the ideal citizen (thus presenting an opportunity to subvert or transform the norm), Butler's work posits such constitutive failings as produced by the norm itself (through a demarcating of the 'other') and indicative (if not productive) of the norm's plasticity and strength. Thus, when the law fails, it is re-imagined and re-tooled but not rejected. The very difference or diversity which demonstrates the law's inadequacy is thus used to legitimise (and reinforce) its borders.

Conclusion

This chapter has sought to investigate the 'conditions of possibility' for (re)conceptualisations of sexual consent within the ancient eras of Athens and Rome as a form of autonomy. Although consent played a significant role in three of the legal categories in which sexual behaviour was regulated in the Classical period, it was not one of autonomy. Instead, consent operated in each of these offence categories as a form of proprietorship in relation to the familial interests of free male citizens. This contrasted with the experiences of the state's outcasts, where consent served to constitute and enforce codes of intelligibility for both juridical and cultural recognition. In each case, the story of autonomy which dominates contemporary theories of consent was destabilised, particularly through a contemplation of those subjectivities for whom neither the ancient nor modern conceptions of consent provided adequate explanation.

This chapter's earlier discussion of sexual offence regulation suggests that within the Athenian polis, consent operated with a presumption that citizens use their bodies reasonably and without shame – a mandate that, as the next chapter

of social and sexual inequality, will be of little use in theorising women's ownership of their sexuality short of radical social and structural change', 29–30.

104 See, for instance, the work of Leticia Sabsay who examines the legal determinations of sex work in Buenos Aires as 'decriminalised' or 'permissible' in certain ('red-light') districts of the city. For Sabsay, these designations are less demonstrative of the law's prohibitive powers than of its ability to demarcate the sexual shape of the public sphere: Leticia Sabsay, 'The Subject of Diversity: Sexual Borders, Citizenship, and the Public Sphere' (Lecture, Cosmopolitanism, Peace, and Conflict Intensive Summer Programme, Utrecht University, 2 February 2010).

will demonstrate, was carried through into the medieval period's treatment of consent (albeit reformulated into a Christian paradigm).[105] This suggests that exploring narratives of consent within contexts that challenge the ahistorical story of consent-as-autonomy can yield alternative accounts of what consent does. Specifically, it reveals that law's use of consent implicates questions of prescriptive subjectivity and socio-political recognition as much as (if not more than) notions of autonomy. Finding these counter-narratives, however, is not easy work. It requires reading against the grain of powerful and pervasive stories of consent that boast the persuasion of the 'common sense'. There is likely no area of law where this autonomy story is more secure than in the field of medical law and its doctrine of informed consent. Reading against this story is the work of the next chapter.

Bibliography

Table of cases

R v Brown [1993] 2 All ER 75
R v Butler [1992] 1 SCR 452
R v Mara [1997] 2 SCR 630

Table of legislation

Criminal Code, RSC 1985, C-46 (Canada)
Sexual Offences Act 2003 (UK)

Secondary sources

Adams JN, *Latin Sexual Vocabulary* (JHUP 1990)
Archard D, *Sexual Consent* (Westview Press 1998)
Arendt H, *The Human Condition* (University of Chicago 1969)
Bauman RA, *Women and Politics in Ancient Rome* (Routledge 1992)
Brisson L, *Sexual Ambivalence: Androgyny and Hermaphroditism in Graeco-Roman Antiquity* (Janet Lloyd tr, University of California Press 2002)
Brown W, *States of Injury: Power and Freedom in Late Modernity* (PUP 1995)
Bullough VL, 'Age of Consent' (2005) 16(2) *JPHS* 25
Bury RG and others (tr), *Plato in Twelve Volumes* (HUP 1968)
Butler J, 'Sexual Traffic' (1994) 6.2+3 *differences* 62

105 Foucault's observations of paederasty in the second volume of the *History of Sexuality* provide some evidence to support this ethos of moderation, suggesting an early Greek view of temperance in the exercise of power where the 'ethics of pleasure' required 'subtle strategies that would make allowance for the other's freedom, his ability to refuse, and his required consent' (n 33) 199. It is important to note, however, that the 'consent' being referenced in Foucault's passage was that of either fully-fledged male citizens or their younger counterparts. The notion that consent, within the ancient context, could have entailed a 'right to refuse' for anyone else would not have been an intelligible contention.

——, *Antigone's Claim: Kinship between Life and Death* (Columbia University Press 2000)

——, 'Co-habitation, Universality and Remembrance: Further Reflections on Israel/ Palestine' (Lecture, Department of Psychosocial Studies, Birkbeck University of London, 24 May 2010)

Butler J and Spivak GC, *Who Sings the Nation State?: Language, Politics, Belonging* (Seagull 2007)

Buxton RG, *Persuasion in Greek Tragedy: A Study of Peitho* (CUP 1982)

Carawan E, *Rhetoric and the Law of Draco* (OUP 1998)

Carey C, 'Rape and Adultery in Athenian Law' (1995) 45(2) *CQ* 407

Cartledge P, Millett P and Todd S (eds), *Nomos: Essays in Athenian Law, Politics, and Society* (CUP 1990)

Cohen D, 'Sexuality, Violence and the Athenian Law of *Hubris*' (1991) 38 *G&R* 171

——, 'Consent and Sexual Relations in Classical Athens' in Angeliki E Laiou (ed), *Consent and Coercion to Sex and Marriage in Ancient and Medieval Societies* (Dumbarton Oaks 1993)

Cole SG, 'Greek Sanctions against Sexual Assault' (1984) 79 *CPhil* 97

Constant B, 'The Liberty of the Ancients Compared with that of the Moderns (1833)' in David Boaz (ed), *The Libertarian Reader* (Free Press 1997)

Cooper C, 'Forensic Oratory' in Ian Worthington (ed), *A Companion to Greek Rhetoric* (Wiley Blackwell 2010)

Dall C, *The College, the Market, and the Court: Women's Relation to Education, Labor and Law* (Lee & Shepard 1867)

Fisher NRE, *Hybris: A Study in the Values of Honour and Shame in Ancient Greece* (Aris & Phillips 1992)

Foucault M, *Discipline & Punish: The Birth of the Prison* (Alan Sheridan tr, Pantheon Book 1977)

——, *The History of Sexuality, Vol 2: The Use of Pleasure* (Robert Hurley tr, Vintage Books 1990)

——, 'The Hermeneutic of the Subject' in Paul Rabinow (ed) *Ethics: Subjectivity and Truth, Essential Works of Foucault 1954–1984* (Penguin 1994)

Gardner HH, 'Ventriloquizing Rape in Menander's *Epitrepontes*' (2012) 39(2) *Helios* 121

Gardner JF, *Being a Roman Citizen* (Routledge 1993)

Gravdal K, *Ravishing Maidens: Writing Rape in Medieval French Literature and Law* (University of Pennsylvania Press 1991)

Haag P, *Consent: Sexual Rights and the Transformation of American Liberalism* (Cornell University Press 1999)

Halperin DM, 'Sexual Ethics and Technologies of the Self in Classical Greece' (1986) 107 *J Phil* 274

——, *One Hundred Years of Homosexuality and other essays on Greek love* (Routledge 1990)

Harris EM, 'Did the Athenians Regard Seduction as a Worse Crime than Rape?' (1990) 40(2) *CQ* 370

Harrison ARW, *The Law of Athens, Vol. 1* (OUP 1968)

Hubbard TK, 'Popular Perceptions of Elite Homosexuality in Classical Athens' (1998) 6(1) *Arion* 48

Hurd H, 'The Moral Magic of Consent' (1992) 2(2) *LEG* 121

Ibbetson DJ and Lewis ADE, *The Roman Law Tradition* (CUP 1994)

Irigaray L, *The Sex Which is Not One* (Catherine Porter tr, Cornell University Press 1985)

Konstan D, 'Between Courtesan and Wife: Menander's *Perikeiromene*' (1987) 41(2) *Phoenix* 122

Laiou AE (ed), *Consent and Coercion to Sex and Marriage in Ancient and Medieval Societies* (Dumbarton Oaks 1993)

Lewis CT, *A Latin Dictionary* (Charles Stewart ed, OUP 1879)

Licht H, *Sexual Life in Ancient Greece* (Routledge 1932)

Loraux N, *Les enfants d'Athéna: Idées athéniennes sur la citoyenneté et la division des sexes* (Maspero 1984)

Moore A and Reynolds P, 'Feminist Approaches to Sexual Consent: A Critical Assessment' in Mark Cowling (ed), *Making Sense of Sexual Consent* (Routledge 2016)

Moses DC, 'Livy's Lucretia and the Validity of Coerced Consent in Roman Law' in Angeliki E Laiou (ed) *Consent and Coercion to Sex and Marriage in Ancient and Medieval Societies* (Dumbarton Oaks 1993)

Murray AT (tr), *Demosthenes with an English Translation* (HUP 1939)

Okin SM, *Justice, Gender, and the Family* (Basic Books 1989)

Omitowoju R, *Rape and the Politics of Consent in Classical Athens* (CUP 2002)

Plutarch, *The Parallel Lives, Vol 1: Theseus and Romulus, Lycurgus and Numa, Solon and Publicola* (Bernadotte Perrin tr, Loeb Classical Library 1914)

Rabinowitz NS, 'Greek Tragedy: A Rape Culture?' (2011) 1 *Eugesta* 1

RAINN, 'Consent Laws' (*RAINN.org*, December 2017) <https://apps.rainn.org/policy/compare/consent-laws.cfm> accessed 30 April 2019

Rawls J, *A Theory of Justice* (HUP 1971)

Robson J, *Sex and Sexuality in Classical Athens* (Edinburgh University Press 2013)

Rowe GO, 'The Many Facets of Hybris in Demosthenes' *against Meidias*' (1993) 114(3) *AJPhil* 397

Rubin GS, 'Thinking Sex: Notes for a Radical Theory of the Politics of Sexuality' in Henry Abelove, Michèle Aina Barale and David M Halperin (eds), *Lesbian and Gay Studies Reader* (Routledge 1993)

Sabsay L, 'The Subject of Diversity: Sexual Borders, Citizenship, and the Public Sphere' (Lecture, Cosmopolitanism, Peace, and Conflict Intensive Summer Programme, Utrecht University, 2 February 2010)

Sawyer DF, *Women and Religion in the First Christian Century* (Routledge 1996)

Sickinger JP, 'Rhetoric and the Law' in Ian Worthington (ed), *A Companion to Greek Rhetoric* (Wiley Blackwell 2010)

Stafford EJ, 'Plutarch on Persuasion' in Sarah B Pomeroy (ed), *Plutarch's 'Advice to the Bride and Groom' and 'A Consolation to His Wife': English Translations, Commentary, Interpretive Essays, and Bibliography* (OUP 1999)

Thirlwall BC, *A History of Greece, Vol. 1* (Longman Rees 1835)

Todd SC, *The Shape of Athenian Law* (OUP 1993)

Xenophon, *Xenophon in Seven Volumes* (Edgar Cardew Marchant and Otis Johnson Todd trs, HUP 1923)

Wertheimer A, *Consent to Sexual Relations* (CUP 2003)

Williams PJ, *The Alchemy of Race and Rights: Diary of a Law Professor* (HUP 1991)

Wolff RP, *Understanding Rawls* (PUP 1977)

3 Medieval medicine

> My God, my God, how soon wouldst thou have me go to the physician, and how far wouldst thou have me go with the physician? I know thou hast made the matter, and the man, and the art; and I go not from thee when I go to the physician.
>
> –John Donne, *Devotions Upon Emergent Occasions* (1624)[1]

The field of medical ethics is one where change is both expected and exigent. Developments in biotechnology and its applications create a host of possibilities for clinical medicine while complicating existing frameworks for treatment and decision-making. Debates concerning reproductive technologies, organ donations and transplants, life-support systems, death assistance, and genetic research represent only some of the places where medicine, law, and ethics converse about the value and limits of human life. Despite the vast differences both between and within these fields, the doctrine of informed consent provides a common platform for these varied analyses, leading some commentators to suggest that 'consent' is the linchpin of bioethical research and its regulation.[2] This pivotal role for consent within medical law and ethics scholarship persists notwithstanding a significant number of problems, often positioned in the literature as deficiencies in the doctrine's level of specificity or scope.[3] Scholars of all stripes question the justificatory bases for consent and whether the requirements for establishing informed consent are sufficiently stringent or extend to an adequate array of arenas of medical research and practice.

Bioethicists are, however, fairly uniform in their view of informed consent as a modern-day construction established against long-standing traditions of paternalism and power within doctor-patient relationships. Histories of the informed consent doctrine often begin with a citation of the Hippocratic Oath, highlighting its implicit endorsement of deception to gain patient trust and a 'doctor knows

1 'Book IV: The Physician is Sent For' in John Donne, *Devotions Upon Emergent Occasions* (first published 1624, John Sparrow ed, CUP 1923) 18.

2 Susan M Wolf, 'Toward a Systematic Theory of Informed Consent in Managed Care' (1999) 35 *Hous LR* 1631.

3 Neil C Manson and Onora O'Neill, *Rethinking Informed Consent in Bioethics* (CUP 2007).

best' approach to decision-making, before moving ahead to an 'emergence' of informed consent in the twentieth century.[4] This has positioned the Nuremberg Code of 1947 as medical law's first appearance of ethical regulations based on informed consent.[5] This view of informed consent as a historically specific and legally created doctrine creates a 'truth' about consent and how it operates in medical law, which is bound to these roots of paternalism and their presumed counterpart of patient autonomy. Informed consent requirements, procedures, and their efficacies are assessed in contemporary scholarship in relation to how well they advance patients' rights to self-determination and choice.[6] Further, even critiques or proposed reforms of the consent doctrine must reference this paternalism debate to be intelligible; they must re-engage with this discourse of individual liberty and its limits.[7] This persists even amidst apparent contradictions created by the ever-increasing demand for more explicit and expansive forms of consent, each aimed at providing patients with greater opportunities for 'free choice'. In a passage that echoes some of the tensions inherent in consent's hypothetical status that were explored in Chapter 1, Manson and O'Neill observe that:

> Explicit consent cannot be necessary, because it is not always possible. Implied consent can be replaced by explicit consent in some, but not all, cases ... [I]t would not be possible to do entirely without implied consent, because

4 See Ruth Faden and Tom Beauchamp, *A History and Theory of Informed Consent* (OUP 1986); Emily Jackson, *Medical Law: Text, Cases, and Materials* (OUP 2009); and Peter J Murray, 'The History of Informed Consent' (1990) 10 *Iowa Orthop J* 104 as examples of this practice.

5 Vollman and Winau, while recognising this as the general view, do depart from it slightly, suggesting evidence of consent-informed guidelines for human experimentation as early as the nineteenth century. See Jochen Vollman and Rolf Winau, 'Informed Consent in Human Experimentation before the Nuremberg Code' (1996) 313 *BMJ* 1445. Similarly, Manson and O'Neill cite the Nuremberg Code as 'the first authoritative statement of consent requirements in biomedical ethics' (n 3) 2, even though they link the doctrine's roots to the European Enlightenment period and early political liberalism's theories of governmental legitimacy. Many American commentators cite the 1914 New York case of *Schloendorff v Society of New York Hospital* 105 NE 92 as the doctrine's first legal appearance, noting Justice Cardozo's holding that every competent adult 'has a right to determine what shall be done with his own body' (92) 'kicked off a struggle to end millennia of physician nondisclosure and decisions for their patients' Wolf (n 2) 1632.

6 The American case of *Canterbury v Spence* 464 F 2d 772 (DC Cir 1972) has been heralded by some scholars as 'the pinnacle of informed consent case law' given its determination that physicians would be held to a standard set by law; Wolf (n 2) 1632. This standard (later characterised as the 'reasonable person' standard) is informed by a 'more robust right grounded in the moral principle of autonomy' rather than a professional standard established by what similarly situated colleagues might disclose; Robert M Veatch (ed) *Cross-Cultural Perspectives in Medical Ethics* (2nd edn, Jones & Bartlett 2000) 146. Veatch describes the *Canterbury* case as one which 'overturn[ed] the more paternalistic Hippocratic professional standard', 158.

7 Note, for instance, the critiques offered by Manson and O'Neill which reject autonomy models (in favour of frameworks for consent which prioritise 'agency' as a form of communicative action) while still recognising the necessity of engaging with the discourse of autonomy in analyses of consent. They state: 'Appeals to informed consent and its role in justifying clinical and research practice are now so well entrenched that their presence, indeed their necessity, and their justification are rarely questioned' (n 3) 2.

> any explicit consenting presupposes and relies on implicit assumptions and agreements – including assumptions about the methods and conventions for requesting, offering and refusing consent.[8]

Thus, while the demand for more specific procedures and forms of consent is often viewed as raising ethical criteria for clinical practice, the effect is a demand for 'formalistic, uniform, and, strictly speaking, impossible procedures and standards'.[9] Consent in this context is tasked with altering an age-old history of paternalism while securing patients' personal and bodily integrity. As a result, medical law has increasingly granted an integral if not all-encompassing role to consent when determining the rights and responsibilities of medical relationships.[10] As noted by Draper and Sorrell, '[i]n comparison to what it asks of doctors, mainstream medical ethics makes very few demands of patients, and these usually begin and end with consent'.[11]

Consent is, therefore, understood in the modern context as an exercise of choice or freedom that each patient is presumed to have. Rethinking informed consent within this frame means tweaking the circumstances in which this choice occurs (eg revisiting the requirements for physician disclosure) rather than examining how this conception of consent prefigures the frame in which it is revisited or whether alternative accounts of the doctrine and its function might exist.[12] Consent as choice or self-determination gains an indisputable status in this narrative, linked to notions of freedom and personal rights. Yet, as Wendy Brown has argued, 'rights are never deployed "freely", but always within a discursive, hence normative context'.[13] This normative context, in terms of informed consent, is deeply entrenched in a liberal grammar of (patient) autonomy, thus making attempts to find understandings of medical consent which do not invoke and reinstate this rights-based foundation rather fruitless – at least in modern scholarship.[14] Hearing a different story will require a context before 'autonomy'

8 Manson and O'Neill (n 3) 12.

9 Manson and O'Neill (n 3) 11.

10 Manson and O'Neill point to empirical research highlighting the prominence of informed consent scholarship in the medical field. They cite their own search results from the database MedLine for the year 2002–2003 where the terms 'informed consent' appear in the titles of more than 300 articles (in English) and in the subject field of more than 1,800 articles (n 3) 1. My own search of the same database (MedLine 1950 to present) for the year 2017–2018 resulted in similar prominence for the terms, with 'informed consent' appearing in the titles of 194 (English language) articles and in the Keyword fields of 2616 articles.

11 Heather Draper and Tom Sorell, 'Patients' Responsibilities in Medical Ethics' (2002) 16(4) *Bioethics* 335, 335.

12 Manson and O'Neill suggest one such alternative account, proposing that consent be viewed as a communicative transaction or 'propositional attitude', although this still positions consent as a waiver of existing legal and ethical requirements – a point which Manson and O'Neill leave uncontested (n 3) 68–77.

13 Wendy Brown, *Left Legalism/Left Critique* (Duke University Press 2002) 422.

14 Martin Pernick argues that the debate between medical and legal values 'derives from attempts to trace the history of "informed consent" as an isolated entity, abstracted from all social and

became, to employ Foucault's words, 'permanently established in the realm of truth' for medical law.[15]

This chapter will continue the project's genealogical investigation of consent by examining a period far removed from the discourses of autonomy operating in contemporary bioethical scholarship – Europe's Middle Ages. Although the term the 'dark ages' has been largely abandoned by historians following the discovery of much intellectual and cultural development during the period, this label continues to be an apt description of the medieval era's reputation in the field of medical ethics.[16] This is even more so when notions of patient autonomy or consent to medical treatment are considered, given the general view of depravity that many medieval and medical historians have held about medical practice of the era. Indeed, as one commentator quipped, 'all medieval medical practice was malpractice'.[17] The period is further plagued by images of supernatural belief systems and charlatan practitioners. One medieval historian noted:

> Because of their simple Christian faith, most medieval folk resorted for healing to saint's relics and superstitious charms. Furthermore, they were misled by medical quacks, old witches with their herbs and incantations, midwives, and blood-letting barbers. Such is the average mental image of medieval medicine.[18]

Yet, despite this reputation, the medieval era can boast a great number of ethical codes for medical practice and physician conduct, including what some scholars have suggested are 'consent forms'. Translations of these texts suggest that they were contracts for medical treatment, each outlining a particular medical act to be performed by a named physician.[19] The *Laws of Valentinus*, enacted in 368 AD,

---

historical context. But changes in medical technology, medical theory, professional power, and social structure all have interacted over time to shape the changing role of the patient in medical decisionmaking' in 'The Patient's Role in Medical Decision Making: A Social History of Informed Consent in Medical Therapy' *President's Commission for the Study of Ethical Problems in Medicine and Biomedical and Behavioral Research, Vol. 3: Making Health Care Decisions* (US Library of Congress 1982) 3.

15 Michel Foucault, *Madness and Civilization: A History of Insanity in an Age of Reason* (Vintage 1965) ix.

16 Loren C MacKinney, 'Medical Ethics and Etiquette in the Early Middle Ages: The Persistence of Hippocratic Ideals' (1952) 26(1) *Bull Hist Med* 1.

17 Madeleine P Cosman, 'Medieval Medical Malpractice: The Dicta and the Dockets' (1973) 49(1) *Bull NY Acad Med* 22. It should be noted that Cosman cites this phrase somewhat disparagingly before examining how erroneous a view of medieval medicine it is. See also Charles Singer, 'Medical Science in the Dark Ages' in Zachary Cope (ed), *Sidelights on the History of Medicine* (Butterworths 1957).

18 MacKinney, 'Medical Ethics' (n 16) 22.

19 Salih Selek, 'A Written Consent Five Centuries Ago' (2010) 36 *J Med Eth* 639. See also Kamel M Ajlouni, 'History of Informed Consent' (1995) 346(8980) *Lancet* 980. Where the scholarship addresses these medical contracts, it does so through the lens of trade and commerce; see: Georges F Fort, *Medieval Economy during the Middle Ages: A Contribution to the History of European Morals, from the Time of the Roman Empire to the Close of the Fourteenth Century* (JW

also sparked a series of regulations over medical practice when the first public surgeon was appointed and paid by the state to administer to the poor.[20] This marked the state's forays into the governance of physician conduct, creating areas of liability and demarcating the correlative consequences for malpractice.[21] Further, these early allocations of medicine to a public domain of regulation fostered an interest in the profession's deontology, spurring many medieval theologians to examine the doctor-patient relationship and its ethical parameters. Contrary to popular characterisations of the period and its medical practices, consent figures prominently in many of these philosophical treatises, most notably in the work of Thomas Aquinas and Nicolas de Cusa.

The following chapter tracks these discussions in pursuit of a different kind of story of consent. Similar to the skewed glance which the exploration of sexual consent among the ancients provided, investigating the uses of consent in a period thought to precede concerns of patient autonomy by centuries should serve to disrupt the ease with which a consent-as-autonomy story can be read. The chapter contains four substantive sections. It begins with a descriptive overview of medieval medicine, including its educational schemes and forms of practice, focussing on the commanding influence (if not monopoly) that the Christian Church can be seen to have exercised over the field both in terms of regulating access to the profession and with respect to what knowledge would be deemed valuable enough to learn. This is in no small part attributable to a particular theological epistemology which ran deep throughout the Middle Ages, invoking a multitude of images of the divine and supernatural forces to explain illness and the path to health. This relationship between science and faith, rationality and belief, is the backdrop of the chapter's second section, designed to provide a historically specific frame within which to contemplate the medieval doctor-patient relationship and the role of consent within it. The chapter's third section considers some other forums where consent figured in medieval thought, including cases of Christian conversion, marriage formation, and trade and commerce. These sources help to construct an understanding of medieval consent as a form of submission (to God), made evident through a regime of self-management. This alternative understanding of consent is examined in the chapter's fourth section where the implications of a conception of consent as an existential act of faith are explored for their modern insights and applications.

Bouton 1883); and Lianna Farber, *An Anatomy of Trade in Medieval Writing: Value, Consent, and Community* (Cornell UP 2006). This economic role of consent is discussed later in this chapter.

20 The decrees of the Visigoths in 504 AD have also been noted as having moved medicine within the purview of 'public health', thus creating a more formalised need to mediate the level of suspicion of the medical profession that was common during the period. See Fort (n 19) 139.

21 Fort discusses a number of these regulations in detail, including those which prescribed death for physicians found in breach of their duty (n 19). See also Cosman's study of medical malpractice cases during the fourteenth and fifteenth centuries in London (n 17).

Medieval medicine: a monastic enterprise

Before the heralded medical centres of Salerno and Chartres, the task of educating and employing physicians fell to monasteries. This was for both ecumenical and economic reasons. In the first instance, ministering to the sick was understood as a form of Christian charity. Medical education and treatment were monopolised by the clergy with monastic infirmaries (which exclusively served members of the religious order) and cleric-run hospices (which treated 'pilgrims' and other 'unfortunate souls') serving as the only hospitals throughout much of the Middle Ages.[22] Disease was also understood as a divine intervention, a demonic or sinful presence in the body that only God might remedy.[23] Who better, then, to administer to the inflicted and decree successful treatment than those called to holy service?

Aside from the Christian ideal of brotherly love and a belief in the divine origin of disease, there were significant economic reasons for monasteries serving as the medieval centres of medical study. They were likely one of the few places of the period which would have had the necessary resources in materials, time, and skill to produce one of the most valuable enterprises of medieval medicine: the illuminated manuscript.[24] Described by some as 'medical catechisms', these manuscripts were thought of as treatises of collected medical wisdom.[25] Produced in monasteries, these texts outlined classical theories and illustrations of human anatomy, trusted plant and herbal sources for remedying known ailments, diagrams denoting known injuries, and guiding principles and techniques for diagnosis and treatment. These manuscripts offer a unique insight into the medieval medical world, particularly as woodcutting technology gained ground and the copying of such texts was made easier, improving their distribution (and signalling the move towards mass medical education).[26]

More specifically, these manuscripts provide a means of understanding how both the study and practice of medicine in the Middle Ages were strongly controlled Christian domains. This dominion can be seen on at least three levels, namely:

22 MacKinney, 'Medical Ethics' (n 16) is clear to note that these centres, quite prominent during the Merovingian period in France, would hardly be recognised as modern-day hospitals.

23 As noted by Fort, '[d]emoniacal aeons or emanations, portraying this diabolical principle of evil, were acknowledged to be the primitive source from which arose the multifarious elements of sorrow and pain, including earthly sufferings, pestilence among men, sickness, and other bodily afflictions, but inflicted with consent of Divinity, whose messengers they were' (n 19) 69.

24 For example, Charles H Talbot describes the onerous task of book production, which 'was not simply a matter of scribbling something down on parchment … for sheep and cattle had to be present to provide the skins. There was a highly technical process involved in transforming the skins to parchment. There was a difficulty, owing to distances between monasteries and intellectual centres, in procuring texts to copy from. And finally there was the physical labour demanded by the mere act of transcription', in his text *Medicine in Medieval England* (Oldbourne 1967) 73.

25 Talbot (n 24) 73.

26 Peter Jones marks this move more specifically with the publication of Vesalius's texts *De humani coporis fabrica* and *Epitome of Defabrica*, both published in 1543. See Peter M Jones, *Medieval Medicine in Illuminated Manuscripts* (British Library 1998).

(i) exclusive access to medical education, (ii) an imposed (and hierarchical) dichotomy between medical theory and its practice, and (iii) a process of 'depaganization' of source material.

Regulating access

The first means by which the church exercised control over medieval medicine was in a stringent regulation of access to the profession. Aside from the obstacle of literacy, aspiring physicians who wished to become educated in the art of medicine had to do so under the tutelage of monks or other clerics. Admission to the medical profession thus came with a number of 'Christian' requirements, including enforced celibacy and prohibitions against marriage.[27] Some commentators have suggested that the anomic conditions that were characteristic of the Middle Ages created a habitual practice of persecution against non-Christian groups in an attempt to secure the 'power and influence of a literate élite'.[28] The Catholic Kings of fifteenth-century Spain, for instance, created laws which required evidence of 'purity of the blood' for all those who wished to learn or practice medicine, effectively prohibiting all non-Christians (and their descendants) from entering the profession.[29] These and similar regulations both established and relied upon prevailing understandings of the 'ideal physician', one which was certainly male, Christian,[30] and university or monastically trained.[31]

Theory over practice

In addition to regulating access to medical education, the Church also exercised control over the medieval medical field at an epistemological level, authorising both eligible 'knowers' and the limits of what could be 'known'. While monasteries offered formal medical education, this instruction was largely a theoretical enterprise which promulgated disdain for the uneducated practitioner (however more useful the latter's knowledge might have been). Scholastic medicine was thought 'so voluminous, so rigorous to learn, so intricate to implement that it required the best minds, not the neighbourhood midwife, the old woodsman who could

27 Ecclesiastical sanction for marriage was given to physicians in 1451. See Fort (n 19).

28 Jon Arrizabalaga, 'The Ideal Medical Practitioner in Counter-Reformation Castile' in Samuel S Kottek and Luis García Ballester (eds), *Medicine and Medical Ethics in Medieval and Early Modern Spain* (Magnes Press 2009) 62.

29 Arrizabalaga (n 28).

30 Arrizabalaga suggests this 'ideal physician' was more specifically Roman Catholic, although this is attributable to the historical context his research focusses on, that is, Counter-Reformation Castile and sixteenth-century Spain (n 28).

31 Even when surgical instruction was first introduced into an institutionalised setting (in Salerno during the thirteenth century) a distinction was drawn between those who studied medicine and those who practiced it, the latter referred to as 'medici manuales', that is, physicians who used their hands. See PM Jones (n 26) 86.

repair a broken bone of dog or man alike, or the leech who knew the herbs'.[32] A decree of the Lateran Council in 1215 which forbade clerics from all major Orders from engaging in the 'base' activities of cautery and surgery also contributed to the devaluing of medieval medicine's more practical components.[33]

This left those interested in the medical field's more technical aspects largely to their own devices. As MacKinney put it: 'If a young man chose to perfect himself in the medical art, he must find an expert'.[34] Practical medical knowledge was thus gained outside of monasteries through systems of apprenticeship. This did little to help the already suspicious reputation of medieval medical practitioners and their association with superstitious or 'quack' practices. The scarcity of available training forced many practitioners to travel, as well, resulting in a 'foreigner' status that was distrusted among many medieval societies.[35]

The period's illuminated manuscripts also provide evidence of medical theory's primacy over its clinical applications.[36] Although the manuscripts served to familiarise readers with accepted bodies of knowledge, they would also have helped to delegitimise others. Users of the manuscripts would have had to have been learned, which many practitioners, such as blood-letters, surgeons, barbers, or apothecaries were not. Further, many of the remedies administered during the period would have employed supernaturally sourced antidotes or pagan rituals, yet these find no place amidst the manuscripts copied by the same scholars who produced prayer books and bibles. MacKinney observes:

> Inasmuch as clerical writers were chiefly interested in religious healing, they gave no details concerning medical practice. An occasional reference to medicines, cauterizing, surgery, and cupping glasses and sponges for blood-letting is about all. Churchmen made little reference even to the simplest instruments which would be necessary to the surgeon.[37]

Evidence of a disjuncture between the way medicine was studied by the church and the means by which it was practiced is also found in the languages in which the illuminated manuscripts were written. The introduction of medieval

32 John M Riddle, 'Theory and Practice in Medieval Medicine' (1974) 5 *Viator* 157, 183.

33 Talbot notes that in some of the northern regions of Italy, which could be characterised as more secular, the teaching of surgery did occur in some university programs but it was rare and difficult to confirm in existing evidentiary sources (n 24) 81.

34 Loren C MacKinney, *Early Medieval Medicine* (John Hopkins Press 1937) 122.

35 David Margalith, 'The Ideal Doctor as Depicted in Ancient Hebrew Writings' (1957) 12 *J Hist Med* 37. MacKinney notes that these 'practitioners of a lower sort' to whom the 'general populace' resorted were called *harioli*. He cites a passage from Gregory de Tours, mentioning 'the *rustic* custom of resorting to "sorcery, potions, and the *ligamenta* of the *harioli*"'. See MacKinney, *Early Medieval Medicine* (n 34) 71 citing Tours' *De Miraculis Sancti Martini*, I 26.

36 Jones is clear to note, however, that such a division is a modern classification of the medical field and would not have been found (explicitly) in these medieval manuscripts (n 26) 28.

37 MacKinney, *Early Medieval Medicine* (n 34) 73.

vernacular into written form, particularly in the areas of science and medicine during the fourteenth and fifteenth centuries, shows a subordinate status for clinical knowledge in relation to the more theoretical pursuits of the church.[38] Prior to the written vernacular, all specialised or professional texts had been composed in Latin, allocating the emerging English language texts to a second-class status – along with their users.[39] As Robbins has remarked:

> This difference in language separated the relatively few university-trained physicians like Chaucer's 'doctor of phisik' from the unlatined others, specifically, the on-the-job-trained surgeon, barber-surgeon, apothecary, apprentice, cunning man, wise woman, lay sister in a convent, and midwife.[40]

Some evidence exists to suggest that medical practitioners themselves may have contributed to the epistemological hierarchy of medical theory over practice in an attempt to establish themselves as 'learned' rather than 'illiterate barbers' and the like.[41]

As the vernacular gained written ground, medical practitioners were able to engage in the composition of medical 'literature', collecting what might be thought of as 'best practices' guides to sit alongside the more conventional (and accepted) works of medical theory. Scholars of both the medieval and modern period were quick to draw a distinction between these collections (described in the literature as 'anthologies') and the more scholastic manuscripts employed in a curricular fashion within monasteries.[42] The latter collection was referred to

38 Linda Ehrsam Voigts, 'Multitudes of Middle English Medical Manuscripts, or the Englishing of Science and Medicine' in Margaret R Schleissner (ed) *Manuscript Sources of Medieval Medicine* (Garland Press 1995). Riddle (n 32) also suggests that this disregard for the clinical applications of medicine was present in the choices made by translators of Greek and Arab texts to include the more philosophical or theoretical works while omitting the practical ones.

39 Other distinctions were drawn in the vernacular, such as the fourteenth-century monikers of 'surgeons of the short robe' and 'surgeons of the long robe', used to denote the practitioner and the university-trained surgeon, respectively. See Clement C Clarke, 'Henri de Mondeville' (1931) 3(6) *Yale J Bio Med* 458, 466.

40 Rossell Hope Robbins, 'Medical Manuscripts in Middle English' (1970) 45(3) *Speculum* 393, 394. Peter Jones has also noted how the manuscripts depict this hierarchical relationship between scholars and practitioners of medicine even in their illustrations where women are shown administering to patients in clinical (yet ancillary) ways (eg 'cupping' the blood during a bloodletting procedure). See PM Jones (n 26) 28.

41 The case of the tenth-century Islamic physician Abū Bakr Muhammed ibn Zakarīyā' al-Rāzī provides an interesting example. Al-Rāzī was a prolific writer who composed a number of theoretical medical treatises. He also kept detailed 'case histories' of the practical treatments he employed with his patients. In a comparison of the two, Cristina Ālvarez-Millān finds stark differences, noting 'that al-Rāzī depended upon medical writings not for the improvement of his craft, but for the raising of his own professional status'. See Cristina Ālvarez-Millān, 'Practice versus Theory: Tenth-Century Cases from the Islamic Middle East' (2000) 13(2) *Soc Hist Med* 293, 306.

42 Faith Wallis, 'Signs and Senses: Diagnosis and Prognosis in Early Medieval Pulse and Urine Texts' (2000) 13(2) *Soc Hist Med* 265.

as the *Articella* and consisted of a series of short texts which were adopted as an official curriculum by many existing universities in France and Italy by the end of the twelfth century.[43] These included Galen's *Isagoge* (outlining his theory of humours) and Hippocrates' texts, *Aphorisms, Prognostics,* and *Regimen in acute diseases*, among others.

Christian alignment

This practice of vesting epistemological authority in early Greek, Roman, and Arab writers could not have been without its theological difficulties for the medieval scholar of medicine. The endorsement of Galen, one of the second century's most prominent physicians, among monastic medical writers seems incongruous with his beliefs in polytheism, his views on the human soul as tripartite, and his criticism of the 'intellectual failings of the Christians'.[44] Some of Galen's works (such as his statements on visual perception) were even labelled as heresy and rejected by members of the medical community in the twelfth and thirteenth centuries.[45] And yet his and other works from the Classical period maintained an authoritative status within medical theory. In fact, departing from these early treatises was regarded as a sign of uneducated and unskilled medical practice.[46] As such, much effort appears to have been taken to move Galen and his works away from the perception of paganism and towards Christian ideals – a task largely left to the clerics who copied and translated his works in the illuminated manuscripts. Few biographical accounts of Galen can be found in these medieval texts, and they are often vague if not ambiguous when they do appear. This granted monastic scholars the 'literary license' to attribute the necessary traits and origins to Galen that would best align with Christian ideals. In some instances, for example, Galen is presented as a contemporary of Christ who, having heard about Christ's miracles of healing, travelled to learn more of the healing art from him.[47]

43 Talbot (n 24).

44 Vivian Nutton, 'God, Galen, and the Depaganization of Ancient Medicine' in Peer Biller and Joseph Ziegler (eds) *Medicine and Religion in the Middle Ages* (York Medieval Press 2001) 19.

45 Fernando Salmón, 'Academic Discourse and Pain in Medical Scholasticism (Thirteenth and Fourteenth Centuries) in Kottek and Ballester (n 28).

46 George Fort, with respect to the enactment of medieval laws aimed at regulating the medical profession, has suggested 'the cause alleged for this stringent law is a positive attestation of the debased condition of the medical men of the period, who apparently preferred to wander from the footsteps of Hippocrates and Galen'. See Fort (n 19) 139.

47 Salmón (n 45) 43 citing Mondini de'Liuzzi lectures in Bologna in 1317. Other accounts include Galen conversing with Mary Magdalene, or learning 'all he knew about women from Cleopatra'; Nutton (n 44) citing a tenth-century Arabic biography of Galen by al-Mubassir ibn Fatik. Nutton also suggests a number of other factors which contributed to Galenic medicine's acceptance in Christian medical frameworks, including Galen's persuasiveness as a rhetorician and his prolific writing career and success at seeing these works disseminated at a time when such intellectual endeavours were increasingly sparse.

This suggests that the church-imposed hierarchy of the theoretical study of medicine over its practice in the medieval era did not serve a scholarly purpose so much as a deontological one. Allying the moral theories which would guide the choices of physicians and patients with Christian ideals was imperative and, at times, explicit. Aside from merely copying and including early Greek authorities, their placement and characterisation within these early treatises suggest attempts to 'Christianise' them or at least bring them into accord with church ideals.[48] The Hippocratic Oath, for instance, which begins with an invocation to Apollo and other Greek gods, was revised to include 'more specifically Christian obligations, emphasizing love and charity'.[49] Ludwig Edelstein has also noted that the Oath's prohibitions on suicide and abortion were atypical of Classical Greece, which did not censure either act until the advent of Christianity at the turn of the first century.[50] These historical incongruities prompted Edelstein to suggest the Oath was a Pythagorean document – a position that is not without its critics.[51] Yet the argument does provide a possible explanation for the enduring authority of the Oath given how well the doctrines of Pythagoreanism align with those of Christianity.[52]

The prominence of Galen and his work in many of these early manuscripts may also be attributable to how well his theory of humorism could be employed as an authority for the Christian view of the human passions and the need to keep them well managed. Galen understood the body to be made up of four substances or 'humors', each corresponding to different fluids in the body (ie black and yellow bile, phlegm, and blood) which might wax and

48 MacKinney notes that despite the explicit condemnation of 'pagan' medicinal practice by the Church, many medieval folk healers continued to employ traditional methods (many of which called upon supernatural or 'magical' powers and properties); however, these were often performed 'under cover of Christian prayers and often with the sign of the cross'. See MacKinney, *Early Medieval Medicine* (n 34) 29.

49 Nutton (n 44) 26. Nutton also observes that in at least three medieval manuscripts, the words of the Hippocratic Oath are written out in the form of a cross.

50 Ludwig Edelstein, 'The Hippocratic Oath' in Owsei Temkin and C Lillian Temkin (eds), *Ancient Medicine: Selected Papers of Ludwig Edelstein* (JHUP 1967). Abortions were prosecuted in antiquity, however, only when the father's right to an heir had been violated, echoing some of the issues raised in Chapter 2 on sexual consent and its role in guarding patrilineage.

51 For a charitable but alternate reading of Edelstein's view, see Owsei Temkin, 'What Does the Hippocratic Oath Say?' in *On Second Thought' and Other Essays in the History of Medicine and Science* (JHUP 2002). See also Steven H Miles, *The Hippocratic Oath and the Ethics of Medicine* (OUP 2005).

52 Life, for instance, was viewed by Pythagoreans as 'a post to be held and defended' to which a person had been divinely appointed. For most of the ancient Greeks, no notion of an immortal soul for which a subject might be held accountable to a divine creator was espoused, rather a multiplicity of gods (each with human failings) could intervene and disrupt human life but not judge it in any eternal sense. The Hippocratic Oath also lists a series of dietary measures which a physician ought to oversee for the 'benefit of the sick' and to 'keep them from injustice' (Edelstein's translation). For Edelstein, this is further evidence of the Oath's Pythagorean origins given the strict dietary and behavioural regiments endorsed by that school of thought (n 50).

wane, depending on diet and activity.[53] When a patient was suffering from a surplus or imbalance of one or more fluids, then his or her personality and physical health were affected. Health was attained through 'complexion', the Latin term for the Greek word 'crasis', meaning a balanced temperament, one not upset by the list of 'non-naturals' Galen identified as correlative to disease, such as food and drink, passions, emotions, and 'accidents of the soul'.[54] Galen and his works make frequent appearances in these early medical manuscripts despite the diminutive clinical benefit his theories would have provided the medieval world. The copying and re-writing of his texts did not serve to advance medical knowledge. It was repetitive and often in conflict with advancements in anatomy or surgery of the day. Its inclusion in medieval manuscripts is therefore an interesting example of the Christian alignment (or 'depaganization' to borrow a term from Vivian Nutton) of these early medical sources. As Nutton puts it:

> [T]he take-over by the later Middle Ages of Galenic-Hippocratic medicine [is not] a story of the triumph of scientific truth over religious obscurantism. Hippocrates was no Copernicus, Galen no Galileo. The effectiveness of Galenic-Hippocratic therapeutics was hotly disputed in the Classical World ... the most popular works among the Carolingians represented a much more practical, non-theoretical type of medicine ... Galenic medicine was far from being the obvious choice it might seem to us, and its eventual triumph owed not a little to its compatibility with Christian, Muslim, and Jewish theology.[55]

This depaganization or re-alignment of ancient medical authorities served to create an exclusively Christian ethic for both medieval medicine's practice and its intellectual history.[56] 'To the Greeks of mediaeval Byzantium, Hippocrates and Galen had become almost divine, worthy of being commemorated in fresco alongside patriarchs and prophets as heralds of Christian truth'.[57] Coupled with a system of social and epistemological stratification on the basis of (monastic) theory and practice, a 'canon' of medieval medicine begins to emerge that takes form within a Christian framework. What, then, is this canonical story of consent?

Perhaps predictably, this narrative is not one of autonomy but submission. There was a prevailing understanding in the Middle Ages of disease as a divine

53 Owsei Temkin, *Galenism: Rise and Decline of a Medical Philosophy* (Cornell University Press 1973).

54 Nancy G Siraisi, *Medieval and Early Renaissance Medicine: An Introduction to Knowledge and Practice* (UCHIP 1990) 101.

55 Nutton (n 44) 19.

56 See Carlos R Galvào-Sobrinho, 'Hippocratic Ideals, Medical Ethics, and the Practice of Medicine in the Early Middle Ages: The Legacy of the Hippocratic Oath' (1996) 51(4) *J Hist Med Allied Sci* 438.

57 Nutton (n 44) 5.

intervention, resulting in an ethic of self-care borrowed from the ancients, where the virtue of balance was preferred to the errors of excess. Within a context where physicians were viewed as agents of the divine, consent was the means by which patients might align themselves with God in the hopes of attaining good health. The next section examines the medieval doctor-patient relationship in further detail, including the relevant legislation and ethical codes of the period. How this scheme and its participants informed medieval uses of consent is explored later in the chapter.

Medieval doctors and their patients: a match made in heaven

Very little has been written about the doctor-patient relationship in the Middle Ages – an oversight which has elicited comment among both medieval and medical historians.[58] Determining how the medieval physician practiced medicine and the ethical principles which guided these routines can be a kind of patchwork project, assembling the various texts and images of the period to form as clear a picture as history may allow. Certainly, the early legislative schemes of the Romans and later the Visigoths at the turn of the sixth century serve as a reasonable backdrop, given their influence on much of the medieval era's approach to medical licensing and regulation.[59] The Romans awarded a number of privileges to doctors who agreed to live within the city limits, including rights of citizenship and some tax exemptions.[60] Yet Roman society had a scattered scheme of medical licensing with few formal restrictions on who could practice medicine or any clear delineation of what requirements were needed to do so. Any number of unskilled persons might enjoy the privileges of the *medici* without any of the training.[61] The *Lex Visigothorum* arose as a response to this lack of medical regulation under the Roman empire. These laws stipulated the requisite conduct for practising physicians, including a number of prohibitions specifically aimed at regulating the doctor-patient relationship. Under the *Lex I Antiqua*, for example, physicians were not permitted to cup or bleed a free or nobly born

58 See, for example, Luis Garcia-Ballester, 'Ethical Problems in the Relationship between Doctors and Patients in 14th Century Spain: On Christian and Jewish Practitioners' in Kottek and Ballester (n 28); and Laurence Brockliss, 'Review of Lawrence I Conrad and others, *The Western Medical Tradition: 800 BC to AD 1800*' (1997) 41(4) *Med Hist* 510.

59 The Laws of Valentinus (368 AD) resulted in the appointment of a public surgeon and a charitable mandate for doctors to treat patients irrespective of their financial circumstances. See Fort (n 19).

60 Physicians were also among the groups exempt from expulsion during periods of famine under Augustus' rule. See Darrell W Amundsen, 'Visigothic Medical Legislation' (1971) 45(6) *Bull Hist Med* 553; Timothy G Sistrunk, 'The Function of Praise in the Contract of a Medieval Public Physician' (1993) 48 *J Hist Med Allied Sci* 320.

61 Sistrunk notes the presence of a concept of negligence in Roman law (*culpa*) which could be used to seek compensation from physicians who had warranted that they had the requisite skill to complete a task but, in effect, did not (n 60).

woman without the presence of her legal guardian or to visit any female patient in her home without a family chaperone.[62] Doctors were also disallowed, under the *Lex II Antiqua*, from entering any prison without official accompaniment so as to prevent the physician from dispensing euthanising drugs.[63] These decrees are largely understood among social and medical historians as having launched, in general, a 'new epoch in legal history' and, more particularly, a contract model for doctor-patient relationships. This is made explicit under the third set of regulations in the Code, *Lex III Antiqua*:

> If anyone should request that a physician treat him for a disease or cure his wound under contract, when the physician has seen the wound or diagnosed the illness, immediately he may undertake the treatment of a sick person under conditions agreed upon and set forth in writing.[64]

Some of these medical contracts have survived, revealing a practice of naming the physician, the patient, the relevant risks and/or liabilities of the procedure, as well as lists of any witnesses to the contract.[65] The introduction of a contractual relationship between doctor and patient was accompanied with a set of rather stringent punishments addressing malpractice, ranging from fines to death depending on the social status of the patient (where 'malpractice' was often inferred from unsuccessful, rather than negligent, treatments).[66]

These legal frameworks, however, provide only one view of the medieval doctor's practice. The physician understood medicine as imposing certain ethical obligations on him, derived from not simply his daily practice but the belief systems of the social world in which it took place.[67] As such, the medieval story of disease as a divine act looms large in these codes aimed at regulating the doctor-patient relationship. Sickness was believed to be the consequence brought

62 *Lex Visigothorum*, Book XI, De Medicis et Aegrotis (*Rec Hist Fr* IV: 434) as cited in MacKinney, *Early Medieval Medicine* (n 34) 174.

63 Fort (n 19).

64 Translation by Amundsen (n 60) 559.

65 Selek (n 19).

66 Fort cites an example from 582 AD where an ancient Teutonic law authorised the kinsmen of nobles to 'pass judgment upon the medical attendant of a defunct', putting them to death where deemed fit. Such was the fate of the physician to Austregild, the Duchess of Burgundy, who was killed following his Lady's death to a sixth-century plague. See Fort (n 19) 350. Amundsen, however, suggests that such acts of retribution 'in kind' were limited and that most of the punishments under the *Lex Visigothorum* were 'relatively mild for the times' (n 60) 561.

67 I employ the male pronoun here, given the prevalence of male physicians during the medieval period. There is evidence, however, of female physicians practicing as early as Antiquity. Medical training for women, however, is thought to have declined during the height of the Middle Ages as 'witch hunts' became more common. As Rhoda Wynn remarks, '[i]n England and France, the passage of licensure laws and the formation of guilds in the 13th century further prohibited women from the practice of medicine. Even midwifery, previously a woman's field, was dominated by men by the 17th century'. See Rhoda Wynn, 'Saints and Sinners: Women and the Practice of Medicine throughout the Ages' (2000) 283(5) *JAMA* 668, 668.

upon by persons who had led sinful or unbalanced lives.[68] Here, the physician's role was merely one of mediator. 'Sufferers could be ministered to and their pain eased, but healing must perforce be left to God or nature'.[69] Further, such healing was unlikely to come where patients refused to submit to God's will and (re) align themselves with the 'good' life, devoid of excess and sin. The 'caladrius' (or 'charadrius') is an interesting symbol of this worldview.[70] A mythical white bird, the caladrius, is thought to have made its first appearance in the second-century text *Physiologus.*[71] Such accounts describe a bird that would visit the sick, foretelling the patient's prognosis. If the bird looked at the patient, she could expect to recover. If the bird looked away, she would not. The description of the bird in the *Physiologus* remarks on its healing attributes:

> [T]he charadrius mentioned in Deuteronomy ... is entirely white with no black part at all. His excrement is a cure for those whose eyes are growing dim and he is found in the hall of kings. If someone is ill, whether he will live or die can be known from the charadrius. The bird turns his face away from the man whose illness will bring death and thus everyone knows that he is going to die. On the other hand, if the disease is not fatal, the charadrius stares the sick man in the face and the sick man stares back at the charadrius, who releases him from his illness. Then flying up to the atmosphere of the sun, the charadrius burns away the sick man's illness and scatters it abroad.[72]

Medieval manuscripts often associate the caladrius with Christ, particularly in marginal decorations of manuscript illustrations.[73] Thus, if the patient was 'aligned' with Christ, able to engage in a reciprocal glance with the divine, balance would be restored and healing would ensue. If, however, the patient could not return the glance, could not 'see eye to eye' with Christ, redemption was lost.

The medieval physician was tasked with overseeing this balancing act. Bloodletting, for instance, was a treatment based on an understanding of the human body as a hydraulic system with the doctor serving to 'fine-tune' the body's fluids.[74] The story of an eleventh-century physician known only by

68 Some commentators debate whether the medieval view of disease as a consequence for sin was attributed to individual acts or humans in general (following the Fall). See Siraisi (n 54), particularly Chapter 1.
69 MacKinney, *Early Medieval Medicine* (n 34) 75.
70 Earle Hackett, 'The Charadrius: A Useful Bird' (1955) 30(11) *Irish J Med Sci* 491. The bird is also sometimes referred to as 'Karadrios'. See Jacques Schnier, 'The Symbolic Bird in Medieval and Renaissance Art' (1952) 9 *Book Psychoanal* 292.
71 Michael J Curley (tr), 'On the charadrius' in *Physiologus: A Medieval Book of Nature Lore* (University of Texas Press 1979) as cited in John Laurence Couper, 'The Healing Bird' (1990) 78 *SA Med J* 485.
72 Curley (n 71) 7–9.
73 PM Jones (n 26).
74 Galen's theory of humours within the human body would likely have served as the context for this understanding. See PM Jones (n 26) 95.

the signature 'John, physician' (which he left on a document in 1046) alludes to the doctor's role as monitor of the human passions. MacKinney describes John as one of King Henry I of France's personal physicians who garnered fame 'from the fact that he lost an important case (no less a personage than his royal master), without losing his own reputation or life'.[75] MacKinney, using two separate accounts of the incident, describes John as having given the king a purgative with strict instructions not to drink anything immediately afterwards. The king disobeyed and died the following day. Despite a suggestion of physician error (in delivering an overdose of purgative), John is said to have 'escaped with a nickname, "the deaf", to remind him of his failure to detect the king's violation of orders in time to avert fatal results'.[76]

This depiction of a requirement in medieval physicians to 'hear' the internal desires of patients suggests doctors were expected to have a heightened level of knowledge or awareness than the average person. Moreover, as some of the discussion in the following section highlights, knowing the truth of another's 'inner will' was a matter thought to belong to God alone (despite the practical difficulties this elusiveness brought to theologians, jurists, and political theorists).[77] A sixth-century letter used for the (royal) appointment and instruction of the Ostrogothic regime's public doctors reads in part:

> The physician helps us when all other helpers fail. By his art he finds out things about a man of which he himself is ignorant; and his prognosis of a case, though founded on reason, seems to the ignorant like a prophecy.[78]

The medieval physician, then, was expected to have some level of transcendent or perhaps 'divine' knowledge. Certainly, a number of medieval sources depict doctors as having been appointed by God. The first known ethical treatise for the doctor-patient relationship, titled 'Practical Ethics of the Physician', was composed in the ninth century by Ishāq ibn 'Alī al-Ruhāwī, an Arab scholar.[79] The text describes the doctor as an agent of Allah, the 'real physician', leaving the 'ethic of the physician [as] an extension of that of a religious man serving his

75 MacKinney, *Early Medieval Medicine* (n 34) 143–144.

76 MacKinney, *Early Medieval Medicine* (n 34) 144.

77 It is also interesting to note that this 'unknowability' of the inner will was acknowledged explicitly by John Locke, leading him to employ tacit consent as a form of compromise. See Chapter 1 for further discussion.

78 Cassiodorus, *Variae*, VI: 19 (MGH Auctores Antiqui, XII) as cited by MacKinney, *Early Medieval Medicine* (n 34) 47.

79 This is, of course, the English translation of al-Ruhāwī's text 'Adab al-tabib' offered by Martin Levey 'Medical Ethics of Medieval Islam with Special Reference to al-Ruhāwī 's "Practical Ethics of the Physician"' (1967) 57(3) *Trans Am Philos Soc* 1. Levey remarks that 'it is also known that al-Ruhāwī was a Christian and compiled two works on Galen' (8), although this knowledge has been questioned by some scholars. See Sahin Aksoy, 'The Religious Tradition of Ishaq ibn Ali al-Ruhāwī: The Author of the First Medical Ethics Book in Islamic Medicine' (2004) 3(5) *JISHIM* 9.

Creator'.[80] St. Augustine made the same claim, positioning Christ as the 'true physician' of souls and bodies.[81] Many medieval manuscripts contain comparable contentions, including translations of the Hippocratic Oath, which suggest physicians must administer to both body and soul.[82] Similarly, MacKinney cites an eighth-century manuscript which uses excerpts from the work of Pope Gregory I, Isidore of Seville, and the Bible to associate medicine with a deific purpose.[83]

This view of the doctor as a divine agent is a marked departure from the physician of Greek antiquity, whose calling and motivations were viewed as purely humanitarian. Understood as the genesis of the model of the doctor-patient relationship of beneficence, the physician of antiquity was motivated by *philanthropia*, or a 'love of humanity', as a means of finding personal fulfilment or the 'good life'.[84] In this context, the physician and the patient were mutually engaged in the medical act, albeit for different ends. Katz contends that while *philanthropia* served as the doctor's motivation, the patient's interest could be kindled with the physician's success at curing what ailed them, understood as *philotechnia*, or love of the medicinal art.[85] The Hippocratic essay 'On Precepts' reflects this when it suggests, 'where there is love of man, there is also love of the art'.[86] This changed with the Middle Ages and the advent of Christianity's influence on medicine and its practice. As Jones has observed:

> In medieval times, divine authority replaced *philanthropia* as the doctor's contribution to the physician-patient unity of will. Faith replaced *philotechnia* as the patient's contribution. The typical routine prior to surgery included the laying out of instruments, prayer with the patient, and finally the technical process of care.[87]

80 Martin Levey, 'Medical Deontology in Ninth Century Islam' (1966) *J Hist Med* 358, 366 (citing Al-Ruhāwī's Adab al-tabib MS, Fols 80a). Al-Ruhāwī also calls physicians the 'guardians of souls and bodies', emphasising the qualities needed in a good physician. In his view, Allah would not choose anyone for the task but rather only 'the foremost of the people in station, highest in rank, greatest in worth, and most truthful in speech' (fols 70b-71a), as cited by Levey, 'Medical Ethics of Medieval Islam' (n 79) 14. Al-Ruhāwī suggests that this divine appointment removes the requirement for any physician to swear by an oath prior to being able to practice, as Allah or God would only select candidates already worthy.

81 Siraisi (n 54) 9.

82 Edelstein (n 50) 35.

83 'Wherefore let us honor the physicians so that they will help us when sick, remembering [the word of] that wise one [Ecclesiasticus 38:1 Vulgate]: "Honor the physician of necessity for the Most High created him ... The Most High created medicine from the earth, and the prudent man will not reject it"' as translated by MacKinney, 'Medical Ethics' (n 19) 5.

84 Kevin B Jones, 'Surgeons' Silence: A History of Informed Consent in Orthopaedics' (2007) 27 *Iowa Orthop J* 115, 116.

85 Jay Katz, 'The Regulation of Human Experimentation in the United States – A Personal Odyssey' (1987) 9(1) *IRB: Eth Hum Res* 1.

86 Chapter 6, as translated by Ludwig Edelstein, 'The Professional Ethics of the Greek Physician' (1956) 30 *Bull Hist Med* 391, 392.

87 KB Jones (n 84) 116.

This, again, highlights the religious backdrop of the medieval doctor-patient relationship. If physicians and their patients understood themselves as engaged in a 'unity of the will' as a result of faith and divine authority, where does this leave consent, the 'linchpin' of the modern era's medical ethics? The following section examines this inquiry in greater detail, exploring three areas of medieval life where consent figured prominently: marriage formation, religious conversion, and trade and commerce.

Medieval consent: coupling, conversion, and commerce

Consent does not figure prominently in medieval law.[88] For the most part, it was a concept treated much the same as it is today, that is, presumed to be present but for evidence of its negation, usually in the form of fraud, duress, or coercion. This creates the familiar difficulty of determining what medieval consent *was* rather than simply what it was *not*. Further, there is a tendency among contemporary scholars to rule out the presence of medieval consent within the doctor-patient relationship on the basis that very little evidence of consent serving as an expression of autonomy can be found in the treatises of the Middle Ages.[89]

Consent was, however, subject to significant commentary among theologians. Perhaps not surprisingly, given the religious backdrop of the medieval doctor-patient relationship, consent was largely regarded as a matter of sacramental concern rather than legal interest.[90] In contrast to the legal approach to consent, with its focus on external factors (eg words spoken and acts performed), the theological view emphasised the state of one's *internal* will. Thomas Aquinas was one of many to identify the central difficulty in such cases: No one but the would-be-consenter and God could know the truth of the external signs of consent.[91] This was, in some circumstances, a concern with theoretical rather than practical consequences. In religious conversion cases, for example, the baptismal act was the signification of the converter's consent and, as Farber notes, while,

> consent thus presented a theoretical difficulty in recognizing conversion, it did not constitute a significant practical problem. People who watched the convert's baptism had no way of knowing whether she had truly consented to the baptism, but at the same time they did not really need to know ... [O]thers could treat her as though she were baptized, and if she were not it would be her sin, not theirs.[92]

88 See Kenneth Varty, 'The Giving and Withholding of Consent in Late Twelfth-Century French Literature' (1986) 12 *Read Mediev Stud* 27 for a discussion of the difficulties in ascertaining the general legal position on any issue during the period, given the breadth of law and custom.

89 As suggested by Katz, 'From the decline of the Greek city states to the 18th century, no major primary or secondary documents on medical ethics ... reveal even a remote awareness of a need to discuss anything with patients that relates to their participation in decision making' (n 85) 7.

90 Farber (n 19).

91 This is the same concern John Locke raised in his own musings on consent, as explored in Chapter 1.

92 Farber (n 19) 95.

The situation was made more complicated, however, with the involvement of a third party, such as in marriage cases or the doctor-patient relationship. In such instances, the 'truth' of one's consent had a more practical consequence, whether that was in terms of establishing a valid marriage or, in the case of medicine, obtaining good health. Of particular concern in these circumstances was the presence of factors that might render one's consent inauthentic, such as the presence of fraud, fear, or pain. Determining how much coercion or duress was needed to negate one's consent was a complicated matter, and medievalists tended to rely on Roman law for these determinations. The Romans used a high standard, requiring extraordinary levels of force to vitiate consent, and medieval lawyers often relied on the maxim that even 'forced will is will'.[93] This represents a distinction the Romans saw between force and compulsion, the former involving no will at all but rather a physical over-powering that results in an undesirable action and the latter understood to be 'a declaration of will which is elicited under pressure'.[94]

This understanding of a forced will (or 'coerced consent', as discussed in Chapter 2) stems from Aristotle's observations on responsibility in the seventh book of his treatise, *Nichomachean Ethics*. Therein, Aristotle considers a moral paradox in Socrates's assertion that 'no person acts against her better judgment'.[95] Aristotle, disagreeing with Socrates, suggests that there are many circumstances where one might act against one's preference, the most prominent of these being dire need. Aristotle offers the example of a captain forced to throw cargo overboard during a severe storm to save the ship and its crew. This was, for Aristotle, still an exercise of will but one that had a 'mixed' character: involuntary in that the external factors had forced the captain into making an undesired choice and yet still voluntary in that they were actions 'worthy of choice' (and, in fact, resulted in one being made).[96] Thus emerges the Roman notion that even a forced choice is a choice. The challenge, of course, lay in determining how much force, duress, or fear might be sufficient to negate the will behind the choice.

The difficulties in assessing these 'coercive' factors were made all the more serious when consent's role in securing a patient's healing was considered. Just as in the case of a sacramental bond, a cure for what ailed the patient was only attainable if a true divine union had been achieved. Such was the contemplation

93 Accursius as cited in Farber (n 19) 95.

94 Herbert A Holstein, 'Vices of Consent in the Law of Contract' (1938) 13 *Tul LR* 560, 569.

95 I am paraphrasing Aristotle in my use of the female pronoun, of course. William David Ross (tr and ed), in his *The Works of Aristotle* (Clarendon 1908), provides the following translation of the original text: 'For Socrates was entirely opposed to the view in question, holding that there is no such thing as incontinence; no one, he said, when he judges acts against what he judges best—people act so only by reason of ignorance' (Book VII:2).

96 For some scholars, it is the 'origin' of the action that directs this view of voluntariness, that is, that the will to throw the cargo overboard originated in the captain (rather than an external force or person). See John M Cooper, 'Aristotelian Responsibility' (2013) 45 *Oxford Stud Ancient Philos* 265, who examines both *Nichomachean Ethics* and *Eudemian Ethics* for his analysis of Aristotle's view of (non)voluntariness.

Thomas Aquinas pursued when he responded to Aristotle's *Nichomachean Ethics* in an attempt to determine whether acts of mixed or forced will might still be considered sinful. For most canonists, the mixed nature of a will was not relevant in determining an act's virtue or sinfulness. 'People never acted according to pure will, they believed, because people are by definition fallen and tied to their bodies'.[97] Thus, a diminished will did not diminish one's responsibility. Instead, such instances were merely signs of the will having been influenced by one's passions or appetites, rather than negated entirely. As Diana Wood has suggested of the medieval period:

> Living a righteous life involved the voluntary limitation of appetites and desires and the avoidance of extremes. The Christian had to live in the world and survive, but this involved a permanent balancing act between the often incompatible needs of body and soul – physical comfort in this world against eternal salvation in the next, material claims against spiritual ones.[98]

This provides some insight into not simply how consent figured in medieval thought but also how knowledge itself was ordered and understood in the Middle Ages. Bakos has described the medieval period as a 'finalistic-teleological Aristotlean-Christian universe', a world where things are what they are for and where all these ends relate to God.[99] Within this frame, people understood the human soul to have two components: the *intellectus*, whereby a person came to think and understand the world around her, and the *voluntas*, which governs human desire and willing. Much of the theology of the medieval period aimed to determine which of these two faculties was superior, and while contemporary readers might view such debates as overly esoteric, Bakos insists that they were of tremendous practical value during the medieval period, given their influence on how one might choose to live one's life.[100] In keeping with the era's teleological quality, these two components to the human soul were understood only in relation to their ends. Thus, any knowledge – including science or medicine – must necessarily find its purpose in the divine. For medievalists, 'the essence of human knowing

97 Farber (n 19) 95.

98 Diana Wood, *Medieval Economic Thought* (CUP 2002) 16.

99 Gergely Tibor Bakos, *On Faith, Rationality, and the Other in the Late Middle Ages: A Study of Nicolas of Cusa's Manuductive Approach to Islam* (Pickwick 2011) 7. Bakos attributes this description to his mentor, Jos Decorte, in *Raak Me Niet Aan* (Pelckmans 2001) 15–20. Paul Vincent Spade offers a similar, perhaps more humourous, description of the period in his entry for 'medieval philosophy' in the *Stanford Encyclopedia of Philosophy*: 'Here is a recipe for producing medieval philosophy: Combine classical pagan philosophy, mainly Greek but also in its Roman versions, with the new Christian religion. Season with a variety of flavorings from the Jewish and Islamic intellectual heritages. Stir and simmer for 1300 years or more, until done' (Summer edn, 2018) <https://plato.stanford.edu/archives/sum2018/entries/medieval-philosophy/> accessed 30 April 2019.

100 For example, Franciscans were known to hold the will in greater esteem than the intellect, while Dominicans espoused the opposite position; Bakos (n 99).

and willing consists of becoming (more and more) a likeness of God'.[101] To seek knowledge merely for its own sake was thought of as a sinful activity in medieval times, understood as a form of vanity or *vana curiositas mundi*, a 'vain curiosity of the world', given its eschewal of the divine.[102] Similarly, to leave the intellect unengaged, to avoid knowing God was to commit the opposite moral sin of pride (or *superbia*), assuming that one knew all there was to know – an acquaintance with the world reserved only for the divine. The desired middle ground between these two points was *sapientia*, a 'wisdom' understood in the medieval period as a competence in practical knowledge, that is, knowing how to live a good or 'godly' life.

This picture of the medieval world as framed within a religious epistemology results in a convergence of knowledge and belief such that there could be 'no sound rationality without sound faith'.[103] Medicine, like any scientific inquiry, was rooted in a quest for divine likeness; to seek truth or further awareness of the world was to seek God. Only His knowledge was true knowledge. As Bakos notes:

> According to the Bible, Christ himself said: 'I am the way, the truth, and the life'. In this biblical dictum, the practice (the way), the epistemological (the truth), and the existential (the life) dimensions of (medieval) knowledge meet.[104]

The difficulty this posed to medievalists, however, lay in the unseen nature of God. Despite the belief of having been created in God's image, human knowledge of the divine was limited by corporeality and its 'blinding' effect.[105] Yet some avenues to divinity remained. Augustine was one of many medieval theologians who espoused the view that divine truth had been revealed to humans in two forms: the Book of Nature (which was unreadable after the Fall) and the Revealed Book, or book(s) of the Bible.[106] This understanding led to a prominent belief in the Middle Ages that the world was replete with symbols of God. Given that human failings prevented an unmediated view of the divine, the search for truth entailed a constant attempt to see the unseen, to interpret the symbols of God which lay hidden in their mundane, earthly forms.[107] Aquinas understood

101 Bakos (n 99) 7.

102 Bakos (n 99) 11.

103 Bakos (n 99) 16.

104 Bakos (n 99) 17.

105 Augustine is often attributed with employing this metaphor of 'seeing' or 'vision' in his explorations of medieval mysticism. See Eileen Serene, 'Demonstrative Science' in Norman Kretzmann, Anthony Kenny and Jan Pinborg (eds), *The Cambridge History of Late Medieval Philosophy* (CUP 1988).

106 Julius Rudolph Weinberg, *A Short History of Medieval Philosophy* (PUP 1964). See also Bakos (n 99).

107 Nicolas de Cusa described this human attempt to understand or know the divine as 'learned ignorance'. See Ferdinand Edward Cranz, 'Nicolaus Cusanus and Dionysius Areopagita' in Thomas M Izbicki and Gerald Christianson (eds), *Nicholas of Cusa and the Renaissance* (Aldershot 2000).

this exercise of mysticism as *cognito dei experimentalis*, or 'knowledge of god through experience'.[108] This amounted to a search for signs in almost all aspects of medieval life, where everything visible might represent the invisible.[109]

This same task was applicable to the human quest for unity with God. Seeking God and aligning one's life with His was the teleological end of all activity in the Middle Ages, including scientific (or medical) pursuits. And while such human acts and ways of knowing were necessarily imperfect, striving for this skewed view of the divine, for a recognition of God in all that was not God was imperative for a good (and healthy) life. This may explain the prominence of beliefs in magic during the medieval period, particularly in terms of medicinal remedies or treatments that were thought to bring good health.[110] In a world replete with hidden signs of the divine, believing in the impossible was entirely rational. As one historian observes:

> The people in medieval Europe who used the term 'magic' thought of it as neither irrational nor nonrational but as essentially rational ... [Those] who used, feared, promoted, or condemned magic, and who identified magic as such, not only assumed it worked but could give (or assumed that authorities could give for them) reasonably specific explanations of how it worked.[111]

Many of these 'magical' practices and rituals were, however, often in conflict with the medical teachings of the church, so Christianity held that God Himself had provided a model for seeking the 'unseen' in John 4:12: 'No man hath seen God at any time. If we love one another, God dwelleth in us, and his love is perfected in us'. Bakos elaborates on this notion:

> God's activity and happiness consists of the fact that He knows and loves Himself (within the Trinity); and that He knows and loves Another than Himself (in the Creation). Since man's task is that of becoming similar to God, man has to arrive at knowledge of and love for God in something other than God ... Through understanding and loving this Other, humans can understand and love God Himself (in this Other).[112]

This openness to the other is understood in Christian theology as agapeic service, that is, an engagement with the other in a state of unselfish love, akin to the love God is understood to have for Himself and humans. Agape is often articulated

108 Jone Salomensen, *Enchanted Feminism: Ritual, Gender, and Divinity among the Reclaiming Witches of San Francisco* (Routledge 2002) 132.

109 de Cusa put it the following way in his 1460 work *De Possest*: 'What is the world but the visible appearance of the invisible God, and what is God but the invisibility of things visible?' as cited in Cranz (n 107) 312.

110 Richard Kieckhefer notes that the writings of both Augustine and Isidore de Seville contain lengthy discussions of magic. See Richard Kieckhefer, 'The Specific Rationality of Medieval Magic' (1994) 99(3) *Am Hist Rev* 813, 815. The works of both Augustine and Seville also contributed to the understanding of medicine as a 'divine art'.

111 Kieckhefer (n 110) 814.

112 Bakos (n 99) 8.

as a groundless or 'unmotivated' love, offered to another without judgment or prerequisites. 'It does not look for anything in man that could be adduced as motivation for it'.[113] Yet, because agape is a divine love, human efforts will necessarily be only approximations, leading to a dominant understanding in Christian theology of faith as the 'human response to God. Through faith, the believer may participate in agape toward the neighbour'.[114] In so doing, the groundwork is laid for achieving a communion with God.[115] This communion with the divine is the goal of *sapienta* – a medievalist's guide to practical living which avoids the sins of excess (and its resultant risks of disease). Bakos suggests that 'in Christianity, agapeic service shown to the Other counts as the noblest and most precious – indeed Divine – activity'.[116]

This suggests that for the medieval subject, unity with the divine was the governing mandate, whether that was achieved through spiritual service to the Other or through 'magic'. This can be seen in a wide array of contexts in the Middle Ages, including a number of forums where 'magic' might seem a bit incongruous for the modern reader, including both medicine and the field of trade and commerce. In both of these contexts, however, the imperative to align oneself with God is the underlying function of 'consent'. The medieval marketplace, in particular, is worth examining for how well it demonstrates a role for consent unassociated with individualism. Instead, the role of consent in the marketplace of the Middle Ages was one of community – understood in terms of the relationships medievalists sought with their neighbours but also in terms of the act of 'communing' with God. Medieval economic thought, Wood observes, was largely a theological enterprise.[117] Labours of the soul were exalted, whereas struggles towards economic betterment were not. Money-making of any kind was generally frowned upon by the church and, in some forms, explicitly prohibited (as the canonical ban on usury in 1311 exemplifies).[118] Yet increased populations in towns and the early forms of industrialisation saw a shift in medieval perceptions towards economic life in the years leading up to the fourteenth century. These developments created tension between the spiritual aims of medieval life and its material circumstances, perhaps best witnessed in the struggles scholars, merchants, traders, and buyers encountered when attempting to determine acceptable pricing schemes for goods and services.[119] As noted, medical practice was far from

113 Anders Nygren, 'Agape and Eros' in Thomas Jay Oord (ed), *The Altruism Reader* (Templeton Press 2007) 68.

114 Colin Grant, 'For Love of God: Agape' (1996) 24(1) *J Rel Eth* 3, 6.

115 Paul K Moser, 'Agapeic Theism: Personifying Evidence and Moral Struggle' (2010) 2 *EJPR* 1.

116 Bakos (n 99) 13.

117 Wood (n 98).

118 Visser and McIntosh note a much longer history to this fourteenth-century ban, citing the Roman Catholic Church's fourth-century ADE prohibition of usury for clergy, extended to the laity in the fifth century and made a general criminal offence under Charlemagne in the eighth century. See Wayne AM Visser and Alastair McIntosh, 'A Short Review of the Historical Critique of Usury' (1998) 8(2) *Acc Bus Finan Hist* 175.

119 EP Thompson has documented some of these moments of tension in his work on the food riots of eighteenth-century England. This work and the insights it offers on shifting notions of the

exempt from these market schemes, as fee regulations, liability provisions, and service contracts (or 'consent forms') rose in response to the general suspicion of physicians and the 'just price' of their craft. Determinations of this price were made by scholars, who tended to employ natural law for its invocations of the divine, and lawyers, who relied on the jurisprudential traditions of the Romans.[120] This resulted in a wide range of approaches to price determination.[121]

Wood notes that price negotiations at any level would often involve an overlap of these models, yet I would argue that *sapienta* is best evidenced in how medievalists reached understandings of the 'just price'. Aristotle's *Nichomachean Ethics* is a key text in these determinations, given its approach to justice as a virtue and the imperative it brought to subjects to act rightly – even where matters of economic advancement were concerned. Virtue, for Aristotle, was a state of mind or disposition (*hexis*) which brought about particular feelings and subsequent actions and relations with others.[122] Further, Aristotle defined virtue as a mean, a condition founded between the vices of excess and deficiency. How this mean might be reached was necessarily contextual. Some circumstances might call for a 'balance' of vices which favoured more anger than another or less reason. Aristotle writes:

> By virtue I mean virtue of character; for this is about feelings and actions, and these admit of excess, deficiency, and an intermediate condition. We can be afraid, for instance, or be confident, or have appetites, or get angry, or feel pity, and in general have pleasure or pain, both too much and too little, and in both ways not well. But having these feelings at the right times, about the right things, toward the right people, for the right end, and in the right way, is the intermediate and best condition, and this is proper to virtue.[123]

Aristotle's critique of the invalid or unequal trade rested on a distinction between the *use* of money and money itself, emphasising that virtue was found (or lost) in the choices made for using money and how well these choices approximated the mean.[124] 'The fact, then, that we might be forced by circumstance

'common good' (and their relationship to understandings of consent) are explored in further depth in Chapter 5. See Edward P Thompson, 'The Moral Economy of the English Crowd in the Eighteenth Century' (1971) 50 *P&P* 76.

120 Wood (n 98).

121 Although three of these emerge from the literature as dominant: (i) the natural price (fixed at the current market value); (ii) the legal price (fixed by the relative public authority); and (iii) the just price (fixed through free negotiation among individuals and thus subject to many factors, including social status).

122 Richard Kraut, 'Aristotle's Ethics' *The Stanford Encyclopedia of Philosophy* (Summer edn, 2018) <https://plato.stanford.edu/archives/sum2018/entries/aristotle-ethics/> accessed 30 April 2019.

123 Aristotle, *Nichomachean Ethics* (Terence Irwin tr, 2nd edn, Hackett 1999) Book II, Chapter 6:2, 1106b.

124 This approach also reflects the Greek understanding of *hubris* and the ability of motivations (or uses of money, in this instance) to alter the (moral) nature of acts.

into a trade we would not make otherwise is a condition of having bodily needs and being subject to circumstances in general, rather than a sign of an invalid contract'.[125] The valid exchange is thus one where each party to the trade feels as though the value for the goods or services traded has been reciprocated. Was the exchange virtuous? Did it avoid extremes? For Aquinas, these circumstantial factors result in negotiations which themselves need to be guided by a principle of 'proportionate reciprocity' in order to achieve an equality of things exchanged – a prerequisite in his mind for communities to be able to live together.

Contemporary scholars will often position consent as the marker of this equality in medieval (and modern) trade arrangements, a signifier of two minds meeting in agreement. Yet, similar to the feeble role that words play in ensuring the formation of marriage or one's religious conversion, medieval consent cannot be tangibly known or made present in language, thus determining its truthfulness in trade presents the same difficulties that it might in the doctor -patient relationship. What mattered more within the medieval era was that parties to a trade or to a contract for medical service had reached some form of 'communion' with one another – not simply for the purposes of being able to, as Aquinas notes, 'live together', but also for the aim of living in the likeness of God (and enjoying the good health this would entail).

This interest in the communion with the divine can also be seen in its practical form in the development of the practice of conciliarism among medieval canonists. Nicolas de Cusa, a fifteenth-century cardinal of the Catholic Church, composed an influential text on conciliar theology in an attempt to reconcile rising conflicts between the pope and competing church councils. De Cusa argued that the practice of reaching concord or consensus within a council mirrored Christ's own marriage with the church, in the way that an initial desire for unity was actualised in the parties' agapeic service to one another. Thus, the council's principle of acting only with the consent of all parties 'was not merely procedural, but was rooted in a shared way of life',[126] not dissimilar to Aquinas's own concern with consent within trade and commerce as the only means by which a community might live together. Bakos, writing on de Cusa's text, *De Concordantia Catholica* (1433), notes:

> Consent here has at least two meanings. First, it is an initial concord in the Catholic faith, and secondly, it refers also to the willingness to consent during the actual discussion. It is thus faith in the form of existential commitment that makes the actual consensus possible.[127]

How does this understanding of consent as an existential act of faith inform the medieval doctor-patient relationship? Moreover, what does this canonical story

125 Farber (n 19) 95–96.
126 Bakos (n 99) 20, writing on de Cusa's conciliar theology.
127 Bakos (n 99) 20.

of consent help us understand about the conditions of possibility of the contemporary consent-as-autonomy story?

The medieval doctor-patient relationship: 'The way, the truth and the light'

When consent appears in medieval medicine, it does so tacitly. Henri de Mondeville, a fourteenth-century surgeon, cautioned physicians against proceeding with a treatment which the patient's family did not endorse or to which the patient was violently opposed, suggesting some consideration of a patient's wishes.[128] Many illustrations within medieval medical manuscripts depict the patient as an active participant in medical procedures, such as holding a urine flask for the physician's analysis or carrying a cupping vessel during instances of bloodletting.[129] This could suggest some level of implicit consent in the medieval doctor-patient relationship. And some scholars have argued that a model of consultation and joint decision-making within doctor-patient relationships was endorsed in Ancient Greece.[130] There are, however, far more explicit statements which seemingly speak against a consideration of a patient's agency in the medieval doctor-patient relationship. The majority of these are found within the context of medicine's divine story which foretold a patient's cure only alongside a patient's obedience to the physician's instructions. As Mondeville wrote:

> The surgeon … should promise that if the patient can endure his illness and will obey the surgeon for a short time he will soon be cured and will escape all of the dangers which have been pointed out to him; thus the cure can be brought about more easily and more quickly … If the patient is defiant, seldom will the result be successful.[131]

128 Mondeville's suggested motive, however, for avoiding such 'unfortunate cases' where patients refuse treatment was for the preservation of the physician's good reputation (and thus livelihood). See Mary Catherine Welborn, 'The Long Tradition: A Study in Fourteenth Century Medical Deontology' in Chester R Burns (ed), *Legacies in Ethics and Medicine* (Science History Publications 1977); Sistrunk (n 60); and Eugene Ashby Hammond, 'Incomes of Medieval English Doctors' (1960) XV(2) *J His Med* 154.

129 PM Jones (n 26).

130 In Book IV of Plato's *The Laws* he describes the differences between relationships among slave-physicians and their slave-patients and the doctor-patient relationship 'befitting of free men'. In the latter case, the physician discusses 'things thoroughly from the beginning in a scientific way and takes the patient and his family into confidence. Thus he learns something from the sufferers … He does not give prescriptions until he has won the patient's support, and when he has done so, he steadily aims at producing complete restoration to health by persuading the sufferer into compliance', as cited in Mark Siegler, 'Searching for Moral Certainty in Medicine: A Proposal for a New Model of the Doctor-Patient Encounter' (1981) 57(1) *Bull NY Acad Med* 56, 68. Siegler goes on to suggest Plato's comments model a 'fully human relationship' between doctor and patient, 'in which technical aspects of care are placed in the context of an appreciation for the most widely construed interests of each', 68.

131 Mondeville as cited by Katz (n 85) 25.

Faden and Beauchamp identify Mondeville's statements as exemplifying the beneficence model of doctor-patient relations, attributing to Mondeville the belief that 'the maintenance of hope [is] of sufficient therapeutic benefit to justify deception'.[132] Certainly, outright deception is found in many medieval codes of conduct, although few in as colourful a language as Mondeville offers, counselling doctors to keep up patients' spirits by the 'music of violas and ten-stringed psaltery, or by forged letters describing the death of his enemies, or if he is a churchman, by telling him that he has been elected to a bishopric'.[133] While these overt recommendations for dishonesty within the doctor-patient relationship suggest an element of paternalism (ie doctor knows best) was present during the medieval period, de Ros notes that outright deception on the part of the physician would not have been regarded favourably in the Middle Ages. '[T]he physician who deceived was seen as doing the patient harm', he writes, 'and was therefore behaving in a morally incorrect way'.[134] Some commentators have suggested that this call for deception among physicians represents a medieval consideration of the patient's role in decision-making practices. Pernick, for instance, maintains that Mondeville's instructions not to accept a case where the patient violently opposed the treatment amount to a prohibition against treating patients without their consent[135] – a contention that both Katz and Faden and Beauchamp dispute, maintaining that the medieval view was that uncooperative patients did not make for successful cases.[136] Instead, deception was counselled only as a means of facilitating a patient's acquiescence. The divine authority thought to have been bestowed upon the physician must have influenced patients' own perceptions of obedience and acquiescence to doctors' knowledge. Is a concept of consent within medieval doctor-patient relationships completely elided here?

The preceding section outlined how acts of faith, in the medieval period, were both rational and highly pragmatic. This was particularly so where one's health was concerned. Control of the appetite and its related passions was prescribed in the Hippocratic Oath for physicians, but it was also an integral component to a patient's ability to 'truly' consent. This was depicted in medieval medical manuscripts, where the margins were often marked with bestiary images. There, animals played the roles of humans who had given in to their passions (always

132 Faden and Beauchamp (n 4) 63.

133 Mondeville as cited by Vern L Bullough, *The Development of Medicine as a Profession: The Contribution of the Medieval University to Modern Medicine* (Hafner 1966) 97.

134 Guillermo Olagüe de Ros, 'The Ethical Manipulation of the Patient in the Ancients Versus Moderns Controversy: The Impact of Giuseppe Gazola's *Il Mondo Ingannato da Falsi Medici (1716) in Spain*' in Kottek and Ballester (n 28) 216. On the same page de Ros comments on how the eighteenth century's use of the term 'deception' held more positive connotations (eg as synonymous with 'error' or 'amenable to correction') than the negative understanding of the word that is 'characteristic of Baroque literature'.

135 Pernick (n 14).

136 This disagreement rests largely on differing interpretations of the medieval physician's interest in obtaining the patient's 'confidence' – a term specifically used by Mondeville and found in other ethical treatises of the era. See Faden and Beauchamp (n 4) 63–64.

to fatal consequence).[137] Similarly, the fabled caladrius would not return the glance of a patient who had inadequately managed these appetites, resulting in a 'misalignment' with God – an imbalance that was often understood through the lens of Galen's humours.

The physician was thus positioned as both a monitor of this human susceptibility to passion in others and as a model of restraint in himself. For Thomas Aquinas, the words spoken or acts performed by the parties involved were secondary considerations to whether a true union had been forged. What mattered was the truth of the parties' internal will – and this couldn't be known, or at least not by any earthly figure.[138] This is a difficult pill to swallow in the twenty -first century, given dominant views of the incongruity of faith and rationality. Within the medieval period's faith-based epistemological frame, however, faith *is* rationality; it is a 'condition of possibility' for reason itself. Believing is the only way to know(ledge of the Divine) and the practical maintenance of a good and healthy life. Coupled with the medieval understanding of the physician as an agent of God and a view of disease as a form of divine intervention visited upon those who had failed to adequately align themselves with Christ, consent within the context of medieval medical practice begins to take shape.

At first glance, one might be tempted to view medieval consent as the rather familiar notion of choice. Yet the specific faith-based epistemology of the medieval era also allows for a reading of consent through the lens of agapeic service to the other. As noted earlier, the view of practicing physicians as 'outsiders' was prevalent during the Middle Ages. Some patients may have considered obedience to their physician's orders as a form of agapeic service. Doctors were, after all, considered to be agents of the divine. Further, while faith is understood within the medieval context as a rational act, it is also an act of obedience; thus the 'choice' medieval medical consent represented was an agreement to align oneself with Christ. This was done in the most immediate of circumstances in the hope of attaining good health or ridding oneself of disease, thus prompting physicians' demands for obedience (and their prescriptions for deception to attain it). As Al-Ruhāwī instructed physicians: 'It is essential that the physician not follow the will of the patient unless it benefits him in his improvement; he should not fear him in this nor any desire in this of his individual rights. On the contrary, it is only God that he fears and entreats'.[139] Thus, while a patient's obedience might have been in pursuit of good health, this was understood to be a joint endeavour between the patient and the physician, where only through communion with one another might unity with the divine (and its ensuing good health) be achieved. The patient's body could be known to the physician. It existed in the realm of the seen. So, too, could the patient's words or stated intentions. The truth of these words, however, was not a matter for human assessment.

137 PM Jones (n 26).

138 Aquinas contends 'the expression of words without inward consent makes no marriage' in *Summa Theologica: Volume V – Part III, Second Section & Supplement* (translated by Fathers of the English Dominican Province, Cosimo Press 2007) 2715.

139 Levey, 'Medical Ethics of Medieval Islam' (n 79) 11 citing Al-Ruhawi.

True knowledge and the healing it might offer were available only in the unseen, the transcendental. Together, in concord, the physician and the patient seek the divine in what is not visible. Through this consent, both might find the divine and live in alignment with God. Healing was the sign of this success – the external indicator of the unknowable inner commitment of the patient.

The emphasis on prognosis (over diagnosis) within medieval medical practice provides some additional support for this view. In the first instance, this dichotomy can be attributed to the Classical Greek practice of making diagnosis subservient to prognosis.[140] While some components to this tradition involved beliefs and practices characterised as 'pagan' by medieval (monastic) scholars (such as the consideration of the planets or the signs of the zodiac in assessing a patient's ailments), the Greeks' ontological reasons for elevating prognosis over diagnosis were fairly compatible with Christian theology. As Pagel explains, for the early Greeks '[t]here is no such thing as disease; there are individuals who fall ill'.[141] Thus, the consideration of an individual's constitution, temperament, or behaviour was important for gaining knowledge of the subject and her nature rather than the (dis)functioning of her organs. Within the medieval context, this would have required access to knowledge only God might know, thus positioning prognosis as a form of 'divine revelation'. Wallis notes that no medieval (Latin) word existed for 'diagnose'; rather the term *cognoscere* is often found in its place, meaning 'I know' or 'I am acquainted with'. She argues, '[t]he word *diagnosis* has no technical connotation for Galen, for example; it simply means knowledge, decision or judgement about *present* matters'.[142] These would have been visible matters – thus the medieval medical manuscript's emphasis on urine analysis, pulse, and other manifest signs of illness. The physician is instructed that the patient's case may be 'easily judged' on these visual symptoms.[143] This judgment is limited by the doctor's own knowledge, resulting in an emphasis on therapeutic treatments; however, a prognosis on the patient's fate was a matter of divine revelation. Following this argument, Wallis likens diagnostic techniques in the Middle Ages to an 'ordeal', a 'means of finding the truth about things which are hidden'.[144] She employs the example of a crime without a witness. The accused is tested; in the typical medieval ordeal this is the application of a hot iron. If the accused's arm is healed in three days, she is innocent. God thus serves as the witness – he sees what is unseeable.[145] Prognosis gains its status as prophecy.

140 PM Jones (n 26). See also Walter Pagel, 'Prognosis and Diagnosis: A Comparison of Ancient and Modern Medicine' (1939) 2(4) *JWCI* 382.

141 Pagel (n 140) 387.

142 Wallis (n 42) 276.

143 This is Wallis's preferred translation of a phrase found in a medical manuscript (circa 900 AD) entitled, 'How you should visit the patient'. She also offers the possibilities of 'attendant circumstances' or 'you will easily understand the patient's condition' (n 42) 276.

144 Wallis (n 42) 276.

145 Wallis also describes the story of the *Ivory Casket*, an account of a text Hippocrates was said to have buried with him that would reveal the secrets of life and death. Wallis notes two important things about this story. The first is how it serves to mystify prognosis as 'esoteric' (or what I would argue is 'divine') knowledge. The second points to the title of Hippocrates' hidden

Within the medieval context, then, consent was a sign of virtue. It was not a simple matter of choice or a stated agreement to share one's inner will with God, but rather it was an act of aligning it with Him, through a balanced and moderate 'application of the movement of appetite to something that is to be done'.[146] Medieval consent does not function as a form of autonomy but rather an existential commitment – a submission to the divine in both will and conduct, measured externally by one's balance of the passions and alignment with Christian ideals. If one did not truly make this commitment, if one lacked the requisite faith, consent (and its promised virtues) was denied. This can be likened to the role of consent among the ancients in marking the boundaries of social and juridical recognition – a status that was also subject to a strict regimen of prescribed behaviours and appetites. The canonical story of consent found in the medieval medical context reveals the onto-epistemological role of consent even more starkly, where certain ways of being served as prerequisites for ways of knowing.[147] Consent is an existential commitment to this schema. It is an act of submission to the terms (of another) that make the very act of submission intelligible.

The suggestion that consent is less about freedom than it is about submission is one that a number of legal and political scholars have made – many of whom were canvassed in Chapter 1. Despite an explicit acknowledgement within many of these critiques that consent serves as a form of subordination to terms set by another (and often in opposition to the interests of the one consenting), the vision of consent as a signifier or enactment of personal freedom is left intact. Further obscured is the role of the consent-as-autonomy story in facilitating this submission. It is only by visiting contexts where contemporary understandings of autonomy simply don't 'work' that this story is disrupted, revealing consent to be less a marker of personal freedom and more a signifier of compliance with dominant norms of intelligibility. In the antiquity context, this submission was to the state, establishing the boundaries of juridical and socio-cultural recognition. The canonical story of consent tells a tale of divine submission that regulates the soul. Is this merely a medieval tale of consent, long since forgotten as the Dark Ages came to a close? Or do some remnants of this onto-epistemological power of consent continue to operate today? Is there still a way in which the 'magic' of consent to transform human error is dependent on an internal alignment with dominant ideals of 'good citizenship' or 'good morality'? How might consent continue to operate today as a site of personal salvation – or damnation – and what form might these prescriptions of subjectivity take? What existential commitment does consent-as-autonomy ask us to make?

---

text, ie *Indicia valetudinum* (or 'Indications of Illness'), noting the legal meaning of 'indicia' as 'grounds of accusation'. Wallis's latter point is interesting for both its depiction of God's knowledge as hidden to humans after the Fall and for its portrayal of illness as indicative or accusatory of a misalignment with Christ (n 42) 276–277.

146 Aquinas, *Summa Theologica* I–II, 15 § 2, as cited in Judith A Barad, 'Aquinas on Faith and the Consent/Assent Distinction' (1986) 24(3) *J Hist Phil* 311, 319.

147 Although medievalists would likely be quick to correct my use of the plural here, suggesting that there was only one way of knowing – God's.

Conclusion

This chapter has examined consent in a period where it operated as an act of faith. This 'skewed glance' of consent has also revealed the role of consent in maintaining both epistemological control over medieval life (and its hereafter) and an ontological control over its inhabitants. By maintaining a monopoly over medieval medicine, the Christian Church could decree who might learn its theories, who might be granted the authority to engage in its practice, and who might benefit from its grace. Medieval consent, following on the heels of an ancient belief in the benefits of moderation, was a virtue – a precursor, perhaps, of contemporary scholars' habit of endowing consent with a transformative power. And while modern-day patients can hardly be said to be trying to attain divinity when they sign consent forms for surgery, they may be trying to beat death, attain immortality, understand the unknowable, view the unseen, or place their bets on magic. These are some of the remnants of the canonical story of consent, unearthed from the medieval medical world.

What happens, then, when these echoed acts of faith are named 'free'? What operations of self-surveillance or submission are obscured when consent is configured as autonomy? Understanding medical law's doctrine of informed consent within a context of power relations is not a new line of thought. Bioethicists and medical legal scholars have long argued that unequal power relationships between the doctor and the patient create significant doubt as to the possibility (or desirability, in some cases) of a fully autonomous patient. As Wilson notes in her examination of the UK use of the 'Expert Patient policy', the 'ideal patient is both compliant and self-reliant'.[148] While this model of self-reliance has roots in the ethic of self-care developed in the medieval period's approach to consent, the contemporary law's treatment of the consenting subject operationalises this ethic within a capitalist logic. This is seen explicitly in the next chapter's investigation of the use of consent within sport – a context that offers another opportunity for a 'skewed glance' at the consent-as-autonomy story.

Bibliography

Table of cases

Canterbury v Spence 464 F 2d 772 (DC Cir 1972)
Schloendorff v Society of New York Hospital 105 NE 92 (NY 1914)

Secondary sources

Ajlouni KM, 'History of Informed Consent' (1995) 346(8980) *Lancet* 980
Aksoy S, 'The Religious Tradition of Ishaq ibn Ali al-Ruhāwī: The Author of the First Medical Ethics Book in Islamic Medicine' (2004) 3(5) *JISHIM* 9

148 Patricia M Wilson, 'A Policy Analysis of the Expert Patient in the United Kingdom: Self Care as an Expression of Pastoral Power?' (2001) 9(3) *Health Soc Care Comm* 134, 138.

Ālvarez-Millān C, 'Practice Versus Theory: Tenth-Century Cases from the Islamic Middle East' (2000) 13(2) *Soc Hist Med* 293

Amundsen DW, 'Visigothic Medical Legislation' (1971) 45(6) *Bull Hist Med* 553

Aquinas T, *Summa Theologica: Volume V – Part III, Second Section & Supplement* (Fathers of the English Dominican Province tr, Cosimo Press 2007)

Aristotle, *Nichomachean Ethics* (Terence Irwin tr, 2nd edn, Hackett 1999)

Arrizabalaga J, 'The Ideal Medical Practitioner in Counter-Reformation Castile' in Samuel S Kottek and Luis García Ballester (eds), *Medicine and Medical Ethics in Medieval and Early Modern Spain* (Magnes Press 2009)

Bakos GT, *On Faith, Rationality, and the Other in the Late Middle Ages: A Study of Nicolas of Cusa's Manuductive Approach to Islam* (Pickwick 2011)

Barad JA, 'Aquinas on Faith and the Consent/Assent Distinction' (1986) 24(3) *J Hist Phil* 311

Brockliss L, 'Review of Lawrence I Conrad and Others, *The Western Medical Tradition: 800 BC to AD 1800*' (1997) 41(4) *Med Hist* 510

Brown W, *Left Legalism/Left Critique* (Duke University Press 2002)

Bullough VL, *The Development of Medicine as a Profession: The Contribution of the Medieval University to Modern Medicine* (Hafner 1966)

Clarke CC, 'Henri de Mondeville' (1931) 3(6) *Yale J Bio Med* 458

Cooper JM, 'Aristotelian Responsibility' (2013) 45 *Oxford StudAncient Philos* 265

Cosman MP, 'Medieval Medical Malpractice: The Dicta and the Dockets' (1973) 49(1) *Bull NY Acad Med* 22

Couper JL, 'The Healing Bird' (1990) 78 *SA Med J* 485

Cranz FE, 'Nicolaus Cusanus and Dionysius Areopagita' in Thomas M Izbicki and Gerald Christianson (eds), *Nicholas of Cusa and the Renaissance* (Aldershot 2000)

Curley MJ (tr), *Physiologus: A Medieval Book of Nature Lore* (University of Texas Press 1979)

de Ros GO, 'The Ethical Manipulation of the Patient in the Ancients versus Moderns Controversy: The Impact of Giuseppe Gazola's *Il Mondo Ingannato da Falsi Medici* (1716) in Spain' in Samuel S Kottek and Luis García Ballester (eds), *Medicine and Medical Ethics in Medieval and Early Modern Spain* (Magnes Press 2009)

Donne J, *Devotions Upon Emergent Occasions* (first published 1624, John Sparrow ed, CUP 1923)

Draper H and Sorell T, 'Patients' Responsibilities in Medical Ethics' (2002) 16(4) *Bioethics* 335

Edelstein L, 'The Professional Ethics of the Greek Physician' (1956) 30 *Bull Hist Med* 391

———, 'The Hippocratic Oath' in Owsei Temkin and C Lillian Temkin (eds), *Ancient Medicine: Selected Papers of Ludwig Edelstein* (JHUP 1967)

Faden RR and Beauchamp TL, *A History and Theory of Informed Consent* (OUP 1986)

Farber L, *An Anatomy of Trade in Medieval Writing: Value, Consent, and Community* (Cornell UP 2006)

Fort GF, *Medieval Economy during the Middle Ages: A Contribution to the History of European Morals, from the Time of the Roman Empire to the Close of the Fourteenth Century* (JW Bouton 1883)

Foucault M, *Madness and Civilization: A History of Insanity in an Age of Reason* (Vintage 1965)

Galvào-Sobrinho CR, 'Hippocratic Ideals, Medical Ethics, and the Practice of Medicine in the Early Middle Ages: The Legacy of the Hippocratic Oath' (1996) 51(4) *J Hist Med Allied Sci* 438

Garcia-Ballester L, 'Ethical Problems in the Relationship between Doctors and Patients in 14th Century Spain: On Christian and Jewish Practitioners' in Samuel S Kottek and Luis García Ballester (eds), *Medicine and Medical Ethics in Medieval and Early Modern Spain* (Magnes Press 2009)

Grant C, 'For Love of God: Agape' (1996) 24(1) *J Rel Eth* 3

Hackett E, 'The Charadrius: A Useful Bird' (1955) 30(11) *Irish J Med Sci* 491

Hammond EA, 'Incomes of Medieval English Doctors' (1960) XV(2) *J His Med* 154

Holstein HA, 'Vices of Consent in the Law of Contract' (1938) 13 *Tul LR* 560

Jackson E, *Medical Law: Text, Cases, and Materials* (OUP 2009)

Jones KB, 'Surgeons' Silence: A History of Informed Consent in Orthopaedics' (2007) 27 *Iowa Orthop J* 115

Jones PM, *Medieval Medicine in Illuminated Manuscripts* (British Library 1998)

Katz J, 'The Regulation of Human Experimentation in the United States – A Personal Odyssey' (1987) 9(1) *IRB: Eth Hum Research* 1

Kieckhefer R, 'The Specific Rationality of Medieval Magic' (1994) 99(3) *Am Hist Rev* 813

Kraut R, 'Aristotle's Ethics' *The Stanford Encyclopedia of Philosophy* (Summer edn, 2018) <https://plato.stanford.edu/archives/sum2018/entries/aristotle-ethics/> accessed 30 April 2019

Levey M, 'Medical Deontology in Ninth Century Islam' (1966) *J Hist Med* 358

———, 'Medical Ethics of Medieval Islam with Special Reference to al-Ruhāwī 's "Practical Ethics of the Physician"' (1967) 57(3) *Trans Am Philos Soc* 1

MacKinney LC, *Early Medieval Medicine* (John Hopkins Press 1937)

———, 'Medical Ethics and Etiquette in the Early Middle Ages: The Persistence of Hippocratic Ideals' (1952) 26(1) *Bull Hist Med* 1

Manson NC and O'Neill O, *Rethinking Informed Consent in Bioethics* (CUP 2007)

Margalith D, 'The Ideal Doctor as Depicted in Ancient Hebrew Writings' (1957) 12 *J Hist Med* 37

Miles SH, *The Hippocratic Oath and the Ethics of Medicine* (OUP 2005)

Moser PK, 'Agapeic Theism: Personifying Evidence and Moral Struggle' (2010) 2 *EJPR* 1

Murray PJ, 'The History of Informed Consent' (1990) 10 *Iowa Orthop J* 104

Nutton V, 'God, Galen, and the Depaganization of Ancient Medicine' in Peer Biller and Joseph Ziegler (eds) *Medicine and Religion in the Middle Ages* (York Medieval Press 2001)

Nygren A, 'Agape and Eros' in Thomas Jay Oord (ed), *The Altruism Reader* (Templeton Press 2007)

Pagel W, 'Prognosis and Diagnosis: A Comparison of Ancient and Modern Medicine' (1939) 2(4) *JWCI* 382

Pernick M, 'The Patient's Role in Medical Decision Making: A Social History of Informed Consent in Medical Therapy' in President's Commission for the Study of Ethical Problems in Medicine and Biomedical and Behavioral Research, *Studies on the Foundations of Informed Consent, Vol. 3: Making Health Care Decisions* (US Library of Congress 1982)

Riddle JM, 'Theory and Practice in Medieval Medicine' (1974) 5 *Viator* 157

Robbins RH, 'Medical Manuscripts in Middle English' (1970) 45(3) *Speculum* 393

Ross WD (tr and ed), *The Works of Aristotle* (Clarendon 1908)

Salmón F, 'Academic Discourse and Pain in Medical Scholasticism (Thirteenth and Fourteenth Centuries) in Samuel S Kottek and Luis García Ballester (eds), *Medicine and Medical Ethics in Medieval and Early Modern Spain* (Magnes Press 2009)

Salomensen J, *Enchanted Feminism: Ritual, Gender, and Divinity among the Reclaiming Witches of San Francisco* (Routledge 2002)

Schnier J, 'The Symbolic Bird in Medieval and Renaissance Art' (1952) 9 *Book Psychoanal* 292

Selek S, 'A Written Consent Five Centuries Ago' (2010) 36 *J Med Eth* 639

Serene E, 'Demonstrative Science' in Norman Kretzmann, Anthony Kenny and Jan Pinborg (eds), *The Cambridge History of Late Medieval Philosophy* (CUP 1988)

Siegler M, 'Searching for Moral Certainty in Medicine: A Proposal for a New Model of the Doctor-Patient Encounter' (1981) 57(1) *Bull NY Acad Med* 56

Singer C, 'Medical Science in the Dark Ages' in Zachary Cope (ed), *Sidelights on the History of Medicine* (Butterworths 1957)

Siraisi NG, *Medieval and Early Renaissance Medicine: An Introduction to Knowledge and Practice* (UCHIP 1990)

Sistrunk TG, 'The Function of Praise in the Contract of a Medieval Public Physician' (1993) 48 *J Hist Med Allied Sci* 320

Spade PV, 'Medieval Philosophy', *The Stanford Encyclopedia of Philosophy* (Summer edn, 2018) <http://plato.stanford.edu/archives/spr2011/entries/liberalism/> accessed 30 April 2019

Talbot CH, *Medicine in Medieval England* (Oldbourne 1967)

Temkin O, *Galenism: Rise and Decline of a Medical Philosophy* (Cornell University Press 1973)

———, *On Second Thought' and Other Essays in the History of Medicine and Science* (JHUP 2002)

Thompson EP, 'The Moral Economy of the English Crowd in the Eighteenth Century' (1971) 50 *P&P* 76

Varty K, 'The Giving and Withholding of Consent in Late Twelfth-Century French Literature' (1986) 12 *Read Mediev Stud* 27

Veatch RM (ed) *Cross-Cultural Perspectives in Medical Ethics* (2nd edn, Jones & Bartlett 2000)

Visser WAM and McIntosh A, 'A Short Review of the Historical Critique of Usury' (1998) 8(2) *Acc Bus Finan Hist* 175

Voigts LE, 'Multitudes of Middle English Medical Manuscripts, or the Englishing of Science and Medicine' in Margaret R Schleissner (ed) *Manuscript Sources of Medieval Medicine* (Garland Press 1995)

Vollman J and Winau R, 'Informed Consent in Human Experimentation before the Nuremberg Code' (1996) 313 *BMJ* 1445

Wallis F, 'Signs and Senses: Diagnosis and Prognosis in Early Medieval Pulse and Urine Texts' (2000) 13(2) *Soc Hist Med* 265

Weinberg JR, *A Short History of Medieval Philosophy* (PUP 1964)

Welborn MC, 'The Long Tradition: A Study in Fourteenth Century Medical Deontology' in Chester R Burns (ed), *Legacies in Ethics and Medicine* (Science History Publications 1977)

Wilson PM, 'A Policy Analysis of the Expert Patient in the United Kingdom: Self Care as an Expression of Pastoral Power?' (2001) 9(3) *Health Soc Care Comm* 134

Wolf SM, 'Toward a Systematic Theory of Informed Consent in Managed Care' (1999) 35 *Hous LR* 1631

Wood D, *Medieval Economic Thought* (CUP 2002)

Wynn R, 'Saints and Sinners: Women and the Practice of Medicine throughout the Ages' (2000) 283(5) *JAMA* 668

4 Modern sport

The Roman people is held together by two forces: wheat doles and public shows.
– Marcus Cornelius Fronto[1]

When Derek Boogaard was first scouted to play major junior hockey at the age of 16, he had already lived more than half his life. Shy and soft-spoken, at seven feet on skates, he was drafted into the National Hockey League (NHL) on his 19th birthday and spent his short career as one of the league's most intimidating enforcers – 'a role for him and his fists, if he was willing to dutifully distribute punishment and quietly absorb pain'.[2] Boogaard certainly held up his end, fighting nearly two hundred times over his career and earning 589 penalty minutes in 277 games.[3] After years of chronic pain, depression, and substance abuse, Derek died in 2011 from an overdose of alcohol and prescription painkillers. An autopsy of his brain revealed chronic traumatic encephalopathy (CTE) – a degenerative brain disease caused by repetitive head trauma.[4] The disease was

1 2.216, as cited in Charles Reginald Haines (tr), *Marcus Cornelius Fronto: Correspondence, Vol. II* (HUP 1920).

2 John Branch, *Boy on Ice: The Life and Death of Derek Boogaard* (HarperCollins 2014) 8. The 'enforcer' role on a hockey team is to protect lead scorers, intimidate opposing players and teams, and engage in on-ice fights when needed (eg to bolster team pride or retaliate for past attacks on key players). Former enforcer Ted Simms describes what 'success' in the league required of him: '[to] be a physical presence; have the ability to fight; have the gift of being able to win [fights] on a consecutive basis; hit; and be able to put fear in an opponent's eyes' as cited in Michael A Robidoux, *Men at Play: A Working Understanding of Professional Hockey* (MQUP 2001) 136. See also Dave Schultz and Stan Fisher, *The Hammer: Confessions of a Hockey Enforcer* (Summit Books 1981); Ross Bernstein, *The Code: The Unwritten Rules of Fighting and Retaliation in the NHL* (Triumph Books 2006).

3 Derek is recorded as having participated in 174 career fights, 61 of which were in the regular season. See Boston University CTE Center, 'Press Release re NHL Player Derek Boogaard' (Boston, 6 December 2011) <www.bu.edu/cte/news/press-releases/december-6-2011/> accessed 22 January 2019.

4 John Branch, 'Derek Boogaard: A Brain Going Bad' *New York Times* (New York, 5 December 2011) <www.nytimes.com/2011/12/06/sports/hockey/derek-boogaard-a-brain-going-bad.html> accessed 30 April 2019. CTE was previously known as 'dementia pugilistica'

progressive in Boogaard's case, and doctors surmised that CTE would have led to dementia as early as his 30s – had he not died at 28.[5]

The year of Derek Boogaard's death, the first concussion-related lawsuit was filed against a professional sports league, the National Football League (NFL). It resulted in the largest class action settlement in sports history.[6] A study released in 2017 by Boston University researchers sampled the brains of 111 deceased former NFL players and found CTE in the brains of all but one of them.[7] More than half of those players with CTE had histories of depression, substance abuse, violence, and feelings of hopelessness, and the most common cause of death among them was suicide.[8] A year prior to the study's release, the NFL's senior vice president for health and safety publicly acknowledged a link between CTE and football-related concussions.[9] This came after years of public denials about the links between long-term brain damage and hits to the head – a line the NHL continues to walk.[10] In 2013, more than three hundred former hockey players filed a class action suit against the NHL for the 'fraudulent concealment' of the game's risks and injuries.[11] The suit was settled in 2018 – with no admission of

---

(or colloquially, 'punch drunk') when it was only associated with boxers. See Daniel Schwartz, 'Are NHL Enforcers' Addictions, Depression a Result of on-ice Brain Trauma?' (*CBC News*, 3 September 2011) <www.cbc.ca/news/canada/are-nhl-enforcers-addictions-depression-a-result-of-on-ice-brain-trauma-1.982100> accessed 11 June 2019.

5 Branch, *Boy on Ice* (n 2) 326–327.

6 A number of administrative problems continue to prevent claimants from accessing pay-outs or obtaining the amounts they anticipated. See Ken Belson, 'After NFL Concussion Settlement, Feeding Frenzy of Lawyers and Lenders' *New York Times* (New York, 16 July 2017) <www.nytimes.com/2017/07/16/sports/football/nfl-concussion-settlement-lawyers.html> accessed 21 January 2019; Rick Maese, 'Dementia Claims in NFL Concussion Settlement are Going Unpaid, Lawyers Say' (*Washington Post*, 20 March 2018) <https://tinyurl.com/y3ff5qnz> accessed 11 June 2019.

7 Jesse Mez and others, 'Clinicopathological Evaluation of Chronic Traumatic Encephalopathy in Players of American Football' (2017) 318(4) *JAMA* 360. The same study found CTE in 7 of the 8 brains of former Canadian Football League (CFL) players.

8 Mez (n 7) 362. Suicide was the most common form of death among study participants who had been diagnosed with mild CTE (27%). Neurodegenerative causes of death were the most common (47%) among those diagnosed with severe CTE.

9 Ken Belson, 'NFL Official Affirms Link between Playing Football and CTE' *New York Times* (New York, 14 March 2016) <www.nytimes.com/2016/03/15/sports/football/nfl-official-affirms-link-with-cte.html> accessed 30 April 2019.

10 John Branch, 'The Tragic Diagnosis They Already Knew: Their Brother Died with CTE' *New York Times* (New York, 3 May 2018) <www.nytimes.com/2018/05/03/sports/nhl-cte-jeff-parker.html> accessed 22 January 2019.

11 *Leeman and others v National Hockey League* (2013) Civil Case No. 13-CV-1856 (DC Dist Ct). This case is largely thought to have been spurred by the $765 million settlement of a similar suit against the National Football League achieved merely three months prior to the commencement of the NHL suit in 2013. The class action status of the players was dismissed in July, 2018 due to "widespread differences" in the legal frameworks.

liability on the part of the league.[12] This has prompted many to describe the NHL as an "athlete beware" culture.[13] Players allege that they do not receive full disclosure of the risks of bodily harm that the game entails, suggesting that 'for decades the NHL has nurtured a culture of violence' while 'purposefully profit[ing]' from it.[14] The league's response rests on the players' voluntary assumption of risk[15], encapsulated in a comment by former NHL enforcer (and career leader in penalty points) Dave 'Tiger' Williams: 'You consent to assault when you lace up your skates. It's what hockey is all about'.[16]

The role of the criminal law in regulating how much harm a person may consent to has long been the subject of public debate. Editorial opinions published in the *New York Times* in 1905 could easily be mistaken for twenty-first-century letters in their call for the reform of football, due to 'concussion of the brain, broken back and other injuries on the football field'[17] that characterise 'the game we have been accustomed to watch with such joy and to discuss with such horror'.[18] There is perhaps no other place in law where rhetoric about the 'common good' and acceptable cultural values is found as explicitly as it is in the criminal law's consideration of consensual bodily harm. As reviewed in Chapter 1, the law's use of consent's preconditions (of voluntariness, knowledge, and rationality) works to authorise some forms of violence while outlawing others. Thus, even

12 Dave Feschuk, 'NHL's Tentative Concussion Lawsuit Another Blow to the Players' *Toronto Star* (Toronto, 12 November 2018) <www.thestar.com/sports/hockey/opinion/2018/11/12/nhls-tentative-concussion-lawsuit-another-blow-to-the-players.html> accessed 22 January 2019.

13 Chris Nowinski, spokesperson for Boston University's CTE Center (and former professional wrestler and varsity football player), remarked about the NHL settlement: 'What this tells you is that it's athlete beware. The message from professional sports is: You're on your own. Once you've left the team, it doesn't matter if you're a legend, once things go south for you, you and your family are on your own', as cited in Feschuk (n 12).

14 Sean Gordon, 'Former Players Sue NHL, Say League Hid Concussion Risks' *Globe & Mail* (Toronto, 25 November 2013) <www.theglobeandmail.com/sports/hockey/former-players-sue-nhl-say-league-hid-concussion-risks/article15599650/> accessed 30 April 2019.

15 See Defendant (NHL)'s Memorandum of Law, *In Re: National Hockey League Players' Concussion Injury Litigation*, MDL No. 14-2551 (Minn Dist Ct, 18 November 2014).

16 Williams's remark was made in 1988 in response to the Canadian case of *R v Ciccarelli* (1989) 54 CCC 3d 121, when Dino Ciccarelli of the Minnesota North Stars was sentenced to one day in jail and a $1000 fine for hitting Toronto Maple Leafs player Luke Richardson, with his stick. See Steve Mertl, 'Vancouver Police Investigate Ugly On-Ice Hit by Canucks Star' *Canadian Press Newswire* (Vancouver, 9 March 2004). Ciccarelli was reported as 'the first National Hockey League player to receive a jail term for an on-ice attack on another player'. See Associated Press, 'Ciccarelli Cited for Assault' *New York Times* (Toronto, 24 August 1988).

17 'Topics of the Times' *New York Times* (New York, 15 October 1905) as cited by Andrew Sharp, 'League of Denial and the Crisis that Never Ends' (*Grantland*, 9 October 2013) <http://grantland.com/the-triangle/league-of-denial-and-the-crisis-that-never-ends/> accessed 22 January 2019. The 1905 editorial argues that the game can't be reformed, only abolished. 'Meanwhile', it concludes, 'concussion of the brain will flourish and broken backs will interfere with the regular course of study at our institution of learning'.

18 'Topics of the Times' *New York Times* (New York, 28 November 1905) 8.

voluntary and well-informed decisions to engage in self-harm can be overridden if the activity in question is deemed to be 'unreasonable' or without social value.

This reveals one of consent's contradictions with respect to the relationship between citizen and state. Vestiges of early liberalism's social contract abound in both legal and philosophical accounts of the liberty individuals should have from state intervention. Each person is thought to be entitled to the 'freedom to be left alone', and consent is meant to enshrine this principle of independence. Yet the law also uses consent to restrict individual liberty when it is exercised in a way that causes harm – to others or oneself. This tension between a principle of non-interference and the state's acts of legal paternalism comes to the fore in sport and play contexts for a number of reasons. Leisure forums are traditionally understood as spaces for social 'time outs'.[19] Indeed, this 'break' from normal behavioural expectations is often cited as a leading virtue of consensual violence.[20] They are also heavily corporeal contexts, so legal interventions within them have consequences for the most intimate spaces of our lives.

Two claims are usually made in favour of the criminal law's application to the spheres of sport and play. The first is some version of the 'rule of law' or a principle of universality, where the law is understood as extending to all persons and activities that fall within the jurisdiction of the state. This is the argument Mill makes in his text *On Liberty* when he asks, 'Where does the authority of society begin? How much of human life should be assigned to individuality, and how much to society?'[21] Mill answers that as 'soon as any part of a person's conduct affects prejudicially the interests of others, society has jurisdiction over it'.[22] It is on this basis that legal paternalism is justified: the law should intervene to prevent individuals from doing harm to *others*. Self-harm is therefore regulated in relation to the potential harm it poses to others, either directly or through an erosion of integral social values and legal norms. This paternalistic role of the criminal law to 'protect people against themselves'[23] was recognised as one of the central distinctions between the role of consent in criminal and civil law in the American case, *State v Brown* (1976):

> While criminal law is designed to protect the interests of society as a whole, the civil law is concerned with enforcing the rights of each individual within the society. So, while the consent of the victim may relieve defendant[s] of liability in tort, this same consent has been held irrelevant in a criminal prosecution, where there is more at stake than a victim's rights.[24]

19 David Gendall, 'The Sport of Boxing: Freedom versus Social Constraint' (1997) 5 *(Waikato Law Review)* 71.

20 See Jennifer A Brobst, 'Why Public Health Policy Should Redefine Consent to Assault and the Intentional Foul in Gladiator Sports' (2015) 29 *JL & Health* 1; Benjamin C Graham and others, 'Member Perspectives on the Role of BDSM Communities' (2015) 53(8) *J Sex Res* 895.

21 John Stuart Mill, *On Liberty* (first published 1859, Elizabeth Rapaport ed, Hackett 1978) 73.

22 Mill (n 21) 73.

23 This is a slight rewording of HLA Hart's description of paternalism as 'the protection of people against themselves' in *Law, Liberty, and Morality* (SUP 1963) 31.

24 *State v Brown* 143 NJ Sup 571, 573 (1976)

Agreement on these stakes is important; some things have to matter to everyone if they are to justify constraints on liberty. This is the second common justification for the law's intervention in sport and play: the enforcement of a common morality. Sir Patrick Devlin is an oft-cited proponent of this view, having argued that law is meant to serve a normalising function, which, in turn, serves to police private immorality.[25] This 'common morality' is what Devlin suggests is 'part of the bondage' that one's participation in a society entails:

> Each one of us has ideas about what is good and what is evil; they cannot be kept private from the society in which we live. If men and women try to create a society in which there is no fundamental agreement about good and evil they will fail; if, having based it on common agreement, the agreement goes, the society will disintegrate. For society is not something that is kept together physically; it is held by the invisible bonds of common thought.[26]

Interestingly, Devlin's argument that society is held together by the 'invisible bonds of common thought' is not unlike the medieval view of consent as the existential commitment that is required before communion can be reached. John Locke's notion of tacit consent seems to have played a similar role, as Chapter 1 delineated, where one's use of the 'common sense' marked one's membership in a community and an agreement to comply with its moral codes and conduct norms. This 'moralising' function of the criminal law is palpable in its regulation of consensual violence, perhaps no better evidenced than the now infamous English case, *R v Brown*.[27] There, the court's assessment of acceptable and unacceptable forms of violence relied on a particular interpretation of 'harm' that many commentators have suggested endorsed hegemonic understandings of masculinity and heteronormativity – all housed within legal definitions of 'reasonableness'.[28] Not unlike the medieval view of consent as a form of submission, might the same paradigm be applicable in the modern legal context – one littered with the premature deaths of professional athletes contracted to play for millions of dollars in a multi-billion-dollar industry?[29] Do criminal law consent cases reveal a prescriptive demand for conformity to dominant norms of intelligible personhood and action?

25 Patrick Devlin, *The Enforcement of Morals* (OUP 1965).

26 Devlin (n 25) 9–10.

27 *R v Brown* [1993] 2 All ER 75.

28 See, for instance, the commentary offered by Michael Thomson in his text, *Endowed: Regulating the Male Sexed Body* (Routledge 2008), in particular, Chapter 6.

29 The National Football League (NFL) alone reported revenue of just over 9.5 billion dollars in 2012. See Monte Burke, 'How the National Football League Can Reach 25 Billion in Annual Revenues' (*Forbes*, 17 August 2013) <http://forbes.com/sites/monteburke/2013/08/17/how-the-national-football-league-can-reach-25-billion-in-annual-revenues/> accessed 24 January 2019.

This chapter pursues these inquiries within criminal law cases that address the limits of consent to harm, focussing primarily on injuries that occur during professional contact sports. Of central concern is the judicial treatment of 'harm' (as a delimiter of consent) in ways that entrench ideals of hegemonic masculinity and establish what 'rational' uses of body capital look like. Certainly, activities involving sex and bondage/domination or sadomasochism (BDSM)[30] are implicated here, too, and have been well explored in the literature in relation to consent,[31] privacy and constitutional rights,[32] socio-medical pathology,[33] and gender identity[34] (among other foci). There are important differences, however, in how the criminal law approaches consent to harm in the nation's bedrooms than on its playing fields, suggesting that the latter context is better suited to finding alternatives to the consent-as-autonomy story.[35] In the first instance, violence within sexual contexts is presumptively illegal in most jurisdictions, 'therefore practitioners must rely on their individual, bodily experiences to outline what encounters are welcomed or not, rather than on formal legal definitions'.[36] This has given consent a fundamental role in the BDSM sphere: it is what distinguishes the community's practices from true violence.[37] Consent also operates explicitly in the BDSM context, involving 'detailed pre-planning in the form of either questionnaires or extensive conversation' about participant desires,

30 Morgan Schumann, in an excellent review of the role of consent in sadomasochistic practices, describes BDSM as an 'umbrella term … compris[ing] a variety of alternative sexual practices including bondage, discipline, domination, submission, sadism, and masochism … [that] "tend to deal with the administration of consensually experienced pain, humiliation, and uses of power, conducted for mutual pleasure"'. See Morgan Schumann, 'Pain, Please: Consent to Sadomasochistic Conduct' (2018) 2018(3) *U Ill L Rev* 1177, 1179 citing J Tuomas Harviainen, 'Information Literacies of Self-Identified Sadomasochists: An Ethnographic Case Study' (2015) 71 *J Doc* 423, 424.

31 Schumann (n 30); Jill D Weinberg, *Consensual Violence: Sex, Sports, and the Politics of Injury* (UCalP 2016); Jordana Greenblatt, '"Cruelty is Uncivilized": Consent, BDSM, and Legal Regulation of the Civil(ized) Subject' in Nikita Dawson and others (eds), *Negotiating Normativity* (Springer 2016); Annette Houlihan, 'When "No" Means "Yes" and "Yes" Means Harm: HIV Risk, Consent and Sadomasochism Case Law' (2011) 20 *Law & Sexuality* 31.

32 Elizabeth Mincer, 'Fifty Shades and Fifty States: Is BDSM a Fundamental Right? A Test for Sexual Privacy' (2018) 26 *Wm & Mary Bill Rts J* 865.

33 Ofer Parchev and Darren Langdridge, 'BDSM under Security: Radical Resistance via Contingent Subjectivities' (2017) 21(1–2) *Sexualities* 194; Kai Lin, 'The Medicalization and Demedicalization of Kink: Shifting Contexts of Sexual Politics' (2016) 20(3) *Sexualities* 302.

34 Brandy L Simula and J Sumerau, 'The Use of Gender in the Interpretation of BDSM' (2017) 22(3) *Sexualties* 452.

35 This is an allusion to the comment famously made to reporters by the (then) Canadian Prime Minster Pierre E. Trudeau, about reforms to Canada's *Criminal Code* in 1967 to decriminalise homosexual acts. 'There is no place for the state in the bedrooms of the nation'. See 'Trudeau's Omnibus Bill' *CBC Digital Archives* (21 December 1967) <www.cbc.ca/player/play/1811727781> accessed 24 January 2019.

36 Weinberg (n 31) 18.

37 Schumann notes that '[p]articipants in BDSM will generally not use the term "violence" and most would strongly object to this categorization' (n 30) 1187.

fears, and limits.[38] BDSM participants also use 'negotiation checklists ... to structure these conversations and ensure clear understanding between partners' as well as '"safe words" that signal withdrawal of consent'.[39] Many scholars have lauded these practices for their recognition and protection of sexual agency, noting that BDSM consent practices have much to offer sexual violence reform projects.[40] It is, however, an approach deeply rooted in the consent-as-autonomy narrative, making alternatives to this story harder to identify.[41]

The role of consent in sporting violence, in contrast, operates *implicitly* in law, and player autonomy is framed within a context of risk management and economic capital. Players are taken to have agreed to bodily harm by voluntarily participating in the game.[42] The impact of this distinction on the role of consent is well articulated by Jill Weinberg in her thoughtful text *Consensual Violence* through a comparison of BDSM activities and mixed martial arts (MMA) competitions:

> The notable difference between BDSM and MMA is the extent to which legal status constructs the meaning and deployment of consent within these communities. When the state does *not* authorize an activity, participants actively construct and regulate consent ... BDSM practitioners consciously invoke legal language to insulate their activities from liability and convey an image of legitimacy to a broader public. By contrast, when the state authorizes an activity like MMA, those engaged in the activity do not construct and regulate consent. Consent becomes an expression of authority where people unknowingly consent to predetermined terms and conditions as a matter of efficiency and formality.[43]

The lack of legal status for BDSM activity leaves its consent configurations outside the formal regulation *and* recognition of the state. This is akin to the

38 Schumann (n 30) 1184. See also Ayesha Kaak, 'Conversational Phases in BDSM Pre-Scene Negotiations' (2016) 2(3) *J Pos Sex* 47.

39 Schumann (n 30) 1184.

40 Theodore Bennett, '"Unorthodox Rules": The Instructive Potential of BDSM Consent for Law' (2018) 4(1) *J Pos Sex* 1; Schumann (n 30); Nafsika Athanassoulis, 'The Role of Consent in Sado-Masochistic Practices' (2002) 8 *Res Publica* 141; Anne Onoma, 'Legal Censure of Unconventional Expressions of Love and Sexuality: Finding a Place in the Law for BDSM' (2017) 28(1) *Hastings WLJ* 25.

41 This is not to suggest there aren't alternative stories of consent to be found in the BDSM context. I do find them harder to hear: Realised sexual autonomy is a grain my feminist self *doesn't want* to read against. This is further troubled by the specter of intimate partner violence that haunts so many of the (so-called) BDSM cases that come before the courts. See Karen Busby, 'Every Breath You Take: Erotic Asphyxiation, Vengeful Wives, and Other Enduring Myths in Spousal Sexual Assault Prosecutions' (2012) 24(2) *CJWL* 328; Dulcinea Pitagora, 'Intimate Partner Violence in Sadomasochistic Relationships' (2016) 31(1) *Sex & RT* 95.

42 Provided the injury is one that could reasonably be expected within the (written and unwritten) rules of the game.

43 Weinberg (n 31) 6.

'ancient outlaws' of Chapter 2, where consent could also be seen to operate in conjunction with socio-legal status. The professional sport context, in contrast, is a heavily regulated forum, thus allowing for an examination of the work that law does to assess the 'reasonableness' of violence that is suffered for profit (but not pleasure).[44] The additional advantage of a genealogical dig into consensual violence in sport is that it provides the opportunity to examine the same 'unwritten codes' of hegemonic masculinity and morality that are at work in BDSM prohibitions while also offering an economic frame of analysis through which the 'consent to play' of professional athletes (like Derek Boogaard) might be better understood.

The following section reviews the criminal law approach to consensual violence, beginning with English common law and tracing the subsequent development of consent-to-injury jurisprudence in North America and other commonwealth countries. Although some reference is made to cases involving consensual violence in sexual contexts, this chapter's primary focus is on the use of consent as a defence to assault charges arising from in-game behaviour.

Harmful horseplay: consent and contact sports

Early common law positions with respect to consensual violence were concerned with the subjective state of mind of the accused and whether it was sufficient to satisfy the mens rea of assault.[45] The victim's agreement to be harmed did not change the illegality of an assault's violence or the danger it posed to the public order, so consent did not arise as a pertinent issue to the determination of criminal liability. Lord Hale, writing in 1778, went so far as to suggest that any death which occurred during a contact sport would constitute manslaughter on the grounds that the accused had intended to cause harm to the opponent.[46] Hale was writing in opposition to another prominent contention at the time put forth by Sir Michael Foster in his 1762 publication *Crown Cases*, which argued that the 'mutual consent' of the parties should vitiate the accused's malicious intention.[47] English courts would later seek a compromise between these two approaches in a trilogy of late nineteenth-century cases (ie *Bradshaw*[48], *Moore*[49],

44 'If we can make sense of rape as a violent, non-consensual act expressed through sex, we can make sense of sadomasochism by analogy, as a sexual consensual act expressed through violence', Athanassoulis (n 40) 153.

45 This has led some commentators to debate whether consent serves as a defence to charges of assault or is better positioned as a justification (ie a negation of the mental element). See Graham Hughes, 'Two Views of Consent in the Criminal Law' (1963) 26 *MLR* 233.

46 Hale mentions the specific contact activities of wrestling and 'cudgens', a martial art performed with a singlestick that was popular in the Middle Ages and continued well into the modern period in Europe. Matthew Hale, *History of the Pleas of the Crown* (E. Rider 1778) 472 as cited in Note, 'Consent in Criminal Law: Violence in Sports' (1976) 75 *Mich LR* 148, 170.

47 Sir Michael Foster, *Crown Cases* (Clarendon 1762) 260.

48 (1878) 14 Cox CC 83.

49 (1898) 14 TLR 229.

and *Coney*[50]), establishing a standard of implied consent which took into account the intent concerns raised by Hale while carving out exceptions for bodily harm incurred during activities which Foster argued were of particular social value.[51] This included any number of 'manly diversions' of the day intended to 'give strength, skill and activity'[52] such as 'friendly exertions of cudgelling, fencing and trials of strength involving wrestling and sparring'.[53] This association of social value with masculine endeavours is perhaps not surprising, given that the first known commentary on the issue of consent in contact sports marked out an exception for playful activities 'done only for disport and trial of manhood'.[54] The nature of these activities and the scope of the 'manly diversion' exception was further developed in the late nineteenth century, as British courts considered the legality of prizefighting[55] and North American courts followed suit.[56] Mill's liberalism looms large in these early demarcations of the legal limits of consensual violence. Where an act could be defined as 'harmless', the principle of non-interference demanded that it fall outside the ambit of state intervention. Changing understandings of 'harm' have resulted in a wide array of 'allowable' forms of bodily harm, such as piercing/tattooing, parental discipline, surgery,[57] 'horseplay' or 'rough housing' outside of a sport context, and some religious or ceremonial acts (eg circumcision, flagellation).[58]

50 (1882) LR 8 QBD 534.

51 Jack Anderson refers to this as the 'implied sporting consent' principle. See Jack Anderson, 'No Licence for Thuggery: Violence, Sport, and the Criminal Law' (2008) 10 *Crim LR* 751.

52 Foster (n 47) 260.

53 Jack Anderson, *The Legality of Boxing: A Punch Drunk Love?* (Birkbeck Law Press, 2005) 40.

54 Michael Dalton, *The Country Justice* (The Company of Stationers, 1635) 246.

55 Prizefighting was effectively banned in Britain following a series of cases where public fighting exhibitions were dissociated from allowable 'manly diversions' on the basis of their potential (and presumed intent) to disrupt the public peace. See Anderson, *The Legality of Boxing* (n 53).

56 See, for instance, the US case of *State v Burnham* (1884) 48 Am Rep 801, in which Foster's category of 'manly diversions' is employed to distinguish between legal sport (in that case, boxing) from events thought to breach the public peace (namely, fist fighting/prizefighting), as cited in Anderson, *The Legality of Boxing* (n 53) 49. Similarly, see *R v Jobidon* [1991] 2 SCR 714, the Supreme Court of Canada case which prohibited consent to a fist fight on the grounds that it held no social value.

57 In *Brown* (n 27), the House of Lords noted that surgeries that were deemed 'necessary' would fall within the exception. This suggests that optional and presumably more normatively complicated surgeries (eg cosmetic, sex reassignment, body modification) might not be deemed sufficiently 'reasonable' for consent. See Peter Alldridge, 'Consent to Medical Surgical Treatment: The Law Commission's Recommendations' (1996) 4 *Med LR* 129; Tracey Elliott, 'Body Dysmorphic Disorder, Radical Surgery, and the Limits of Consent' (2009) 17(2) *Med LR* 149.

58 Some commentators have suggested that Lord Templeman's claim that ritual circumcision fell within the lawful exceptions to violent offences was *obiter dictum*. See, for example, Marie Fox and Michael Thomson, 'A Covenant with the Status Quo? Male Circumcision and the New BMA Guidance for Doctors' (2004) 31(8) *J Med Eth* 463. See also the New Zealand Court of Appeal case, *R v Lee* [2006] 5 LRC 716 involving a fatal 'exorcism' and the court's consideration of the role of consent to religious practice.

The criminal law's use of the harm principle in its approach to consensual violence has been codified in a number of jurisdictions, all of which limit how much and what kinds of harm a person can (legally) consent to.[59] Sport has long fallen within these exempted grounds, and even 'healthy horseplay' is subject to legal limits, most notably a standard of reasonableness.[60] Courts assess the 'rationality' of consent to harm using two (related) factors: the severity of the harm and the public's interest in the violent activity. The majority in *Brown* suggested that 'common sense' would dictate a point where the harm incurred would cross a line whereafter considerations of consent would be 'irrelevant'.[61] This is in keeping with the discussion in Chapter 1 of the role of 'common sense' in producing and enforcing views about what 'normal' behaviour, desires, and identities look like. Certainly, the meaning that 'common sense' has been given jurisprudentially lends credence to this claim. As one commentator has remarked: 'In addition to the cognitive, volitional, and formal requirements, the appropriate act of tacit consent must meet the criterion of generality ... something virtually every person does'.[62] A dominant interpretation of this generality principle in the criminal law's articulations of consent is a 'regularity of behaviour', that is, an assumption about the gestures and actions which can be expected from people on the basis of convention.[63] Treated in law as a standard of common sense,[64] implied consent relies on shared understandings of gestures or circumstances from which particular significations are interpreted as acts of volition or informed choice. There are cases, for instance, where the law has recognised silence or

59 See 2.11(2) of the American *Model Penal Code* or s 83(2) of the *Criminal Code of Canada*, RSC 1985, which exempts particular sports (eg mixed martial arts) from the definition of 'prizefights' (and their consent prohibition).

60 For a review of the relevant offences commonly triggered by sports-related violence, see Angela Baxter, 'Hockey Violence: The Canadian Criminal Code and Professional Hockey' (2006) 31(2) *Man LJ* 281 (for Canadian offences); Christo Lassiter, 'Lex Sportiva: Thoughts Towards a Criminal Law of Competitive Contact Sport' (2007) 22(1) *St John's J Legal Comm* 35 (for coverage of applicable American offences); and Stefan Fafinski, 'Consent and the Rules of the Game: The interplay of civil and criminal liability for sporting injuries'. (2005) 29 *JCL* 414 and Jack Anderson, *The Legality of Boxing* (n 53), particularly Chapter 4 (for relevant UK offences).

61 Marianne Giles, '*R v Brown:* Consensual Harm and the Public Interest' (1994) 57(1) *MLR* 101, 108.

62 Edward A Harris, 'From Social Contract to Hypothetical Agreement: Consent and the Obligation to Obey the Law' (1992) 92 *Colum L Rev* 651, 660.

63 John A Simmons, 'Political Obligation and Consent' in Franklin Miller and Alan Wertheimer (eds), *The Ethics of Consent: Theory and Practice* (OUP 2009) 316.

64 As Miller has put it: '[V]alid consent in ordinary life is often implicit or tacit. We presume that competent adults will know what they are consenting to when they offer a token of unforced consent, absent deception, based on either common-sense understanding of how the world works or an expectation that it is up to them to undertake inquiry about whether what they consent to is in their interest', Franklin G Miller, 'Consent to Clinical Research' in Miller and Wertheimer (n 63) 380.

body language as a form of implied consent based on the circumstances in which it occurred.[65]

This is particularly prominent in the criminal law's regulation of sporting violence, given that the amount of force and risk of injury in most contact sports is sufficient to pass the threshold of assault or battery. Broken jaws and collarbones, separated shoulders, facial lacerations, and concussions are common in ice hockey, where body checking and stick or puck contact contribute to and escalate both the incidents and severity of in-game injuries.[66] This might explain the predominance of Canadian jurisprudence in the area of consent in sport, given the velocity, aggressive style of play, and average size of the players in both amateur and professional ice hockey games.[67] Echoing Lord Hale's early consideration of the mental element in assessing criminal liability, courts in every commonwealth jurisdiction have struggled with determinations of intent amidst the common threshold-meeting injuries in heavy contact sports. As one Canadian court put it in *Green* (1970), the first case in history to see criminal charges laid against a professional (NHL) player for an in-game fight:

> One now gets to the most difficult problem of all, in my opinion: since it is assumed and understood that there are numerous what would normally be called assaults in the course of a hockey game, but which are really not assaults because of the consent of the players in the type of game being played, where do you draw the line?[68]

The *Green* case concerned an altercation between Wayne Maki of the St. Louis Blues and Ted Green of the Boston Bruins. Both players were charged with assault following an on-ice fight, although neither case led to a conviction on

65 Emily Jackson offers the example of an outstretched arm offered to a nurse holding a needle. See Emily Jackson, *Medical Law: Text, Cases, and Materials* (OUP 2009) 219. This same circumstance was the subject of the 1891 American case, *O'Brien v Cunard Steamship Co*, where the charge of battery (for injuries sustained from a vaccination on a passenger ship) was unsuccessful following the court's determination that the passenger's outstretched arm constituted a valid form of (implied) consent: 154 Mass 272, 28 NE 266 (1891)

66 Markku Tuominen and others, 'Injuries in Men's International Ice Hockey: A 7-year Study of the International Ice Hockey Federation Adult World Championship Tournaments and Olympic Winter Games' (2015) 49 *Br J Sports Med* 30, which found body checking and stick/puck contact caused 60.7% of the injuries.

67 Although some might envision American football to be a more dangerous game given the larger (on average) size of its players, a 2003 study done by researchers at the neurosurgical unit of Toronto's St Michael's hospital found that '[d]irect fatality and injury rates for football are half those for hockey: 1.8 per 100 000 football players in high school and 7.0 per 100 000 in college. Nonfatal catastrophic spinal cord and brain injury rates are 2.6 per 100 000 hockey players and 0.7 per 100 000 football players among high school athletes'. See Anthony Marchie and Michael D Cusimano, 'Bodychecking and Concussions in Ice Hockey: Should our Youth Pay the Price?' (2003) 169(2) *CMAJ* 124. These rates would presumably increase (for both sports) in the professional realm.

68 *R v Green* (1970) 16 DLR (3d) 137 (Ont Prov Ct), 142. See also *R v Maki* (1970) 14 DLR (3d) 164 (Ont Prov Ct).

the basis that the incident was construed as 'part of the game'. When acquitting Green, the court stated:

> I think within our experience we can come to the conclusion that this is an extremely ordinary happening in a hockey game and the players really think nothing of it. If you go behind the net of a defenceman, particularly one who is trying to defend his zone, and you are struck in the face by that player's glove, a penalty might be called against him, but you do not really think anything of it; it is one of the types of risk one assumes.[69]

Five years later, a Manitoba court took judicial notice of the same difficulty in *Watson* (1975), a case involving a fight in a minor league hockey game:

> Hockey is a fast, vigorous, competitive game involving much body contact. Were the kind of body contact that routinely occurs in a hockey game to occur outside the playing area or on the street, it would, in most cases, constitute an assault to which the sanctions of the criminal law would apply. Patently when one engages in a hockey game, one accepts that some assaults which would otherwise be criminal will occur and consents to such assaults. It is equally patent, however, that to engage in a game of hockey is not to enter a forum to which the criminal law does not extend. To hold otherwise would be to create the hockey arena a sanctuary for unbridled violence to which the law of Parliament and the Queen's justice could not apply. I know of no authority for such a proposition.[70]

This rhetoric of acts and intentions which would otherwise be considered criminal being merely 'part of the game' has circulated in the legal treatment of sports violence for decades.[71] In some instances, it has been used to establish the reasonableness of the players' actions or, in others, to vitiate their intent.[72] This

69 *Green* (n 68) 140.

70 (1975) 26 CCC (2d) 150, [20]. Similar commentary can be found in the early English cases regarding the violent nature of football. For instance, Justice Hawkins in the 1898 case *Bradshaw* noted, 'Football is a lawful game, but a rough one, and persons who play it must be careful to restrain themselves so as not to do bodily harm to any other person': (n 48) 229. See also the judicial commentary in *Mayer* (1985), a Manitoba provincial court case involving a fight between the accused and another player in the course of a junior hockey game. The court remarked: 'It is not injury that determines the existence of the crime of assault in hockey games, but rather it is the act itself and the circumstances under which the act is performed which is determinative of the existence of a crime … Lack of serious injury is often more luck and good fortune than intent and in the case before me, it is not thanks to the accused that extremely serious injury did not result from his attack on the complainant', [1985] 41 Man R (2d) 73, [15].

71 American Courts have adopted the same view of violence as 'commonplace' in hockey. See *McKichan v St. Louis Hockey Club LP*, 967 SW 2d 209 (Mo Ct App 1998); and the commentary offered in Patricia K Thornton, 'Rewriting Hockey's Unwritten Rules: *Moore v Bertuzzi*' (2009) 61 *Me L Rev* 205, 214–215.

72 This was explicitly the case in *Green*, where the court held that the accused's act of swinging his stick at Maki was 'instinctive' and thus lacking in intent; see Note (n 46) 161.

contextual approach to consent in sport has been prominent in Canadian courts' treatment of in-game assaults and has been replicated in other commonwealth jurisdictions.[73] In the English Court of Appeal case *Barnes*,[74] the Court (somewhat contentiously, as some have argued)[75] suggested that the 'threshold level' for criminality in sporting contexts might not always be triggered by conduct that was 'outside the rules' nor even conduct that warranted 'being penalized ... a warning or even a sending off'.[76] *Barnes* referenced the 1989 Canadian case *Cey* in an attempt to identify an objective test for this criminal threshold.[77] In *Cey*, the accused cross-checked[78] his opponent into the boards during an amateur ice hockey game, resulting in a number of facial injuries. The Saskatchewan Court of Appeal established a set of factors to be considered when assessing the victim's implied consent, each aimed at aiding the court in determining whether the activity in question involved 'such a high risk of injury and such a distinct probability of serious harm as to be beyond what, in fact, the players commonly consent to, or what, in law, they are capable of consenting to'.[79] These factors represent a kind of modified objective test, given their inclusion of the victim's subjective state of mind as well as a series of other game-specific circumstances. The court in *Ciccarelli* phrased these as:

(a) The nature of the game played; whether amateur or professional league and so on;
(b) The nature of the particular act or acts and their surrounding circumstances;
(c) The degree of force employed;
(d) The degree of risk of injury;
(e) The state of mind of the accused.[80]

These principles provide some frame for interpreting the legal preconditions that are applied to consent, namely: knowledge, reasonableness, and voluntariness.

73 American Courts have limited implied consent to sporting violence to those injuries that are 'reasonably foreseeable' as part of playing the game – akin to the Canadian use of a player's 'reasonable expectations of play'.
74 *R v Barnes* [2005] 1 Cr App Rep 507.
75 Anderson, 'No Licence for Thuggery' (n 51).
76 *Barnes* (n 74) [15].
77 *R v Cey* (1989) 48 CCC 3d 480 (Sask CA).
78 'Cross-checking' is defined in the National Hockey League's Rulebook as 'The action of using the shaft of the stick between the two hands to forcefully check an opponent' (Rule 59.1, NHL Official Ice Hockey Rules) <www.nhl.com/ice/page.htm?id=26351> accessed 28 January 2019. A 'check' is a defensive move employed to disrupt an opposing player's possession of the puck.
79 *Cey* (n 77) [31]. Interesting in the court's analysis is the conflation of consenting *capacity* with concerns about law's legitimacy. This points to how the law's requirements about who *can* consent are situated within a context of state interests (in shaping the bodies and activities of the citizenry) rather than individualised abilities or rights.
80 *Ciccarelli* (n 16) 126. When the court applied these factors in Ciccarelli's case (one involving an on-ice assault during a professional hockey game), the accused was found guilty, sentenced to one day in jail, and fined $1,000.

The criminal law's defence of consent has long recognised a person's free will in consenting to particular activities; however, to be considered valid, consent must be given voluntarily. As noted in Chapter 1, this level of volition is assessed in conjunction with what a reasonable person can be considered to have done with the knowledge she had at the time. English courts have adopted this Canadian standard where, as Lord Mustill put it in *Brown* (1993), 'some level of violence is lawful if the recipient agrees to it ... enquiring whether the recipient could really have tacitly accepted a risk of violence at the level which actually occurred'.[81] This approach is not meant to override considerations of duress, where both force and threats of force will be regarded as sufficient to vitiate consent.[82] Nor is it meant to remove the possibility of findings of recklessness or wilful blindness – both of which would serve to negate a player's 'reasonable expectations'.[83] Instead, these findings represent negations of consent's central components (ie knowledge, voluntariness, and reason). Consent operates when players can be shown to have known what the risks of injury were and voluntarily chose to engage in the activity for a 'good reason'. As the NHL stated in their response to the class action lawsuit filed by former players: 'Publicly available information related to concussions and their long-term effects, coupled with the events that had transpired – that is, the players incurring head injuries – should have allowed (players) to put two and two together'.[84]

How then to determine what players knew or ought to have known when participating in the sport? David Archard uses 'game' language explicitly when addressing this question in the broader context of consent's operative scope noting that

> the simplest and most plausible model [of consent] is that of 'playing by the rules of the game'. If I take part in an activity which is constituted by some set of rules, then I may be taken as agreeing to abide by those rules. More generally, I may be taken as agreeing to accept what, normally and reasonably, may be expected to follow from taking part in this rule-governed behaviour.[85]

81 *Brown* (n 27) 592H-593D as cited in Law Commission (UK), *Consent and Offences against the Person* (Law Com No. 134, 1994) 21.

82 See, for instance, the Canadian sexual assault case *R v Martin* (1980) 53 CCC (2d) 250, where the court maintained 'the line between using force to overcome a woman and using a serious threat to prevent her from offering resistance is too fine to be the basis of a legal distinction' (256). This position has been widely accepted in English law as establishing consent as vitiated by duress. See UK Law Comm Paper (n 81) 52.

83 See *R v McSorley* [2000] BCPC 117, where the Crown argued that if McSorley had not deliberately struck the victim in the head he had been reckless as to the danger of doing so. The court noted, 'Recklessness in this case may be likened to wilful blindness - ignoring a known risk' [60].

84 Defendant (NHL)'s Memorandum of Law, *In Re NHL* (n 15) 26.

85 David Archard, *Sexual Consent* (Westview Press 1998) 8.

But what about in-game violence that *does* deviate from the rules? Instances of 'fighting' in sports presents an interesting case study for examining the law's definition of 'reasonable' violence.

Foul play: Fighting in sports

> [T]he nature of any assault offence imports the notion of violence, and violence certainly is not something that is countenanced in the Canadian society.
>
> – *R v Bertuzzi*[86]

> I went to a fight last night and a hockey game broke out.
>
> – common Canadian joke[87]

When assessing what injuries are reasonably foreseeable risks of playing a game, it is common to see courts take judicial notice of not only the official rules of the sport but also the 'playing culture' of the game, which might include unwritten codes of conduct and player customs.[88] Many Canadian cases have explicitly recognised that the physical nature of most contact sports will involve a certain degree of 'routine body contact'[89] and that a player's participation in the activity will be held to represent an implied consent to this bodily contact as well as other acts of aggression or violence which can be deemed to be 'closely related to the play'.[90] In many cases, this includes physical altercations between players. In the Canadian case *Leyte* (1973), the accused had knocked the victim into a wall and then hit him twice with his fists during a game of handball. Acquitting the accused of assault charges, the court noted that the 'competitive' nature of the sport should have left the victim aware that he 'may be hit in one of many ways and must be deemed to consent thereto so long as the reactions of the players are instinctive and closely related to the play and whether or not a foul is being committed'.[91]

Identifying 'unwritten' players' codes with respect to fighting in sports has proven to be a complex matter, demonstrated by two high-profile Canadian cases involving on-ice fights in NHL hockey games, *R v McSorley*[92] and *R v Bertuzzi*.[93] Marty McSorley was charged with assault with a weapon after having

86 *R v Bertuzzi*, 2004 BCPC 472 (CanLII) [3].
87 John Branch attributes a version of this joke to comedian Rodney Dangerfield who 'famously said that he went to a boxing match and a hockey game broke out' in *Boy on Ice* (n 2) 55.
88 *Cey* (n 77). See also David Archard, '"A Nod's as Good as a Wink": Consent, Convention, and Reasonable Belief' (1997) 2 *LEG* 273.
89 *Watson* (n 70).
90 *R v Leyte* [1973] 13 CCC (2d) 458 (ON Prov Ct).
91 *Leyte* (n 90) 459.
92 *McSorley* (n 83).
93 *Bertuzzi* (n 86).

'slashed' an opposing player, Donald Brashear, with his hockey stick.[94] Brashear fell to the ice, suffered a seizure, and lost consciousness, suffering from a grade 3 concussion.[95] In finding McSorley guilty, the trial judge took notice of the discrepancies presented at trial between the official position taken by the NHL (as per the Rulebook) that slashing was an illegal act in hockey subject to penalty and the position taken by McSorley and other players who submitted evidence that slashing was an accepted means of starting a fight – another illegal yet unwritten component to hockey. The trial judge stated:

> [T]hose written rules are only part of the picture. There is also an unwritten code of conduct, agreed to by the players and officials, that is superimposed on the written rules. This code of conduct deals mainly with situations where the written rules are breached, and the code then comes into play. For example, the written rules prohibit slashing with the stick, but the unwritten code says that slashing is permissible as long as it is during play, and not to the head … Another example deals with fighting.[96]

Fighting, although officially an illegal component to the game of professional ice hockey, is the subject of 22 rules in the NHL's Rulebook which examine and delineate various acts of on-ice aggression into the minutia.[97] Similarly, as Patrick Thornton observed, '[t]he word "enforcer" or "hockey goon" does not appear in the … National Hockey League (NHL) rulebook. However, every player and coach knows the meaning of those words'.[98] The court in *McSorley* took note of the accused's frankness with respect to his role in the game, observing that '[i]t was his job to fire up the team, and he did so by fighting

94 'Slashing', according to the National Hockey League's (NHL) Official rulebook (2018–2019), is 'the act of a player swinging his stick at an opponent, whether contact is made or not'. The rulebook goes on to exempt 'non-aggressive stick contact to the pant or front of the shin pads' from penalty but asserts that any 'forceful or powerful chop with the stick on an opponent's body, the opponent's stick, or on or near the opponent's hands that, in the judgment of the Referee, is not an attempt to play the puck, shall be penalized as slashing' (n 78) Rule 61.1.

95 *McSorley* (n 83) [59].

96 *McSorley* (n 83) [18]–[19].

97 See Rules 46.1–46.22 in NHL Rulebook (n 78). Examples include dictations on which players drop their gloves first (46.11) or demonstrate a 'menacing attitude or posture' (46.11) as well as the removal of jerseys or penalties for not having a jersey 'tied down' during a fight (46.13).

98 Thornton (n 71) 206. Enforcers are players who are big, powerful, and adept at fighting but who are often critiqued for not being particularly skilled hockey players (although some distinction is made between enforcers and the even less-skilled category of 'goons'). Take, for instance, well-known 'tough guy' Derek Boogaard, who, over six seasons in the NHL, totalling 277 games, accrued 589 penalty minutes and took part in 174 fights but scored only three goals in his entire professional career. The role of the enforcer on a team is to protect lead scorers, intimidate opposing players and teams, and engage in on-ice fights when needed (to bolster team pride or retaliate for past attacks on key players). Some scholars refer to these players as 'private rule enforcers', alluding to their role in maintaining the unwritten code of violence and aggression that operates in hockey.

Brashear - obviously a formidable undertaking by which the other players should have been inspired'.[99] McSorley's claims of being an 'enforcer' on the team were not backed up at trial by his coach or officials of the NHL, all of whom argued that fighting – and fighters – were not a sanctioned or official part of hockey. McSorley was convicted of assault, suspended for the remainder of the season and one additional year, and never played in another NHL game again.

Four years later, a similar incident occurred during a game between the Vancouver Canucks and the Colorado Avalanche when Vancouver's Todd Bertuzzi punched Colorado's Steve Moore in the head from behind. Moore fell to the ice immediately and suffered fractures to two vertebrae, some facial lacerations, and a concussion.[100] Bertuzzi maintained that he had been instructed to engage Moore in a fight in retaliation for a hit the Canucks' star player had received from Moore in an earlier game,[101] yet similar to the *McSorley* case, 'hockey's unwritten rule dealing with enforcers and hockey's code of retaliation' was not recognised by the NHL.[102] Rather, Bertuzzi's team was fined $250,000 by League, and its commissioner, Gary Bettman, announced on an international sports television broadcast: 'The message we're sending is that this is not part of our game, it has no place in our game and it will not be tolerated in our game'.[103] The court in *McSorley* remarked on the ambiguity this creates for players:

> So the rules of the NHL game of hockey consist of the written rules in the rulebook, a coexisting unwritten code of conduct impliedly agreed to by

99 *McSorley* (n 83) [84]. The court goes further than this, observing that McSorley was ordered out onto the ice with only twenty seconds left in the game with specific instructions to fight. 'There was no line change - he was the only player sent out. From his experience, and knowing his role on the team, this was a clear message to him to go out and finish things with Brashear' [86].

100 *Bertuzzi* (n 86) [21].

101 Thornton (n 71) includes an excerpt from Bertuzzi's deposition in support of this view (at 211):

Q. And as I understand in the dressing room there's a board and it has the roster of the opposing team, it has all their names and numbers?
A. Yes there is.
Q. And by, when you say pointing, pointing at my client on the board, that he's actually pointing to Steve Moore, number 36?
A. Yes he was.
Q. All right, and can you tell me what his tone of voice was when he said it?
A. He wasn't obviously very happy, I think he was pissed off at everything that was going on to begin with. So obviously he was pretty angry.
Q. All right, and did that play a role in your decision to go after Steve Moore in the third period?
A. I think it influenced him being challenged by a lot of players yes.

102 Thornton observes that '[l]eading up to the match, several Canucks made statements to the effect that they would retaliate against Moore. In fact, the threats became so well known that NHL Commissioner Gary Bettman and Executive VP and Director of NHL Hockey Operations, Colin Campbell, attended the game' (n 71) 211.

103 Rick Westhead, 'Bertuzzi Suspended for Season and Playoffs' *New York Times* (New York, 12 March 2004) D1 as cited in Thornton (n 71) 208. Bettman has, however, publicly acknowledged fighting as part of the game in other places, see Thornton (n 71) 216. This paradox has not gone

> the players and officials, and guidelines laid down by the officials from game to game. It is within this somewhat indefinite framework that players must play the game.[104]

These cases reveal that the task of determining the parameters of what is 'reasonable' or 'normal' in sporting violence is both daunting and ripe for normative bias. Similarly, the various tests and factors used by the courts to establish the bounds of 'reasonable violence' do not work to remove what appears to be an over-riding principle of public policy considerations within the jurisprudence. As noted by the UK Law Commission in its 1994 Report on Consent:

> The law clearly reserves the right to say that some activities do not qualify for special exemption at all; just as it reserves the right to say that, within a lawful sport, public policy requires that injury caused by some of the sport's practices, even though accepted by the injured player, should be dealt with as criminal in nature.[105]

The bodily contact incurred in physically demanding and fast-paced sports such as ice hockey, rugby, and (American) football is more than sufficient to meet the harm threshold for criminal liability – even when it is played within the confines of the game's rules. In some instances, the mental state of the players could also satisfy criminal intent requirements, particularly when the view of fighting as 'part of the game' is considered. Former NHL player and federal member of Canada's parliament Ken Dryden has noted that aggressive intent is an included characteristic of the game:

> What is the possible intent of hitting someone into the boards from behind, except to injure? There is no other understanding. The same for a hit to the head. You can stop someone dead in his tracks with a hit to the shoulder or hip. The only reason to hit someone on the head is to hurt him. Even if you say, 'Well, I didn't want to really hurt him', you wanted to shake him up, put him off his game, intimidate him, just not put him in hospital. But the intent to injure is there.[106]

---

unnoticed by sports commentators. As Michael Farber notes, 'The sickening irony is this: If before the mugging Moore had chosen simply to turn and fight Bertuzzi, who had been stalking Moore, tugging on his jersey and goading him throughout the third period of a lopsided game, Moore wouldn't have ended up face-first in a pool of his own blood with two broken vertebrae in his neck and a concussion. The two players could have pounded on each other for a while, and the world would have paid no notice. Because in the National Hockey League there is acceptable violence and unacceptable violence, a distinction that makes sense in the skewed, internal logic of the sport but is inexplicable to almost everyone outside the game's cocoon', Michael Farber, 'Code Red' (*Sports Illustrated*, 22 March 2004) <www.si.com/nhl/2014/08/19/si-vault-code-red-todd-bertuzzi-steve-moore-attack-nhl-violence> accessed 28 January 2019.

104 *McSorley* (n 83) [24].

105 UK Law Comm Paper (n 81) 22–23.

106 Ken Dryden, 'Saving the Game' *Globe & Mail* (27 March 2004) A19. Intent is what seals the conviction in *McSorley*. The court concludes its judgment with a comment on the accused's state

Former NFL linebacker Ray Lewis has made similar observations about the intention underlying players' actions in the hard-hitting sport of football and makes a direct link to players' assumptions of risk and the impact this can have on the consent to play:

> When you get that type of hit on a player, trust me, the game is not the same after that – and the player is not the same, either. That player is going to ask himself, Will I pay the price? Do I really want to get hit that hard again? And that's what the game is about. The long runs, the touchdowns and all that, that's the glamour. But the game is about taking a man down, physically and mentally.[107]

Still, the definition of these acts as 'harmful' depends on a judicial consideration of public policy in addition to the perceived reasonableness of player expectations. How do these inform one another? Is public policy always reasonable? The jurisprudence in the area of sport and play provides an interesting case study for these inquiries. The court in the *McSorley* case declared some injuries too 'perverse' to be eligible for consent, stating 'there are some actions which can take place in the course of a sporting conflict that are so violent it would be perverse to find that anyone taking part in a sporting activity had impliedly consented to subject himself to them'.[108] Yet despite the explicit recognition of in-game fighting among players and commentators of hockey, the courts have not always found such instances to fall within the reasonable expectations of play, but nor have they equated in-game violence with the social disutility of fist-fighting (as was done in the barroom brawl case *Jobidon*).[109] Something about violence in sport must be of 'use' to the state.

In some of its earliest articulations, the rejection of the defence of consent to self-inflicted bodily harm reflected foundations of political liberalism where state legitimacy was grounded in the consent of its political subjects. Liberty was a sacred principle such that a person could consent to anything other than severing one's own limb(s).[110] Blackstone's *Commentaries on the Laws of England* explains

---

of mind: 'He had an impulse to strike him in the head. His mindset, always tuned to aggression, permitted that. He slashed for the head … An NHL player would never, ever miss. Brashear was struck as intended. Mr. McSorley, I must find you guilty as charged', *McSorley* (n 83) [108]–[109].

107 Tim Layden, 'The Big Hit' (*Sports Illustrated*, 30 July 2007), <www.si.com/vault/2007/07/30/100157949/the-big-hit> accessed 28 January 2019.

108 *McSorley* (n 83) [70]. This was the same terminology employed by the House of Lords in *Brown* when dismissing the possibility of consent. See Lord Lowry's judgment: 'What the appellants are obliged to propose is that the deliberate and painful infliction of physical injury should be exempted from the operation of statutory provisions the object of which is to prevent or punish that very thing, the reason for the proposed exemption being that both those who will inflict and those who will suffer the injury wish to satisfy a perverted and depraved sexual desire', *Brown* (n 27) 99.

109 *Jobidon* (n 56).

110 Studies of the legal limits of extreme body modification practices (eg scarification, tongue-splitting) and elective amputations provide interesting contexts for thinking about contemporary examples of this principle. See Rachel Clement, 'Consent to Body Modification in Criminal Law' (2018) 77(3) *CLJ* 451; Daniel Bansal, 'Bodily Modifications and the Criminal

this was to prevent deprivation to 'the king of the aid and assistance of one of his subjects'.[111] Might contemporary public policy discourse within the case law be achieving the same end? Judicial treatments of consent in cases involving voluntary self-harm have emphasised the general principle that interference with individual liberty is justified only where a strong reason to do so exists, invoking language of the 'common good' or public interests to construct the content of this reason. How is the state's interest in producing and maintaining eligible subjects serviced by these configurations of 'harm'? What is 'reasonable' about sporting violence? The following sections explore these questions, reviewing the relationship between contact sports, ideals of masculinity, and the use of body capital.

'No sissy stuff': harm and hegemonic masculinity in sport

Sport has long been recognised as a ground where cultural norms take root, where 'civilization arises and unfolds in and as play'.[112] This is, perhaps predictably, not a value-neutral process. A glance at other dominant social ethos (Michael Oriard offers the examples of 'mass culture' or 'consumer culture') suggest ways that these are 'rooted in conspicuous playfulness of a kind that Huizinga considered not truly playful at all'.[113] Rather, they provide a structure or schematisation for human relations – a frame for interpreting (and prescribing) specific subjectivities and their ontologies. 'Norms articulate knowledge and power, cognitive and normative expectations, and this articulation is reflexive; normative expectations make the world visible in a particular way'.[114] Histories of play detail how it can be used to discipline social relations or alter cultural assumptions.[115] Fundamentally understood as an activity that is 'not serious' and immersed in the realm of the imaginary, play can be posited as outside of or apart from 'reality'. This allows it to be understood as timeless, ahistorical, and apolitical – traits which also make it easy to position sport and play as objective and authoritative about social life. Play is able to assume a presocial status, fortifying it against critique – it is simply 'natural' or 'always been this way'.[116] In this way, play and its organisational structure

Law' (2018) 82(6) *JCL* 496; Theodore Bennett, 'It's But a Flesh Wound: Criminal Law and the Conceptualisation of Healthy Limb Amputation' (2011) 36(3) *Alt LJ* 158.

111 *Wright's Case* (Leicester Assizes 1604) reported in Joseph Henry Beale, *Cases on Criminal Law* (3rd edn, Harvard Law Review Publishing Assn 1915) 209 as cited in Richard L Binder, 'Consent Defense: Sports, Violence, and the Criminal Law' (1976) 13(2) *Am Crim L Rev* 235, 236.

112 Johan Huizinga, *Homo Ludens: A Study of the Play-Element in Culture* (Beacon Press 1950), ix.

113 Michael Oriard, *Sporting with the Gods: The Rhetoric of Play and Game in American Culture* (CUP 1991), x.

114 Alain Pottage, 'Foucault's Law by Ben Golder and Peter Fitzpatrick (Review)' (2011) 74 *MLR* 159, 160.

115 Michael Thomson notes how modern sporting beliefs can be traced to the public school system of nineteenth-century England, where 'folk games were sequestered and transformed by a ruling-class ethos that demanded order and standardization'; (n 28) 129.

116 Judith Butler has cautioned that the 'invocation of a nonhistorical 'before' becomes the foundational premise that guarantees a presocial ontology of persons' in *Gender Trouble: Feminism and the Subversion of Identity* (10th ann edn, Routledge 1999) 5.

of human roles and relations becomes common sense.[117] These assumptions, in turn, inform judicial interpretations of the 'reasonable expectations' players of a game might have about its inherent risks and acceptable levels of harm – key components to the availability of the defence of consent.

Perhaps one of the most prevalent components of this 'common sense' is a prescriptive form of masculinity. Sport and play have long been recognised as formative places for the development and entrenchment of gender schematics.[118] Working from Judith Butler's formulation of gender as a performance, sex roles are understood not to be stable signifiers of a particular way of being but rather 'repeated stylization[s] of the body … within a highly rigid regulatory frame that congeal over time to produce the appearance of substance'.[119] Certainly, the organisation of play into modern sport meets the requirement of just such a frame of social (and ontological) regulation. In particular, sport's contributions to cultural understandings of masculinity have served as an operative means of privileging some subjects while excluding others. As some scholars have remarked, 'sport has been one of the most significant means by which gender boundaries have been marked'.[120] Michael Thomson employs the example of the Victorian period's public school system to highlight how values of aggression, competitiveness, order, and discipline were pitted as ideals of masculinity through the introduction of organised sport in the curriculum. He notes how sex segregation in recreational activities among students produced 'natural' traits and skills that 'firmly secure[d] the feminine within the sphere of the home and of reproduction. Her physical frailty and weakness left her unfit for challenging exercise and the rigors of sport. The competitive public arena was naturally the world of men'.[121] Christine Skelton, remarking on the same period, notes how football was viewed (by the capitalist class) as 'beneficial' to working-class men as it kept them 'away from the pubs after collecting their wages Saturday lunchtime'.[122] Other scholars have suggested that the incorporation of football in physical education curriculum at the public school level served as a 'political strategy to teach upper and middle class males to be leaders and to induce discipline in working class males'.[123]

117 Thomson, remarking on the Victorian education system and its standardisation of play into school sport, suggests that '[t]he Victorians translated these learnt understandings of what sport meant into common sense cultural assumptions' (n 28) 120.

118 Huizinga does note a difference between 'sport' and 'play' (or 'games') that reflects the former's relation to capitalist interests, see Huizinga (n 112) 222–223. This idea is further explored in this chapter's third section, 'Capitalism with the Gloves Off'.

119 Butler (n 116) 43–44.

120 David Rowe, Jim McKay and Toby Miller, 'Panic Sport and the Racialized Masculine Body' in Jim McKay, Michael A Messner and Donald Sabo (eds), *Masculinities, Gender Relations, and Sport* (Sage 2000) 249.

121 Thomson (n 28) 129.

122 Christine Skelton, '"A Passion for Football": Dominant Masculinities and Primary Schooling' (2000) 5(1) *Sport Educ Soc* 5.

123 Skelton (n 122) 7, referring to Sara Delamont, *Sex Roles and the School* (Routledge 1980); and Christine Heward, *Making a Man of Him* (Routledge 1988).

The encouragement of young boys to participate in sport, while young girls are expected to take up more passive activities didn't end with the Victorian era, as many scholars of sex segregation in education and athletics maintain.[124] In addition to the explicit division between male and female roles in modern sport, studies of both sport participation and the 'business' of sport (including its televised coverage and the professional careers it offers) continue to be male-dominated regimes.[125] Masculinities scholar Michael Kimmel has remarked on this, noting that '[s]ports has become both metaphor and reality of American masculinity – its language dominates other discourses as metaphor, while sports have become increasingly important among young boys as the arena of demonstration and proof'.[126]

This postulation of the sports arena as a 'proving ground' for young men has an extraneous effect of establishing particular traits of male superiority for both on and off the field.[127] These cultural accounts of gender can adhere to produce behavioural codes which dictate not simply how one should act but effectively who one is.[128] This is the normative quality of masculinity definitions which offer a standard of what men *ought* to be, often with reliance on essentialist understandings of sex roles and differences. These traits, in turn, inform judicial assessments of the kinds of activities that can be considered 'rational' or desirable for men to engage in, which, in turn, serve to establish the limits of the consent defence in sports violence cases. Perhaps more insidious, however, is the role the consent-as-autonomy story plays in cementing this idealised subjectivity. Connell's theory of hegemonic masculinity maintains that not all masculinities are equally practiced, valued, or even available.[129] Instead, it is hegemonic masculinity that is 'the pattern of masculinity which is most honoured, which is most associated with authority and power, and which – in the long run – guarantees the collective privilege of men'.[130] When assessing the 'reasonableness' of harm incurred during a sporting activity, courts will often rely on these idealised traits of 'manliness' when determining that a player's choice to subject himself to in-game violence is not simply a rational exercise of his autonomy but a culturally desirable one.

124 See David S Cohen, 'No Boy Left Behind? Single-Sex Education and the Essentialist Myth of Masculinity' (2009) 84 *Ind LJ* 135; and also David S Cohen, 'Keeping Men "Men" and Women Down: Sex Segregation, Anti-Essentialism, and Masculinity' (2010) 33 *Harv J Law & Gen* 509; and Raewyn Connell, 'Masculinity Construction and Sports in Boys' Education: A Framework for Thinking about the Issue' (2008) 13(2) *Sport Educ Soc* 131.

125 See, for example, Michael A Messner, Michele Dunbar, and Darnell Hunt, 'The Televised Sports Manhood Formula' (2000) 24(4) *J Sport Soc Iss* 380.

126 Michael Kimmel, 'Foreword' in McKay, Messner and Sabo (n 120) xiii.

127 Thomson (n 28).

128 Raewyn Connell, *Masculinities* (Polity Press 1995).

129 This is akin to the claim made by Jill Weinberg in her book *Consensual Violence*, that 'not all consent is created equal and not all consent is viewed as equal' (n 31) 5.

130 Connell, *Masculinities* (n 128) 133.

One of the dominant examples of these normative frameworks of masculinity was provided in Robert Brannon's oft-cited 'blueprint of manhood' wherein he offers a four-fold typology of idealised male roles, each of which can be actively seen in sport, particularly the culture of high-contact sports.[131] Brannon's criterion of 'no sissy stuff' is sometimes cited as the 'first and foremost' principle of idealised masculinity.[132] It demands the rejection of all things 'feminine', where femininity is understood to be indicative of weakness, passivity, and emotional sensitivity.[133] Men must not resemble women in their appearance or emotive responses, thus giving minimal attention to hygiene, body work, and physical attire.[134] By way of contrast, Sandra Bartky has remarked on the notion of idealised femininity that is at work in appearance norms for women. She notes that a 'woman's skin must be soft, supple, hairless, and smooth; ideally, it should betray no sign of wear, experience, age, or deep thought'.[135] Hegemonic masculinity requires the adoption of an opposite aesthetic, where physical 'wear and tear' is heralded as the mark of a 'real man'. This conforms to Brannon's criterion that 'real men' engage in an ethos of 'give 'em hell', exalting hostility and risk-taking. Men are expected to 'exude an aura of manly daring and aggression' while aiming for power, thrills, and success ('the big wheel') which is often measured in capitalist terms.[136] Moreover, men are expected to do this as 'a sturdy oak', showing little to no emotions, specifically vulnerability.

Many scholars have noted the ill effects each of these ideals can have on men's health, creating normative pressure to conceal illness, refrain from discussing symptoms, and refuse medical advice or treatment.[137] In some instances, the

131 Robert Brannon, 'The Male Sex Role: Our Culture's Blueprint for Manhood, What It's Done For Us Lately' in Deborah Sarah David and Robert Brannon (eds), *The Forty-Nine Percent Majority: The Male Sex Role* (Addison-Wesley 1976).

132 Michael Kimmel, 'Issues for Men in the 1990s' (1992) 46 *U Miami L Rev* 671, 674.

133 Sadly, while Brannon's framework is more than forty years old, ample evidence exists to suggest that these notions of hegemonic masculinity continue to find an audience. A 2011 commentary by *National Post* columnist Christie Blatchford entitled 'Where Have All the Manly Men Gone? Toronto, City of Sissies' laments the 'male as delicate creature' after witnessing a group of 10–12-year-old boys greeting one another with (gasp!) hugs. She explicitly links this deficiency in masculinity to a lack of sporting prowess, suggesting 'Toronto likes its men delicate, slender and arch, not sportif unless le sport in question is maybe badminton' (10 December 2011) A29.

134 Sandra Bartky's work links (women's) appearance work to a Foucauldian conception of discipline to suggest ways in which regimes of diet, exercise, and beautification produce 'docile bodies'. Arguably, these standards (when coupled with normative definitions of masculinity) have the same disciplinary effect on men. See Sandra Lee Bartky, *Femininity and Domination: Studies in the Phenomenology of Oppression* (Routledge 1990).

135 Bartky (n 134) 98.

136 Michael Kimmel describes 'the big wheel' ideal as 'he who has the most toys when he dies, wins'. See Kimmel, 'Issues for Men' (n 132) 674.

137 See, for example, Will H Courtenay, 'Constructions of Masculinity and Their Influence on Men's Well-Being: A Theory of Gender and Health' (2000) 50(10) *Soc Sci Med* 1385.

demand for player toughness and the presumption that professional athletes will 'play through the pain' have been the basis for claims of civil negligence, demonstrating how idealised masculinity informs judicial understandings of 'reasonableness' in sport contexts.[138] In the English case *Brady v Sunderland Association Football Club Ltd*,[139] the plaintiff was a professional footballer who was playing for the defendant club when he suffered a career-ending injury during a game. Brady claimed that the football club had been negligent in failing to address his complaints of pain, which resulted in inadequate treatment for the injury. The Court of Appeal dismissed the claim, finding that the club's assumption (that Brady's injuries were not as serious as he made out) was reasonable, particularly in light of the rarity of the plaintiff's condition and the inconsistency with which the player complained about the pain. This finding was reached despite the Queen's Bench Division decision explicitly acknowledging evidence that when the player complained of pain, he was admonished by his coach for having a 'bad attitude' and demonstrating a poor work ethic. Brady described this in his witness statement as follows:

> [The coach] was telling me that I had an attitude problem and in particular in relation to training. I didn't really realise there was something physically wrong. I just wasn't able to keep up all the time. From time to time I would try and explain to him in training sessions why I was unable to keep up but he did not want to listen and told me it was to do with my attitude. Over the following month his opinion about my attitude seemed to harden … He told me that he wasn't going to put up with any more nonsense. He told me that I couldn't stop and to keep going. He then sent the other players off in a different direction and he ran with me along the coast lecturing me about my attitude and telling me I just didn't like hard work.[140]

The 'reasonableness' of playing while injured is informed by these cultural assumptions about masculinity as well as the economic frame within which players' decisions to 'play through the pain' are made. Professional athletes are applauded by sports media and made more valuable to the team when they can sustain injuries without losing game time.[141] Player accounts often point to the coercive context in which their returns to the game are made. Clint Malarchuk, a former NHL goalie, famously suffered a near-fatal injury during a game when

138 For an examination of how violent 'horseplay' is constructed as natural (and idealised) masculine behaviour within labour arbitration discourse, see Joan Sangster, 'Just Horseplay? Masculinity and Workplace Grievances in Fordist Canada, 1947–70s' (2014) 26 *CJWL* 330.

139 [1998] EWCA Civ 1780.

140 [1998] QBD 2 April 1998 (transcript), citing from plaintiff's witness statement [11].

141 See Paul McCoun, 'The 10 Greatest Examples of Hockey Tough' (*Bleacher Report*, 12 January 2010) <https://bleacherreport.com/articles/324477-the-10-greatest-examples-of-hockey-tough#slide7> accessed 28 January 2019, where numerous players are commended for returning to play after sustaining serious injuries.

his carotid artery was sliced by an opposing player's skate blade.[142] He lost 1.5 litres of blood, received more than 300 stitches, and returned to play a game ten days later. Hegemonic masculinity looms large in Malarchuk's account of the roots of his 'toughness', but so, too, does the game's economic context:

> Throughout my career, I was always paranoid about missing games because of an injury. It took a lot to keep me out. I often played hurt. Look at the picture of me clutching my neck when my jugular got cut, and you'll see I had a cast on my hand. I was playing with a broken thumb. My dad taught me to fight, but my mom made me tough. *Be tough, be tough.* The first time I remember getting hurt in a hockey game was when I was eight ... I writhed around on the ice, gasping for air ... That was exactly what she said to me. 'You want to lie there and get attention? Or do you want to be a man and skate to the box?' ... I carried that with me throughout my career. If I went down, I didn't stay down. I tried to play through every injury, and if I couldn't, I came back as fast as humanly possible. I took pride in that for a long time. But most of that was rooted in fear. Any honest player will tell you that. A fear of losing your job, of being traded or going unsigned. Or of some damn rookie coming in and taking your job. So you bite the bullet and play hurt.[143]

A further (and often most prominent) component of hegemonic masculinity is compulsive heterosexuality, denoted most often by an explicit rejection of homosexuality. Similar to the proscription against 'sissy stuff', idealised masculinity often asserts itself through homophobia and the characterisation of non-conforming males as gay.[144] Kimmel, in his research on this issue, cites an interview with rap musician Eminem to illustrate the social authority of hegemonic masculinity's heterosexist script:

> The lowest degrading thing that you can say to a man ... is to call him a faggot and try to take away his manhood. Call him a sissy. Call him a punk. 'Faggot' to me doesn't necessarily mean gay people. 'Faggot' to me just means taking away your manhood.[145]

142 In a chilling account of the incident, Malarchuk provides a graphic depiction of how 'the game must go on' when he describes riding by ambulance as his replacement 'stood in the dark red crease and crouched as the puck dropped ... He played in a pool of my blood', Clint Malarchuk and Dan Robson, *A Matter of Inches: How I Survived the Crease and Beyond* (Triumph 2014) 87.

143 Malarchuk (n 142) 100.

144 See Michael Kimmel 'Masculinity as Homophobia: Fear, Shame, and Silence in the Construction of Gender Identity' in Nancy Cook (ed), *Gender Relations in Global Perspective: Essential Readings* (Canadian Scholars Press 2007).

145 Richard Kim, 'Eminem – Bad Rap?' (*The Nation*, 5 March 2011) 5 as cited by Michael Kimmel and Matthew Mahler, 'Adolescent Masculinity, Homophobia, and Violence: Random School Shootings, 1982–2001' (2003) 46 *Am Behav Sci* 1439, 1445–1446.

This practice is prominent in sports rhetoric among both players and commentators. The requirement within hegemonic masculinity that men 'give 'em hell' has led some masculinities scholars to suggest that '[v]iolence is the single most evident marker of manhood'.[146] The use of the moniker 'Cindy' among online critics to describe professional hockey player Sidney Crosby when observations about his playing style and behaviour failed to conform to the 'tough guy' ideal of masculinity serves as a good example.[147] After Crosby (a player who is widely recognised as one of the top players in the league)[148] suffered a severe concussion following hits to the head in back-to-back games during the 2010–2011 season, he was removed from the playing roster for over ten months, prompting remarks that he was a 'wimp' who was failing to 'man up'.[149] Similarly, identical Swedish twins Henrik and Daniel Sedin, who both play ice hockey for the Vancouver Canucks, were labelled the 'Sedin Sisters' by sports media and opposing players for failing to initiate physical contact with players on the ice.[150] North America's recent debate about the role of fighting in ice hockey has also sparked rhetoric that reinforces these idealised notions of maleness where 'good' players are expected to take risks, not shy away from on-ice violence, and 'play through the pain'. This attitude is well evidenced in CBC sports commentator Mike Milbury's (offensive) lament in 2009 that

146 Kimmel, 'Masculinity as Homophobia' (n 144) 215.

147 Allain observes that these comments often alleged that Crosby was a 'whiner', noting that '[d]uring the 2008/09 playoffs, The *Ottawa Citizen* directed their readers to a "sign in the arena (that) said: I Whine Less Than Crosby, held by a baby"', Kristi A Allain, 'Kid Crosby or Golden Boy: Sidney Crosby, Canadian National Identity, and the Policing of Hockey Masculinity' (2011) 46 *Int Rev Soci Sport* 3, 15.

148 Wayne Gretkzy himself opined (during Crosby's years in the amateur leagues) that he expected Sidney could break his playing records, adding that he was the best player Gretzky had known since Mario Lemieux. See Gare Joyce, *Sidney Crosby: Taking the Game by Storm* (Fitzhenry & Whiteside 2005).

149 See 'Sidney Crosby out Indefinitely Again with Concussion Symptoms' (*Ohio Valley Athletics*, 12 December 2011) <www.ovathletics.com/home/sidney-crosby-out-indefinately-again-with-concussion-symptoms/9254> accessed 28 January 2019.

150 Pierre LeBrun, 'Surprised by Sedin? You shouldn't be' (*ESPN NHL*, 3 February 2010) <http://sports.espn.go.com/nhl/columns/story?columnist=lebrun_pierre&id=4883674> 28 January 2019; Adam L Jahns, 'Dave Bolland Calls Sedin Brothers "Sisters"' *Chicago Sun-Times* (Vancouver, 14 December 2011). The Sedin brothers have also been called 'Thelma and Louise' by hockey commentator Mike Milbury, to which Daniel Sedin remarked, 'We don't really worry about those kind of comments. He made a bad comment about us, calling us women. I don't know how he looks at women. I would be pretty mad if I was a woman', as reported by Eric Duhatschek, 'Canucks' Sedin Brothers Rebuff Mike Milbury after Thelma and Louise Jab' (*Globe and Mail*, 11 June 2011) <www.theglobeandmail.com/sports/hockey/globe-on-hockey/canucks-sedin-brothers-rebuff-mike-milbury-after-thelma-louise-jab/article615071/> accessed 28 January 2019. As Kristi Allain remarks: 'As Canadian national identity is tied to men's ice hockey, it is not surprising that particular styles of masculinity – that is, hard hitting, fearless and aggressive play – are privileged over what is considered to be more effeminate ways of expressing masculinity – that is, skating, passing and other skilled maneuvers' (n 147) 13.

banning fights in hockey would lead to the 'pansification' of the sport.[151] Research studies have made similar findings. A textual analysis of American televised sporting events found that

> [a]thletes who are "playing with pain", "giving up their body for the team", or engaging in obviously highly dangerous plays or manoeuvers were consistently framed as heroes; those who removed themselves from games due to injuries had questions raised about their character, their manhood.[152]

This relationship between the sporting world, manhood, and homophobia has been identified by some scholars as forming a kind of 'sporting masculinity', where hegemonic masculine ideals are bolstered through and within sport.[153] Not only does sports rhetoric and playing culture dictate how young boys are to become men through its rules, commentary, and direct instruction, but it also cements hegemonic understandings of men as tough, aggressive risk-takers by admonishing alternative models of 'being male'. This is found explicitly in the juridical treatment of 'harm' in decisions addressing the limits of consensual violence, where 'harm' is configured as a failure to enact hegemonic masculinity. The *Brown* (1993) case offers one of the clearest instances of this (re)construction of the harm principle where, as Thomson suggests, 'sporting language and imagery is deployed in a judicial setting to distance, marginalise, and ultimately penalise an already subordinate masculinity'.[154] The subordinate masculinity in *Brown* was, of course, homosexuality, further complicated by the introduction of consensual sadomasochistic activity. Interestingly, much of the appellants' behaviour in *Brown* conforms to the ideals of hegemonic masculinity. Participants enthusiastically engaged in aggressive acts of violence where the risk of injury was 'played through' by a group of men seeking thrills and power. These events took place over a ten-year period during which time no participant had ever sought medical treatment for any of the injuries they sustained, nor did anyone voice complaint or 'wimp out'.[155] Yet the court in *Brown* goes to great lengths to move the behaviour of the appellants away from the domain of hegemonic masculinity, which, as Thomson has argued, is accomplished by constructing the appellants as not simply

151 As reported in William Houston, 'Gay Rights Group Outraged by CBC's Use of "Pansification"' (*Globe and Mail*, 28 January 2009) <www.theglobeandmail.com/sports/gay-rights-group-outraged-by-cbcs-use-of-pansification/article1148084/> accessed 30 April 2019. See also Justin Gus Foote, Michael L Butterworth and Jimmy Sanderson, 'Adrian Peterson and the 'Wussification of America': Football and Myths of Masculinity' (2017) 65(3) *Comm Q* 268.

152 Messner (n 125) 387.

153 Thomson (n 28).

154 Thomson (n 28) 135.

155 Charges in *Brown* were laid after police found videotaped evidence of the accused persons' activities during a search on an unrelated matter. None of the participants themselves had filed a complaint or sought police action.

'unmanly' but also unhealthy.[156] This is a familiar technique for the maintenance of hegemonic masculinity:

> The 'homosexual' becomes one who has transgressed the boundaries not only of the sexual, but also of the civilized, through acts of depravity that require the reaffirmation of social norms. The events are symbolic in that they reaffirm definitions of normalcy, and are designed to expurgate the gay men from the realm of the social to a pathologised sphere of decay, illness, and to an unavoidably brutal, and ironically, seductive death.[157]

Given this construction, 'consent' must be removed from the appellants' capacity. It is the marker of the normal, the civilised, the 'man' of contemporary society. To leave the 'homosexual' eligible to consent would be to disrupt the frame of exclusion and privilege necessary for the preservation of an idealised masculinity – not unlike the disavowal of autonomy among those without sufficient status in ancient Greece. Thus, despite sadomasochism's esteem for pain, toughness, violence, and the enjoyment thereof, the court in *Brown* is unable to reconcile this with the heterosexual demands of hegemonic masculinity. Instead, the court distances the appellants' conduct from the acceptable and 'reasonable' forms of violence that occur in organised sports on the basis of the former's lack of masculinity. Not only is the appellants' activity without 'good reason', but it is deemed to be against the public's interest on the basis of being unhealthy and harmful (by way of deviating from the 'manly diversions' of sport and skills contests).[158]

Brown is a case which has received significant criticism from legal scholars and commentators, particularly with respect to what is perceived to be blatant homophobia in the court's reasoning.[159] Contrasting judicial approaches to other forms of 'rough horseplay' outside of the sadomasochistic realm, however, reveals similar considerations of harm and hegemonic masculinity.[160] The English case of *Jones* (1986) involved a group of teenaged boys on a youth club playground.[161] The older boys in the group took hold of two younger children and, after some

156 Thomson (n 28) 136. For further examination of how 'sporting sexuality' is policed, see the work of Shari Lee Dworkin and Faye Linda Wachs on HIV-positive athletes: '"Disciplining the Body": HIV-Positive Male Athletes, Media Surveillance, and the Policing of Sexuality' in Susan Birrell and Mary G MacDonald (eds), *Reading Sport: Critical Essays on Power and Representation* (Northeastern University Press 2000).

157 Carl F Stychin, *Law's Desire: Sexuality and the Limits of Justice* (Routledge 1995) 117.

158 This is made explicit in the *Brown* judgment when the court cites Swift J in *Donovan* (n 27).

159 This argument was specifically made at the European Court of Human Rights (ECHR) when it was alleged that a contrast between *Brown* and the *R v Wilson* [1996] 2 Cr App Rep 241 (where the court recognised a wife's capacity to consent to being branded by her husband with a hot iron) revealed a bias in English law against homosexuals. The ECHR, however, rejected this contention. See Anderson, *The Legality of Boxing* (n 53) 99.

160 See Lois Bibbings, 'Boys Will be Boys: Masculinity and Offences against the Person' in Lois Bibbings and Donald Nicolson (eds), *Feminist Perspectives on Criminal Law* (Cavendish 2000).

161 (1986) 83 Cr App R 375.

brief 'play fighting' (as one of the participants described it) involving a headlock, some punching, and some kicking, managed to throw the two young boys in the air. Each landed on the ground, one suffering a ruptured spleen (which required immediate surgery and hospitalisation) and the other, a broken arm. In exempting the activity from criminal liability on the basis that it fell within the established grounds of 'horseplay', the court argued that this was merely an example of typical boyhood mischief. While recognising the activity was likely to cause injury, the court dismissed the need for criminal sanction, suggesting that

> though they anticipated that they might get the odd bruise, *as boys do in playground roughness* ... [t]hey thought that it was being taken as a joke by their victims. True, their victims protested and claimed that they were being hurt, but that was common form among the boys in order to achieve an escape.[162]

A similar approach was taken in another English case, *R v Aitken*, where the appellants were officers in the Royal Air Force who were celebrating the conclusion of their flight training.[163] After consuming a large quantity of alcohol, the appellants began to set fire to the fire-resistant suits of two officers who, the court relays, 'treated it as a joke'.[164] Later in the night, one of the officers indicated that he was retiring to bed at which point the appellants poured white spirit on the victim and ignited it, resulting in serious burns. In characterising these events as 'rough and undisciplined horseplay', the court found a basis for the victim's (implied) consent due to his 'knowledge of the course which celebration evenings such as the one in question was likely to take', holding that 'his continued presence with the others demonstrated an acceptance by him that horseplay of the nature perpetrated upon him might well take place'.[165] It is hard to imagine the court taking this approach to implicit consent (while sleeping) in any other instance of criminal assault without reliance on normative understandings of masculinity and 'horseplay'.[166]

Judicial use of the 'rough horseplay' exception in defence of consent cases has garnered significant criticism among legal commentators, some suggesting it amounts to nothing more than a 'bully's charter'.[167] Their position highlights

162 *Jones* (n 161) 377 (my emphasis).

163 [1992] 1 WLR 1006.

164 *Aitken* (n 163) 1009.

165 *Aitken* (n 163) 1020. The fact that the victim's 'continued presence' took place while he was asleep is not mentioned by the court.

166 In *R v JA*, the Supreme Court of Canada explicitly ruled against this view of tacit consent. JA, while engaging in consensual sexual intercourse with his partner, KD, placed his hands around her neck and choked her until she was unconscious. KD testified to having consented to the choking, but the Court disallowed the possibility of consent being present while in an unconscious state: [2011] 2 SCR 440.

167 Chris Clarkson and Heather Keating, *Criminal Law: Text and Materials* (5th edn, Sweet & Maxwell 2003) 295.

the juridical practice of equating 'harm' with non-conformity to hegemonic masculinity by placing it in a context of homophobia:

> This seems to be a bully's charter. It is extremely far-fetched to suggest that boys being held by several others *to prevent them running away* are genuinely consenting to being thrown in the air. To say that boys in such a situation can consent to *grievous bodily harm,* but that sado-masochists, who are genuinely consenting, cannot consent to *actual bodily harm* provides an interesting insight into the way some of our judiciary view the world. Violence in the playground or barrack-room is what is expected and normal in the male world; it is a 'manly diversion'. Two men wishing to express their sexuality together and in private are not doing the sort of thing 'real men' do. It is an 'evil thing' and 'uncivilised' and cannot be the subject of valid consent.[168]

This association of social violence (that would normally trigger the criminal law) with the 'rough horseplay' that common law exemptions have recognised is often an explicitly gendered one. Take, for instance, the Canadian (2006) case *R v Beahm* where the accused held a knife to an employee's throat while on the job.[169] Although the court did not allow the defence of consent, it was not on the grounds that this behaviour fell outside the ambit of allowable social violence but instead was untenable given the surrounding circumstances and their influence on what the victim could reasonably have expected.[170] The judgment situates the inquiry within the context of hegemonic masculinity from the onset, opening with the following paragraph:

> The fishing industry in Newfoundland and Labrador was traditionally dominated by males. As such these males, in attempts to show their male prowess or for other male generated reasons, would at times engage in verbal and physical jousting in the work place. This would take the form of verbal comments, both in general and more colourful language, and in everything from minor poking and bumping of one person against another to more engaging physical activity.[171]

These cases point to the ways in which dominant understandings of masculinity are used to distinguish allowable forms of violence from those that will incur

168 Clarkson and Keating (n 167) 295–296 as cited in Alan Reed, 'Case Comment: Non Consensual Horseplay and Involuntary Manslaughter' (2005) 157 *Crim Law* 1, 2 (emphasis in original). Reed makes a similar comment about these cases, suggesting '[t]he courts apparently believe that young people have a need for the sort of rough horseplay that occurs in school playgrounds and in military barracks, usually among males' (2).

169 [2006] NJ No. 207.

170 These included that the accused and complainant were not friends, had not wrestled or 'jousted' in the past, and that some animosity was observed after the incident. The court also makes multiple mentions of the accused's non-Canadian citizenship, perhaps to disassociate him from the local context or culture (wherein such 'male prowess' took place).

171 *Beahm* (n 169) 207.

criminal liability. These views of 'manliness' are often positioned as so commonplace, so 'natural' as to be beyond explanation – they are merely the expected outcomes of 'male community life'.[172] Sport remains an essential component of this male community where it is often 'mobilized as a signifier of appropriate (that is, hegemonic) masculinity'.[173] Thus, where the horseplay of young men can be likened to sport (with allusions to rules or 'tacitly agreed understandings or conventions'),[174] consent is permissible. Further, the invocation of consent works to naturalise these ideals by positioning the activity as one that the participants *chose* to partake in. Consent serves as the 'badge' or public statement of a masculinity that assumes risk, endures pain, and welcomes violence without complaint or sign of vulnerability. But it is only in circumstances where these traits are enacted in ways that do not challenge hegemonic masculinity that they are deemed not to be 'harmful' or contrary to public policy. What socially utile end does this 'ideal man' serve?

The following section examines how this cultural conditioning of the traits of desirable masculinity is deployed in service to state interests of capitalism. It explores a second juridical construction of harm in sports cases, that is, the misuse of body capital.

Capitalism with the gloves off: consent and body capital in sport

For as much as sport can be seen as a forum for the construction and maintenance of cultural understandings of masculinity, it is arguably even better understood as a site of struggle – between winners and losers, participants and spectators, amateurs and professionals, and elite and populist classes of activity.[175] Moreover, these struggles are both political and corporeal, waged with certain authorised bodies and with certain allowable uses of those bodies. Like any exercise of disciplinary power, sport employs expert knowledge to facilitate desired outcomes of these struggles, including medical professionals; coaches and trainers; and, in some instances, the courts.[176] The professional sports

172 Interesting to note is Lord Mustill's language in this characterisation of 'male community life' where he suggests that the 'criminal law cannot be *too tender* about the susceptibilities of those involved', invoking notions of Brannon's 'no sissy stuff' ideal, *Brown* (n 27) 110.

173 Thomson (n 28) 139.

174 *Blake v Galloway* [2004] 3 All ER 315. In this case, two teenagers were throwing bark chippings at one another until one of them (Blake) was hit in the eye, causing serious injury. The court exempted the action from liability on the grounds that '[t]he horseplay had been conducted in accordance with tacitly agreed understandings or conventions which were objectively ascertainable by [the victim]', thus distancing the acts from recklessness or wilful blindness – a move not unlike much of the judicial rhetoric on fighting conventions in contact sports.

175 Pierre Bourdieu, 'Sport and Social Class' (1978) 17(6) *Soc Sci Info* 819.

176 Bourdieu identifies a number of these 'agents engaged in the struggle over the definition of sporting uses of the body', including clergy, doctors, health specialists, and 'educators in the broadest sense (marriage guidance counsellors, etc.), pacemakers in matters of fashion and taste (couturiers, etc.)' (n 175) 826–827.

associations and administrative bodies that govern sporting activities are also vested with the power to discipline players and practices that might fail to conform to official (and unofficial) rules of play. As noted within the context of sport's role in enforcing ideals of hegemonic masculinity, these 'rules of play' also apply off the field where players are expected to conform to standards of 'toughness' with a stoic tolerance of pain. These standards are enforced through both formal and informal social controls, the latter of which often proves the most influential. Concealing injuries and 'playing through the pain' are not simply expected of players but are acts deemed reasonable both for the avoidance of personal ridicule[177] and the establishment of a hard-working reputation.

This points to a particular characteristic of modern sport as a form of labour where, as Loïc Wacquant has suggested, sport 'looks like a cross among prostitution, the performing arts, soldiering, and bartering'.[178] Attitudes towards pain among players and spectators of heavy-contact sports provide a useful example. Aside from the insistence that injured players 'man up' (or the reverse scenario examined earlier where players are emasculated for failing to do so), a class frame is often employed to portray players who do 'play through the pain' as more hard-working and thus valuable. Kristi Allain's work has noted the use of the term 'lunch pail' players in ice hockey leagues[179] to refer to players who '[l]ike their working-class equivalents ... are thought to do "dirty" and unglamorous jobs on the ice' and are understood to be 'less about beauty, and more about grit'.[180] While this work rhetoric is prominent in a number of sports contexts, it is most prevalent in professional leagues where athleticism is assessed on the basis of occupational achievements (themselves often signified by risk-taking, violence, and injury). Nick Trujillo, in his study of American baseball, identifies a number of factors which contribute to the understanding of sport-as-work, including the differentiation of sport from play[181] and the commodification of players, where they are 'sold' or 'traded' in a competitive marketplace.

Understanding the professional sporting world as a marketplace is not an imaginative exercise, particularly when the high-end salaries and ancillary benefits

177 See the comments made by players interviewed in a 2006 study conducted by Martin Roderick who relay the measures undertaken by many professional footballers to hide injuries (and the degree of pain they caused) from teammates and coaching staff so as to avoid the reputation of being a 'poor player': Martin Roderick, 'Adding Insult to Injury: Workplace Injury in English Professional Football' (2006) 28(1) *Soc Health & Illness* 76.

178 Loïc Wacquant, 'A Fleshpeddler at Work: Power, Pain, and Profit in the Prizefighting Economy' (1998) 27 *Theory Soc* 1, 2.

179 Allain (n 147) 14.

180 Bruce Arthur, 'Case of Beauty and the Beast; Crosby Plays, But Ovechkin is a Performer' *National Post* (Pittsburgh, 11 May 2009) S1 as cited in Allain (n 147) 14.

181 Nick Trujillo, 'Hegemonic Masculinity on the Mound: Media Representations of Nolan Ryan and American Sports Culture' (1991) 8(3) *Crit Stud Mass Comm* 290. Trujillo cites the work of William A Sadler who observed how athletes themselves view their sports activities as labour, including the characterisation of practice sessions as 'workouts'; William A Sadler, 'Competition Out of Bounds: Sport in American Life' in Andrew Yiannakis and others (eds), *Sport Sociology: Contemporary Themes* (Kendall/Hunt 1976).

of pro athletes are considered. The introduction of in-game violence, however, alters the standard view of sport-as-work. In a book detailing his career as an NHL enforcer, Georges Laraque writes about the stresses and difficulties of being 'paid to fight':

> [Most] tough guy[s] in the league would rather do anything but fight on the ice. They would love to score tons of goals, become more and more talented, and earn bigger salaries, all the things hockey players dream of the moment they become hockey players. And I was one of those. I never enjoyed fighting. I did it because it was my job and the only way for me to keep playing in the NHL. Period ... I could be injured, hurting everywhere — it didn't matter. If I had to go, I simply had to.[182]

Similar accounts have been given by other enforcers, each noting the stress and anxiety associated with their 'jobs' as in-game fighters.[183] In some instances, a player's refusal to engage in violent conduct results in the end of his or her professional sporting career.[184] This has led many to comment on the exploitive nature of sport, described by Wacquant as 'show business with blood',[185] a factor further complicated when the distinctive class locations of many contact sports players are considered. Boxers, for instance, have been noted as largely coming from 'poor, working-class backgrounds. Many are members of minority groups for whom boxing may seem to be one of the few ways out of the misery they were born into'.[186] The use of a class analysis allows for a view of the differential stakes at risk in sport violence where subproletarian players, 'shorn of all social and economic security, subjected to the cycles of employment in unskilled and

182 Georges Laraque and Pierre Thibeault, *Georges Laraque: The Story of the NHL's Unlikeliest Tough Guy* (Viking Canada 2011) 151–152.

183 Although enforcers are most commonly found in ice hockey leagues, other sports also employ their use, including basketball and American football. See Jeffrey A Citron and Mark Ableman, 'Civil Liability in the Arena of Professional Sports' (2003) 36(2) *UBC L Rev* 193; and C Antoinette Clarke, 'Law and Order on the Courts: The Application of Criminal Liability for Intentional Fouls During Sporting Events' (2000) 32 *Ariz St LJ* 1149.

184 The case of professional ice hockey player Paul Mulvey is one of the more famous instances of this occurring. During a 1982 game when Mulvey was playing for the Los Angeles Kings, a fight broke out on the ice. Mulvey was on the bench at the time and was ordered out onto the ice by his coach, Don Perry, with the directive to fight. Mulvey (who had just returned to active play following a recent suspension) refused. His coach accused him of being a coward and unwilling to defend his teammates and allegedly threatened that Mulvey would never play professional hockey again. The threat would prove true: Mulvey was benched for the remainder of the game, demoted to the minor leagues, and never played for the NHL again. See Clarke (n 183) 1160.

185 Loïc Wacquant, 'Whores, Slaves, and Stallions: Languages of Exploitation and Accommodation among Boxers' (2001) 7(2–3) *Body Soc* 181.

186 Michael A Messner and Donald F Sabo, *Sex, Violence & Power in Sports: Rethinking Masculinity* (Crossing Press 1994) 77. Colin Radford also notes that boxing has largely been perceived by participants as an 'escape from hard labor – or, as it is more likely to be these days, unemployment'. See Colin Radford, 'Utilitarianism and the Noble Art' (1988) 63 *Philosophy* 63, 70.

unstable labour', are frequently forced into less rationalised management of body capital in pursuit of socio-economic betterment.[187] As the boxing club manager of Wacquant's study points out to him, 'if you want to know who's at d'bottom of society, all you gotta do is look at who's boxin'.[188]

Within this context of labour exploitation, how is the 'freedom to consent' meant to be understood? The law's interventions into the sporting realm are rare and hinge on determinations of whether the harm exceeded what public policy or 'good reason' will allow players to consent to. Despite the psychological burdens and the dangers associated with violent confrontation (often when players have pre-existing injuries), normal protections by way of work safety standards or even legal sanctions are not applicable to the sports context unless the conduct can be deemed to fall outside the reasonable expectations of play. Coupled with the criminal law's use of the 'public interest' as a delimiter of consent, the effect is to construct certain forms of violence as 'reasonable'. This establishes not just what is acceptable (and valuable) on the playing field but also within the surrounding social order itself. In some of the more contact-oriented sports, (such as rugby, ice hockey, or American football), 'the borders between the permissible and the inadmissible are not always very clear-cut. Both are inherently violent'.[189] This distinction is even more difficult when the unwritten codes of players are considered. Some have suggested unsanctioned violence is best defined alongside a notion of 'fair play', where something 'that is not supposed to come to light, to be exposed, because it is not directed to the unfolding of the game but to the private goals of rage or revenge, to "get at" a specific opponent, to "prove" oneself'.[190] However, most players' accounts of unwritten codes and their own expectations of in-game violence don't adhere to this classification, particularly when the ideals of hegemonic masculinity are considered. As one commentator observed with respect to the unwritten code in rugby: 'You do not allow yourself or your team-mates to be publicly brutalized by an opposing team in the course of play. You are duty bound to level the score'.[191] This accords with ice hockey players' (and fans') accounts of fist-fighting as 'part of the game' of hockey and the goals of intimidation and retaliation, which many contact sports players report as inciting (and justifying) in-game violence.[192] Further, these characterisations of violence in sport as merely 'part of the game' are not made by spectators or players alone but have also formed part of judicial

187 Loïc Wacquant, *Body & Soul: Notebooks of an Apprentice Boxer* (OUP 2004) 131. Wacquant makes reference to the case of Mike Tyson, suggesting that 'it would be difficult to overstate the influence of the Tyson phenomenon on boxing in the black ghetto in the late 1980s' as an example of the class (and racial) frame in which boxing and its clubs exist (43 n31). Bourdieu (n 175) has also commented on how sporting careers are often the sole means of upward mobility for the working classes.

188 Wacquant, *Body & Soul* (n 187) 42.

189 Andre Brink, 'South Africa's Dirty Old Habits Die Hard' *Weekly Mail & Guardian* (30 June 1995) 22.

190 Brink (n 189) 29.

191 John H Kerr, *Rethinking Aggression in Sport* (Routledge 2005) 67.

192 Kerr (n 191).

determinations of criminal liability. As noted by the British Columbia Provincial Court in its sentencing of Todd Bertuzzi (a professional ice hockey player) for his assault against an opposing player:

> I am not so naïve as to suggest that fights are not a part of hockey. I will leave aside the issue of whether they should be, but the fact of the matter is that hockey is a sport in which there is significant physical contact, and in certain circumstances fighting is considered to be part of the game. It is not a sanctioned part of the game, but it is a part of the game.[193]

Where physical violence does garner criticism in sports circles, it is rarely because the violence has reached an unprecedented level but rather because it was for the wrong ends. In other words, it is where players have misused their body capital. Loïc Wacquant has observed the practice of 'managing' body capital that is prevalent among both amateur and professional boxers where the French expression '*payer de sa personne*' is an apt description of a pugilist's ethic.[194] He notes how successful boxing careers are dependent on 'a rigorous management of the body, a meticulous maintenance of each one of its parts ... an extraordinarily efficient relation to the specific capital constituted of one's physical resources'.[195] Moreover, the use or misuse of one's body capital serves as the foundation for critiques among players about the reasonableness of in-game violence. Wacquant cites an example of a boxer in his study, Curtis, who was criticised by his peers for going too many rounds with a rather vicious opponent. 'Curtis ain't gonna go too far if he lets hisself get beat up by guys like that, if he don't know how to *economize hisself* better than that. It's a long road', one of the other boxers confides in Wacquant, drawing attention to the capitalist model that not only instructs determinations of reasonable or rational physical violence but is supported by them.[196] Against this backdrop, players' decisions to engage in violence (which would otherwise be illegal) so as to maintain employment, intimidate an opposing team, garner revenge for past losses or attacks on key players, or simply to assert personal pride are rational, for 'good reason', and not sufficiently harmful to trigger the criminal law. Instead, they are examples of a player's estimable work ethic and occupational ambition.[197]

193 *Bertuzzi* (n 86) [35]. It's also worth noting that the same court (albeit four years earlier) made mention of the accused's motives of regaining team pride as justification for an in-game fight which resulted in a conviction for aggravated assault with a weapon. See *McSorley* (n 83).

194 Wacquant, *Body & Soul* (n 187).

195 Wacquant, *Body & Soul* (n 187) 127.

196 Wacquant, *Body & Soul* (n 187).

197 In many instances, these acts of physical aggression are further rationalised on the basis that such confrontations are 'natural' for men, thus further cementing violence and risk as components of an idealised masculinity. See Lindsay Fitzclarence and Christopher Hickey, 'Learning to Rationalize Abusive Behaviour through Football' in Christopher Hickey, Russell Matthews, and Lindsay Fitzclarence (eds), *Where the Boys Are: Masculinity, Sport and Education* (Deakin University Press 1998).

This is recognised in contemporary judicial treatments of the defence of consent alongside a recognition of the 'nature' of sport and its participants. In keeping with idealised notions of masculinity, court decisions on the applicability of the consent defence in cases where bodily harm has been incurred during sporting activity often include commentary on the inherent competitiveness of sport and the 'naturalness' with which it heightens aggression, risk-taking behaviour, and the 'passions' of its participants. Where in-game violence can be linked to these qualities, the defence of consent is often permitted, irrespective of the degree of injury or level of violence employed. Take, for instance, a recent decision of a Canadian provincial court where the accused faced charges of assault causing bodily harm after having kicked the complainant repeatedly in the face (while wearing cleats) during an amateur soccer game.[198] The complainant suffered serious injuries, including severe facial lacerations and long-term breathing difficulties. In dismissing the charge and allowing the defence of consent, the trial judge relied on assumptions about how participants in such a 'competitive setting' could easily be caught up in 'the heat of the match'.[199] This was deemed a central component to the (amateur) game's 'playing culture'. Thus, despite a finding that the accused had used 'reckless force', it was determined to be in service to 'a legitimate sporting interest in both players striving to gain control of the ball; one to score, the other to defend'.[200] The judge, in allowing the defence of consent, makes note of the accused's lack of intent; however, this can only be understood within the context of the playing culture the judge establishes – one that celebrates risk and injury in pursuit of victory:

> Struggle for control of the ball is part of the essence of soccer, particularly close to a goal. In such a competitive setting as was the match here, it cannot be said that players do not consent to the high risk of injury and the potential of receiving reckless force from an opponent in such a struggle for a loose ball in the penalty area proximate to one side's goal. [The accused] was quite within his rights under the playing culture of soccer to pursue his scoring chance.[201]

Where, however, harm is incurred in circumstances that either challenge these 'legitimate' uses of body capital or don't support them, consent is rarely permitted. One common instance of this is found in cases where the violence occurs after play has stopped or where victory is deemed unlikely.[202]

198 *R v Adamiec* [2013] MJ No. 325 (Man QB).
199 *Adamiec* (n 198) [5].
200 *Adamiec* (n 198) [48].
201 *Adamiec* (n 198) [51]. A similar finding was reached in the *Green* and *Maki* cases (n 68) on the basis that the assault took place while both players were trying to gain possession of the puck.
202 See, for instance, *R v Gray* [1981] S.J. No. 1429 (Sask Prov Ct), where the defence of consent was prohibited on the grounds that the accused had acted 'when play [was] not under way' [16]. A similar scenario took place in the American case *State v Floyd*, 466 NW 2d 919 (Iowa Ct App 1990).

Although these cases speak to the contemporary context, the interpretation of 'harm' as linked to body capital has long-standing roots in the common law treatment of the defence of consent to harm. As early as 1604, the defence of consent was limited to acts that would not deny the king the corporeal use of his subjects and their limbs.[203] This limitation was explicitly linked to the criminal law's consideration of the 'public interest' in the 1882 English case *Coney*, where in denying the defence of consent to participants of a prize fight, Hawkins J noted:

> [I]t is not in the power of any man to give an effectual consent to that which amounts to, or has a direct tendency to create, a breach of the peace; so as to bar a criminal prosecution. In other words, though a man may by his consent debar himself from his right to maintain a civil action, he cannot thereby defeat proceedings instituted by the Crown in the interests of the public for the maintenance of good order. He may compromise his own civil rights, but he cannot compromise the public interests.[204]

In this instance, the social utility of sport hinges on the perceived dangers it might foster among its participants and its spectators. One of the earliest judicial delineations of the social utility of sport eliminates activities undertaken solely for profit for exactly this reason. In a 1763 English text, Sir Michael Foster distinguishes between 'cudgelling or wrestling' and 'prize-fighting and public boxing matches or any other exertions … of the like kind which are exhibited for lucre' on the basis that the latter 'serve no valuable purpose' but rather encouraged 'a spirit of idleness and debauchery'.[205] Although the criminal law's approach to sport-for-profit has changed dramatically, these early cases demonstrate a long-standing preoccupation with the misuse of body capital within judicial determinations of consent and its limits.

Bourdieu has argued that one's relation to one's body marks a particular class *habitus* or set of attitudes and values, where the use of body capital is the mark of the disenfranchised not simply because of a lack of other available resources (as in Wacquant's subproletarian pugilists) but also because of the ethos that such corporeal use represents. Bourdieu notes that

> weight-lifting, which is supposed to develop the muscles, was for many years, especially in France, the favourite working-class sport; nor is it an accident that the Olympic authorities took so long to grant official recognition to weightlifting, which, in the eyes of the aristocratic founders of modern sport, symbolized mere strength, brutality and intellectual poverty, in short the working classes.[206]

203 *Wrights Case* (n 111).

204 *Coney* (n 50) 553.

205 Foster (n 47) 260 as cited in Binder (n 111) 239. Binder elaborates on the exclusion of prize-fighting, suggesting it was the heightened possibility that such events would result in a breach of the peace that drove the sense of the activity's social disutility.

206 Bourdieu (n 175) 836.

This suggests that the legal regulation of sport serves a disciplinary function, influencing how the body of the 'lunch pail' athlete is shaped and valued and, in turn, how the rules and parameters of sporting practice, including its violence, are set and enforced. Not only does this represent a differential valuation of bodies within sport according to the supply they can offer a politicised social demand, but it also hints at the ethos produced through this process. Michael Robidoux provides some insight on this in his study of sporting activities during the British settlement period in Canada, noting that

> [t]he intent of making sport and physical activity more socially democratic was threefold: to acquire levels of control over increased amounts of leisure time made possible by industrialization and a shorter workweek; to reduce class conflict by enabling male participants of various backgrounds to compete on an equal playing field; and to build a physically fit yet subordinate workforce, ensuring maximum levels of industrial production.[207]

Sport can thus be seen to operate as a site for the negotiation of hegemony. In a recent study of early North American sporting events, Kenneth Cohen explores how the public spaces of athletic events in frontier America created opportunities for socialisation across class lines but argues against the view that sport merely mirrored already existent class relations. Instead, the sporting events staged in public taverns, fields, and raceways of the newly independent United States created a shared culture (of risk) which served to entrench capitalist ideology.

> In posh 'refined' sporting spaces, the old tenets of gentility – which privileged mental skill over physical force, heterosocial accord over homosocial discord, and urged an etiquette based on self-control to enforce these priorities – were reaffirmed and men of all ranks abided by strictures of politeness. In coarse 'physical' spaces, however, confrontations frequently degenerated into fistfights instead of arguments. Each type of space served particular purposes in a risk culture linking sport to business, as men sought to establish both their reputation and their raw manliness in the throes of a boom-and-bust economy riddled with rampant failure and decreasing opportunities for advancement. Since failure, stagnation, and hardening class lines threatened men's reputations and their very masculinity, 'various classes of persons' resorted to the two types of sporting environments to recuperate both.[208]

Cohen's study takes note of how sport was initially employed by the bourgeoisie of early America with the intention of fostering deference among the lower classes, that is, a sense of respect and reverence for the social and cultural authority

207 Michael A Robidoux, 'Imagining a Canadian Identity through Sport: A Historical Interpretation of Lacrosse and Hockey' (2002) 115(456) *J Amer Folk* 209, 212.

208 Kenneth Cohen, '"To Give Good Sport": The Economic Culture of Public Sporting Events in Early America, 1750–1850' (PhD dissertation, University of Delaware 2008) 9.

of the business elite. Many of the sporting events were supported as a show of philanthropy, and investors created 'genteel' spaces from which to consume the coarseness of physical sport (rather than participate in it).[209] Predictably, this fostered enmity among the excluded, effectively shifting investor aims of deference to economic and political return. Cohen observes that in this way, sport served as the site where a capitalist ideology could take root, 'heightening the contest for status that lured people to participate even as the expense and bureaucracy needed to stage these activities hardened the power and control of wealthy Americans'.[210]

This demonstrates a use of sport to 'condition the savage body' while using the defence of consent to entrench the ideologies that such social divisions could be justified upon. Where individuals act in pursuit of idealised masculinity and profit, their acts of aggression, risk, and violence are intelligible. Where, however, individuals act in ways that challenge these values, their behaviours lack the 'good reason' that enables recognisable consent. Much like the requirements in ancient Greece that one conform to the requirements of citizenship before one's consent could be intelligible (and juridically effective), contemporary treatments of consent are accompanied by normative preconditions which operate in service to the state. Hegemonic masculinity demands a commodification of the body, put to use for the pursuit of profit. Provided these ideals are what has motivated a player's choice to incur bodily harm, the violence will be deemed to have sufficient social utility to allow the defence of consent. Where, however, the harm incurred has not been in accordance with these masculine ideals or the bodily harm suffered was the result of foolhardiness, the errors of this 'mismanaged' self are the player's to bear.

In this way, consent on the present-day sports field operates in a manner similar to its functions in the previous chapter's historical periods – it demands conformity to certain prescribed identities and behaviours in order to be intelligible. Yet, in the contemporary context, there is an additional capitalist logic which operates through the 'public utility' exemption to the consent defence. Poor decision-making, miscalculated risk, and a mismanagement of body capital are an individual's error in judgment and the consequences fall not to the state to remedy but within the realm of individual responsibility. As John Fiske observed with respect to televised portrayals of masculinity, the conception of ideal maleness as ceaseless labour, boundless achievement, and propensity for risk creates a 'superhuman' archetype, its own inaccessibility necessary 'to keep men striving for more and more achievement in order to maintain the "naturalness" of the ideological concept of progress which is so central to capitalism'.[211]

209 This distinction between consumption and participation of/in sport is one made by Bourdieu (n 175) when noting the commodification of sport-as-spectacle.

210 K Cohen (n 208) 686. Bourdieu also argued that 'in sport as in music, extension of the public beyond the circle of amateurs helps to reinforce the reign of the pure professionals' (n 175) 829.

211 John Fiske, *Television Culture* (Methuen 1987) 210.

This quality of 'inaccessibility' echoes the fictional role consent is understood to have in liberal accounts of state legitimacy, as examined in Chapter 1. The consent-as-autonomy story relies on the presumption that each person has the right to self-govern, that is, to act in the world as one wishes. Yet this freedom is limited by a prohibition against harming others, the nature of which is informed by unwritten codes of practice and cultural norms of intelligibility. Autonomous action must therefore conform to these codes to not simply be allowed but to be recognisable as autonomy. One must be a certain kind of person and act in a certain kind of way to be free. The law's treatment of consent in sport and play contexts thus mirror the acts of submission seen in the medieval medical context, where despite an understanding of the impossible promise consent makes (of autonomy or of union with the Divine), it is pursued nonetheless.

Conclusion

This chapter's examination of how the criminal law approaches charges of bodily harm incurred during sporting activity demonstrates how the defence of consent is used to produce and entrench a code of conduct for players which makes it both rational and laudable to subject oneself to violence, provided it bolsters cultural, social, and economic capital. This marks a preservation of not only a (privileged) hegemonic masculinity but one in service to capitalism. Sports, constructed as a marketplace, is a domain where rules and attitudes are established to assess what is 'harm' and what is simply 'fair play'. Consent operates within this context as a normative principle that moralises the punishment of those who haven't amassed sufficient 'human capital'.[212] Consent is denied to those players who haven't learned how to 'man up' or 'play through the pain', or to those who have expended their body capital in ways that don't contribute to hegemonic ideals or reveal disjointedness in the rationality of the market or the natural equality of economic man.

Are these the new conditions of possibility for consent as it operates today? How does the consent-as-autonomy story and its promise of 'freedom' operate within a capitalist logic? The following chapter explores these inquiries through a more in-depth examination of neoliberal rationality and its influence on the current operations of consent in both criminal and medical law.

Bibliography

Table of cases

Blake v Galloway [2004] 3 All ER 315

Brady v Sunderland Association Football Club Ltd [1998] EWCA Civ 1780

212 Loïc Wacquant, 'Three Steps to a Historical Anthropology of Actually Existing Neoliberalism' (2012) 20 *Soc Anth* 66. See also Wacquant's 2007 text, *Punishing the Poor: The Neoliberal Government of Social Insecurity* (Duke University Press 2007).

Brady v Sunderland Association Football Club Ltd [1998] QBD 2 April 1998
In Re National Hockey League Players' Concussion Injury Litigation MDL No. 14–2551 (Minn Dist Ct, 2014)
Leeman and others v National Hockey League (2013) Civil Case No. 13-CV-1856 (DC Dist Ct)
McKichan v St. Louis Hockey Club LP, 967 SW 2d 209 (Mo Ct App 1998)
O'Brien v Cunard Steamship Co, 154 Mass 272, 28 NE 266 (1891)
R v Adamiec [2013] MJ No. 325 (Man QB)
R v Aitken [1992] 1 WLR 1006
R v Barnes [2005] 1 Cr App Rep 507
R v Beahm [2006] NJ No. 207 (Nfld Prov Ct)
R v Bertuzzi (2004) 26 CR 6th 71 (BCPC)
R v Bradshaw (1878) 14 Cox CC 83
R v Brown [1993] 2 All ER 75
R v Cey (1989) 48 CCC 3d 480 (Sask CA)
R v Ciccarelli (1989) 54 CCC 3d 121 (Ont Dist Ct)
R v Coney (1882) LR 8 QBD 534
R v Donovan [1934] 2 KB 498
R v Gray [1981] S.J. No. 1429 (Sask Prov Ct)
R v Green (1970) 16 DLR (3d) 137 (Ont Prov Ct)
R v JA [2011] 2 SCR 440
R v Jobidon [1991] 2 SCR 714
R v Jones (1986) 83 Cr App R 375
R v Lee [2006] 5 LRC 716 (NZ CA)
R v Leyte [1973] 13 CCC (2d) 458 (Ont Prov Ct)
R v Maki (1970) 14 DLR 164 (Ont Prov Ct)
R v Martin (1980) 53 CCC (2d) 250 (ONCA)
R v Mayer [1985] 41 Man R (2d) 73 (Prov Ct)
R v McSorley [2000] BCPC 117
R v Moore (1898) 14 TLR 229
R v Watson (1975) 26 CCC (2d) 150 (Ont Prov Ct)
R v Wilson [1996] 2 Cr App Rep 241
State v Burnham (1884) 48 Am Rep 801
State v Floyd 466 NW 2d 919 (Iowa Ct App 1990)
State v Limon No. 1999–CR-2892 (144th Jud Dist Ct Bexar Co Texas 2000)
Wright's Case (Leicester Assizes 1604)

Table of legislation

Criminal Code, RSC 1985, C-46 (Canada)
Model Penal Code § 2.11 (United States)

Secondary sources

———, 'Topics of the Times' *New York Times* (New York, 15 October 1905)
———, 'Topics of the Times' *New York Times* (New York, 28 November 1905)
———, 'Trudeau's Omnibus Bill' *CBC Digital Archives* (21 December 1967) <www.cbc.ca/player/play/1811727781> accessed 24 January 2019

Allain KA, 'Kid Crosby or Golden Boy: Sidney Crosby, Canadian National Identity, and the Policing of Hockey Masculinity' (2011) 46 *Int Rev Soci Sport* 3

Alldridge P, 'Consent to Medical Surgical Treatment: The Law Commission's Recommendations' (1996) 4 *Med LR* 129

Anderson J, *The Legality of Boxing: A Punch Drunk Love?* (Birkbeck Law Press 2005)

———, 'No Licence for Thuggery: Violence, Sport, and the Criminal Law' (2008) 10 *Crim LR* 751

Archard D, '"A Nod's as Good as a Wink": Consent, Convention, and Reasonable Belief' (1997) 2 *LEG* 273

———, *Sexual Consent* (Westview Press 1998)

Arthur B, 'Case of Beauty and the Beast; Crosby Plays, But Ovechkin is a Performer' *National Post* (Pittsburgh, 11 May 2009)

Associated Press, 'Ciccarelli Cited for Assault' *New York Times* (Toronto, 24 August 1988)

Athanassoulis N, 'The Role of Consent in Sado-Masochistic Practices' (2002) 8 *Res Publica* 141

Bansal D, 'Bodily Modifications and the Criminal Law' (2018) 82(6) *JCL* 496

Bartky SL, *Femininity and Domination: Studies in the Phenomenology of Oppression* (Routledge 1990)

Baxter A, 'Hockey Violence: The Canadian Criminal Code and Professional Hockey' (2006) 31(2) *Man LJ* 281

Beale JH, *Cases on Criminal Law* (3rd edn, Harvard Law Review Publishing Association 1915)

Belson K, 'NFL Official Affirms Link between Playing Football and CTE' *New York Times* (New York, 14 March 2016) <www.nytimes.com/2016/03/15/sports/football/nfl-official-affirms-link-with-cte.html> accessed 30 April 2019

———, 'After NFL Concussion Settlement, Feeding Frenzy of Lawyers and Lenders' *New York Times* (New York, 16 July 2017) <www.nytimes.com/2017/07/16/sports/football/nfl-concussion-settlement-lawyers.html> accessed 30 April 2019

Bennett T, 'It's But a Flesh Wound: Criminal Law and the Conceptualisation of Healthy Limb Amputation' (2011) 36(3) *Alt LJ* 158

———, '"Unorthodox Rules": The Instructive Potential of BDSM Consent for Law' (2018) 4(1) *J Pos Sex* 1

Bernstein R, *The Code: The Unwritten Rules of Fighting and Retaliation in the NHL* (Triumph Books 2006)

Bibbings L, 'Boys Will be Boys: Masculinity and Offences against the Person' in Lois Bibbings and Donald Nicolson (eds), *Feminist Perspectives on Criminal Law* (Cavendish 2000)

Binder RL, 'Consent Defense: Sports, Violence, and the Criminal Law' (1976) 13(2) *Am Crim LR* 235

Blatchford C, 'Where Have All the Manly Men Gone? Toronto, City of Sissies' *National Post* (10 December 2011) A29

Boston University CTE Center, 'Press Release re NHL Player Derek Boogaard' (Boston, 6 December 2011) <www.bu.edu/cte/news/press-releases/december-6-2011/> accessed 30 April 2019

Bourdieu P, 'Sport and Social Class' (1978) 17(6) *Soc Sci Info* 819

Branch J, 'Derek Boogaard: A Brain Going Bad' *New York Times* (New York, 5 December 2011) <www.nytimes.com/2011/12/06/sports/hockey/derek-boogaard-a-brain-going-bad.html> accessed 30 April 2019

———, *Boy on Ice: The Life and Death of Derek Boogaard* (HarperCollins 2015)

———, 'The Tragic Diagnosis They Already Knew: Their Brother Died with CTE' *New York Times* (New York, 3 May 2018) <www.nytimes.com/2018/05/03/sports/nhl-cte-jeff-parker.html> accessed 30 April 2019

Brannon R, 'The Male Sex Role: Our Culture's Blueprint for Manhood, What It's Done For Us Lately' in Deborah Sarah David and Robert Brannon (eds), *The Forty-Nine Percent Majority: The Male Sex Role* (Addison-Wesley 1976)

Brink A, 'South Africa's Dirty Old Habits Die Hard' *Weekly Mail & Guardian* (30 June 1995) 22

Brobst JA, 'Why Public Health Policy Should Redefine Consent to Assault and the Intentional Foul in Gladiator Sports' (2015) 29 *JL & Health* 1

Burke M, 'How the National Football League can Reach 25 Billion in Annual Revenues' (*Forbes*, 17 August 2013) <http://forbes.com/sites/monteburke/2013/08/17/how-the-national-football-league-can-reach-25-billion-in-annual-revenues/> accessed 30 April 2019

Busby K, 'Every Breath You Take: Erotic Asphyxiation, Vengeful Wives, and Other Enduring Myths in Spousal Sexual Assault Prosecutions' (2012) 24(2) *CJWL* 328

Butler J, *Gender Trouble: Feminism and the Subversion of Identity* (10th ann edn, Routledge 1999)

Citron JA and Ableman M, 'Civil Liability in the Arena of Professional Sports' (2003) 36(2) *UBC L Rev* 193

Clarke CA, 'Law and Order on the Courts: The Application of Criminal Liability for Intentional Fouls during Sporting Events' (2000) 32 *Ariz St LJ* 1149

Clarkson C and Keating H, *Criminal Law: Text and Materials* (5th edn, Sweet & Maxwell 2003)

Clement R, 'Consent to Body Modification in Criminal Law' (2018) 77(3) *CLJ* 451

Cohen DS, 'No Boy Left Behind? Single-Sex Education and the Essentialist Myth of Masculinity' (2009) 84 *Ind LJ* 135

———, 'Keeping Men "Men" and Women Down: Sex Segregation, Anti-Essentialism, and Masculinity' (2010) 33 *Harv J Law & Gen* 509

Cohen K, *"To Give Good Sport": The Economic Culture of Public Sporting Events in Early America, 1750–1850* (PhD dissertation, University of Delaware 2008)

Connell RW, *Masculinities* (Polity Press 1995)

——, 'Masculinity Construction and Sports in Boys' Education: A Framework for Thinking about the Issue' (2008) 13(2) *Sport Educ Soc* 131

Courtenay WH, 'Constructions of Masculinity and Their Influence on Men's Well-Being: A Theory of Gender and Health' (2000) 50(10) *Soc Sci Med* 1385

Dalton M, *The Country Justice* (The Company of Stationers, 1635)

Delamont S, *Sex Roles and the School* (Routledge 1980)

Devlin P, *The Enforcement of Morals* (OUP 1965)

Dobinson I and Thorpe D, 'What's Wrong with the Commissioner? Some Lessons from Downunder' (2009) 19(1) *Seton Hall J S&EL* 105

Dryden K, 'Saving the Game' *Globe & Mail* (27 March 2004) A19

Duhatschek E, 'Canucks' Sedin Brothers Rebuff Mike Milbury after Thelma and Louise Jab' (*Globe and Mail*, 11 June 2011) <www.theglobeandmail.com/sports/hockey/globe-on-hockey/canucks-sedin-brothers-rebuff-mike-milbury-after-thelma-louise-jab/article615071/> accessed 30 April 2019

Dworkin SL and Wachs FL, '"Disciplining the Body": HIV-Positive Male Athletes, Media Surveillance, and the Policing of Sexuality' in Susan Birrell and Mary G MacDonald

(eds), *Reading Sport: Critical Essays on Power and Representation* (Northeastern University Press 2000)
Elliott T, 'Body Dysmorphic Disorder, Radical Surgery, and the Limits of Consent' (2009) 17(2) *Med LR* 149
Fafinski S, 'Consent and the Rules of the Game: The Interplay of Civil and Criminal Liability for Sporting Injuries'. (2005) 29 *JCL* 414
Farber M, 'Code Red' (*Sports Illustrated*, 22 March 2004) <www.si.com/nhl/2014/08/19/si-vault-code-red-todd-bertuzzi-steve-moore-attack-nhl-violence> accessed 28 January 2019
Feschuk D, 'NHL's Tentative Concussion Lawsuit Another Blow to the Players' *Toronto Star* (Toronto, 12 November 2018) <www.thestar.com/sports/hockey/opinion/2018/11/12/nhls-tentative-concussion-lawsuit-another-blow-to-the-players.html> accessed 22 January 2019
Fiske J, *Television Culture* (Methuen 1987)
Fitzclarence L and Hickey C, 'Learning to Rationalize Abusive Behaviour through Football' in Christopher Hickey, Russell Matthews and Lindsay Fitzclarence (eds), *Where the Boys Are: Masculinity, Sport and Education* (Deakin University Press 1998)
Foote JG, Butterworth ML and Sanderson J, 'Adrian Peterson and the "Wussification of America": Football and Myths of Masculinity' (2017) 65(3) *Comm Q* 268
Foster M, *Crown Cases* (Clarendon 1762)
Fox M and Thomson M, 'A Covenant with the Status Quo? Male Circumcision and the New BMA Guidance for Doctors' (2004) 31(8) *J Med Eth* 463
Gendall D, 'The Sport of Boxing: Freedom Versus Social Constraint' (1997) 5 *Waikato LR* 71
Giles M, '*R v Brown:* Consensual Harm and the Public Interest' (1994) 57(1) *MLR* 101
Gordon S, 'Former Players Sue NHL, Say League Hid Concussion Risks' *Globe & Mail* (Toronto, 25 November 2013) <www.theglobeandmail.com/sports/hockey/former-players-sue-nhl-say-league-hid-concussion-risks/article15599650/> accessed 30 April 2019
Graham BC and others, 'Member Perspectives on the Role of BDSM Communities' (2015) 53(8) *J Sex Res* 895
Greenblatt N, '"Cruelty is Uncivilized": Consent, BDSM, and Legal Regulation of the Civil(ized) Subject' in Nikita Dawson and others (eds), *Negotiating Normativity* (Springer 2016)
Haines CR (tr), *Marcus Cornelius Fronto: Correspondence, Vol. II* (HUP 1920)
Hale M, *History of the Pleas of the Crown* (E Rider 1778)
Harris EA, 'From Social Contract to Hypothetical Agreement: Consent and the Obligation to Obey the Law' (1992) 92 *Colum L Rev* 651
Hart HLA, *Law, Liberty, and Morality* (SUP 1963)
Harviainen JT, 'Information Literacies of Self-Identified Sadomasochists: An Ethnographic Case Study' (2015) 71 *J Doc* 423
Heward C, *Making a Man of Him* (Routledge 1988)
Houlihan A, 'When "No" Means "Yes" and "Yes" Means Harm: HIV Risk, Consent and Sadomasochism Case Law' (2011) 20 *Law & Sexuality* 31
Houston W, 'Gay Rights Group Outraged by CBC's Use of "Pansification"' (*Globe and Mail*, 28 January 2009) <www.theglobeandmail.com/sports/gay-rights-group-outraged-by-cbcs-use-of-pansification/article1148084/> accessed 30 April 2019
Hughes G, 'Two Views of Consent in the Criminal Law' (1963) 26 *MLR* 233

Huizinga J, *Homo Ludens: A Study of the Play-Element in Culture* (Beacon Press 1950)
Jackson E, *Medical Law: Text, Cases, and Materials* (OUP 2009)
Joyce G, *Sidney Crosby: Taking the Game by Storm* (Fitzhenry & Whiteside 2005)
Kaak A, 'Conversational Phases in BDSM Pre-Scene Negotiations' (2016) 2(3) *J Pos Sex* 47
Kerr JH, *Rethinking Aggression in Sport* (Routledge 2005)
Kim R, 'Eminem – Bad Rap?' (*The Nation*, 5 March 2011) <www.thenation.com/article/eminem-bad-rap/> accessed 30 April 2019
Kimmel M, 'Issues for Men in the 1990s' (1992) 46 *U Miami L Rev* 671
———, 'Foreword' in Jim McKay, Michael A Messner and Donald Sabo (eds), *Masculinities, Gender Relations, and Sport* (Sage 2000)
———, 'Masculinity as Homophobia: Fear, Shame, and Silence in the Construction of Gender Identity' in Nancy Cook (ed), *Gender Relations in Global Perspective: Essential Readings* (Canadian Scholars Press 2007)
Kimmel M and Mahler M, 'Adolescent Masculinity, Homophobia, and Violence: Random School Shootings, 1982–2001' (2003) 46 *Am Behav Sci* 1439
Labuschagne P, '"Violence" in Sport and the *Violenti Non Fit Injuria* Defence: A Perspective on the Death of the Cricket Player Phil Hughes' (2018) 21 *PELJ* 1 <https://papers.ssrn.com/sol3/papers.cfm?abstract_id=3151299> accessed 18 January 2019
Laraque G and Thibeault P, *Georges Laraque: The Story of the NHL's Unlikeliest Tough Guy* (Viking Canada 2011)
Lassiter C, 'Lex Sportiva: Thoughts Towards a Criminal Law of Competitive Contact Sport' (2007) 22(1) *St John's J Legal Comm* 35
Law Commission (UK), *Consent and Offences against the Person* (Law Com No. 134, 1994)
Layden T, 'The Big Hit' (*Sports Illustrated*, 30 July 2007) <www.si.com/vault/2007/07/30/100157949/the-big-hit> accessed 28 January 2019
LeBrun P, 'Surprised by Sedin? You shouldn't be' (*ESPN NHL*, 3 February 2010) <http://sports.espn.go.com/nhl/columns/story?columnist=lebrun_pierre&id=4883674> accessed 28 January 2019
Lin K, 'The Medicalization and Demedicalization of Kink: Shifting Contexts of Sexual Politics' (2016) 20(3) *Sexualities* 302
Maese R, 'Dementia Claims in NFL Concussion Settlement are Going Unpaid, Lawyers Say' (*Washington Post*, 20 March 2018) <www.washingtonpost.com/sports/redskins/dementia-claims-in-nfl-concussion-settlement-are-going-unpaid-lawyers-say/2018/03/20/00e635bc-2c7f-11e8-8ad6-fbc50284fce8_story.html> accessed 21 January 2019
Malarchuk C and Robson D, *A Matter of Inches: How I Survived the Crease and Beyond* (Triumph 2014)
Marchie A and Cusimano MD, 'Bodychecking and Concussions in Ice Hockey: Should Our Youth Pay the Price?' (2003) 169(2) *CMAJ* 124
McCoun P, 'The 10 Greatest Examples of Hockey Tough' (*Bleacher Report*, 12 January 2010) <https://bleacherreport.com/articles/324477-the-10-greatest-examples-of-hockey-tough#slide7> accessed 28 January 2019
Mertl S, 'Vancouver Police Investigate Ugly On-Ice Hit by Canucks Star' *Canadian Press Newswire* (Vancouver, 9 March 2004)
Messner MA, Dunbar M and Hunt D, 'The Televised Sports Manhood Formula' (2000) 24(4) *J Sport Soc Iss* 380
Messner MA and Sabo DF, *Sex, Violence & Power in Sports: Rethinking Masculinity* (Crossing Press 1994)

Mez J and others, 'Clinicopathological Evaluation of Chronic Traumatic Encephalopathy in Players of American Football' (2017) 318(4) *JAMA* 360

Mill JS, *On Liberty* (first published 1859, Elizabeth Rapaport ed, Hackett 1978)

Miller FG, 'Consent to Clinical Research' in Franklin Miller and Alan Wertheimer (eds), *The Ethics of Consent: Theory and Practice* (OUP 2009)

Mincer E, 'Fifty Shades and Fifty States: Is BDSM a Fundamental Right? A Test for Sexual Privacy' (2018) 26 *Wm & Mary Bill Rts J* 865

Note, 'Consent in Criminal Law: Violence in Sports' (1976) 75 *Mich LR* 148

Ohio Valley Athletics Staff, 'Sidney Crosby out Indefinitely Again with Concussion Symptoms' (*Ohio Valley Athletics*, 12 December 2011) <www.ovathletics.com/home/sidney-crosby-out-indefinately-again-with-concussion-symptoms/9254> accessed 30 April 2019

Onoma A, 'Legal Censure of Unconventional Expressions of Love and Sexuality: Finding a Place in the Law for BDSM' (2017) 28(1) *Hastings WLJ* 25

Oriard M, *Sporting with the Gods: The Rhetoric of Play and Game in American Culture* (CUP 1991)

Parchev O and Langdridge D, 'BDSM under Security: Radical Resistance via Contingent Subjectivities' (2017) 21(1–2) *Sexualities* 194

Pitagora D, 'Intimate Partner Violence in Sadomasochistic Relationships' (2016) 31(1) *Sex & RT* 95

Pottage A, 'Foucault's Law by Ben Golder and Peter Fitzpatrick (Review)' (2011) 74 *MLR* 159

Radford C, 'Utilitarianism and the Noble Art' (1988) 63 *Philosophy* 63

Reed A, 'Case Comment: Non Consensual Horseplay and Involuntary Manslaughter' (2005) 157 *Crim Law* 1

Robidoux MA, *Men at Play: A Working Understanding of Professional Hockey* (MQUP 2001)

———, 'Imagining a Canadian Identity through Sport: A Historical Interpretation of Lacrosse and Hockey' (2002) 115(456) *J Amer Folk* 209

Roderick M, 'Adding Insult to Injury: Workplace Injury in English Professional Football' (2006) 28(1) *Soc Health & Illness* 76

Rowe D, McKay J and Miller T, 'Panic Sport and the Racialized Masculine Body' in Jim McKay, Michael A Messner and Donald Sabo (eds), *Masculinities, Gender Relations, and Sport* (Sage 2000)

Sadler WA, 'Competition Out of Bounds: Sport in American Life' in Andrew Yiannakis and others (eds), *Sport Sociology: Contemporary Themes* (Kendall/Hunt 1976)

Samson C, 'No Time Like the Present: Why Recent Events Should Spur Congress to Enact a Sports Violence Act' (2005) 37 *Ariz St LJ* 949

Sangster J, 'Just Horseplay? Masculinity and Workplace Grievances in Fordist Canada, 1947–70s' (2014) 26 *CJWL* 330

Schultz D and Fisher S, *The Hammer: Confessions of a Hockey Enforcer* (Summit Books 1981)

Schumann M, 'Pain, Please: Consent to Sadomasochistic Conduct' (2018) 2018(3) U Ill L Rev 1177

Schwartz D, 'Are NHL Enforcers' Addictions, Depression a Result of On-Ice Brain Trauma?' (*CBC News*, 3 September 2011) <www.cbc.ca/news/canada/are-nhl-enforcers-addictions-depression-a-result-of-on-ice-brain-trauma-1.982100> accessed 21 January 2019

Sharp A, 'League of Denial and the Crisis that Never Ends' (*Grantland*, 9 October 2013) <http://grantland.com/the-triangle/league-of-denial-and-the-crisis-that-never-ends/> accessed 22 January 2019

Simmons JA, 'Political Obligation and Consent' in Franklin Miller and Alan Wertheimer (eds), *The Ethics of Consent: Theory and Practice* (OUP 2009)

Simula BL and Sumerau J, 'The Use of Gender in the Interpretation of BDSM' (2017) 22(3) *Sexualties* 452

Skelton C, '"A Passion for Football": Dominant Masculinities and Primary Schooling' (2000) 5(1) *Sport Educ Soc* 5

Stychin CF, *Law's Desire: Sexuality and the Limits of Justice* (Routledge 1995)

Thomson M, *Endowed: Regulating the Male Sexed Body* (Routledge 2008)

Thornton PK, 'Rewriting Hockey's Unwritten Rules: *Moore v Bertuzzi*' (2009) 61 *Me L Rev* 205

Trujillo N, 'Hegemonic Masculinity on the Mound: Media Representations of Nolan Ryan and American Sports Culture' (1991) 8(3) *Crit Stud Mass Comm* 290

Tuominen M and others, 'Injuries in Mens' International Ice Hockey: A 7-year Study of the International Ice Hockey Federation Adult World Championship Tournaments and Olympic Winter Games' (2015) 49 *Br J Sports Med* 30

Vecsey G, 'College Athletes Move Concussions into the Courtroom' *New York Times* (New York, 29 November 2011) <www.nytimes.com/2011/11/30/sports/ncaafootball/college-players-move-concussions-issue-into-the-courtroom.html> accessed 30 April 2019

Wacquant L, 'A Fleshpeddler at Work: Power, Pain, and Profit in the Prizefighting Economy' (1998) 27 *Theory Soc* 1

———, 'Whores, Slaves, and Stallions: Languages of Exploitation and Accommodation among Boxers' (2001) 7(2–3) *Body Soc* 181

———, *Body & Soul: Notebooks of an Apprentice Boxer* (OUP 2004)

———, *Punishing the Poor: The Neoliberal Government of Social Insecurity* (Duke University Press 2007)

———, 'Three Steps to a Historical Anthropology of Actually Existing Neoliberalism' (2012) 20 *Soc Anth* 66

Weinberg JD, *Consensual Violence: Sex, Sports, and the Politics of Injury* (UCalP 2016)

Westhead R, 'Bertuzzi Suspended for Season and Playoffs' *New York Times* (New York, 12 March 2004) D1

Wilkinson P, 'Assault with a Deadly Elbow' (*Rolling Stone*, 22 June 2000) <www.rollingstone.com/culture/culture-news/assault-with-a-deadly-elbow-191330/> accessed 30 April 2019

5 The political economy of consent

The previous chapters have focussed on three of the subject areas where law contends with the notion of consent, namely: the regulation of sex, the requirements for lawful medical treatment, and defences to assault. Examining these uses of consent within unconventional contexts revealed that consent has operated quite differently than the story of consent-as-autonomy might suggest. Whether a guardian of proprietary and patrilineal interests, a path to spiritual enlightenment through submission to the Other, or an enactment of hegemonic masculinity, these forms of consent do not appear to produce or facilitate personal freedom so much as they represent acts of submission to conformist ontologies and identities. Yet, the understanding of consent as an attestation of autonomy prevails. Amidst the evidence unearthed in previous chapters of these alternative understandings and functions of consent, it seems important to determine how this autonomy story has become both dominant and obscuring of all other narratives. Further, what purpose does this obfuscation serve?

In an effort to address this central inquiry, this chapter is organised in three parts. It begins with a brief exploration of the current logic within which consent operates today: neoliberalism. This portion of the chapter is meant to position neoliberalism as more than a theory of economic activity and instead a form of political and legal rationality. Foucault's concept of governmentality can be thought of as the engine that drives an analysis of this kind, where an understanding of how power operates to both produce and delimit intelligible personhood necessitates an examination of the political rationalities that support these compulsory subjectivities.[1] As such, a component of the first section of this chapter includes an overview of Foucault's own observations on neoliberalism and the market as a site of truth, moving to a fuller examination of what freedom (and autonomy as 'self-governance') might mean within this regime. As part of this analysis, neoliberal rationality is positioned as a foundationalist discourse, where the ahistorical story of capitalism is explored for the contribution it makes to securing market rationality as 'common sense' in the

1 Wendy Brown, in her own analysis of contemporary neoliberalism, cites Foucault as the source for the view that neoliberalism is better understood as a 'political rationality' than a 'bundle of economic policies with inadvertent political and social consequences'. See *Edgework: Critical Essays on Knowledge and Politics* (PUP 2005) 38.

modern era and the implications this has for the role which consent is allotted in contemporary law.

The second section of the chapter seeks to test the prevalence of this neoliberal rationality within contemporary deployments of consent in each of the legal areas examined in previous chapters: namely consent to sex, informed consent to medical treatment, and the role of consent in regulating violence in sport. This section explores two of the central components of neoliberal rationality as they operate through consent in these legal areas, namely: individualism and responsibilisation. As part of this discussion, the law's deployment of social utility and risk is examined for its contribution to neoliberal understandings of the self. The chapter concludes with a discussion of the implications of a legal doctrine of consent that is entrenched and enacted within a capitalist logic, paying particular attention to its consequences for identity, where self-governance and risk management become the centrepieces of the consenting (neoliberal) subject. The chapter is thus concerned with the politics of consent and how they operate to not only naturalise particular (economic) rationalities and ontologies but to also produce the subjects needed to enact them. In this respect, it is engaged in the political economy of consent.

Neoliberal rationality: touched by an invisible hand

In order for a narrative to secure its place as a foundationalist discourse, it must do more than simply out-voice other accounts. It must secure itself as truth. As Foucault suggested in his own exploration of the rise of neoliberalism in his lectures at the Collège de France in 1979, part of the success story of neoliberalism is its ability to naturalise the very social conditions it requires to survive. Thomas Lemke furthers this point when he suggests that neoliberalism is 'a political project that endeavors to create a social reality that it suggests already exists'.[2] There are two components to such an endeavour. The first is the task of obscuring the social and political events, processes, and customs which made it possible for a different way of acting and being in the world to develop. These are the 'conditions of existence' for neoliberalism. In the case of the consent-as-autonomy story, this has meant positioning the underlying components of classical liberalism (self-interest, self-regulation, and possessive individualism) as both 'natural' (in terms of what human beings inherently want or do) and 'ahistorical', that is, as coming into existence merely as a result of the development or evolution of these natural human tendencies.

A second – and related – component to the establishment of a foundationalist discourse is the creation of a (necessarily) fictitious subject for whom these tendencies *are* natural and thus 'rational'.[3] This not only creates a pre-social and

2 Thomas Lemke, 'Foucault, Governmentality, and Critique' (2002) 14(3) *Rethinking Marxism* 49, 60.

3 The medieval fiction of the 'constant man' as well as contemporary law's use of the 'reasonable person' are good examples of this ahistorical and pre-social subject put to regulatory use in this fashion.

ahistorical ontology (which itself serves to obscure alternate subjectivities), but it also provides justification for the norms of intelligibility that establish the 'normal rules of play' among citizens of the state. Thus, certain constraints on what a person may do (or be) within a neoliberal world are not only deemed rational on the basis that such actions or desires are not what 'normal' people 'naturally' want to do, they are also removed from the realm of what is desirable in the first instance. It should therefore hardly be necessary to force populations to abide by 'the rules', given that they merely represent what 'everyone knows everyone wants'.[4]

Neoliberalism – as both a set of economic policies and their underlying political rationality – fulfils each of these two components of a foundationalist discourse. In the first instance, it benefits from the ahistorical story of capitalism told by classical economic liberalism, which has 'naturalised' the neoliberal subject. This, in turn, has served to imbue the principles of self-interest, wealth maximisation, possessive individualism, and competition with a ubiquitous truth, allowing for prescriptions about what human beings are (and should be) that are then used to delimit the boundaries of acceptable desires, wills, and actions. The previous chapter's examination of the defence of consent within the contemporary sporting context provides some evidence of this, demonstrating how modern-day uses of consent function within a logic where it is rational to subject oneself to violence – provided it bolsters cultural, social, and economic capital. This lends credence to Wendy Brown's claim that in the contemporary sphere of existence, 'not only is the human being configured exhaustively as homo economicus, but all dimensions of human life are cast in terms of a market rationality'.[5]

Yet, neoliberalism is not the only foundationalist discourse at work in the law's treatment of consent. As delineated in Chapter 1, the autonomy narrative that is so closely associated with consent is also positioned as ahistorical and 'natural' – both in terms of what human beings might want and in terms of what constitutes 'normal' personhood. Further, the ways in which these two foundationalist discourses work in tandem are rarely investigated. Instead, the conditions of existence for the consent-as-autonomy narrative are obscured, leaving its liberal origins (and its role within the ideology of capitalism) unexplored. It should then not be surprising that consent is itself cast in proprietary terms, where autonomy is often described as a form of 'self-ownership'. What, then, becomes of exercises of freedom when envisioned as dispositions of commodities? Who, in contemporary legal treatments of consent, is entitled to 'self-own'? What does autonomy mean in a neoliberal world? To address these inquiries, some preliminary work needs to be done to disrupt the ahistorical status of the consent-as-autonomy narrative. This necessitates a brief investigation into the emergence of classical

4 As Lori Beaman has remarked in her study of Canadian courts' treatment of religious objections to medical treatment, '"Everybody knows that" is a difficult position to counter', *Defining Harm: Religious Freedom and the Limits of the Law* (UBC Press 2008) 95.

5 Brown, *Edgework* (n 1) 40.

liberalism, its impact on the practices of the medieval market, and the conditions of existence for capitalist thought. The following subsections chart this course.

The market rationality: an origin-less story

Best evidenced by the cardinal principle of laissez-faire, classical liberalism conceptualises freedom in opposition to constraint (ie freedom *from* as opposed to freedom *to*). Within this frame, the capitalist state is understood as merely the 'natural' consequence of removing barriers to free action, effectively leaving markets (and their actors) 'free' to develop as they might be naturally inclined to do. As Ellen Meiksins Wood has observed, in 'most accounts of capitalism and its origins, there really *is* no origin'.[6] Instead, capitalism is presented as inevitable, omnipresent, or simply lying dormant in wait for its release from any variety of restrictive conditions.[7] This is certainly the argument underlying one of the more common explanations for the rise of capitalism: the end of feudalism. In such formulations, capitalism is positioned as merely 'an acceleration of universal and transhistorical, almost *natural*, tendencies' where 'industrialization is the inevitable outcome of humanity's most basic inclinations'.[8] Lost in these accounts are the coercive acts of the state that were necessary to shift pre-capitalist social relations into a divisive system of competitive labour, namely 'forcibly stripping peasants of their land'.[9] This produced a class of persons wholly dependent on the market who might not 'have been compelled to attain an average rate of profit in the manner of a modern capitalist, but production for profit beyond their own subsistence needs was the condition of their continued access to the land and a *presupposition* of production for their own subsistence'.[10]

An endemic theory of neoliberalism (ie as an inevitable development of the basic human characteristics of greed and need) would thus seem to owe

6 Ellen Meiksins Wood, *The Origins of Capitalism: A Longer View* (Verso 2002) 4.

7 Wood notes a series of 'chains' that capitalism is often characterised as having been 'released' from, including feudalism and 'the parasitic powers of lordship, or the restrictions of an autocratic state. Sometimes they are cultural or ideological: perhaps the wrong religion' (n 6) 4. See, in particular, Chapter 1 of her 2002 text for further discussion of the dominant explanations for capitalism's development, including the commercialisation model (where capitalism is the natural outcome of human practices), the demographic model (where capitalism is the result of the laws of supply and demand), and the world systems theory (where capitalism is explained through increased globalisation and incremental 'value-added' processes, such as various technological advancements). While Wood is careful not to fully dismiss these explanations, she does point to each model's reliance on an ahistorical notion of capitalism, which ignores the necessary changes in social relations that precede these other developments.

8 Wood (n 6) 5.

9 Vivek Chibber, 'Remembering Ellen Meiksins Wood' (*Jacobin*, 15 January 2016) <www.jacobinmag.com/2016/01/ellen-wood-obituary-chibber-retreat-from-class-origins-of-capitalism-marxist> accessed 29 January 2019.

10 Ellen Meiksins Wood, 'Capitalism's Gravediggers' (*Jacobin*, 5 December 2014) <www.jacobinmag.com/2014/12/capitalisms-gravediggers/> accessed 29 January 2019.

something to the origin-less story of capitalism.[11] This claim to an inherent or intuitive nature is further cemented by a fairly opaque view of neoliberalism's own genesis – something that some commentators have suggested is facilitated by the name 'neoliberalism' itself. '[F]ree trade and "competitive advantage" is 200 years old', Paul Treanor reminds us. 'There is nothing "neo" in [this] liberalism'.[12] And yet, there are dangers in understanding neoliberalism as merely an extended, saturated form of capitalism or the natural evolution of an ever-expanding practice of rationalisation.[13] Such views tend to overlook the very direct forms of intervention governments make to further the neoliberal agenda, obscuring the intricate relationship between the market and the state. Wendy Brown, for instance, notes that despite the contributions Marx's theory of capital and Weber's rationalisation thesis make to contemporary understandings of neoliberalism, 'neither brings into view the historical-institutional rupture it signifies, the form of governmentality it replaces and the form it inaugurates, and hence the modalities of resistance it renders outmoded'.[14]

Brown's analysis directs attention to the all-encompassing quality of neoliberal rationality, its presence in every aspect of contemporary human existence, while highlighting how this permeation relies on an underestimation of it as a 'constructivist project'.[15] Thus, while neoliberalism envisions and assesses all components of human behaviour and subjectivity within the confines of a market rationality, it doesn't leave these factors to chance, nor does it place faith in the 'invisible hand' of the classical liberal model. Rather, the 'hand' of neoliberalism is an active agent, intervening in social policy, legal reforms, and countless initiatives at both the domestic and international levels. The state itself must behave as a market; its policies and initiatives must be defensible as cost-wise and economically productive. Neoliberalism is both the directive for the state to act in the interests of the market and the underlying logic which grants such initiatives legitimacy.[16] Further, neoliberalism is also actively involved in

11 Many scholars have laboured to track the origins of neoliberalism in more specific detail than is needed here. See, in particular, David Harvey's 2007 text, *A Brief History of Neoliberalism*, where he suggests the 'neoliberal turn' in global politics was a response to 'the catastrophic conditions that had so threatened the capitalist order in the great slump of the 1930s': (OUP 2007) 9.

12 Paul Treanor, 'Neoliberalism: Origins, Theory, Definition' (Research Paper, Personal Blog, 12 December 2005) < http://web.inter.nl.net/users/Paul.Treanor/neoliberalism.html > accessed 29 January 2019.

13 It may be useful to note that Foucault distinguishes between classical liberalism and its 'neo' counterpart on the basis that the first envisioned a socio-political realm based on the human activity of *exchange*, whereas he viewed neoliberalism as focussed more on *competition*. For a more in-depth discussion of this distinction, see Jason Read, 'A Genealogy of Homo-Economicus: Neoliberalism and the Production of Subjectivity' (2009) 6 *Fouc Stud* 25.

14 Brown, *Edgework* (n 1) 45.

15 Brown, *Edgework* (n 1) 40.

16 Foucault notes this as a form of sovereignty founded on economic activity rather than divine authority, historical conquest, or paternal benevolence – foundations that were relied on in historical understandings of consent seen in previous chapters. See, for instance, his discussion

the 'dissemination of social norms designed to facilitate competition, free trade, and rational economic action on the part of every member and institution of society'.[17] The neoliberal 'hand' is not as readily visible as its level of involvement in contemporary human existence suggests it should be.

The neoliberal subject: a normative ontology

The norm-setting practices of neoliberalism are a significant means by which neoliberal rationality establishes itself as a foundationalist discourse. As David Harvey has argued, to gain dominance, an ideology or 'way of thought' must embed its 'conceptual apparatus' into the common sense, thus removing it from scrutiny or resistance. This apparatus must contain valorised ideals, those that 'appeal to our intuitions and instincts, to our values and desires', and Harvey contends that neoliberalism's selection of individual freedom and human dignity was a wise one, given their 'compelling and seductive' character.[18] Yet, if neoliberalism is a new dog, this is an old trick. The ability to obscure its conditions of existence through the dissemination of legitimising norms has been a key component to capitalism's widespread survival, given the inherent contradictions within the system itself.[19] The expansion and prosperity of capital does not benefit the many but rather the few – and even then it is on the basis of exploitation. Thus, the system necessitates the production and maintenance of this exploited class, on the one hand, and a means of disciplining this population so as to avoid its rebellion, on the other. The true triumph of the system thus lies not in its ability to coerce populations or to manage widespread revolt but rather to generate ideological adoption of the system and its 'conceptual apparatus' among its subordinated classes.[20] Surely, this is the contribution liberalism makes to the neoliberal

---

of *raison d'Etat* in his 10 January 1979 Collège de France lecture in *The Birth of Biopolitics: Lectures at the Collège de France 1878–1979* (Michel Senellart ed, Graham Burchell tr, Picador 2008). Wendy Brown observes how this economically based notion of legitimacy manifests itself even in challenges to state action where anti-war protests in the United States were debated on the grounds that they were 'expensive disruptions' creating 'unacceptable costs for financially strapped cities'. She suggests that this demonstrates how within a neoliberal rationality, 'the value of public opinion and protest should be measured against its dollar costs', *Edgework* (n 1) 51. For Brown, this represents a conjoining of the interests of neoliberalism and imperialism – a relationship that is facilitated by a market rationality of 'efficiency'.

17 Brown, *Edgework* (n 1) 41.

18 Harvey (n 11) 5.

19 This hints at what Wood identifies as capitalism's 'paradox of freedom', where despite heralding 'choice' as the pre-eminent principle of a market economy (where freedom is thought to be perfected in the supply-demand aspects of commercialism), the origin-less story of capitalism and its ensuing logic of inevitability negates, from the onset, any notion of 'choice' (n 6). Wendy Brown has made a similar argument with respect to the paradoxes that liberalism (and its prioritising of rights) creates. See Wendy Brown, 'Suffering Rights as Paradoxes' (2000) 7(2) *Constellations* 230.

20 This usually extends to critiques of the system as well. Wood observes that even Marxist analyses of the emergence of capitalism 'conced[e] too much to standard histories of capitalist

project, championing notions of freedom, autonomy, and equality such that neoliberalism becomes 'that which we cannot not want'.[21] For Brown, neoliberalism's normative force lies in its effort to subject every dimension of socio-political life to an economic rationality, not simply on the basis that it is efficient to do so, but that it is also *right.*[22] Morality, within neoliberalism, simply *is* economic rationality. It is 'configured entirely as a matter of rational deliberation about costs, benefits, and consequences'.[23] This serves to construct a particular ontology that is in service to neoliberal rationality. The 'good citizen', within a moral paradigm based on economic rationality, is an entrepreneur.[24] She must engage in a strict regime of managing risks according to a calculated assessment of the costs and benefits of each proposed action. To recall the phrasing of a sporting coach from the previous chapter, the moral responsibility of the neoliberal subject is to 'economise oneself'.[25] Failure to do so, to 'navigate impediments to prosperity', is an indicator of a 'mismanaged life'.[26]

This model of a moral obligation to 'manage' oneself according to a normative ontology should strike the reader as familiar. As discussed in Chapter 3, the need to effectively balance one's appetites and desires was an integral component to medieval understandings of health and salvation. Within the medieval frame,

---

development' when they focus on changes in technology or trade activities, attributing changes to the labour force (and modes of production) to developments in industrialisation (n 6) 66. Instead, Wood maintains that '[w]hat created the drive to intensify exploitation was not the emergence of steam or the factory system but rather the need inherent in capitalist property relations to increase productivity and profit' (n 6) 67. This points to the power of origin-less stories in the production and maintenance of foundationalist discourses.

21 Gayatri Chakravorty Spivak, *Outside in the Teaching Machine* (Routledge 1993) 44. In the same chapter, Spivak notes that it 'is hard to acknowledge that liberal individualism is a violating enablement'. Wendy Brown, when citing this exact excerpt, suggests that it demonstrates how Spivak is 'keenly aware of what liberalism cannot deliver, what its hidden cruelties are, what unemancipatory relations of power it conceals in its sunny formulations of freedom and equality', 'Suffering Rights' (n 19) 230.

22 Brown, *Edgework* (n 1). Bruno Anili also suggests that liberalism is able to gain validity on the basis of common usage, arguing that '[l]iberal discourse sounds intuitively "right" because it sounds familiar, because the content that it articulates conforms to the expression that it employs'. See Bruno Anili, 'Beyond Liberal Discourse: Meta-Ideological Hegemony and Narrative Alternatives' (PhD dissertation, University of Oregon 2010) 68.

23 Brown, *Edgework* (n 1) 42.

24 This is what Ong has identified as the 'market criteria on citizenship', whereby political belonging (and the distribution of rights and benefits) is determined on the basis of a person's marketable skills rather than membership to a nation state. See Aihwa Ong, *Neoliberalism as Exception: Mutations of Citizenship and Sovereignty* (Duke University Press 2007). This leaves those whose skills are not deemed to have sufficient economic value outside the realm of citizenship or, to use Judith Butler's phrasing, those who are 'stateless within the state'. See Judith Butler and Gayatri Chakravorty Spivak, *Who Sings the Nation State?: Language, Politics, Belonging* (Seagull 2007) 16.

25 This is a paraphrasing of the words of Loïc Wacquant's boxing coach who critiqued one of the rookie boxers for failing to '*economize hisself*'. See Loïc Wacquant, *Body & Soul: Notebooks of an Apprentice Boxer* (OUP 2004) 146.

26 Brown, *Edgework* (n 1) 42.

however, many of the values esteemed within a contemporary neoliberal context would have been considered vices. Greed, profit maximisation, competition, increased privatisation, and possessive individualism were conditions of appetites the medieval 'good citizen' needed to constrain. This is the crux of consent's role in the context of medieval medicine. It was the marker of the well-balanced or 'managed' life. In his own analysis of the decline of ecclesiastical authority during the eighteenth century, Foucault argued that pastoral power was merely taken up in another form. 'It was no longer a question of leading people to their salvation in the next world', Foucault argued, 'but rather ensuring it in this world'.[27] This new context meant a shift in the meaning of 'salvation' from one focussed on the after-life to one rooted in the values of an emergent economic rationality: wealth, security, and the liberty to pursue these on an individualised basis. In the words of Margaret Thatcher: 'Economics are the method but the object is to change the soul'.[28]

This shift in political and ontological rationality warrants closer reflection for the insights it offers on the role the consent-as-autonomy narrative plays in the contemporary neoliberal context. The glance backwards to the medieval world in Chapter 3 allows for a clearer picture of how consent served as a means of both defining virtue and facilitating conformity to this standard. The sick suffered because they had been sinful. Poor health was the marker of an unbalanced life. Consent was the means of remedying this, through conformity to a dominant (and Christian) way of being. Similarly, the Ancient context examined in Chapter 2 demonstrates how consent marked the boundaries of 'good citizenship' both in terms of who was entitled to consent and what consent served to protect (ie patrilineage and citizenship). What conformist subjectivities does consent serve today? To what end is its promise of autonomy? Gerald Cohen asked a similar question in a lecture he gave at the London School of Economics in 1980 when he sought to understand how certain kinds of liberals and libertarians could defend private property on the basis of an understanding of 'freedom' that did not recognise the 'unfreedom' of private ownership itself.[29] He answered this query by suggesting that at the heart of this position is a tendency to treat private property 'as part of the structure of human existence in general, and therefore as ... *merely as things are*'.[30] Yet, to 'think of capitalism as a realm of freedom is to overlook half of its nature'.[31]

The relevance of this for the consent-as-autonomy story is well evidenced by the change in medieval trade practices alongside the emergence of liberalism's classical economic theories. The medieval marketplace was a setting of both stringent regulation and customary practices.[32] It was not a design of profit

27 Michel Foucault, 'The Subject and Power' (1982) 8(4) *Crit Inq* 777, 784.
28 As cited in Harvey (n 11) 23.
29 Gerald A Cohen, 'Freedom, Justice, and Capitalism' (1981) 126 *New Left Rev* 3.
30 Cohen (n 29) 9 (emphasis in original).
31 Cohen (n 29) 10.
32 Edward P Thompson has described these as: 'The farmers should bring their corn in bulk to the local pitching market; they should not sell it while standing in the field, nor should they

but of community sustenance.[33] Bread was a staple in most medieval diets. As such, there were a number of statutory and customary provisions which strictly regulated how the growth and sale of grain, flour, and corn should operate. Both millers and bakers were thought of as 'servants of the community, working not for a profit but for a fair allowance'.[34]

Foucault assesses these characteristics of the medieval market as indicative of a model of distributive justice, where 'the market operated to ensure that, if not all, then at least some of the poorest could buy things as well as those who were more well-off'.[35] This echoes some of the observations made by Lianna Farber with respect to the role of consent in medieval trade where consent was less about establishing voluntariness in trade transactions[36] (as it is commonly employed in contemporary contract law) and more about the contemplation of 'need' and what could be considered a 'just price'.[37] Where prices were set far above what the seller could reasonably be deemed to require for sustenance (or where usury was paid out of compulsion), consent was not possible. Again, this is not because the consent given for the trade might be considered 'involuntary' (a tempting – but retrospective – reading of consent) but rather because it was not in alignment with the 'common good' or, as Thompson might suggest, the customs the community held in common.[38] It was these customs that created the crowd's 'legitimising notion' which prompted riotous action when the market price was deemed too high. This moral imperative was rooted in a shared understanding of traditional customs and the wider consensus of the community. This consensus had significant force – rioters were frequently able to control the market price of food (often through violent protest) without fear of sanction from authorities who, as Thompson describes, were made 'prisoners of the people' as a result.[39] Thompson's work details a number of highly descriptive examples, many of which dispel the more common explanation that riots

withhold it in the hope of rising prices. The markets should be controlled; no sales should be made before stated times, when a bell would ring; the poor should have the opportunity to buy grain, flour, or meal first, in small parcels, with duly supervised weights and measures. At a certain hour, when their needs were satisfied, a second bell would ring, and larger dealers (duly licensed) might make their purchases' in *Customs in Common* (New Press 1991) 193–194.

33 Thompson cites a 1768 pamphlet describing a farmer's attendance at the market as 'a material part of his duty; he should not be suffered to secret or to dispose of his goods elsewhere' as evidence of this. See Thompson, *Customs in Common* (n 32) 198.

34 Thompson, *Customs in Common* (n 32) 194.

35 Foucault, *The Birth of Biopolitics* (n 16) 30.

36 Lianna Farber, *An Anatomy of Trade in Medieval Writing: Value, Consent, and Community* (Cornell University Press 2006) 94–95. Farber attributes this to two central sources which influenced medieval authors' considerations of voluntariness, that is, classical Roman law and Aristotle's *Nichomachean Ethics* – both of which endorsed the maxim, 'forced will is will'.

37 Farber traces much of this through an examination of medieval authors' writings on usury (n 36) 93–97.

38 This is similar to the medieval medical forum, where consent was understood to be the means by which the sick could bring themselves into alignment with Christ (and/or Christian ideals held 'in common').

39 Thompson, *Customs in Common* (n 32) 189.

were attributable to mere hunger or 'rebellions of the belly'(particularly where crowds entered mills or bakeries to destroy the goods rather than steal them).[40] Instead of a (capitalist) picture of inadequate supply to meet demand, these riots demonstrate a community for whom maximisation of profit through pricing was an unfamiliar and immoral practice. This is what Thompson has described as 'the moral economy of the crowd' – an informal system by which a community ensured the poor could eat.[41] This was how the 'just price' of goods was set. Thompson explains:

> It is of course true that riots were triggered off by soaring prices, by malpractices among dealers, or by hunger. But these grievances operated within a popular consensus as to what were legitimate and what were illegitimate practices in marketing, milling, baking, etc. This in turn was grounded upon a consistent traditional view of social norms and obligations, of the proper economic functions of several parties within the community, which, when taken together, can be said to constitute the moral economy of the poor.[42]

This moral economy was altered with the emergence of classical liberalism. Well encapsulated in Adam Smith's *The Wealth of Nations*, this new theory called upon members of the market to simply 'leave it alone', abandoning the strict regulations of the medieval economy so as to allow the market to function on its own accord – a strategy, according to Smith and his disciples, which would permit the market to flourish rather than flounder amidst excessive and unneeded constraint. This was the work of Smith's notorious 'invisible hand', an unseen coordinator of the various individual interests and demands of the market's participants, facilitating prices to ebb and flow according to the desires and distastes of human nature.[43] This had the further effect of granting the market and its activity a certain epistemological authority.[44] If the market was merely functioning

40 Thompson, *Customs in Common* (n 32) 230–235. One particularly vivid example from West Cornwall is relayed where crowds were witnessed 'visiting farms with a noose in one hand and an agreement to bring corn to reduced prices to market in the other' 229.

41 Edward P Thompson, 'The Moral Economy of the English Crowd in the Eighteenth Century' (1971) 50 *P&P* 76. Foucault elaborates on this point, suggesting that the systems of regulations that the medieval market had in place to ensure the presence of the 'just price' (and the absence of fraud) 'meant that the market was essentially, and really functioned as, a site of justice, a place where what had to appear in exchange and be formulated in the price was justice', *Birth of Biopolitics* (n 16) 31.

42 Thompson, 'The Moral Economy' (n 41) 78–79.

43 It is worth noting that some scholars have questioned the role of the 'invisible hand' in Smith's work. See, for instance, Emma Rothschild's work which argues that Smith's use of the 'invisible hand' (in all three places where it appears in his works) is, at best, ironic and that it is not a concept that he would have endorsed without sardonicism. Emma Rothschild, 'Adam Smith and the Invisible Hand' (1994) 84(2) *Am Econ Rev* 319.

44 As Foucault has observed, Smith's 'invisible hand' was a remnant of 'a theological conception of the natural order', *Birth of Biopolitics* (n 16) 278. This suggests that the market was granted a sort of divine authority as well.

according to a set of 'natural' laws, the resulting prices (and commercial activity) must be, in some sense, true.[45]

This had far wider-reaching effects than mere price-setting. The truth-telling power of the market also served to delineate what it meant to be a 'good citizen', effectively de-moralising the crowd's economy in favour of a supply and demand model of the common good. Central to this task was situating Smith's market economy as 'amoral' so as to give it the appearance of objectivity. As Thompson has suggested:

> It should not be necessary to argue that the model of a natural and self-adjusting economy, working providentially for the best good of all, is as much a superstition as the notions which upheld the paternalist model … Whereas the first appeals to a moral norm – what *ought* to be men's reciprocal duties – the second appears to say: 'this is the way things work, or would work if the State did not interfere.[46]

Here, the force of invoking an ahistorical truth ('this is the way things work') is rather apparent. The market rationality gains a sense of inevitability, thus obscuring modes of resistance – for how does one challenge that which has always been?[47] This is perhaps best demonstrated by the difficulty the contemporary reader has of envisioning an alternative to the self-interested and profit-driven human nature presumed (and produced) by free market rationalities. Thompson notes that:

> It is not easy for us to conceive that there may have been a time, within a smaller and more integrated community, when it appeared to be 'unnatural' that any man should profit from the necessities of others, and when it was assumed that, in time of dearth, prices of 'necessities' should remain at a customary level, even though there might be less all round.[48]

45 In Foucault's words, 'When you allow the market to function by itself according to its nature, according to its natural truth, if you like, it permits the formation of a certain price which will be called, metaphorically, the true price, and which will still sometimes be called the just price, but which no longer has any connotations of justice', *Birth of Biopolitics* (n 16) 31.

46 Thompson, *Customs in Common* (n 32) 203. It should be noted that Thompson is careful to point out that several years of debate about corn regulation laws resulted in a repeal of the legislation against forestalling (ie selling in advance of market stalls) four years prior to the publication of Smith's work.

47 In keeping with the religious values of the medieval period, proponents of Smith's theory characterised its opponents as 'enemies both to God and man, opposite both to Grace and Nature'. See Thompson, *Customs in Common* (n 32) 254, citing a 1648 text.

48 Thompson, *Customs in Common* (n 32) 252–253. David Harvey echoes this sentiment in slightly more generalised language (in a chapter titled 'The Construction of Consent') when he suggests that as neoliberalism made its way into common-sense understandings, '[t]he effect in many parts of the world has increasingly been to see it as a necessary, even wholly "natural" way for the social order to be regulated' (n 11) 41.

Studies like Thompson's reveal that despite accounts of capitalism and its market rationality as having always been or, perhaps more aptly, being merely the result of allowing persons to 'act freely', there are alternative accounts of how communities might live together and the 'natures' of those that live within them. Further, the 'freedom fable' told by classical liberalism has had observable effects on prevailing attitudes about not simply how the market ought to operate but also about what constitutes 'good' citizenship and 'normal' human behaviours and desires, suggesting 'there is nothing merely economic about economics'.[49] The medieval subject stands in stark contrast to the liberal one which took its place – a subject described by Wendy Brown as 'fiercely autonomous and diffident … unencumbered by anyone or anything, independent in both senses of the term (free of dependents and dependency in civil society). [The liberal subject] is not oriented toward relationships and persons but toward self and things'.[50] The 'birth' of this *homo economicus* was met with a capitalist calculus for all aspects of the human condition, including the means by which law assessed criminal responsibility and meted out penalties.[51] 'Crime and punishment were meant to be exchanged as costs and benefits like any other commodity, and punishment was an economic disincentive to crime'.[52] Surely within this frame, where human beings are self-interested, profit-seeking, and driven by rational choice, the exercising of one's will, the rules of self-governance, and the very meaning of freedom itself must also have economic 'worth'.[53] The last chapter's examination of the consent defence in sport provides some evidence of a prevailing notion in the contemporary context that to be 'free' one must be able to expend one's property, one's body capital as one wishes. This is the bedrock of the libertarian position and

49 Judith Butler and Athena Athanasiou, *Dispossession: The Performative in the Political* (Polity Press 2013) 39. Butler elaborates on this idea with a suggestion that to regard the economic domain as autonomous is to accept certain claims of 'economic science and calculation' that neoliberalism puts forth. She likens this to an earlier point made by Marx 'that one of the achievements of capitalism was the analytic distinction between the domain of the social and the domain of the economic' – a divide that is only traversed when neoliberalism is understood as a political rationality: 40–41.

50 Wendy Brown, *States of Injury: Power and Freedom in Late Modernity* (PUP 1995) 149.

51 The work of both Nicola Lacey and Alan Norrie provides ample evidence of this. Note, in particular, Lacey's account of the shift in law's emphasis (for the purpose of determining criminal responsibility) from a medieval preoccupation with 'character' to the Enlightenment's interest in 'capacity'. The former represents a valuing of 'status' and the role of communal judgments (and customs); whereas the latter is a 'quasi-contractual' understanding of criminal responsibility, one that prioritises the *choices* the law's subjects make. See Nicola Lacey, 'In Search of the Responsible Subject: History, Philosophy and Social Sciences in Criminal Law Theory' (2001) 64(3) *MLR* 350; Nicola Lacey, 'Responsibility and Modernity in Criminal Law' (2001) 9(3) *J Pol Phil* 249; Alan Norrie, *Crime, Reason and History* (3rd edn, PUP 2014).

52 Norrie (n 51) 26.

53 This may be the basis for Wendy Brown's caution against envisioning social and political autonomy as 'that which can be tinkered with independently of developments in the forces of capitalism' (n 50) 11. She notes that 'for Marx, liberalism is to capitalism something institutionally securing, discursively naturalizing, ideologically obscuring, and historically perpetrating the power of the dominant' (n 50) 82.

its view of private property as the embodiment of freedom. 'Unless people are free to make contracts and to sell their labour, or unless they are free to save their incomes and then invest them as they see fit, or unless they are free to run enterprises when they have obtained the capital, they are not really free'.[54]

This suggests a grid of (economic) intelligibility is at work in law, wherein human nature and action are evaluated for their (neoliberal) rationality. Consent must presumably also conform to this calculus. Consider, for instance, the observation Erik Olin Wright has made about consent as a 'cost smart' means of exploiting labour (given the expensive 'overhead' in extracting it coercively).[55] Or, Randy Barnett's claim that consent ensures maximum economic efficiency in contractual transactions.[56] While the contemplation of consent in a cost-benefit rubric may not appear as incongruous in contexts of labour relations or contract, what happens to law's use of consent in the criminal and medical fields when its neoliberal logic is considered?

Consent within a capitalist logic: revisiting criminal and medical law

Rose and Miller, in the following excerpt, identify the core of neoliberalism's moral epistemology, whereby what is thought to be ethically estimable and 'naturally' possible is in congruence with what is economically viable:

> Those who could not carry their contractual obligations were now to appear 'anti-social', and to be confined under a new legitimacy. The scandalous and bizarre were to be placed under a revised medical mandate, in asylums that promised to cure and not merely to incarcerate. Law-breakers and malefactors were no longer to have the status of bandits or rebels, but were to become transgressors of norms motivated by defects of character amenable to understanding and rectification.[57]

Wendy Brown makes a similar point with respect to the normative ontology that a neoliberal rationality entrenches and propagates, through which the moral

54 Gerald Gaus and Shane D Courtland, 'Liberalism' in *The Stanford Encyclopedia of Philosophy* (Spring edn, 2011) <http://plato.stanford.edu/archives/spr2011/entries/liberalism/> accessed 30 April 2019.

55 Erik Olin Wright, 'Foundations of a Neo-Marxist Class Analysis' in Erik Olin Wright (ed), *Approaches to Class Analysis* (CUP 2005) 29–30. To be clear, Wright is not advocating this position. He presents this so-called 'endogenous theory of the formation of consent' as one of the 'theoretical pay-offs' that a Marxist class analysis (ie one that explores the notion of 'class' using the concepts of exploitation and domination) can bring to the table when the more normative (ie capitalism is oppressive and/or bad) claims are not as desirable.

56 Randy E Barnett 'Consenting to Form Contracts' (2002) 71(3) *Fordham L Rev* 627.

57 Nikolas Rose and Peter Miller, 'Political Power Beyond the State: Problematics of Government' (1992) 43(2) *Brit J Soc* 173, 180. Rose and Miller write about the liberal doctrine of 'freedom' and its role in producing the normative subjectivities needed to 'make liberalism operable'.

responsibilities (and understandings) of citizenship are economically defined.[58] Consent does not operate independently of this frame.[59] Rather, as the observations made by Rose and Miller suggest, when a political rationality takes on a moral form, it gains the power to inform the aims and uses of government itself. Ideals such as 'freedom' or 'justice' take on particular ('economised') meanings within a neoliberal rationality and so, too, do the laws which are enacted in their name. Thus, the 'good citizen' is defined within an economic calculus – a framework that is also used to define what it means to be a 'good patient' (in medical law), a 'good player' (on the sports field), and a 'good girl' (in adjudications of sexual assault).

This points to two of the central ways consent can be seen to operate within (and as a component to) neoliberal rationality. The first is through invocations of the 'common good' and legal interpretations of public or social utility – key factors in law's delineation of the scope and content of consent. The second is the extension of this neoliberal 'good' onto individual ontologies, whereby certain behaviours and subjectivities are prescribed (and valorised), while others are not. Under the law's rubric of 'reasonableness', those actions (and actors) that best conform to neoliberal values of efficiency, calculated risk, and self-management are deemed 'capable' of consenting. The rest are excluded from this legal performance of autonomy. The following two sections examine each of these factors that are used in the jurisprudence to limit consent (ie social utility and capacity) in further detail.

Social utility in a neoliberal world

As discussed in previous chapters, judicial limits are often placed on consent in the name of social utility, where claims to autonomy (via consent) are over-ruled on the basis that the activity the accused persons were engaged in is found to have no 'good reason'. These social utility arguments were initially used by the courts to rule against the availability of the defence of consent in circumstances where bodily harm was incurred merely for the sake of profit.[60] Judicial views on boxing have since changed, as has the broad prohibition against exhibitions of sport for profit, and courts now explicitly acknowledge the 'good reason' of

58 Brown, *Edgework* (n 1).

59 Vanessa Munro has argued that while social contract theorists, relying on the work of both Hobbes and Locke, posit consent as the 'master of law' this is a problematic claim. She contends that 'the assertion that consent is the master of law neglects or at least trivializes the complex and powerful ways in which the dictates of law and institutions of the state, once established, operate to construct the very mechanisms of, and parameters for communicating, consent'. See Vanessa E Munro, 'Constructing Consent: Legislating Freedom and Legitimating Constraint in the Expression of Sexual Autonomy' (2009) 41 *Akron LR* 923, 926.

60 *R v Coney* (1882) LR 8 QBD 534. See also Sir Michael Foster's summary of the courts' treatment of this issue in his 1763 text, *Crown Cases* (Clarendon 1762). The American case, *Commonwealth v. Collberg* 119 Mass 350 (SC 1876) also ruled out the consent defence in boxing matches on the same basis, equating it with prizefighting.

such events. This can be observed in the oft-cited Supreme Court of Canada judgment in *Jobidon*, where Gonthier J (writing for the majority) remarked:

> The policy of the common law will not affect the validity or effectiveness of freely given consent to participate in rough sporting activities, so long as the intentional applications of force to which one consents are within the customary norms and rules of the game. Unlike fist fights, sporting activities and games usually have a significant social value; they are worthwhile.[61]

Although the court does not elaborate on the 'significant social value' of sporting activities in *Jobidon*, the cases surveyed in the previous chapter demonstrated how contemporary courts distinguish between assault and sport on the basis of the latter's quality as a 'manly pursuit'. Further, these cases provide evidence that the early profit-seeking exclusion delineated in *Coney* has not survived in contemporary treatments of the social utility of contact sports. Instead, the law's treatment of violence that erupts on the professional playing field is adjudicated in ways that align with neoliberal ideals of calculated risk, the 'manly pursuit' of profit, and the unavailability of the consent defence for those players who have not adequately 'economised' their body capital.

This reveals that while claims to the 'public interest' are somewhat of a staple in the law's dealings with consent, it is not a static category. Instead, understandings of what might be useful to society or 'good' for everyone are shifting concepts, as evidenced by the very different functions and values ascribed to consent in Ancient Greece, the medieval marketplace, or the contemporary sports field. Following the widespread adoption of classical liberalism and its endorsement of the social contract, consent has been inseparably connected to notions of the 'common good'. Freedom to act in the world is constrained by what's good for everyone else living in it. But as these communities change, so, too, does the conceptualisation of what will be of the most social value or use.

What, then, is socially utile in a neoliberal world? What does neoliberalism value? Certainly, the components of individualism and its resultant responsibilisation play a central role in the neoliberal understanding of the 'common good', as do unfettered trade, competition, calculated risk, profit maximisation, and governmental policies principled in non-interference. Yet, for all of its inferences about facilitating the ways in which citizens might live in the company of others, the neoliberal conception of what might be commonly good has very little to do with community. Rather, independence reigns supreme in neoliberal rationality, where individuals are 'left alone' to make their own decisions and live with the resulting consequences. The neoliberal ethic is thus a self-regarding one, rooted in the claim of universal self-interest. And while many commentators have suggested there is a need to temper this self-interest with some sense of 'civic virtue' so as to foster more social (if not distributive) justice or to preserve

61 *R v Jobidon* [1991] 2 SCR 714, 766–767.

the sustainability and legitimacy of the market itself,[62] the 'economic morality' of neoliberalism conflates the good with the entrepreneurial. In such equations, civic virtue itself becomes a private, self-regarding matter.[63]

The previous chapter's discussion of the consent defence in sporting contexts provides some evidence of this economically motivated notion of social utility, where what is thought to be 'good' is also that which fosters competitive aggression; effective risk management; and, perhaps above all, freedom of choice. Within a neoliberal rationality, however, this freedom is understood through a consumerist lens, aptly described by David Harvey as the 'liberty of consumer choice'.[64] Autonomy is thus an all but limitless ability to commodify. For instance, when asked to comment on the increasing incidents of neurological disorders among professional athletes, the co-director of Boston University's Center for the Study of Traumatic Encephalopathy (himself a former professional athlete) suggested that the league organisations were 'trading money for brain cells'.[65] Within a neoliberal rationality, this is a fair trade. After all, *homo economicus* is, above all else, an entrepreneur of herself. This is a model of 'goodness' that some have argued has replaced the so-called 'Protestant work ethic' where labour itself (of the mind and body) was valued as a means of pursuing the good life.[66] Instead, the 'modern citizen is not that of the producer but of the consumer' where personal fulfilment, social good, and moral virtue are pursued through 'purchasing power'.[67] This is a power to both buy and sell – be that barley or brain cells. Freedom within this rubric is not a liberty to labour,

62 See Barry Smart, *Economy, Culture, and Society* (Open University Press 2003).

63 This stands in stark contrast to the community-based model of civic virtue espoused in the medieval market, where contemplations of one's needs (versus 'greeds') were essential to determining the 'just price'. See Farber (n 36) and Thompson, *Customs in Common* (n 32). Similarly, criminal responsibility was a matter of one's character, established by testimony of one's community members. As noted by Nicola Lacey, 'the key question was whether the guilty defendant was a corrigible member of the law-abiding community', thus enforcing a 'community consensus' model of criminality; Lacey, 'In Search of the Responsible Subject' (n 51) 362.

64 Harvey (n 11) 42.

65 John Branch, 'Derek Boogaard: A Brain Going Bad' *New York Times* (New York, 5 December 2011) <www.nytimes.com/2011/12/06/sports/hockey/derek-boogaard-a-brain-going-bad.html> accessed 30 April 2019. This has become a frequently cited quotation in both the social and academic commentary on sports violence. See, for instance, Hanna Kong's article, which employs this phrase in its title (despite no reference to Chris Nowinski in the piece itself): Hanna Kong, 'For the Love of the Game: Trading Money for Brain Cells' (2013) 2(1) *Miss Sports LR* 115.

66 Max Weber commented on the way in which a capitalist logic transformed the Protestant work ethic into an ideology that constrained freedom rather than enhanced it, noting: 'The Puritan wanted to work in a calling; we are forced to do so. For when asceticism was carried out of monastic cells into everyday life, and began to dominate worldly morality, it did its part in building the tremendous cosmos of the modern economic order… In Baxter's view the care for external goods should only lie on the shoulders of the "saint like a light cloak, which can be thrown aside at any moment". But fate decreed that the cloak should become an iron cage', *Protestant Ethic and the Spirit of Capitalism* (Talcott Parsons tr, first published 1930, Routledge 2005) 123.

67 Nikolas Rose, *Governing the Soul: The Shaping of the Private Self* (Routledge 1990) 102.

but rather a liberty to consume. 'Choice' is a selection from a range of options that are 'marketed' and promoted.[68] It is a freedom to make use of one's body capital by selling or trading it for the best possible return.

The description of the accused which the court offers in one of the first criminal prosecutions of an athlete for in-game violence provides some evidence of this monetarily driven conception of social utility and the proper use of body capital. In the Canadian case of *Green* (discussed in detail in Chapter 4), the court described Green as 'a man who is very experienced in his sport, a man who undoubtedly plays boisterously, *as he is paid to*; he is well known and his reputation is well known, and other players respect that reputation, as they have to in the circumstances'.[69] The accused's act of violence is validated for the court by the fact that he receives financial compensation for his behaviour – an understanding that is supported by the game itself, where 'enforcers' are hired specifically to engage in on-ice fighting.[70] Further, the court doesn't describe the accused's actions as violent or assaultive, but rather as 'boisterous play', keeping stride with the common law's tradition of valuing aggression and physical force in 'manly pursuits'. This is solidified in the *Green* judgment when the court explains its reasons for acquittal (on the basis of implied consent), noting that 'Mr. Green's action was instinctive, and … more protective in his own interests than anything else of his own safety. Having regard to those circumstances, I find Mr. Green not guilty'.[71]

This suggests that while hegemonic masculinity and pursuit of profit are valued in sport, they are even more estimable when sought in the face of personal risk (and for the aim of self-interest). And while commentators might herald physical aggression and bodily contact as values in and of themselves in

68 Nik Rose presents a view of modern life as structured entirely around the notion of 'choice' where '[e]ntry into family life is represented as occurring out of the love that two individuals voluntarily declare for each other; remaining within marriage is a matter of decision rather than conformity to an eternally binding undertaking; having or not having children should, it appears, be a personal choice. Leisure has been invented as the domain of free choice *par excellence*. However constrained by external or internal factors, the modern self is institutionally required to construct a life through the exercise of choice from among alternatives' (n 67) 227.

69 *R v Green* [1971] 16 DLR (3d) 137 (1970, Ont Prov Ct), [16] (emphasis added). Green and his opponent, Wayne Maki, were each tried for the same incident (*R v Maki* (1970) 16 DLR (3d) 137 (Ont Prov Ct)). Their cases are often cited in Canadian jurisprudence as they represent the first time members of the National Hockey League (NHL) were criminally charged for in-game violence.

70 Brent Severyn, a former NHL enforcer describes in-game violence as his 'trade' and notes that new, young players didn't threaten his place on the team but, in his words, his 'livelihood'. He remarks, 'Tough guys have to be on at all times, ready to handle every new young player who wants to take their jobs and livelihoods … An enforcer must also have a feel for how a game is unfolding and continually take stock of his team's emotional state. … The score also determines when you apply your trade'. There is also some ambiguity about whether his role on the team was about ice hockey or fighting when he suggests 'I might as well have left my stick and gloves on the bench'. See Brent Severyn, 'An Enforcer's Life is a Daily Battle' *Sports Illustrated* (21 September 2011) <www.si.com/nhl/2011/09/21/brent-severynenforcerlife> accessed 29 January 2019.

71 *Green* (n 69) [22].

sport, these components are often described in economic terms, whereby pain is regarded as a 'currency' with which young men might 'purchase' masculine identities.[72] In fact, it is difficult to find discussions of the social utility of sport which *don't* cite its economic value.[73] The very first page, for instance, of a 2001 text entitled *Sport Matters*, under the heading 'The social significance of sport', reads as follows:

> There is no need to support the contention that sport is significant by reference to facts and figures ... Think, for example, of the following: the attention regularly devoted to sport in the mass media; the amounts of money, public and private, spent on sport; the dependency of business on sport for advertising; the growth of state involvement in sport for reasons as diverse as a desire to combat spectator violence and contribute to health or national prestige; the numbers of people who regularly take part in sport as performers or spectators, to say nothing of those who are directly or indirectly dependent on it for their livelihoods.[74]

In this description, the significance of sport seems grounded in a neoliberal understanding of social utility, where value is determined on the basis of economic return. Within this calculus, freedom is the opportunity to pursue profit, commodify one's body, and risk injury – for the right price.

This equation of costs versus benefits is one of the central mechanisms of neoliberal rationality and is extended to all aspects of the socio-political world, including determinations of the value of human life itself. There is perhaps no place where this is more poignantly evidenced than in the field of medical law where the language of 'cost savings' or 'resource allocation' is explicit in deliberations about medical treatment, quality of life, and the requisite procedures for informed consent. For some bioethicists, this is attributable to a particular character that 'best interests' considerations take on within a neoliberal rationality. Jill Fisher has noted that neoliberalism spawns a cultural logic wherein 'what is good for industry' is also what is deemed good for the citizenry.[75] This

72 Michael Gard and Robert Meyenn, 'Boys, Bodies, Pleasure and Pain: Interrogating Contact Sports in Schools' (2000) 5(1) *Sport, Educ & Soc* 19.

73 See, for example, John CH Jones, Kenneth G Stewart and Randy Sunderman, 'From the Arena into the Streets: Hockey Violence, Economic Incentives, and Public Policy' (2006) 55(2) *Am J Econ & Soc* 231. The authors explore the positive correlation between in-game violence and spectator attendance at professional ice hockey games and the legal implications that flow from this. The article begins with a quotation from a former player who went on to become a general manager of a team, Bobby Clark, which reads, 'If they cut down on violence too much, people won't come out to watch... violence sells'.

74 Eric Dunning, *Sport Matters: Sociological Studies of Sport, Violence, and Civilization* (Routledge 2001) 1.

75 I have paraphrased Fisher slightly here so as to broaden the scope of her comments. Fisher's article looks specifically at pharmaceutical trials in the United States, thus her wording reads: 'what is good for industry must be good for America'. See Jill A Fisher, 'Coming Soon to a

logic grants considerations of the 'public purse' an equal (if not central) stake in a number of bioethical debates, including decisions concerning the withdrawal of life-sustaining treatment. Some of the legal commentary on a high-profile Canadian case, *Rasouli v Sunnybrook Health Sciences Centre*,[76] illustrates this.

Hassan Rasouli, a retired mechanical engineer, immigrated to Canada from Iran in April 2010. In August of the same year, he was diagnosed with a benign brain tumour and underwent surgery in October 2010 to have it removed. In the days following the surgery, Rasouli suffered an infection (bacterial meningitis), which resulted in significant neurological damage, respiratory failure, and reduced consciousness.[77] He was placed on life-support and designated as being in a persistent vegetative state (PVS), with no prognosis for recovery. In December 2010, his physicians sought consent from Rasouli's substitute decision maker (SDM) to remove the life-support and transfer him to palliative care. Rasouli's SDM was his wife, Dr Salasel, a qualified physician who disagreed with the attending physicians' prognosis. She maintained that Rasouli would regain cognitive ability and denied consent to withdraw treatment.[78] Amidst disputes with Rasouli's physicians about whether or not the SDM's consent was required to withdraw treatment, Dr Salasel (Rasouli's wife and SDM) sought an injunction to prevent the withdrawal of life-support.[79] This injunction was granted at the trial level and re-affirmed at the Court of Appeal. An appeal of this judgment was heard by the Supreme Court of Canada in December 2012 and almost a year later, the Supreme Court affirmed the decision of the Court of Appeal, finding that the consent of Rasouli's SDM was needed to withdraw treatment.[80]

The case has solicited a fair amount of commentary among legal scholars, bioethicists, and public opinion about the value of life and the circumstances in which consent can and should be required. Arguments about social utility (traditionally a delimiter of consent in criminal law) have figured prominently in these discussions, often presented within a neoliberal rhetoric. Hilary Young, for instance, frames the issue in the following way:

> No one wants to deny care to a patient who could materially benefit from it, but advances in technology allow health practitioners to keep people alive even when there is no realistic prospect of improvement to their underlying condition. As a result, life-sustaining treatment *can* be provided, but as

Physician Near You: Medical Neoliberalism and Pharmaceutical Clinical Trials' (2007) 8(1) *Harv Health Pol Rev* 61, 64.

76 *Cuthbertson v. Rasouli* (2011) ONCA 482.

77 *Cuthbertson v Rasouli (Litigation Guardian of)*, SCC Docket No. 34362 (10 July 2012) (Factum of the Respondent) [9–12].

78 Interestingly, Rasouli did regain some abilities, resulting in a removal of the PVS (persistent vegetative state) designation and a re-designation of 'minimally conscious'. This change in his condition has not altered his attending physicians' prognosis of recovery.

79 Rasouli's physicians cross-applied for an order, confirming that no consent was required for withdrawal of treatment; Factum of the Appellant (n 77) [6].

80 *Cuthbertson v Rasouli* [2013] 3 SCR 341.

> potential returns diminish and costs (including to the patient, in terms of invasiveness and suffering, as well as to the public purse) increase, it is not obvious that such treatment *should* be provided.[81]

Many arguments of this ilk are found in the literature discussing end-of-life care, often with reference to the term 'medical futility', where proposed treatments are deemed to be 'irrational' or lacking in 'good reason' on the basis that they are unlikely to improve a patient's condition. Underlying this standard of reasonableness is an economic vision of (social) utility that defines the value of life with the labour (and ensuing product) it might provide. As Tom Koch has noted, the 'invocation of cost as a rational criterion for limiting acceptable levels of care for the chronically and terminally ill is rooted in the late nineteenth century redefinition of individual worth as a quotient of employability and productivity'.[82] Thus, determinations of medical futility rest on an understanding of 'improvement' (of the patient's condition) that is not about extending life (as Hassan Rasouli's request for continued treatment would do) so much as it is about providing treatment for patients who might cease to be economically burdensome.[83] These monetary concerns are also attributed a 'common sense' status in the legal and bioethical commentary on medically 'futile' cases, allowing the state's economic interests to be positioned on equal footing with arguments about the sanctity of life, religious objections to treatment, and patient autonomy.[84] Arguments about state resources and the gross expenditures on health care operate on the presumption that given the scarcity of these resources, allocations should be done for the greatest good. Yet, these contentions rely on a particular vision of what this social good is – one that values economic productivity above all else. In such a formulation, reasonableness or 'rational' decision-making is a matter of cost efficiency.

Despite the prevalence of concerns about health care resource allocations, courts have been reluctant to engage in explicit cost-benefit analyses in consent-based medical cases. In most instances, following an acknowledgement of the economic concerns, the courts have deferred to legislatures on the matter.

81 Hilary Young, 'Why Withdrawing Life-Sustaining Treatment Should Not Require Rasouli Consent' (2012) 6(2) *MJLH* 54, 58–59 (emphasis in original).

82 Tom Koch, 'Care, Compassion, or Cost? Redefining the Basis of Treatment in Ethics and Law' (2011) 39(2) *JLM&E* 130, 131.

83 Koch provides a famous example of a case where physician assessments of medical futility (based on an economic notion of productivity) were grossly mistaken: Stephen Hawking. At the age of 21, he was given no more than two years to live. Interventions to prolong his life were thought to be 'futile', and yet despite ongoing physical debilitation, Hawking went on to become one of the world's leading physicists and researchers (n 82) 134.

84 The author of a 2012 article in the *University of Toronto Medical Journal* states the matter almost defiantly: 'Beyond the ethical and religious issues regarding the termination of medical treatment for the critically ill, there are serious economic issues – *yes, economic issues* – that cannot be ignored' (emphasis in original). See Eric Nauenberg, 'Beyond the *Golubchuk* Case: The Issue of Intergenerational Trends in Medical Expenditures' (2012) 90(1) *UTMJ* 12, 12.

The House of Lords decision in *Bland* (1993) is a good example of this practice. Anthony Bland was a spectator who was crushed and asphyxiated at a football game when the stadium's overcrowding safety measures failed.[85] As a result of the injuries he sustained at the stadium, Bland went into a PVS for more than three years before his physicians (with the consent of his family) sought a court declaration that removing Bland's life-support systems would not constitute a criminal offence. In their decision, the House of Lords made explicit note of the financial considerations of maintaining Bland's current condition, although they deferred judgment on these matters to Parliament, stating (under the heading 'Best interests of the community'):

> Threaded through the technical arguments addressed to the House were the strands of a much wider position, that it is in the best interests of the community at large that Anthony Bland's life should now end. The doctors have done all they can. Nothing will be gained by going on and much will be lost ... The large resources of skill, labour and money now being devoted to Anthony Bland might in the opinion of many be more fruitfully employed in improving the condition of other patients, who if treated may have useful, healthy and enjoyable lives for years to come ... This argument was never squarely put, although hinted at from time to time. In social terms it has great force, and it will have to be faced in the end. But this is not a task which the courts can possibly undertake. A social cost-benefit analysis of this kind ... must be for Parliament alone, and the outcome of it is at present quite impossible to foresee.[86]

Courts have seemingly come a long way since the turn of the twentieth century when such deference wasn't needed in the face of a more prevalent and widespread 'economic mind'. In the now famous case of *Buck v Bell* (1927), involving the forced sterilisation of a so-called 'feeble-minded' woman, Oliver Wendell Holmes wrote explicitly about the state's interest in restricting the number of economically dependent citizens. Framing the issue entirely as a matter of 'public welfare', Justice Holmes declared:

> We have seen more than once that the public welfare may call upon the best citizens for their lives. It would be strange if it could not call upon those who already sap the strength of the State for these lesser sacrifices ... in order to prevent our being swamped with incompetence. It is better for all the world if, instead of waiting to execute degenerate offspring for crime or to let them starve for their imbecility, society can prevent those who are manifestly unfit from continuing their kind ... Three generations of imbeciles are enough.[87]

85 *Airedale NHS Trust v. Bland* [1993] AC 789.
86 *Airedale* (n 85) 896.
87 *Buck v Bell* 274 US 200 (1927) 207.

The words of Justice Holmes are jarring, particularly when juxtaposed with the more cautious language of the House of Lords in *Bland* (1993); yet, the clarity of the court's position in *Buck v Bell* and its underlying economic motivations suggests that consent in the modern era performs a similar function as it has in past ages, that is, a prescription of normative subjectivity rather than an expression of personal autonomy. Holmes's meaning is clear: some persons are more deserving of life than others and the determinant of this desert is economic productivity. While contemporary medical jurisprudence may have toned done its rhetoric, the underlying principles of market morality remain operative when social utility is in play, even when pitted against hallmark principles of medical ethics, such as patient autonomy or personal dignity.[88] Where the treatment or procedure that is the subject of a patient's consent (or refusal thereof) is deemed to be too expensive or an inefficient use of state funds, social utility demands that it be over-ridden or disallowed. The Canadian case of *Golubchuk v Salvation Army Grace General Hospital*[89] provides a contemporary example of this rationality at work.

The facts of the *Golubchuk* case share some similarity with those of *Rasouli.* Samuel Golubchuk was an 84-year-old Orthodox Jew who suffered severe brain damage following a fall in 2003. After several years of deteriorating health, Mr Golubchuk was placed on life-support at the Salvation Army Grace General Hospital in Winnipeg, Manitoba. Although he did have brain function, the level of this functioning was a point of dispute between Mr Golubchuk's attending physicians and his family. The physicians advised Golubchuk's children that they intended to remove him from life-support. Consent to do so was refused on

88 Take, for instance, the 2011 decision of the UK Supreme Court with respect to a community care plan for Elaine McDonald in the case *R (On the Application of McDonald) v Royal Borough of Kensington and Chelsea* [2011] UKSC 33. McDonald was 67 years old and had suffered a stroke several years before the proceedings, which left her with severely restricted mobility. Due to a bladder dysfunction, McDonald needed to urinate frequently over the course of a night. Her mobility difficulties often presented a problem in this regard for her, including several falls, one of which broke both of her hips. When she was released from hospital, her local authority, the Royal Borough of Kensington and Chelsea (RBKC) underwent a needs assessment for her and, as part of an interim care plan, provided her with funding for a temporary caretaker to assist her in getting to and from a commode during the night. Her final needs assessment, however, resulted in a decrease of allotted funds on the basis that RBKC found it was 'preferable' that she use incontinence pads (at a significantly lower cost than that of a night-time caretaker). RBKC argued that McDonald's care had been 'changed to reflect [her] needs', suggesting that incontinence pads would provide McDonald with 'greater safety, independence, and privacy' – hallmark principles of neoliberalism. McDonald disagreed, contending that she was not incontinent and that to be treated as such was to infringe on her sense of personal dignity. In a letter notifying McDonald of the change in funds, RBKC stated, 'The council has a duty to provide care, but we must do so in a way that shows regard for use of public resources'. McDonald sought judicial review of the council's decision, but at each stage of appeal, the decision of the RBKC was upheld. For a review of Lady Hale's dissenting opinion and the judicial backlash it received, see Helen Carr, 'Rational Men and Difficult Women: *R (On the Application of McDonald) v Royal Borough of Kensington and Chelsea* [2011] UKSC 33' (2012) 34(2) *JSWFL* 219.

89 [2008] MJ No. 54 (Man QB).

religious grounds.[90] Golubchuk's children sought an injunction from the court to prevent the disconnection. This injunction was granted on a temporary basis, awaiting full disposition of the matter at trial; however, Mr Golubchuk died (naturally in hospital) before the trial took place. During the legal battle, Golubchuk's physicians argued that consent was not needed to withdraw treatment – a principle that the Manitoba College of Physicians and Surgeons endorsed in a guideline it released in 2008 in response to the court injunction in Golubchuk's case.[91] This guideline stated that the final decision to withdraw treatment is one that lies with the attending physician and not with the family.[92] While this position received a fair amount of critical reception among bioethicists and legal scholars for its 'affront to the guiding principles of Western medical ethics: patient autonomy and human freedom',[93] other commentators defended the position for its 'good sense'. Bernard Dickens, in response to the case, remarked that '[i]f the patient's life cannot be saved in a meaningful way and if intervention would deny resources that would benefit other patients … then the doctor is justified in clinical judgment to withhold treatment. Clinical judgment is not negotiated with patients'.[94] Some ethicists have argued that cost considerations form part of a physician's professional and ethical duties, where 'in addition to [the] role as caregiver, the physician is a gate-keeper who must subordinate the interests of an individual patient if necessary to attain societal cost containment objectives'.[95] Austin Sarat and Jennifer Culbert, in their examination of state violence and assisted death, observe that:

> In a regime dedicated to putting and keeping life in order and safe, the state may still exercise the right to death associated with the classic sovereign. To do so, however, it has to describe those who will be put to death as incorrigible monsters or as biological hazards so that their demise and final disposal can be represented as an unpleasant but necessary task that the state reluctantly but decisively undertakes for the well-being of its citizens.[96]

90 *Golubchuk* (n 89) [8–9]. The primary ground was that removing the ventilation tubes would amount to a hastening of death, which Golubchuk's family argued was prohibited by Orthodox Jewish law.

91 For (critical) commentary on this guideline, see Jocelyn Downie and Karen McEwan 'The Manitoba College of Physicians and Surgeons Position Statement on Withholding and Withdrawal of Life-Sustaining Treatment (2008): Three Problems and a Solution' (2009) 17(1) *Health LJ* 115.

92 Alan Bruce Jotkowitz, Seymour M Glick and Ari Z Zivotofky, 'The Case of Samuel Golubchuk and the Right to Live' (2010) 10(3) *Am J Bioeth* 50.

93 Jotkowitz (n 92) 53.

94 Robert Cribb, 'Lawsuit Could Set Precedent about End-of-Life Decision' (*Toronto Star*, 4 September 2010) <www.thestar.com/news/gta/2010/09/04/lawsuit_could_set_precedent_about_endoflife_decisions.html> accessed 29 January 2019.

95 Maxwell J Mehlman, 'Patient-Physician Relationship in an Era of Scarce Resources: Is There a Duty to Treat?' (1993) 25(2) *Conn L Rev* 349, 352.

96 Austin Sarat and Jennifer L Culbert, *States of Violence: War, Capital Punishment, and Letting Die* (CUP 2009) 6, as cited in James A Tyner, *Violence in Capitalism: Devaluing in an Age of Responsibility* (University of Nebraska Press 2016) 82–83.

James Tyner offers the examples of 'the disabled and the elderly – two figures that are progressively understood as market failures within the neoliberal state' for whom the 'injunction to "die sooner" is becoming hauntingly clear'.[97] In this context, Justice Holmes's decision in *Buck v Bell* does not seem so distant a past.

Not only do economic conceptions of social utility influence determinations of medical futility and quality of life,[98] but there is also evidence to suggest this prevailing market morality serves to transform the kinds of subjects that are 'free' to consent and the functions this consent is meant to perform. Jill Fisher has argued that 'medical neoliberalism' represents a commodification of both health care and its delivery that effectively converts patients into consumers.[99] Aside from the emphasis on individualism that this consumer model propagates (discussed in further detail in the following section), there is a shift in what consent is understood to do when patients are thought to be 'buying' health products or services. Rather than an expression of patient autonomy, consent becomes a guard against physician liability. It marks the moment of consumer choice and the shifting of responsibility for the consequences of that choice from health care providers to health care consumers. Fisher notes:

> Unlike patients, consumers seeking health care bear the responsibility for the choices they make – or fail to make – regarding their health. Because they are positioned as having the right to make choices about health care, consumers also have the obligation to utilize whatever products and services are available to ensure health or to treat illness and disease. This is not to say that medical professionals are not liable for malpractice claims. If anything, assessing the appropriateness of care is another burden on consumers, and malpractice suits serve as a means to make claims that the products and services they sought were not delivered as promised.[100]

Consent in this configuration serves as a legal 'flak jacket' – a term employed by Lord Donaldson in the English case *W (a minor)*,[101] referring to the protection against liability that consent confers on physicians against 'the litigious'.

97 Tyner (n 96) 182, citing Margaret Morganroth Gullette, *Agewise: Fighting the New Ageism in America* (UCHIP 2011) 50.

98 For a review of cases that define 'quality of life' with economic productivity, see Koch (n 82). Among other similar cases, Koch describes a trend in the 1990s that denied organ transplants to patients with Down's Syndrome 'because it was believed such persons were socially burdensome and thus less worthy than normal people', 135.

99 Fisher, 'Coming Soon' (n 75).

100 Fisher, 'Coming Soon' (n 75) 65.

101 [1992] 4 All ER 627; [1993] Fam 64, 78. Lord Donaldson uses the term when revising an analogy he had employed in an earlier case (*Re R (a minor) (wardship; consent to treatment)* [1992] Fam 11) of consent as a 'key', suggesting that he now preferred 'the analogy of the legal "flak jacket" which protects the doctor from claims by the litigious … Anyone who gives him a flak jacket (that is, consent) may take it back, but the doctor only needs one and so long as he continues to have one he has the legal right to proceed'.

Margaret Brazier has described this model of consent in the following way: 'Once consent is obtained, the doctor is protected from legal gunfire. Consent protects his [sic] back'.[102] The flak jacket was only one of two functions Lord Donaldson viewed consent as serving in medical law. The first was a clinical one, described in the judgment in a fashion strikingly similar to the role ascribed to consent in medieval codes of ethics governing the doctor-patient relationship. 'The clinical purpose', Lord Donaldson stated, 'stems from the fact that in many instances the co-operation of the patient and the patient's faith or at least confidence in the efficacy of the treatment is a major factor contributing to the treatment's success'.[103] In the medieval period, obtaining the patient's consent was thought to be integral to the success of the treatment, even if obtained through deception. The giving of consent, in a medieval context steeped in religious conviction, took on a ritual form. Rather than an expression of freedom, the medievalist viewed consent as submission (to God, via the other). Although most of this religious context has been replaced by a clinical and positivist one, ritual persists in the contemporary process of informed consent. Ethnographic studies of patients' experiences with the consent process affirm the notion that the informed consent form is viewed as merely a 'technicality' or routine part of the intake or assessment procedures patients experience prior to treatment, rather than a moment for substantive discussion or autonomy.[104] Market morality forms the backdrop of this patient experience. A conception of the physician's time as limited (and more 'valuable' than that of the patient) and hospital resources as strained contributes to patients' perceptions that compliance is the most expedient way forward.[105] As noted by a participant in a 2006 ethnographic study of the reasons women consent to surgery: '[T]he last thing they need is somebody turn round and saying "I've changed my mind I don't want to have this", because it messes you know all their sort of thing up'.[106] At times, this perception can shift to a direct feeling of coercion, evident in the words of another participant in the same study:

> Yeh, because they were there really pressurising me. It was like I was signing for a loan or something, and they had got this pen and they go 'right then are you ready to sign' and you just feel like they are stood there, waiting for

102 Margaret Brazier, 'Organ Retention and Return: Problems of Consent' (2003) 29 *J Med Eth* 30.

103 *W (a minor)* (n 101) 76.

104 Mary Dixon-Woods and others, 'Why Do Women Consent to Surgery, Even When They Don't Want to: A Qualitative Study' (2006) 1 *Clin Eth* 153; Philip Meredith, 'Patient Participation in Decision-Making and Consent to Treatment: The Case of General Surgery' (1993) 15(3) *Soc Health & Illness* 315. One participant in Dixon-Woods's study encapsulates this view in the following comment: 'Well they're [consent forms] all standard, standard protocol, isn't it, what you have to do, and I just go with the flow and sign 'em', 155.

105 Dixon-Woods cites Strong's (1979) study on the ceremonial nature of the clinic as support for this point, suggesting that 'power is produced and maintained in the doctor–patient relationship through the ritualized nature or ceremonial order of the doctor–patient encounter, which may mask power differentials through the imperative to preserve an apparently harmonious encounter' (n 104) 155.

106 Participant 14, as cited in Dixon-Woods (n 104) 155.

> me [...] they had got a load of other patients and I am thinking well you really haven't got time to, they are busy which I do appreciate that they are busy.[107]

This suggests that within a frame of 'common economic sense', patients are aware of an unwritten code of conduct that encourages acquiescence and discourages argumentation, conflict, or active questioning, all in the name of effective resource management and cost efficiency. To act outside the ambit of these rules is to risk losing one's status as a 'good patient', thereby losing a perception of one's reasonableness and, in turn, one's capacity to consent. This is not unlike accounts from young women who claim to have difficulty saying 'no' when negotiating sexual encounters as a result of the 'unwritten rules' about sexual norms, gender roles, and social expectations.[108] To act assertively, to 'own' one's desire, to change one's mind or to stop a sexual encounter once it has begun is to risk losing one's reputation as a 'good girl', just as to shy away from aggressive behaviour on the playing field or to misuse one's body capital is to risk losing one's status as a 'good player'. These acts of non-conformity with the unwritten rules are the makings of *Buck v Bell*'s 'undesirables'; those subjects for whom consent is not available due to a lack of (neoliberal) reason or social utility. Consenting subjects must govern themselves accordingly to be granted the *capacity* to consent, and this governance requires strict adherence to a neoliberal rationality.

The capacity to consent: an act of self-governance

Neoliberalism, acting as political rationality, serves as a form of governmentality insofar as it operates through what Foucault has called 'technologies of the self'.[109] Broadly defined, these are methods through which a state or ruling class is able to govern others by requiring (both juridically and ethically) that citizens exercise self-control, in essence, governing themselves.[110] This ethic of *self*-governance stems from two central components to neoliberal rationality: individualism and responsibilisation. Built on the model of the self-interested individual of classical liberalism, neoliberal rationality posits a social world made up of atomistic agents, each tasked with self-determination. One's life circumstances, in a neoliberal world, are thought to be the consequences of one's actions and one's choices. Predictably, this is one of the elements of neoliberalism that sustains

107 Participant 15, as cited in Dixon-Woods (n 104) 155.

108 Anastasia Powell, 'Amor fati? Gender Habitus and Young People's Negotiation of (Hetero) sexual Consent' (2008) 44(2) *J Soc* 167.

109 Both Wendy Brown, *Edgework* (n 1) and Thomas Lemke, 'Foucault, Governmentality' (n 2) make this point.

110 '[G]overning people', Foucault argues, 'is not a way to force people to do what the governor wants; it is always a versatile equilibrium, with complementarity and conflicts between techniques which assure coercion and processes through which the self is constructed or modified by [it]self' as cited in Lemke, 'Foucault, Governmentality' (n 2) 53.

the greatest critique from communitarians, where the argument that human life is inherently social (rather than individualistic) is used to buttress claims that the complex web of inter-relationships among and within communities should be the basis for legal and political action.[111] Further, ignoring these relational components to human life allows neoliberal regimes to set aside the ways in which different social groups might enjoy undue privilege, or work to oppress and exclude others.[112]

Hand-in-hand with the emphasis on individualism is the process of responsibilisation that neoliberalism puts in play. Neoliberal rationality espouses the view that individuals should be set free from the over-reaching arm of big government and left to their own pursuits, each aided (or marred) by the strengths and weaknesses of the individual. The heart of neoliberal autonomy is the freedom to pursue one's own interests and control one's own destiny (to the best of one's abilities), without the interference of state regulation. In this configuration, individuals who achieve less success or experience more hardship are merely the victims of their own failings. The state, having 'left alone' its citizens to their own pursuits, can hardly be blamed for their lack of success; rather, according to the neoliberal story, such disappointments are merely the result of the 'natural' order of things where some individuals simply have *more* than others: more skill, more competency, more luck, more ambition, more expertise.[113] These categories of 'more' are the stuff of human capital and, unlike other commodities, are indivisible from the person who possesses them. '[M]ade up of two components: an inborn physical-genetic predisposition and the entirety of skills that have been acquired as the result of "investments" in the corresponding stimuli: nutrition, education, training and also love, affection, etc', citizens become entrepreneurs of themselves, seeking to gain ever greater return on their 'investments'.[114] Individuals are thus expected to 'take responsibility' for their own lives, recognising their own strengths and weaknesses, and managing these effectively so as to reap the greatest benefit at the lowest cost.

These elements of individualism and responsibility lie at the heart of neoliberal rationality and, when coupled with the principle of non-interference, result in an imperative to 'look after one's self'. Within this ethic of self-care, individuals are tasked with making good choices, avoiding 'bad' risks, and assuming

111 For an approach to autonomy that takes these concerns seriously, see Jennifer Nedelsky, 'Reconceiving Autonomy: Sources, Thoughts, and Possibilities' (1989) 1 *Yale J L & Fem* 7; and Catriona MacKenzie and Natalie Stoljar (eds), *Relational Autonomy: Feminist Perspectives on Autonomy, Agency, and the Social Self* (OUP 2000).

112 See, for instance, Nicola Lacey's essay, 'Community in Legal Theory: Idea, Ideal, or Ideology?' in *Unspeakable Subjects: Feminist Essays in Legal and Social Theory* (Hart Publishing 1998).

113 Note the lack of structural excesses (eg more money, more opportunity). Within neoliberal rationality, these inequities are the result of individual successes/weaknesses, work ethic, and 'natural' talents.

114 Thomas Lemke, '"The Birth of Biopolitics": Michel Foucault's lecture at the Collège de France on Neo-liberal Governmentality' (2001) 30(2) *Econ & Soc* 190, 199.

'reasonable' ones. This standard of reasonableness, however, is rooted in neoliberal ideals of social utility and value. Some endeavours will simply be deemed too 'costly' – either, in the medical context, because of the toll a particular treatment might take on hospital resources (with an inefficient rate of return) or, in the criminal law context, because the prospects of criminalisation are simply too high to warrant an action in the first instance.[115] In some circumstances, unreasonably risky behaviour will be that which falls outside the normal 'rules of play', an ambit, of course, which varies depending on the socio-legal context. On the sports field, for example, although professional athletes are expected to risk injury during the course of a game, they must do so in a way that doesn't reduce the overall value of their body capital. The athlete's body is both capital and the tool to obtain it; therefore reasonableness demands a certain 'corporeal thrift' in its usage. As Wacquant has observed, 'one must make use of one's body without using it up'.[116] This also serves to delineate what forms of self-care (and surveillance) will be deemed 'rational'. Take, for example, the following description offered of the body work of boxers:

> The boxer comes to consider his body, especially his hands, as his stock-in-trade. Boxers have varied formulas for preventing their hands from excess swelling, from excessive pain, or from being broken. This does not mean a hypochondriachal interest, because they emphasize virility and learn to slough off and to disdain punishment.[117]

This passage speaks both to the ideals of hegemonic masculinity that the last chapter found endorsed in criminal law's assessment of 'harm' in sports violence cases and to the commodification and maximisation of capital that neoliberal rationality demands.[118] This same 'conservation ethic' forms part of the *habitus* around sexuality for young women, many of whom are counselled (both socially and culturally) to 'save' themselves for marriage, reinforcing the 'value' ascribed to women for their bodies (and use thereof).[119] When women and athletes do

115 This notion of criminal conviction as a 'cost' is one put forth by Richard Posner in his positive economic analysis of sexual assault. See Richard Posner, *Sex and Reason* (HUP 1992) – a book that solicited a great deal of feminist critique. For a collection of these, see (1993) 25(2) *Conn L Rev*.

116 Wacquant (n 25) 130.

117 S Kirson Weinberg and Henry Arond, 'The Occupational Culture of the Boxer' (1952) 57(5) *Am J Soc* 460, 462; as cited by Wacquant (n 25) 129.

118 In his description of the relationship between the boxer and the trainer, Wacquant highlights these components of neoliberal rationality: 'One of the major functions of the pair formed by the trainer and the manager is to modulate and adjust the trajectory of their charge over time so as to optimize the "return on pugilist investment" of the trio, that is, the ratio between the corporeal capital stacked and the dividends procured by fights in the form of money, ring experience, notoriety, and usable contacts with influential agents in the field such as promoters' (n 597) 140.

119 See Catharine MacKinnon, *Toward a Feminist Theory of the State* (HUP 1989), in particular, Chapter 9.

not protect their 'stock-in-trade', they are deemed to have taken unreasonable risks and are deserving of the consequences. As Wacquant notes, departures from this regime of 'corporeal discipline' are 'promptly interpreted as the direct cause of [the boxer's] failings in the ring'.[120]

These 'failings' clearly extend beyond the sports arena to form an integral part of the law's assessment of the limits of consent. Within a neoliberal rubric, persons are expected to engage in a strict regime of risk management, undertaking only those hazards that, on a cost-benefit analysis, are expected to yield sufficient profit to warrant the risk. This means there are some risks that will not be seen as 'reasonable' within a neoliberal rationality. Engaging in these excludes a subject from consent, marking the act (and actor) as 'undesirable' or 'without good reason'. These circumstances of 'excessive' or 'unreasonable' risk are seen as too harmful or without adequate social utility to allow for the invocation of consent. This is not unlike the process of Christian alignment that was demanded of medieval patients so as to bring them good health. In the contemporary period, all things must be 'aligned' with neoliberal ideals of reason and social value (or face the consequences). In this calculus, 'harm' is not a violation of bodily integrity, a creation of coercive circumstances, or a disavowal of personhood, but rather an interference with each individual's ability to self-govern, where self-governance is understood as a form of economic management of the self. If a person chooses to mismanage herself, it is her freedom to do so; but the ensuing damage is her responsibility to bear.

One of the loci where the neoliberal requirement of responsible risk management meets consent most explicitly is in the legal and social regulation of sex. Sexual assault law has a long history of presuming 'good girls' will avoid risky situations.[121] Determinations of what kinds of behaviours or circumstances will constitute 'high risk' have largely been informed by stereotypical assumptions about female sexuality and gender roles, if not Victorian values of propriety.[122] At times, these cultural assumptions have been judicially recognised both for the harm they create for women and the difficulties they present to a variety of evidentiary and investigatory matters, such as determinations

120 Wacquant (n 25) 147.

121 See, for example, Melanie Randall, 'Sexual Assault Law, Credibility, and "Ideal Victims": Consent, Resistance, and Victim Blaming' (2010) 22(2) *CJWL* 397; Lise Gotell, 'Rethinking Affirmative Consent in Canadian Sexual Assault Law: Neoliberal Sexual Subjects and Risky Women' (2008) 41(4) *Akron LR* 865; Elizabeth Sheehy, 'From Women's Duty to Resist to Men's Duty to Ask: How Far Have We Come?' (2000) 20(3) *CWS* 98.

122 The now infamous words of Justice McClung of the Alberta Court of Appeal in the landmark Canadian case, *Ewanchuk* (1998) 13 CR (5th) 324 (Alta CA), represent a good example of this value system at work in judicial discourse. Writing for the majority in a confirmation of the trial court's acquittal of the accused, McClung J noted, 'it must be pointed out that the complainant did not present herself to Ewanchuk or enter his trailer in a bonnet and crinolines', [4]. Notably, McClung is the grandson of women's rights activist, Nellie McClung – one of the 'Famous Five' who launched the so-called 'Person's Case' that sought to have women declared 'persons' under the law in 1929. See *Edwards v AG Canada* [1930] AC 124.

of credibility and under-reporting levels.[123] One such instance, the Supreme Court of Canada case of *Seaboyer*, is significant because of the legislative reforms it launched in Canada, including the first statutory definition of consent within Canada's *Criminal Code* and a list of circumstances in which consent is not possible.[124]

These provisions were interpreted for the first time in the *Ewanchuk* (1999) case, where the Supreme Court of Canada rejected a doctrine of implied consent for sexual assault. In a separate (concurring) judgment, Justice L'Heureux-Dubé noted that the 'case is not about consent, since none was given'.[125] Instead, the case was characterised as being about stereotypes of female sexuality, which rely on the notion that women say 'no' when they really mean 'yes'.[126] As a result, *Ewanchuk* instituted what has been called an 'affirmative consent' model where 'consent' must be communicated in a positive and express manner.[127] While this has led some commentators to describe the *Ewanchuk* case as the 'no means no' decision, others have suggested it might more aptly be understood as a judgment that confirmed 'only yes means yes' given its endorsement of a positive consent standard.[128] Moreover, *Ewanchuk* established the principle that the *absence* of consent (for the purposes of establishing the *actus reus* of sexual assault) is

123 See, for instance, the Supreme Court of Canada case, *R v Seaboyer* [1991] 2 SCR 577, which recognised sexual assault as the most underreported crime with an estimated reporting rate of 6%. A 2017 Statistics Canada study estimated there were more than 600,000 annual sexual assaults (based on self-reported data); see Shana Conroy and Adam Cotter, 'Self-reported Sexual Assault in Canada, 2014 [85-002-X]' *Juristat* (Statistics Canada 2017). The 2014 General Social Survey found that only 5% of these were reported to police – a rate 'that has remained unchanged over the past decade. This makes sexual assault the violent crime least likely to be reported to police. By comparison, over one in three (38%) physical assaults were reported to police', Cristine Rotenberg, 'Police-reported Sexual Assaults in Canada, 2009 to 2014: A Statistical Profile [85-002-X]' *Juristat* (Statistics Canada 2017) 4.

124 Section 273.1(1) of the *Criminal Code* defines consent as 'the voluntary agreement of the complainant to engage in the sexual activity in question'. It forms a central component of the *Code*'s delineation of sexual assault provisions. This is in keeping with a number of other jurisdictions. For a survey of these in the UK, US, and Australia, see Terry Goldsworthy, 'Yes Means Yes: Moving to a Different Model of Consent for Sexual Interactions' (*The Conversation*, 29 January 2018) < https://theconversation.com/yes-means-yes-moving-to-a-different-model-of-consent-for-sexual-interactions-90630 > accessed 30 January 2019.

125 *R v Ewanchuk* [1999] 1 SCR 330, [82].

126 Justice McLachlin (who later served as the Chief Justice of Canada's Supreme Court from 2000 to 2017) noted this explicitly in her concurring reasons, suggesting the implied consent doctrine 'rests on the assumption that unless a woman protests or resists, she should be "deemed" to consent … On appeal, the idea also surfaced that if a woman is not modestly dressed, she is deemed to consent. Such stereotypical assumptions find their roots in many cultures, including our own. They no longer, however, find a place in Canadian law', *Ewanchuk* (n 125) [103–104].

127 For a fuller explanation of this model, see Gotell, 'Rethinking' (n 121) and Lise Gotell, 'Canadian Sexual Assault Law: Neoliberalism and the Erosion of Feminist inspired Law Reform' in Clare McGlynn and Vanessa E Munro (eds), *Rethinking Rape Law: International and Comparative Perspectives* (Routledge 2010).

128 Rakhi Ruparelia, 'Does "No" Mean Reasonable Doubt: Assessing the Impact of *Ewanchuk* on Determinations of Consent' (2006) 25(1–2) *CWS* 167.

determined from the subjective standpoint of the complainant.[129] Provided the complainant is found credible, the court's inquiry shifts to the accused and the state of mind he had at the time of the offence. To satisfy the *mens rea* of sexual assault, the Crown must establish either that the accused knew the complainant was *not* consenting or that he did not take reasonable steps to ensure she was.[130] As the Court noted in *Ewanchuk*, 'the trier of fact may only come to one of two conclusions: the complainant consented or not. There is no third option'.[131]

The court's treatment of the defence of an 'honest but mistaken belief in consent' was clear about the need for an accused to rely on more than mere body language or assumptions when assessing whether or not the complainant was, in fact, consenting. As the majority judgment in *Ewanchuk* stated:

> In order to cloak the accused's actions in moral innocence, the evidence must show that he believed that the complainant <u>communicated consent to engage in the sexual activity in question</u>. A belief by the accused that the complainant, in her own mind wanted him to touch her but did not express that desire, is not a defence. The accused's speculation as to what was going on in the complainant's mind provides no defence.[132]

In rejecting a doctrine of implied consent, the *Ewanchuk* decision established a standard of explicit consent, where affirmative agreement on the part of the complainant for the sexual activity in question must be obtained by the accused. Critics of the decision raised concerns about the practicality of such a standard, given the social awkwardness of having to gain permission for each stage of a sexual encounter, and the potential detriment the affirmative consent model might have on 'seduction' or customary sexual overtures – speaking, perhaps, to the power of prevailing gender norms and codes of intelligibility about sex.[133] Others have praised the decision for the move it makes away from a view of sexual consent as a failure to resist and towards an explicit, voluntary expression of desire.[134] While, on one hand, this new approach to sexual consent has signalled a move away from the cultural assumptions about female sexuality that have previously informed beliefs about what constitutes a 'good girl' or the 'ideal rape victim', the standard of reasonableness that is applied to judicial determinations

129 *Ewanchuk* (n 125) [26].

130 The court in *Ewanchuk* relied on an earlier judgment of L'Heureux-Dubé's in the *Park* (1995) case, where she explained the mental element of the offence of sexual assault as 'not only satisfied when it is shown that the accused knew that the complainant was essentially saying "no", but is also satisfied when it is shown that the accused knew that the complainant was essentially not saying "yes"', *Park* [1995] 2 SCR 836, [39] as cited in *Ewanchuk* (n 125) [45].

131 *Ewanchuk* (n 125) [31].

132 *Ewanchuk* (n 125) [46] (emphasis in original).

133 Don Stuart, '*Ewanchuk*: Asserting "No Means No" at the Expense of Fault and Proportionality Principles' (1999) 22 CR (5th) 39. Elaine Craig refutes these claims in her article 'Ten Years after *Ewanchuk* The Art of Seduction is Alive and Well: An Examination of the Mistaken Belief in Consent Defence' (2009) 13(3) *CCLR* 247.

134 Sheehy (n 121); Gotell, 'Canadian Sexual Assault Law' (n 127).

of the mistake defence continues to operate within a neoliberal rationality, to the detriment of rape complainants. As Lise Gotell has observed:

> Recent Canadian decisions recognize sexual autonomy, but in a form that is consistent with individuated norms of criminal law. Normative sexual interaction is reconceived as being like an economic transaction and good sexual citizens are reconfigured to resemble rational economic actors assuming responsibility for their actions and the risks that they take.[135]

Despite the impetus to eliminate harmful stereotypes about women and their sexuality from sexual assault law (and the criminal justice system's response to it), the neoliberal components of individualism and responsibilisation function to maintain victim-blaming practices in the law's dealings with consent through an adherence to its autonomy story. Canadian Courts have also set parameters for the 'honest mistake' defence, requiring that it be 'reasonable', not based on intoxication, or held in the face of wilful blindness or recklessness.[136] Unfortunately, judicial interpretations of what 'reasonable' mistaken beliefs in consent look like tend to focus less on the steps the accused took and more on the victim's traits and behaviours (and the presumed effect these had on an accused's perception of consent).[137] As Justice L'Heureux-Dubé noted in the *Ewanchuk* case, in response to the comments made by the appellate court judge about the complainant's style of dress, her living arrangements, and her status as an unmarried mother:

> [O]ne might wonder why [McLung J] felt necessary to point out these aspects of the trial record. Could it be to express that the complainant is not a virgin? Or that she is a person of questionable moral character because she is not married and lives with her boyfriend and another couple? These comments made by an appellate judge help reinforce the myth that under such circumstances, either the complainant is less worthy of belief, she invited the sexual assault, or her sexual experience signals probable consent to further sexual activity. Based on those attributed assumptions, the implication is that if the complainant articulates her lack of consent by saying "no", she really does not mean it and even if she does, her refusal cannot be taken as seriously as if she were a girl of "good" moral character. "Inviting" sexual assault, according to those myths, lessens the guilt of the accused.[138]

135 Gotell, 'Canadian Sexual Assault Law' (n 127) 216.

136 *Criminal Code of Canada*, RSC 1985, C-46, s 273.2. See also the UK's *Sexual Offences Act* 2003, s 75.

137 For a thorough and insightful (albeit, disheartening) examination of this issue, see Elizabeth A Sheehy, 'Judges and the Reasonable Steps Requirement: The Judicial Stance on Perpetration against Unconscious Women' in Elizabeth A Sheehy (ed), *Sexual Assault in Canada: Law, Legal Practice and Women's Activism* (University of Ottawa Press 2012).

138 *Ewanchuk* (n 125) [89]. Lucinda Vandervort has observed that in some instances, even making the defence of 'honest belief' available to a jury to consider represents a 'flagrant example of the

Even where these myths do not present themselves in judicial discourse as explicitly as they did in *Ewanchuk,* the credibility of rape complainants is assessed as a matter of risk management. Did she exhibit 'questionable judgment'?[139] Did she drink too much, leaving her 'disinhibited' or feeling 'flirty'?[140] Did she engage in 'bizarre' or 'abnormal' behaviours without 'good reason'?[141] Was she 'foolish' or old enough to know better?[142] Lise Gotell has suggested these investigations into the 'risky' behaviour of rape complainants represent a 'revised form of victim-blaming'.[143] This is well evidenced by a passage in a 2008 Canadian case where two men were convicted after drugging and sexually assaulting a woman (J.M.) they met in an online chatroom:

> J.M. communicated with a stranger who contacted her out of the blue on the internet. She flirted with him and foolishly agreed to meet, giving him her name, address, and telephone number. She knew that he had mentioned

---

preference for, and the tendency to revert to, "local common sense" and "local social norms" in legal interpretation, in defiance of decades-long efforts by the Supreme Court of Canada to clarify the law on the point at issue'; Lucinda Vandervort, 'Lawful Subversion of the Criminal Justice Process? Judicial, Prosecutorial, and Police Discretion in *Edmondson, Kindrat,* and *Brown*' in Sheehy, *Sexual Assault in Canada* (n 137) 140. Vandervort has also written about the exculpatory rhetorical power of the term 'honest belief', see 'Honest Beliefs, Credible Lies, and Culpable Awareness: Rhetoric, Inequality, and *Mens Rea* in Sexual Assault' (2004) 42(4) *Osgoode Hall LJ* 625.

139 Lise Gotell has noted the use of this discourse in cases even where convictions have been reached, as was the case in *R v CRN* [1999] OJ No. 3918 where the court stated, 'It is not unfair, I think to say, putting herself in this setting was of questionable judgment, questionable maturity, careless and without much concern for her personal security' [14], as cited in Gotell, 'Rethinking' (n 121) 879. This discourse also appears in cases where the 'poor risk manager' is not the complainant but her caretaker, as was the circumstance in the case *R v KRB* [2005] AJ No. 1329 where the mother of a child who had been sexually assaulted by her father was critiqued for the 'questionable judgment' she displayed in not foreseeing the assault [18].

140 In the case *R v JR* [2006] OJ No. 2698, despite finding the complainant's testimony compelling and thus determining that she did not consent, the court considered her level of intoxication and her testimony that being drunk had 'made her "flirty" in the past and that she had done things while drunk that she later regretted' as factors relevant to the accused's defence of an honest but mistaken belief in consent. This defence was rejected, however, and the accused was convicted – although one of the factors the court found most compelling in believing the complainant did not consent was the fact that she had had an abortion a few days earlier and was told by a physician to avoid intercourse.

141 Lise Gotell has noted the presence of these discursive moves in the Manitoba Court of Appeal case, *R v AJS* (2005) 192 Man R (2d) 4, where the court questioned the behaviour of the complainant, an aboriginal woman living in severe poverty in a remote, rural community, when she visited the accused to borrow a lawnmower. Gotell cites the court's inquiry: 'Why would she put herself at risk of being raped for the sole reason of borrowing a lawnmower to cut the grass?' [17] as cited in Gotell, 'Canadian Sexual Assault Law' (n 127) 217.

142 In reviewing the sentence for an offender who had sexually assaulted the complainant (in addition to choking her), the British Columbia Court of Appeal in *R v Baker* [1990] BCJ No. 1995 made the following observation: 'The complainant was not a very young woman. She was approximately 35 years of age. She was probably extremely foolish in entering the residence at that hour of the morning but that does not justify the assault upon her', 1996.

143 Gotell, 'Canadian Sexual Assault Law' (n 127) 217.

> bringing alcohol and drugs and she did contemplate the possibility of a sexual encounter with him. When he showed up at the residence with his friend, she voluntarily got into the car ... J.M'.s continued attempts to minimize her provocative and foolish behaviour stemmed from her intense embarrassment that she allowed herself to get into the situation in the first place.[144]

While most legal scholars would be quick to argue consent operates differently in sexual circumstances than it does on a sports field,[145] these assessments of sexual assault complainants' risk management behaviour suggest the same line of thinking is at work in both contexts. Consent in the sports arena is confined to the 'reasonable expectations of play'. As such, by stepping onto the ice, a hockey player is deemed to have consented to a certain degree of force or injury, provided it occurs in a circumstance that is 'usual' or falls within the normal rules of the game. In a study examining the public discourse surrounding the *Ewanchuk* case, Wright cites the following Letter to the Editor that was submitted to a national newspaper by a Canadian lawyer:

> Actions speak louder than words. What on earth was the female complainant doing engaging in mutual massage with a man she had never met before in the privacy of his own trailer? And yes, her rather skimpy attire would do nothing to discourage his allegedly unwanted advances in the course of the massage.[146]

Here, the reference to 'reasonable expectations' is all but explicit. The complainant's clothing, her act of entering the accused's trailer (under the auspices of a job interview), and her engagement in 'mutual' massage (throughout which she repeatedly told the accused 'no') are all viewed as indicators of poor risk management, leaving her responsible for the consequences of these 'choices'. Consent is hardly an expression of autonomy in a context where it need not be uttered at all. Rather, in the course of the 'normal rules of play', women are denied consent precisely because they are deemed to be always giving it.[147]

144 *R v Sadaatmandi* [2008] BCJ No. 405, [86] as cited in Gotell, 'Canadian Sexual Assault Law' (n 127) 217. See also Tracey Lindberg, Priscilla Campeau, and Maria Campbell, 'Indigenous Women and Sexual Assault in Canada' in Sheehy, *Sexual Assualt in Canada* (n 137) for an analysis of three cases involving the sexual assault of a 12-year-old aboriginal girl by three non-aboriginal men. The authors identify a series of (irrelevant) 'risk' factors (pertaining to the victim) that were considered by the courts in their adjudication of the accused's guilt (eg level of intoxication, history of sexual abuse, experience in sex work).

145 Cheryl Hanna, 'Sex is Not a Sport: Consent and Violence in Criminal Law' (2001) 42(2) *BCL Rev* 239.

146 John Mahony, 'Judgment Day' *National Post* (3 March 1999) A19 as cited in Joanne Wright, 'Consent and Sexual Violence in Canadian Public Discourse: Reflections on *Ewanchuk*' (2001) 16(2) *Can J L & Soc* 173, 182.

147 This is an argument Carole Pateman has made, suggesting that to 'begin to examine the unwritten history of women and consent brings the suppressed problems of consent theory to the

Perhaps most problematically, these judicial assessments of a complainant's level of life 'mismanagement' persist even where significant statutory reforms have been implemented with an aim for improving definitions of 'consent' and eliminating reliance on stereotypical views of women and their sexuality. The Scottish case *HM Adv v Mutebi*[148] is a good example. The complainant had become significantly intoxicated at a friend's home before visiting a nightclub in Glasgow where she continued to drink. She left the nightclub, and CCTV footage demonstrated that she was visibly intoxicated and unstable on her feet. She returned to her flat, and while her memory of events is not entirely clear, she recalled meeting the accused (a stranger) outside her flat, kissing him, and then 'coming to' in her bed amidst forcible penetration by the accused. The complainant testified she pushed against his chest, said 'no' repeatedly, and then 'succeeded in wriggling away'.[149] The accused then left the flat (after stealing the complainant's mobile phone and £170 from her wallet). The case was one of the first to reach the Appeal Court following significant statutory revisions to the meaning of 'consent' under the *Sexual Offences Act* and the circumstances in which consent could be vitiated (including excessive intoxication). Despite these reforms, the conviction of the accused for sexual assault was overturned at the Court of Appeal on the basis of the 'reasonableness' of the accused's mistaken belief in consent. Rather than establish that the complainant's state of intoxication was severe enough to vitiate consent (thus moving to an assessment of what steps the accused might have taken to establish his 'reasonable' albeit mistaken belief in consent), the court appears to take the complainant's severe intoxication level as evidence 'that it was likely that she would have consented to have sex with a stranger who she met on the street while very drunk, rather than regarding this as something out of the ordinary or improbable'.[150]

Similar reasoning is found in many sexual assault cases involving intoxicated complainants.[151] The decision of a provincial court judge in the 2017 Canadian case, *R v Al-Rawi*, made national headlines after the accused, a taxi driver charged with the sexual assault of a heavily intoxicated fare, was acquitted in a decision that included the remarks: 'Clearly a drunk can consent' and 'A lack of

---

surface. Women exemplify the individuals who consent theorists have declared are incapable of consenting. Yet, simultaneously, women have been presented as always consenting, and their explicit nonconsent has been treated as irrelevant or has been reinterpreted as "consent"'. See Carole Pateman, *The Disorder of Women* (Polity Press 1989) 150.

148 *Rogers Mutebi v Her Majesty's Advocate* [2013] HCJAC 142.

149 *Mutebi* (n 148) [2].

150 Lindsay Farmer, 'On the Misinterpretation of the *Sexual Offences Act* 2009: *HM Adv v. Mutebi*' (*Oblique Intent*, 12 November 2013) < http://obliqueintent.blogspot.com/2013/11/on-misinterpretation-of-sexual-offences.html > accessed 30 January 2019.

151 See Sharon Cowan, 'The Trouble with Drink: Intoxication, (In)capacity, and the Evaporation of Consent to Sex' (2008) 41(4) *Akron LR* 899; and Janine Benedet, 'The Sexual Assault of Intoxicated Women' (2010) 22(2) *CJWL* 435.

memory does not equate to a lack of consent'.[152] The accused had picked up the complainant downtown after a night of heavy drinking. She was found by police unconscious and incontinent in the back seat of the accused's cab far from her home 'or any address she was familiar with … naked from the waist down, with her breasts exposed'. The accused was found with his pants undone 'between the complainant's open legs. The police saw him trying to hide the complainant's urine-soaked pants between the console and front seat'.[153] Despite explicit acknowledgement of the complainant's severe intoxication, her apparent incapacity (and a comment that the accused was 'not somebody I would want my daughter driving with'), the trial judge was unable to find an absence of consent.[154] Instead, the court alludes to the complainant's poor risk management and lowered inhibitions, invoking the tried-and-true stereotype of the 'regretful slut'. Referring to evidence from the forensic alcohol specialist (that showed the complainant's blood-alcohol level to be three times the legal limit), the court noted that alcohol 'tends to reduce inhibitions and *increases risk-taking behaviour*. And this often leads to people agreeing, and to sometimes initiating, sexual encounters, only to regret them later when they are sober'.[155]

This rationality prevails in the discourse of sexual assault prevention campaigns, where women are cautioned against walking alone at night, dressing provocatively, drinking too much, or leaving one's drink unattended in mixed company. The 'good girl' will choose the well-lit route, will carry her handbag with cell phone and money close, and, above all, follow her instincts.[156] These discourses are a part of the wider crime prevention literature that 'implores us to reduce our possibilities of encountering crime. Indeed, it is a duty of good citizenship'.[157] Aside from positioning women as inherently rapeable,[158] these

152 *R v Al-Rawi* (unreported, 2017). Transcript of audio recording of verdict available: <www.cbc.ca/news/canada/nova-scotia/halifax-cab-driver-sex-assault-acquittal-judge-decision-transcript-1.4008375> accessed 30 January 2019.

153 *R v Al-Rawi*, 2018 NSCA 10, [3–6].

154 The trial judge's decision was overturned on appeal and ordered a second trial, which began in January 2019.

155 *Al-Rawi*, NSPC (n 152). For further discussion of this case, see Elaine Craig, *Putting Trials on Trial: Sexual Assault and the Failure of the Legal Profession* (MQUP 2018) 37–38.

156 Examples of these kinds of scripts in sexual violence prevention literature are abundant. To take merely one example, the New York State Police advise, on their website, that to prevent sexual violence, women ('while dating') should abstain from alcohol use, never accept beverages from someone they don't trust, carry money for taxis or phone calls, and 'follow your instincts: If a place or the way your date acts makes you nervous or uneasy, get out'. See 'Crime Prevention: Date Rape' <www.troopers.ny.gov/Crime_Prevention/Violence/Date_Rape/> accessed 30 January 2019. See also: Elizabeth A Stanko, 'Safety Talk: Conceptualizing Women's Risk Assessment as a "Technology of the Self"' (1997) 1(4) *Theo Crim* 479, for an examination of UK police warnings to women about safety. Fiona Vera-Gray also offers an insightful analysis of women's safety work in *The Right Amount of Panic: How Women Trade Freedom for Safety* (Polity 2018).

157 Stanko (n 156) 486.

158 Sharon Marcus, 'Fighting Bodies, Fighting Words: A Theory and Politics of Rape Prevention' in Judith Butler and Joan Scott (eds), *Feminists Theorize the Political* (Routledge 1992).

scripts reinforce a view of sexual assault as an individualised problem.[159] In congruence with neoliberal rationality, violence against women is not a social issue deserving of governmental intervention but rather an individual woman's responsibility to guard against; to live her life in 'proper alignment' (to echo the medieval view of the consenting patient) so as to avoid injury. Provided a rape complainant has not led a 'mismanaged' life, she will be entitled to give (and refuse) consent.

A similar approach is taken in the prevention literature for sexually transmitted diseases, where individuals are tasked with 'taking responsibility' for not simply their own health, but that of others. This responsibility is heightened with the use of the criminal law, as seen in cases of HIV transmission where failure to disclose one's positive status has resulted in convictions for aggravated assault[160] and criminal negligence.[161] These convictions have been steadily rising, even in jurisdictions without HIV-specific legislation.[162] In these cases, the complainant's consent to sexual intercourse is retroactively reneged on the basis that it was improperly or inadequately informed. Further, in each case, the risk presented by the offender's conduct is positioned as a danger to the public at large, and the result of a failure of the individual's responsibility to take adequate care in managing the risk of infection. It is this latter aspect of the criminal law's foray into the regulation of health risks that has elicited the greatest criticism from anti- or de-criminalisation advocates. While some argue the criminal law is simply an inept tool for addressing public health concerns,[163] others have suggested the law's interventions serve to further stigmatise those already suffering from HIV and AIDS.[164] The law's response to these critiques has largely followed a route of soft

159 Conversation analysis studies have also suggested that 'just say no' strategies in sexual violence prevention campaigns serve to further enforce male norms of women's sexuality. Based on an analysis of refusals found in day-to-day conversation, Kitzinger and Frith remark that 'it should not … be necessary for a woman to say "no" for her to be understood as refusing sex'. See Celia Kitzinger and Hannah Frith, '"Just Say No?" The Use of Conversation Analysis in Developing a Feminist Perspective on Sexual Refusal' (1999) 10(3) *D&S* 293. Instead, these policies can create assumptions about women that reinforce myths about their inherent submissiveness or low self-esteem.

160 *R v Cuerrier* [1998] 2 SCR 371. See also *R v Williams* [2003] 2 SCR 134, where the charge of aggravated assault was reduced to attempted aggravated assault on the basis that the Court could not determine the exact point in time at which the victim became infected.

161 *R v Mercer* [1993] NJ No. 198 (Nfld CA).

162 Patrick O'Byrne, 'Criminal Law and Public Health Practice: Are the Canadian HIV Disclosure Laws an Effective HIV Prevention Strategy?' (2012) 9(1) *Sex Res & Soc Pol* 70.

163 See Edwin Cameron, 'Criminalization of HIV Transmission: Poor Public Health Policy' (2009) 14(2) *HIV/AIDS Pol Law Rev* 63; and Edwin Cameron, Scott Burris and Michaela Clayton, 'HIV is a Virus, Not a Crime: Ten Reasons Against Criminal Statutes and Criminal Prosecutions' (2008) 11(7) *J Int AIDS Soc* 1 <http://www.ncbi.nlm.nih.gov/pmc/articles/PMC2635346/pdf/1758-2652-11-7.pdf> accessed 30 January 2019.

164 See Erin Dej and Jennifer M Kitty, '"Criminalization Creep": A Brief Discussion of the Criminalization of HIV/AIDS Nondisclosure in Canada' (2012) 27(1) *Can J L & Soc* 55; and Lucinda Vandervort, 'HIV, Fraud, Non-Disclosure, Consent and a Stark Choice: *Mabior* or Sexual Autonomy?' (2013) 60(2) *CLQ* 301.

paternalism, not unlike that of Mill's traveller about to cross a broken bridge. Rather than prevent her from crossing altogether, the soft paternalist merely seeks to ensure she is aware of the risks. This lies at the heart of the English Court of Appeal's decision to quash the conviction in *Dica* (2005),[165] a case where the defendant had unprotected sex with two women while aware of his HIV-positive status. Rather than prohibit the defence of consent on the basis that it was given under false pretences (as the Supreme Court of Canada held in *Cuerrier*), the court suggested the issue was whether the women had consented to the *risk* of infection, separating this from their consent to sex. '[R]isks have always been taken by adults consenting to sexual intercourse', the court argued, citing sexually transmitted infections and unwanted pregnancies as examples. 'Modern society has not thought to criminalise those who have willingly accepted the risks'.[166]

The Court in *Dica* draws a distinction, then, between consenting to bodily harm (which might not be permitted on public policy grounds) and consenting to the risk of this harm. The latter circumstance, the court held, was too great an imposition on personal autonomy.[167] Implicit in this view of consent is the responsibilised individual, tasked with managing the risks s/he may encounter in life so as to yield the best outcomes. Note, for instance, the testimony of the complainants under cross-examination in the case, *R v Konzani*,[168] where the appellant had been convicted at trial on three counts of inflicting grievous bodily harm after failing to disclose his HIV-positive status to three different women (who were later infected). In the transcript of the trial, the defence cross-examined one of the complainants as follows:

Q. What did you know about him before you agreed to have sex with him?
A. Not much …
Q. Did you realise you were taking a risk of becoming pregnant.
A. Yeah.
Q. Were you prepared to take that risk?
A. Yeah.
Q. Did you realise you were taking a risk of catching a disease?
A. Yeah.
Q. And were you prepared to take that risk? …
A. Yes, I was, yeah.[169]

The same line of questioning was put to the second complainant at trial:

Q. You also realise that by having unprotected sex you risk catching an infection?
A. Yes …

165 [2005] All ER 593.
166 *Dica* (n 165) [50].
167 *Dica* (n 165) [52].
168 [2005] 2 Cr App R 14.
169 *Konzani* (n 168) [13].

Q. ... That too is a risk that you took.
A. Yes.
Q. That risk included the risk of contracting HIV didn't it?
A. Yes, but I didn't think about it at the moment.
Q. That means at the time you had unprotected sex?
A. Yes. ...
Q. But there was no discussion about HIV or tests or anything before you had sex?
A. Yes.
Q. You agree that there was no discussion?
A. Yes.[170]

In these excerpts, consent is positioned as a form of risk assumption, where the responsibility for 'getting informed' lies with the complainant (ie the 'risk taker' in the *Dica* Court of Appeal's vision of the inherently risky activity of sexual intercourse).[171] This is the same approach adopted by members of the HIV-positive community themselves, as documented in a 2005 ethnographic study of 'barebackers',[172] each of whom expressed the view that one's health was a personal responsibility that included being both informed and knowledgeable about the sexual choices one was making. Consent thus serves as a marker of this responsibility, as one of Adam's HIV-positive participants noted: 'When you consented to it ... if your other partners were willing to participate, it [condomless sex] was just a given. I just assumed that they take responsibility for their actions if they're willing to go along with it'.[173] This responsibilisation model persisted even where partners were consenting under false information, as demonstrated by another one of Adam's HIV-positive participants who reported the following exchange: 'I said, "I'm positive. It's, you know, your ball game then. No problem." And he said, well, his quote was, "I'm a top and I have less risk of catching it". All right. And I said, "Well, that's your choice. It's a high risk. It's always your choice"'.[174] Similar findings were reported by Michael Bartos in a 2002 study of safe-sex practices among HIV-positive persons in

170 *Konzani* (n 168) [20].
171 This stands in stark contrast to the 'duty to disclose' standard endorsed by the Supreme Court of Canada in *Cuerrier* and, notably, by Konzani's third victim who responded to similar questioning under cross-examination as follows: '**Q:** But you were actually on the subject of talking about HIV in Africa. Would it have been easy for you to ask him if he ... **A:** No, it would have been easier for him to tell me. That's what I think. He had...I didn't have the responsibility to ask him. He had the responsibility to tell me'. See *Konzani* (n 168) [27].
172 'Barebacking' refers to the practice of intentionally engaging in unprotected sex with new or unknown partners. Some scholars distinguish between this (self-labelled 'barebacking' practice) and the 'wider range of unplanned, episodic, unprotected sexual encounters' that occur. See Barry D Adam, 'Constructing the Neoliberal Sexual Actor: Responsibility and Care of the Self in the Discourse of Barebackers' (2005) 7(4) *Cult Health & Sex* 333, 334.
173 Adam (n 172) 340.
174 Adam (n 172) 340.

Australia, where it was argued that the self-interest promoted among the study's participants is not indicative of a 'callous disregard or reckless[ness]' but rather speaks to the prevalence of a neoliberal 'common sense' around consent that creates 'fewer bonds of social obligation' or duties of care to others.[175] Instead, it is a particular neoliberal view of autonomy that underlies these practices, one rooted in individualised risk management.

What is lost in such accounts of autonomy are, of course, the social and environmental inequalities that might affect one's choices or how the contexts in which these choices occur might themselves limit the available options. Jill Fisher offers the example of clinical pharmaceutical trials, wherein the prevalent 'economic sense' that prioritises health care costs over health care needs (if it doesn't equate the two), positions clinical research as a 'responsible choice' for those who require medical treatments they cannot afford. Fisher elaborates:

> [P]articipation in clinical trials becomes almost a duty for those who have no other access to health care because it is available as a 'choice'. By privileging the individual and choice, a health care system mediated by neoliberal policies and cultural sensibilities tends to obscure the inequalities to which those who participate in clinical trials tend to be subject. Within this frame, the systematic use of the uninsured or economically disenfranchised people as human subjects in pharmaceutical clinical development is not seen as being exploitive, but is instead positioned as an opportunity for members of those groups.[176]

This positioning also has a direct effect on the role of informed consent. While premised as a guardian of patient autonomy, this conceptualisation presupposes a certain level of autonomy that many of the participants of clinical trials simply don't have. Most studies on informed consent within these settings have shown that subjects' decisions to participate occur long before the consent form is presented or discussed and that such processes have little to no impact on study participation.[177] This has led Fisher to characterise the so-called 'ready to recruit' populations that pharmaceutical trials attract as 'ready to consent' – an observation that calls into question many of the reform strategies that bioethicists propose as a means of enhancing patient autonomy through consent.[178] For Fisher, such calls for more process-oriented approaches to informed consent or

175 Michael Bartos, 'HIV-Positive Gay Men's Risk Assessment and the Changing Meanings of HIV Infection' in Michael Hurley (ed), *Cultures of Care and Safe Sex amongst HIV Positive Australians* (Australian Research Centre in Sex, Health, and Society 2002) 45, 54 as cited in Adam (n 172) 344.

176 Fisher, 'Coming Soon' (n 75) 69.

177 Fisher, 'Coming Soon' (n 75). See also Jill A Fisher, *Medical Research for Hire: The Political Economy of Pharmaceutical Clinical Trials* (Rutgers 2009).

178 Jill A Fisher, '"Ready to Recruit" or "Ready to Consent" Populations?: Informed Consent and the Limits of Subject Autonomy' (2007) 13(6) *Qual Inq* 875.

the 'partnership' model proposed by Robert Veatch and others, while laudable, don't speak to the realities of participants' experiences, particularly in the clinical trial setting. While Veatch has suggested that 'partners' in decision-making processes are entitled to know about benefits and risks, the purpose of the study, its underlying theory, and so on, assessing these factors is made more difficult in a context where the study is designed by the physician and the economic needs of patients serve to characterise their participation as 'responsible' choices. Fisher suggests this 'indicates that the process of informed consent actually begins *before* potential human subjects are informed about the purpose, risks, and benefits of any given study'.[179] But accounts from patients themselves suggest the problem with consent is not *when* it is requested but the context of inequality in which it occurs. As noted by Dixon-Woods following a qualitative study of 25 women on their experiences with consenting to surgery: 'Women's accounts emphasise that it is the *procedure* of consenting that is instrumental in producing their docility, and thus subverts the original intention of the consent process in ensuring their autonomy'.[180] This procedure is one which takes place within a neoliberal rationality, where state resources, considerations of human capital[181] (and its management) as well as the 'ceremonial order of the clinic' serve to constrain the freedom patients have to explore alternatives or make 'non-normative' choices.[182] Put quite simply, patients are aware of 'the rules' and consenting – even amidst uncertainty[183] or pain[184] or fear[185] – is how one maintains the status of being a 'good patient'.

179 Fisher, 'Ready to Recruit' (n 178) 879.

180 Dixon-Woods (n 104) 157.

181 Capital is derived from the differential valuation of time and experience among patients versus doctors but also, as Dixon-Woods suggests, 'from specialist technical knowledge and skill … and the routines and tacit rules of the hospital and encounters between "lay people" and "professionals"' (n 104) 157.

182 Take, for instance, the account of refusing consent that is offered by one of Dixon-Woods's participants whose profession was in health sciences, offering her a greater degree of capital than any of the study's other patients: '[The nurse] puts the consent form in front of me and it's got laparotomy. I went, "Whoa, I'm not having that, that's major surgery". [She] was lovely afterwards [once the doctor arrived] but she weren't very nice before. No, no I wasn't complying and therefore, you know, she didn't want to know basically, I wasn't making things very easy for them. But I think I was within my rights to question what they were doing and to voice my opinions, saying, "No I'm not having it done". […] I found it quite easy to say no to the doctors, because I've worked with doctors therefore I felt a different relationship with them, but I should imagine it could be quite frightening. But I wasn't, I didn't feel intimidated at all by them. (laughs) Not one little bit' (n 104) 156.

183 'I'm just questioning you know, "God I just signed this form", why (laughs) you know yeah, it's weird. […] No, no, I wasn't saying yes I wanna go for a caesarean, I was just told to sign this form and so I signed this form', Participant 23 in Dixon-Woods (n 104) 155.

184 'I think the pain was taking over, I don't think I was completely in, and I was on morphine anyway, I was having gas and air, so I don't think I was completely compos mentis as such', Participant 26 in Dixon-Woods (n 104) 156.

185 'I didn't, I couldn't see, I couldn't see it, my mum held the pen to the paper where the box was and I just squiggled. [I] was scared, I cried, as soon as I did it. I cried cause I wasn't sure what I'd let myself in for', Participant 17 in Dixon-Woods (n 104) 156.

These are concerns bioethicists and medical legal scholars have wrestled with for years, often noting the systemic inequalities of the doctor-patient relationship as a central motivating factor in reform strategies aimed at improving the informed consent process so as to increase patient autonomy. Yet what is overlooked in such analyses is the role which the autonomy story of consent plays in both producing and sustaining this context of inequality. Where consent can be seen to construct particular frames of subjectivity as intelligible, namely those that possess the characteristics of responsibilised neoliberal rationality, positioning consent as a choice that is made by rational, calculating, and 'free' individuals obscures how this 'choice' is 'in large part circumscribed, if not pre-determined, by the rules of the game in [that] particular field and the power relations contained therein'.[186]

The consent-as-autonomy story is a narrative about a type of liberty that is understood to be both hypothetical and potentially 'harmful' when left unrestrained. Even in the most ardent of anti-paternalism arguments, some means of limiting the choices of individuals is thought necessary. Taking account of the 'public interest' or 'common good' is the generally accepted way of establishing these parameters of autonomy – a practice well demonstrated in judicial treatments of consent. Yet, when the 'good' is understood to be that which is also economically 'rational', the limits to what one might consent to (or of what 'knowledge' would be reasonable to have before making a choice) is also that which makes 'good economic sense'. This is perhaps the most compelling evidence of how consent operates as a form of self-governance, where one's freedom to act is limited by the frame of (neoliberal) intelligibility that positions consent as a choice in the first instance. This narrative proclaims persons to be 'free' to consent to whatever they wish (provided they only wish acts or circumstances that conform to neoliberal understandings of social utility and 'good reason'). As Catharine MacKinnon has argued, there is 'an unnoticed slippage' from the ideals of freedom that consent is meant to signify to the law's 'actual rules that tacitly reflect and impose inequalities', resulting in consent having 'an appeal it does not earn'.[187]

Conclusion

This chapter has attempted to demonstrate that, while consent is often positioned in law and political theory as a signifier of inalienable freedom, it is a liberty that is heavily circumscribed by the norms of neoliberal rationality. Consent is limited to circumstances that are judicially determined to be of social utility and not harmful, where both 'social utility' and 'harm' are defined within an economic calculus. Where subjects consent in contexts that run counter to this rationality's unwritten rules (eg in situations that are too high risk or lacking in 'good reason') they are all the more distasteful for what these 'choices' demonstrate about the

186 Dixon-Woods (n 104) 156–157.

187 Catharine A MacKinnon, 'Defining Rape Internationally: A Comment on *Akayesu*' (2006) 44(3) *Colum J Transnat'l L* 940, 955.

would-be-consenter's 'mismanaged' life. Consenting in such contexts is a kind of *hubris*, to echo the view in Antiquity, and, as the medieval period suggests, such 'sinfulness' can only lead one to further ill. As Aquinas might argue, the social world is not privy to the inner wills of its citizens. Thus, true salvation can only be achieved on one's own, through an exercise in self-regulation. Within a neoliberal context, individuals are 'left alone' to self-own and self-inspect, aligning themselves with 'common sense' values, and managing their risky behaviours in as cost-efficient a manner as possible.

In this way, the submissive operation of consent evidenced in the historical periods examined in previous chapters does not seem so distant a past. Contemporary consent also appears as a means of submitting to an economic frame, wherein the 'good' that governs determinations of social utility is akin to the 'good' individuals might strive for in their own self-management regimes. Where corporeal commodification is a *rational* act, the effective management of this capital is what marks one as a member of the neoliberal community. To take risks that are not economically viable, to mismanage one's body capital, is to take one out of balance or out of alignment with neoliberal ideals. To position consent as a choice serves to legitimise this calculation. It also serves to offload the responsibility for the various social conditions and relations which might impede agency or constrain choice to the individual and away from the state.

This is the new 'art of government' that Foucault examined in his study of the emergence of neoliberalism, where the authoritative arm of the state was replaced with a production and management of freedom.[188] Subjects are free insofar as they exercise freedom in ways that are in alignment with the maintenance of the (neoliberal) order. As a proclaimed embodiment of this freedom, consent is not simply a means of governing, but of doing so under the guise of self-direction. It is, to employ the words of Foucault, 'a limited use of an empty liberty'.[189] And while it is hardly a new line of thought to position political power and the dominant ideologies that support it as enabled more by the consent of the masses than the coercive force of the state,[190] consent itself is left unmarked in these analyses as is its promise of 'autonomy'. Legal scholars and reformers from all sides of the political spectrum debate how consent might be tweaked or

188 Foucault, *Birth of Biopolitics* (n 16).

189 Michel Foucault, *Madness and Civilization: A History of Insanity in an Age of Reason* (Richard Howard tr, Vintage 1965) 261.

190 While this explanation is typical of classical liberal and social contract theorists, Marxists and Gramscian scholars have also noted the role of consent in establishing (perceptibly legitimate) state authority. Even Machiavelli's *The Prince* advocates the avoidance of hatred from the masses, seemingly recognising that the power to govern lies ultimately in the will of the people. For further discussion, see the work of Heather Ingham who offers some interesting insights on the figure of Chiron, the centaur, in *The Prince*, suggesting that he represents the balance between a ruler's use of force with that of law, the latter presumably grounded in popular consent. See H Ingham, 'Machiavelli and the Interpretation of the Chiron Myth in France' (1982) 45 *JWCI* 217. (I am indebted to Andrew Moore for this point on Machiavelli's text.)

re-tooled, while others argue it is no more than an 'illusion'.[191] Yet the story of autonomy that is told about consent remains untouched. The vision is that if we can only 'get it right', self-realisation, self-governance, and personal integrity will be ours. The previous chapters have attempted to demonstrate the long history consent has had as a form of submission to dominant norms of intelligibility. The question that remains is perhaps the most important: why, in present day, should it be necessary for us to understand consent as something else? Perhaps more to the point, what purpose is served by positioning this submission as autonomy? It is to this inquiry that the concluding chapter turns its focus.

Bibliography

Table of cases

Airedale NHS Trust v Bland [1993] AC 789
Buck v Bell 274 US 200 (1927)
Commonwealth v Collberg 119 Mass 350 (Mass Sup Ct 1876)
Cuthbertson v Rasouli (2011) ONCA 482
Cuthbertson v Rasouli [2013] 3 SCR 341
Edwards v AG Canada [1930] AC 124
Golubchuk v Salvation Army Grace General Hospital [2008] MJ No. 54 (Man QB)
R (on the app of McDonald) v Royal Borough of Kensington and Chelsea [2011] UKSC 33
R v AJS (2005) 192 Man R (2d) 4
R v Al-Rawi (unreported, NSPC 2017)
R v Al-Rawi 2018 NSCA 10
R v Baker [1990] BCJ No. 1995 (BCCA)
R v Coney (1882) LR 8 QBD 534
R v CRN [1999] OJ No. 3918 (Ont SCJ)
R v Cuerrier [1998] 2 SCR 371
R v Dica [2005] All ER 593
R v Ewanchuk (1998) 13 CR (5th) 324 (Alta CA)
R v Ewanchuk [1999] 1 SCR 330 (SCC)
R v Gardner (2005) EWCA Crim 1399
R v Green [1971] 16 DLR (3d) 137 (Ont Prov Ct)
R v Jobidon [1991] 2 SCR 714
R v JR [2006] OJ No. 2698 (Ont SCJ)
R v Konzani [2005] 2 Cr App R 14
R v KRB [2005] AJ No. 1329 (Alta Prov Ct)
R v Mercer [1993] NJ No. 198 (Nfld CA)
R v Park [1995] 2 SCR 836
R v Sadaatmandi [2008] BCJ No. 405 (BCSC)
R v Seaboyer [1991] 2 SCR 577
R v Williams [2003] 2 SCR 134
Re R (minor) (wardship; consent to treatment) [1992] Fam 11
Re W (minor) (medical treatment) [1992] 4 All ER 627
Rogers Mutebi v Her Majesty's Advocate [2013] HCJAC 142

191 Daniel I O'Neill, Mary Lyndon Shanley and Iris Marion Young, *Illusion of Consent: Engaging with Carole Pateman* (Penn State University Press 2008).

Table of legislation

Criminal Code, RSC 1985, C-46 (Canada)
Sexual Offences Act 2003 (UK)

Secondary sources

Adam BD, 'Constructing the Neoliberal Sexual Actor: Responsibility and Care of the Self in the Discourse of Barebackers' (2005) 7(4) *Cult Health & Sex* 333

Anili B, 'Beyond Liberal Discourse: Meta-Ideological Hegemony and Narrative Alternatives' (PhD dissertation, University of Oregon 2010)

Barnett RE, 'Consenting to Form Contracts' (2002) 71(3) *Fordham L Rev* 627

Bartos M, 'HIV-Positive Gay Men's Risk Assessment and the Changing Meanings of HIV Infection' in Michael Hurley (ed), *Cultures of Care and Safe Sex amongst HIV Positive Australians* (Australian Research Centre in Sex, Health, and Society 2002)

Beaman L, *Defining Harm: Religious Freedom and the Limits of the Law* (UBC Press 2008)

Benedet J, 'The Sexual Assault of Intoxicated Women' (2010) 22(2) *CJWL* 435

Branch J, 'Derek Boogaard: A Brain Going Bad' *New York Times* (New York, 5 December 2011) <www.nytimes.com/2011/12/06/sports/hockey/derek-boogaard-a-brain-going-bad.html> accessed 30 April 2019

Brazier M, 'Organ Retention and Return: Problems of Consent' (2003) 29 *J Med Eth* 30

Brown W, *States of Injury: Power and Freedom in Late Modernity* (PUP 1995)

———, 'Suffering Rights as Paradoxes' (2000) 7(2) *Constellations* 230

———, *Edgework: Critical Essays on Knowledge and Politics* (PUP 2005)

Butler J and Athanasiou A, *Dispossession: The Performative in the Political* (Polity Press 2013)

Butler J and Spivak GC, *Who Sings the Nation State?: Language, Politics, Belonging* (Seagull 2007)

Cameron E, 'Criminalization of HIV Transmission: Poor Public Health Policy' (2009) 14(2) *HIV/AIDS Pol Law Rev* 63

Cameron E, Burris S and Clayton M, 'HIV is a Virus, Not a Crime: Ten Reasons against Criminal Statutes and Criminal Prosecutions' (2008) 11(7) *J Int AIDS Soc* 1 <www.ncbi.nlm.nih.gov/pmc/articles/PMC2635346/pdf/1758-2652-11-7.pdf> accessed 30 January 2019

Carr H, 'Rational Men and Difficult Women: *R (On the Application of McDonald) v Royal Borough of Kensington and Chelsea* [2011] UKSC 33' (2012) 34(2) *JSWFL* 219

Cohen GA, 'Freedom, Justice, and Capitalism' (1981) 126 *New Left Rev* 3

Conroy S and Cotter A, 'Self-reported Sexual Assault in Canada, 2014 [85-002-X]' *Juristat* (Statistics Canada 2017)

Cowan S, '"Freedom and Capacity to Make a Choice": A Feminist Analysis of Consent in the Criminal Law of Rape' in Vanessa E Munro and Carl F Stychin (eds), *Sexuality and the Law: Feminist Engagements* (Routledge 2007)

———, 'The Trouble with Drink: Intoxication, (In)capacity, and the Evaporation of Consent to Sex' (2008) 41(4) *Akron LR* 899

Craig E, 'Ten Years after *Ewanchuk* The Art of Seduction is Alive and Well: An Examination of the Mistaken Belief in Consent Defence' (2009) 13(3) *CCLR* 247

———, *Putting Trials on Trial: Sexual Assault and the Failure of the Legal Profession* (MQUP 2018)

Cribb R, 'Lawsuit Could Set Precedent about End-of-Life Decision' (*Toronto Star*, 4 September 2010) <www.thestar.com/news/gta/2010/09/04/lawsuit_could_set_precedent_about_endoflife_decisions.html> accessed 29 January 2019

Dej E and Kitty JM, '"Criminalization Creep": A Brief Discussion of the Criminalization of HIV/AIDS Nondisclosure in Canada' (2012) 27(1) *Can J L & Soc* 55

Dixon-Woods M and others, 'Why Do Women Consent to Surgery, Even When They Don't Want to: A Qualitative Study' (2006) 1 *Clin Eth* 153

Downie J and McEwan K, 'The Manitoba College of Physicians and Surgeons Position Statement on Withholding and Withdrawal of Life-Sustaining Treatment (2008): Three Problems and a Solution' (2009) 17(1) *Health LJ* 115

Dunning E, *Sport Matters: Sociological Studies of Sport, Violence, and Civilization* (Routledge 2001)

Farber L, *An Anatomy of Trade in Medieval Writing: Value, Consent, and Community* (Cornell UP 2006)

Farmer L, 'On the Misinterpretation of the *Sexual Offences Act* 2009: *HM Adv v Mutebi*' (*Oblique Intent*, 12 November 2013) <http://obliqueintent.blogspot.com/2013/11/on-misinterpretation-of-sexual-offences.html> accessed 30 January 2019

Fisher JA, 'Coming Soon to a Physician Near You: Medical Neoliberalism and Pharmaceutical Clinical Trials' (2007) 8(1) *Harv Health Pol Rev* 61

———, '"Ready to Recruit" or "Ready to Consent" Populations?: Informed Consent and the Limits of Subject Autonomy' (2007) 13(6) *Qual Inq* 875

———, *Medical Research for Hire: The Political Economy of Pharmaceutical Clinical Trials* (Rutgers 2009)

Foucault M, *Madness and Civilization: A History of Insanity in an Age of Reason* (Richard Howard tr, Vintage 1965)

———, 'The Subject and Power' (1982) 8(4) *Crit Inq* 777

———, *The Birth of Biopolitics: Lectures at the Collège de France 1878–1979* (Michel Senellart ed, Graham Burchell tr, Picador 2008)

Gard M and Meyenn R, 'Boys, Bodies, Pleasure and Pain: Interrogating Contact Sports in Schools' (2000) 5(1) *Sport, Educ & Soc* 19

Gaus G and Courtland SD, 'Liberalism', *The Stanford Encyclopedia of Philosophy* (Spring edn, 2011) <http://plato.stanford.edu/archives/spr2011/entries/liberalism/> accessed 30 April 2019

Goldsworthy T, 'Yes Means Yes: Moving to a Different Model of Consent for Sexual Interactions' (*The Conversation*, 29 January 2018) <https://theconversation.com/yes-means-yes-moving-to-a-different-model-of-consent-for-sexual-interactions-90630> accessed 30 January 2019

Gotell L, 'Rethinking Affirmative Consent in Canadian Sexual Assault Law: Neoliberal Sexual Subjects and Risky Women' (2008) 41(4) *Akron LR* 865

———, 'Canadian Sexual Assault Law: Neoliberalism and the Erosion of Feminist inspired Law Reform' in Clare McGlynn and Vanessa E Munro (eds), *Rethinking Rape Law: International and Comparative Perspectives* (Routledge 2010)

Hanna C, 'Sex is Not a Sport: Consent and Violence in Criminal Law' (2001) 42(2) *BCL Rev* 239

Harvey D, *A Brief History of Neoliberalism* (OUP 2007)

Ingham H, 'Machiavelli and the Interpretation of the Chiron Myth in France' (1982) 45 *JWCI* 217

Jones JCH, Stewart KG and Sunderman R, 'From the Arena into the Streets: Hockey Violence, Economic Incentives, and Public Policy' (2006) 55(2) *Am J Econ & Soc* 231

Jotkowitz AB, Glick SM and Zivotofky AZ, 'The Case of Samuel Golubchuk and the Right to Live' (2010) 10(3) *Am J Bioeth* 50

Kitzinger C and Frith H, '"Just Say No?" The Use of Conversation Analysis in Developing a Feminist Perspective on Sexual Refusal' (1999) 10(3) *D&S* 293

Koch T, 'Care, Compassion, or Cost? Redefining the Basis of Treatment in Ethics and Law' (2011) 39(2) *JLM&E* 130

Kong H, 'For the Love of the Game: Trading Money for Brain Cells' (2013) 2(1) *Miss Sports LR* 115

Lacey N, *Unspeakable Subjects: Feminist Essays in Legal and Social Theory* (Hart 1998)

———, 'In Search of the Responsible Subject: History, Philosophy and Social Sciences in Criminal Law Theory' (2001) 64(3) *MLR* 350

———, 'Responsibility and Modernity in Criminal Law' (2001) 9(3) *J Pol Phil* 249

Lemke T, '"The Birth of Biopolitics": Michel Foucault's lecture at the Collège de France on Neo-liberal Governmentality' (2001) 30(2) *Econ & Soc* 190

———, 'Foucault, Governmentality, and Critique' (2002) 14(3) *Rethinking Marxism* 49

Lindberg T, Campeau P and Campbell M, 'Indigenous Women and Sexual Assault in Canada' in Elizabeth A Sheehy (ed), *Sexual Assault in Canada: Law, Legal Practice & Women's Activism* (University of Ottawa Press 2012)

MacKenzie C and Stoljar N (eds), *Relational Autonomy: Feminist Perspectives on Autonomy, Agency, and the Social Self* (OUP 2000)

MacKinnon CA, *Toward a Feminist Theory of the State* (HUP 1989)

———, 'Defining Rape Internationally: A Comment on *Akayesu*' (2006) 44(3) *Colum J Transnat'l L* 940

Mahony J, 'Judgment Day' *National Post* (3 March 1999) A19

Marcus S, 'Fighting Bodies, Fighting Words: A Theory and Politics of Rape Prevention' in Judith Butler and Joan Scott (eds), *Feminists Theorize the Political* (Routledge 1992)

Mehlman MJ, 'Patient-Physician Relationship in an Era of Scarce Resources: Is There a Duty to Treat?' (1993) 25(2) *Conn L Rev* 349

Meredith P, 'Patient Participation in Decision-Making and Consent to Treatment: The Case of General Surgery' (1993) 15(3) *Soc Health & Illness* 315

Munro VE, 'Constructing Consent: Legislating Freedom and Legitimating Constraint in the Expression of Sexual Autonomy' (2009) 41 *Akron LR* 923

Nauenberg E, 'Beyond the *Golubchuk* Case: The Issue of Intergenerational Trends in Medical Expenditures' (2012) 90(1) *UTMJ* 12

Nedelsky J, 'Reconceiving Autonomy: Sources, Thoughts, and Possibilities' (1989) 1 *Yale J L & Fem* 7

New York State Police, 'Crime Prevention: Date Rape' <www.troopers.ny.gov/Crime_Prevention/Violence/Date_Rape/> accessed 30 January 2019

Norrie A, *Crime, Reason and History: A Critical Introduction to Criminal Law* (3rd edn, CUP 2014)

O'Byrne P, 'Criminal Law and Public Health Practice: Are the Canadian HIV Disclosure Laws an Effective HIV Prevention Strategy?' (2012) 9(1) *Sex Res & Soc Pol* 70

O'Neill DI, Shanley ML and Young IM, *Illusion of Consent: Engaging with Carole Pateman* (Penn State University of Press 2008)

Ong A, *Neoliberalism as Exception: Mutations of Citizenship and Sovereignty* (Duke University Press 2007)

Pateman C, *The Disorder of Women* (Polity Press 1989)

Posner RA, *Sex and Reason* (HUP 1992)

Powell A, 'Amor fati? Gender Habitus and Young People's Negotiation of (Hetero)sexual Consent' (2008) 44(2) *J Soc* 167

Randall M, 'Sexual Assault Law, Credibility, and "Ideal Victims": Consent, Resistance, and Victim Blaming' (2010) 22(2) *CJWL* 397

Read J, 'A Genealogy of Homo-Economicus: Neoliberalism and the Production of Subjectivity' (2009) 6 *Fouc Stud* 25

Rose N, *Governing the Soul: The Shaping of the Private Self* (Routledge 1990)

Rose N and Miller P, 'Political Power Beyond the State: Problematics of Government' (1992) 43(2) *Brit J Soc* 173

Rotenberg C, 'Police-reported Sexual Assaults in Canada, 2009 to 2014: A Statistical Profile [85-002-X]' *Juristat* (Statistics Canada 2017)

Rothschild E, 'Adam Smith and the Invisible Hand' (1994) 84(2) *Am Econ Rev* 319

Ruparelia R, 'Does "No" Mean Reasonable Doubt: Assessing the Impact of *Ewanchuk* on Determinations of Consent' (2006) 25(1–2) *CWS* 167

Sarat A and Culbert JL, *States of Violence: War, Capital Punishment, and Letting Die* (CUP 2009)

Severyn B, 'An Enforcer's Life is a Daily Battle' *Sports Illustrated* (21 September 2011) <www.si.com/nhl/2011/09/21/brent-severynenforcerlife> accessed 29 January 2019

Sheehy EA, 'From Women's Duty to Resist to Men's Duty to Ask: How Far Have We Come?' (2000) 20(3) *CWS* 98

———, 'Judges and the Reasonable Steps Requirement: The Judicial Stance on Perpetration against Unconscious Women' in Elizabeth A Sheehy (ed), *Sexual Assault in Canada: Law, Legal Practice and Women's Activism* (University of Ottawa Press 2012)

Smart B, *Economy, Culture, and Society* (Open University Press 2003)

Spivak GC, *Outside in the Teaching Machine* (Routledge 1993)

Stanko EA, 'Safety Talk: Conceptualizing Women's Risk Assessment as a "Technology of the Self"' (1997) 1(4) *Theo Crim* 479

Stuart D, '*Ewanchuk*: Asserting "No Means No" at the Expense of Fault and Proportionality Principles' (1999) 22 CR (5th) 39

Thompson EP, *Customs in Common* (New Press 1991)

Treanor P, 'Neoliberalism: Origins, Theory, Definition' (Research Paper, Personal Blog, 12 December 2005) <http://web.inter.nl.net/users/Paul.Treanor/neoliberalism.html>

Tyner JA, *Violence in Capitalism: Devaluing in an Age of Responsibility* (University of Nebraska Press 2016)

Vandervort L, 'Honest Beliefs, Credible Lies, and Culpable Awareness: Rhetoric, Inequality, and *Mens Rea* in Sexual Assault' (2004) 42(4) *Osgoode Hall LJ* 625

———, 'Lawful Subversion of the Criminal Justice Process? Judicial, Prosecutorial, and Police Discretion in *Edmondson, Kindrat,* and *Brown*' in Elizabeth A Sheehy (ed), *Sexual Assault in Canada: Law, Legal Practice & Women's Activism* (University of Ottawa Press 2012)

———, 'HIV, Fraud, Non-Disclosure, Consent and a Stark Choice: *Mabior* or Sexual Autonomy?' (2013) 60(2) *CLQ* 301

Vera-Gray F, *The Right Amount of Panic: How Women Trade Freedom for Safety* (Polity 2018)

Wacquant L, *Body & Soul: Notebooks of an Apprentice Boxer* (OUP 2004)

Weber M, *Protestant Ethic and the Spirit of Capitalism* (Talcott Parsons tr, first published 1930, Routledge 2005)

Weinberg SK and Arond H, 'The Occupational Culture of the Boxer' (1952) 57(5) *Am J Soc* 460

Wood EM, *The Origins of Capitalism: A Longer View* (Verso 2002)

——, 'Capitalism's Gravediggers' (*Jacobin*, 5 December 2014) <www.jacobinmag.com/2014/12/capitalisms-gravediggers/> accessed 29 January 2019

Wright EO, 'Foundations of a Neo-Marxist Class Analysis' in Erik Olin Wright (ed), *Approaches to Class Analysis* (CUP 2005)

Wright J, 'Consent and Sexual Violence in Canadian Public Discourse: Reflections on *Ewanchuk*' (2001) 16(2) *Can J L & Soc* 173

Young H, 'Why Withdrawing Life-Sustaining Treatment Should Not Require Rasouli Consent' (2012) 6(2) *MJLH* 54

Conclusion

Margaret Atwood's poem, 'Dream 1: The Bush Garden', offers a dark vision of reaping what is sown. Its last stanzas offer the promise of a fruitful harvest, but not without warning:

> Around my feet
> the strawberries were surging, huge
> and shining
>
> When I bent
> to pick, my hand
> came away red and wet
>
> In the dream I said
> I should have known
> anything planted here
> would come up blood.[1]

Consent might be thought of as legal ground surging with bright and desirable aims. It is meant to be an enactment of personal freedom, a guardian of bodily integrity, and an expression of free will. This vision of consent is difficult to interrogate. Apart from the appeal of these fundamental values, their relationship to consent is something that has been 'put to memory'.[2] Yet, try as it might, the law's attempts to bring consent's promise of autonomy to fruition have not had great yield. Real-life experiences of agreeing to sex, surgery, or a sports contract rarely involve feelings of freedom. Instead, consent is understood as a demand, an imposition, a liability waiver, or a ritualistic 'matter of course'.[3] Patients express feelings of fear and submission when describing the informed consent process with remarkable similarity to women's accounts of unwanted sex, or to the

1 Margaret Atwood, 'Dream 1: The Bush Garden' in *The Journals of Susanna Moodie* (OUP 1970).

2 This is a reference to HLA Hart's description of legal concepts that have an 'open texture'. See 'Analytical Jurisprudence in Mid-Twentieth Century: A Reply to Professor Bodenheimer' (1957) *105 U Pa L Rev* 953.

3 Marwan Habiba and others, 'Women's Accounts of Consenting to Surgery: Is Consent a Quality Problem' (2004) 13(6) *BMJ* 422, 424.

stories told by professional athletes negotiating another contract to shed blood for public sport and spectacle.[4] Players, patients, and women know there are 'rules to the game' and consent is something they are expected to 'go along with'.[5] If this is consent's touted autonomy, it is a rather impoverished freedom.

The previous chapters provide some evidence that, despite the ubiquity of the consent-as-autonomy story, it is a relatively recent conceptualisation. Furthermore, the book's investigations revealed a number of narratives of consent that differed substantially from accounts of personal freedom. Certainly, the diversity of functions assigned to consent lends some credence to the notion that it might mean and do different things than emblemise individual agency. It is used to 'morally transform' wrong acts,[6] to safeguard against liability,[7] to establish the fairness of a trade or agreement,[8] or to cement political legitimacy. With consent, a trespass is a visit, a theft is a gift, an assault is a welcomed touch, and an act of state force is law. Yet, amidst this wide range of operations and explicit commentary on consent's protean nature, the 'common sense' of consent never changes. This book has sought to understand why.

The challenges of interrogating the consent-as-autonomy story stem from its dominance, ahistoricity, and widespread appeal. Autonomy is not simply the most prevalent way of understanding consent, but the *only* way. It is what Joan Scott has called a 'foundational discourse', where certain presumptions or principles are unquestionable, often unstated, and used to 'authorize and legitimize analysis; indeed analysis seems not to be able to proceed without them'.[9] In the case of the consent-as-autonomy story, these underlying values are desirable ideals. Few principles have been as 'compelling and seductive' as personal autonomy.[10] Consent, viewed as a homeland for this idealised form of personal agency, holds an almost sacred place in both law and political theory and its defence is all but automatic for most legal scholars. The narrative of consent-as-autonomy therefore makes for easy listening – so much so that it often 'goes without saying'. There is, however, much to be found in what is left unsaid about consent. The pervasive claim in law about consent's 'ambiguous'

4 Women often distinguish between 'unwanted sex' and 'non-consensual sex', even when describing the coercive circumstances of each. See, for example, Emily J Thomas, Monika Stelzl and Michelle N LaFrance, 'Faking to Finish: Women's Accounts of Feigning Sexual Pleasure to End Unwanted Sex' (2017) 20(3) *Sexualities* 281.

5 Jennifer Katz and Vanessa Tirone, 'Going Along With It: Sexually Coercive Partner Behavior Predicts Dating Women's Compliance with Unwanted Sex' (2010) 16(7) *VAW* 730. See also Habiba (n 3) 424; and Christian Boissinot, 'Fisticuffs: When Do We Say Enough's Enough' in Scott Irving, Normand Baillargeon and Christian Boissinot (eds), *Hockey and Philosophy* (Univeristy of Ottawa Press, 2015).

6 Heidi Hurd, 'The Moral Magic of Consent' (1992) 2(2) *LEG* 121.

7 *Re W (minor) (medical treatment)* [1992] 4 All ER 627.

8 Randy E Barnett, 'A Consent Theory of Contract' (1986) 86 *Colum L Rev* 269.

9 Joan Wallach Scott, 'Experience' in Judith Butler and Joan Wallach Scott (eds), *Feminists Theorize the Political* (Routledge 1992).

10 David Harvey, *A Brief History of Neoliberalism* (OUP 2007).

meaning or 'shifting content'[11] gives consent an elasticity: it can be stretched to allow a wide range of activity or shrunk to prohibit even the simplest of freedoms. The rules of this flexibility, however, are normative, rooted in historically specific values, and the liberties that they referee are not enjoyed equally. The capacity for self-governance is therefore not granted to everyone. And while consent's preconditions and processes have been subject to able critique, consent's underlying promise of autonomy has been left intact.

The current inquiry thus necessitated venturing to contexts where this autonomy narrative might not be heard as easily; where the social and legal relations might differ enough to allow for a disruption in the consent-as-autonomy tale. As a means of framing this methodological route, I employed Foucault's approach of genealogy, where consent could be positioned as an historical artefact, unhinged from some of the presumptions that enable and entrench its contemporary foundation in autonomy. Rather than offer a comprehensive history of consent as a legal concept, this book aimed to provide a 'history of the present' for consent, examining the conditions of possibility for contemporary understandings and uses of consent. As Foucault described this task:

> What I am trying to do is grasp the implicit systems which determine our most familiar behavior without our knowing it. I am trying to find their origin, to show their formation, the constraint they impose upon us; I am therefore trying to place myself at a distance from them and to show how one could escape.[12]

The book began in familiar territory, where the autonomy story was presented in Chapter 1 as the contemporary 'canon' of consent law. This included an examination of the legal requirements for establishing consent to sex, informed consent to medical treatment, and the role of consent in sport, with a focus on the three 'preconditions' of consent that dominate the jurisprudence in criminal law and medical law. These key components of voluntariness, rationality, and knowledge were reviewed within the context of long-standing debates about legal paternalism and the limits to legitimate state interference in the decision-making capacity of 'free' individuals. This review revealed a number of contradictions in the consent-as-autonomy story, where despite proclamations of universality, consent is a highly regulated sphere of freedom that is only available to certain kinds of subjects. While critical legal scholars, communitarian theorists, and feminists have criticised the way these requirements for consent have been applied by the courts, all of these accounts leave the meaning of consent (as autonomy) uncontested. In the latter half of Chapter 1, I argued that this is attributable to the

11 Peter Westen, *The Logic of Consent: The Diversity and Deceptiveness of Consent as a Defense to Criminal Conduct* (Ashgate 2004).

12 John K Simon, 'A Conversation with Michel Foucault' (1971) 38(2) *Partisan Review* 192 as cited by David Garland, 'What is a "History of the Present"? On Foucault's Genealogies and their Critical Preconditions' (2014) 16(4) *Pun & Soc* 365, 369.

'common sense' status that the autonomy story has gained in the modern period. To hear something different, we would need to look in unfamiliar places.

The first of these was explored in Chapter 2, with an examination of the role of consent in the legal regulation of sex in Antiquity. Focussing on three broad classifications of sexual offences in Classical Athens and Rome at the turn of the first century, this chapter demonstrated that in a historical context where personal and political autonomy was a right enjoyed only by free male citizens, consent functioned as a marker and gatekeeper of community membership. 'Ancient' consent served to mark legally recognisable citizens while ensuring their exclusive access to female sexuality (and its procreative ends). This role of consent as a guardian of patrilineal interests also operated to constitute the boundaries of the public domain and those who were entitled to live within it, suggesting the ways in which consent serves as a delimiter of normative subjectivity. Those who were excluded from the state on the basis of non-conforming identities and behaviours demonstrated that, despite an ability to live 'free' from state interference, these ancient outlaws were not intelligible as autonomous, nor were they capable of giving or refusing consent. Instead, their acts of independence lacked both coherence and cultural influence, often serving to further shame, rather than liberate, the non-conforming subject.

The book then turned its focus to the informed consent doctrine in medical law – one of the most secured discourses of autonomy in consent scholarship. In an attempt to find a different story of how consent might have operated within the medical field, I examined the doctor-patient relationship in the so-called 'dark age' of medieval medicine. This allowed a picture of medieval medicine to emerge as a domain controlled by the Christian Church through a strict regulation of access to medical education and its curriculum. Favouring theory over practice, this enterprise of monastic medicine worked to align many of the popular medical treatises of the ancient period (such as the works of Galen and Hippocrates) with a Christian ethic. This was aided by the theological epistemology that was prevalent during the medieval period and which fostered an explanation for health and sickness that was rooted in divine intervention. If the ill sought healing, they would need to find it in God. How might this view have influenced the medieval doctor-patient relationship and the codes of ethics through which physicians held themselves to account? The medieval physician was an agent of God. This, coupled with other medieval understandings of consent in religious conversion cases, marriage formation, and trade and commerce, provided an understanding of consent within the medical context of the Middle Ages as a form of submission (to God). I argued in the conclusion to Chapter 3 that this was effected through a strict regime of self-management, itself enforced by community norms and standards – not unlike contemporary regimes of patient self-care that operate today.

Self-supervision also arose in Chapter 4 through an investigation of the role of consent in establishing legal and illegal forms of bodily harm, and a focus on the use of the criminal law to regulate violence in sports. In these cases, the victim is held to have consented to the injury by agreeing to play the game, provided the harm (and the game) is deemed reasonable and socially useful.

The modern sports context demonstrates that when these limits are defined using capitalist logics, 'harm' emerges as a misuse of body capital. Consent, rather than an act of agency, is made a license for corporeal commodification (that can be revoked when used for the 'wrong' ends). The criminal law's reliance on a 'public interest' standard thus produces a normative framework for players in which subjecting the body to high-risk violence in pursuit of social, cultural, and economic capital is both rational and *good*. What is more, the exploitive and coercive conditions that influence athletes' decisions to 'play through the pain' are concealed by a discourse of risk management (and voluntary assumption of those risks) that is enabled and entrenched by the individualism at the heart of consent's autonomy narrative.

My efforts in Chapter 5 were to demonstrate how criminal and medical law engage in the same arguments of social utility and risk management when considering the availability of consent. I argued that the ahistorical status of capitalism contributes to the neoliberal definitions of the 'self' that have been naturalised through the consent-as-autonomy story, enabling the history of consent as a form of submission (and its modern-day remnants) to remain hidden from view. The contemporary subject enjoys a 'freedom' to consent, provided her acts and choices ultimately serve a neoliberal understanding of the 'common good'. This offers a view of consent-as-license to regulated uses of the body.[13] Licensing has been recognised by some scholars to be a means through which self-governing bodies are created, 'allow[ing] governments to ensure that certain spaces, activities and people are under constant surveillance and are subject to immediate disciplinary measures' without the appearance of state interference.[14] This highlights a number of important observations about the modern association of consent with autonomy.

The first of these observations lies in one of the key objectives of the neoliberal state. Akin to the laissez-faire doctrine of classic liberal theory, neoliberal rationality presents itself as ahistorical and inevitable. It is merely the result of leaving citizens to make their own decisions. The consent-as-autonomy story enables a particularly disciplined form of corporeal commodification, as seen in the case law that addresses bodily harm in criminal and medical contexts. This use of the body is understood through a lens of 'choice', thus removing any contemplation of the state's interest or directive power in this economic constitution of subjectivity and its bodily deployment. The effect is to position neoliberal rationality as the 'natural' outcome of leaving citizens to self-govern, moving the conditions of possibility for a neoliberal order beyond the frame of inquiry and contestation.

Second, this corporeal commodification is 'naturalised' through an understanding of consent-as-autonomy. The result is the transfer of responsibility for the risks and harms that result from this economic calculus and its 'use' of human capital from the state to the private citizen. This masks the inequalities

13 See, for instance, Michelle J Anderson, 'From Chastity Requirement to Sexuality License: Sexual Consent and a New Rape Shield Law' (2002) 70(1) *Geo Wash L Rev* 51.

14 Mariana Valverde, 'Police Science, British Style: Pub Licensing and Knowledges of Urban Disorder' (2003) 32(2) *Econ & Soc* 234, 236.

and coercive circumstances that limit and direct individual choice in ways that marginalise certain subjects and behaviours while privileging others. For Wendy Brown, this takes the notion of self-responsibility to new heights, where 'the rationally calculating individual bears full responsibility for the consequences of his or her action no matter how severe the constraints on this action'.[15] The consent-as-autonomy story thus acts to enforce what Wacquant has described as a 'laissez faire et laissez passer' model for bodily harm and self-commodification which, while seemingly non-invasive for the 'dominant class' and its idealised subjectivities, 'turns out to be paternalist and intrusive for the subaltern'.[16] This is a key component to the common 'unfortunate but not unfair' legal argument used to recognise inequality in opportunity or circumstance while denying state and social responsibility for these conditions of 'poor fortune'.[17] Where one can be said to have 'chosen' an act (via consent), the consequences – however unfair or reproachable – are the individual's to bear. The social or economic conditions which might have influenced this choice are not relevant factors in this equation. Take, for instance, the arguments put forward by the Canadian government in the Supreme Court of Canada's 2013 case assessing the constitutionality of the *Criminal Code*'s prostitution prohibition provisions.[18] In a judgment declaring the provisions to be invalid, the Supreme Court summarised one of the government's central claims as follows:

> The Attorneys General of Canada and Ontario argue that prostitutes choose to engage in an inherently risky activity. They can avoid both the risk inherent in prostitution and any increased risk that the laws impose simply by choosing not to engage in this activity. They say that choice — and not the law — is the real cause of their injury.[19]

Although the Supreme Court dismisses these arguments, they are a poignant example of how the discourse of 'choice' can elide the socio-political and personal conditions that might constrain or unduly influence a decision to engage in

15 Brown offers the examples of a 'lack of skills, education, and child care in a period of high unemployment and limited welfare benefits'. Wendy Brown, *Edgework: Critical Essays on Knowledge and Politics* (PUP 2005) 42.

16 Loïc Wacquant, 'Three Steps to a Historical Anthropology of Actually Existing Neoliberalism' (2012) 20 *Soc Anth* 66, 74.

17 The comments made by the American bioethicist, Tristram Englehardt, Jr at the 1984 Shattuck Lecture, are a good example: 'Differences in need, both medical and financial, must be recognized as unfortunate … However, it must be understood that though unfortunate circumstances are always grounds for praiseworthy charity, they do not always provide grounds, by that fact, for redrawing the line between the circumstances we will count as unfortunate but not unfair and those we will count as unfortunate and unfair', H Tristram Englehardt, 'Allocating Scarce Medical Resources and the Availability of Organ Transplantation: Some Moral Presuppositions' (1984) 311 *NE J Med* 66, 71.

18 *Canada (AG) v Bedford*, 2013 SCC 72.

19 *Bedford* (n 18) [79].

sex work.[20] The 'consensual' participation of professional athletes in violence that is configured as 'part of the game' is another case in point, particularly given the circumstances which influence these players' participation and the cultural norms which construct this aggression and its risks as both reasonable and desirable.

Third, the indivisible association of consent with autonomy allows it to benefit from the myth of liberalism's non-interference principle. Chapters 4 and 5 demonstrated the ways in which consent operates in the contemporary context as a means of regulating the methods of and limits to corporeal commodification. Consent, although positioned as a liberty or 'right', is restricted to those who conform to dominant norms of idealised subjectivity. Sexual agency, for instance, is available only to those who conform to cultural understandings of the 'good girl'. The risky behaviours of the rape complainant who drinks too much, walks alone at night, or dresses 'like a slut' are used to discredit and deny her capacity to (refuse) consent.[21] Likewise, consent is made unavailable to the 'bad patient' who asks too many questions or wants to discuss 'unreasonable' therapies or religious beliefs; or to the lazy or wimpy athlete who, after failing to play by the (written and unwritten) rules of the game, deserves what he gets. Akin to the medieval story of consent explored in Chapter 3, the power to consent (or withhold it) is available only to those who can align themselves with the model of the 'good patient', the 'good player', or the 'good girl'. When consent operates in this manner, the disciplinary measures of neoliberal rationality are made invisible, leaving 'liberal sensibilities' unoffended. This is the work of the autonomy narrative, its mythic promise of non-interference stated rather succinctly by Don Herzog:

> The liberal state doesn't tell us how to lead our lives. It doesn't insist that we be devoted to any one religion; indeed it is indifferent to whether we're religious at all. It doesn't instruct us on the merits of competing life plans, on whether it's better to pursue fame, money, or a nondescript happiness. Provided we don't harm others, the liberal state allows us to pursue our proudest aspirations – or to bask mindlessly in cathode rays emanating from our television sets. It is silent on a host of issues.[22]

The state *does*, however, have quite a lot to say about how citizens should lead their lives, and consent plays a crucial role in establishing what these normative

20 This is made explicit in a subsequent paragraph in the judgment where the Court states: 'Whether because of financial desperation, drug addictions, mental illness, or compulsion from pimps, [sex workers] often have little choice but to sell their bodies for money. Realistically, while they may retain some minimal power of choice – what the Attorney General of Canada called "constrained choice" – these are not people who can be said to be truly "choosing" a risky line of business' (n 14) [86]. Jessica Elliott explores this same argument within the context of human trafficking in her book, *The Role of Consent in Human Trafficking* (Routledge 2014).

21 Joetta L Carr, 'The SlutWalk Movement: A Study in Transnational Feminist Activism' (2013) 4 *J Fem Sch* 24.

22 Don Herzog, *Happy Slaves: A Critique of Consent Theory* (UCHIP 1989) 148.

ways of being and acting are. Yet, these prescriptions are neither visible nor subject to interrogation through the consent-as-autonomy story. When consent is configured as individual agency, there is little room to examine the state's role (or its interests) in defining and policing the 'unwritten rules' that govern its use. This has certainly been of benefit to the neoliberal order. As Judith Butler has observed:

> This presumption in law of a discrete individual with perspicacious and deliberate autonomy was crucial to all forms of economic contract, and to the possibility of devising and implementing laws that held individuals accountable for contracted goods and services, or indeed for criminal deeds. The legal apparatus that supported the economic functioning of the market and a regime of criminal law required an operative idea of the fully volitional subject at the same time that it made provisions for those who were less than competent to understand or honor a civil contract.[23]

Some legal scholars have already called for a displacement of consent in statutory treatments of sexual assault, where it is argued that an emphasis on the presence of coercion[24] or desire[25] might operate in more equitable ways. Bioethicists maintain that a redefinition of informed consent as an ongoing process, rather than a moment of decision or choice, is needed.[26] And many legal commentators have begun to suggest that sports violence is more aptly addressed in civil actions than through the defence of consent in criminal law. Yet, what many of these reform strategies have in common is an uninterrogated commitment to the consent-as-autonomy story.

One of the book's central discoveries has been a much longer and richer history of consent than contemporary scholarship suggests this 'twentieth-century doctrine' should have. Moreover, very little of it is about personal agency. Importantly, these alternate roles of consent – as a marker of cultural belonging, a right of access to female sexuality, a license to self-commodification, and a submission to dominant (and often oppressive) norms of intelligibility – continue to operate today, albeit under the rubric of autonomy. The notion of freedom as not just an ideal but also an ideology has been amply explored within critical legal scholarship for decades. While understanding one's role in

23 Judith Butler, 'Sexual Consent: Some Thoughts on Psychoanalysis and the Law' (2011) 21(2) *Colum J Gen & L* 3, 17.

24 See Catharine MacKinnon, 'Defining Rape Internationally: A Comment on *Akayesu*' (2006) 44(3) *Colum J Transnat'l L* 940; Katie O'Byrne, 'Beyond Consent: Conceptualising Sexual Assault in International Criminal Law' (2011) 11(3) *Int CLR* 495.

25 Lani Anne Remick, 'Read Her Lips: An Argument for a Verbal Consent Standard in Rape' (1993) 141(3) *U Pa L Rev* 1103; Michael Gill, *Already Doing It: Intellectual Disability and Sexual Agency* (U Minnesota Press 2015); Michelle Fine, 'Sexuality, Schooling, and Adolescent Females: The Missing Discourse of Desire' (1988) 58(1) *Harv Educ Rev* 29.

26 See, for example, Lorne E Rozovsky and Fay A Rozovsky, *The Canadian Law of Consent to Treatment* (3rd edn, Butterworths 2003)

a social or political order in terms of submission was prevalent in pre-modern times, modernity has been characterised by a ubiquitous belief in freedom.[27] The historical contexts explored in Chapters 2 and 3 make it a bit easier to identify consent's role in producing unequal power relations and compulsory subjectivities. Chapters 4 and 5, however, reveal a contemporary narrative of consent-as-submission, (albeit to a neoliberal order rather than a divine one). The central difference between these pre-modern and modern conceptions of consent is in the latter's commitment to freedom, to understanding everything – even submission – as an act of autonomy. The 'problem' with consent, then, is not in how it is defined, communicated, or limited, but rather its indivisible, unquestionable association with autonomy, itself a relic of a particular historical moment where the commodification of the body and the individualisation of responsibility were embedded into the 'common sense'. The alternative views of consent offered in this book provide an opportunity to contest this.

The way forward, then, may not be in redefinition or reinvention projects, but rather in what Alan Norrie has suggested is a call for the law to be more honest, even if that means having to be a bit 'meaner'.[28] Consent's freedom fable may be its most true (and dangerous) magic. Dispelling it will require acknowledging the unwritten codes that make saying 'no' to unwanted sex unintelligible. It will entail examining the social ethos that renders pain-for-profit desirable and naming the unspoken rules about 'desirable' human life. Anything planted in consent is likely to remain bloodied until then. Hope, as Audre Lorde reminds us, may not be in breaking new ground, but in revisiting the familiar:

> Sometimes we drug ourselves with dreams of new ideas … But there are no new ideas still waiting in the wings to save us as women, as human. There are only old and forgotten ones, new combinations, extrapolations and recognitions from within ourselves, along with the renewed courage to try them out.[29]

Bibliography

Table of cases

Canada (AG) v Bedford 2013 SCC 72
Re W (minor) (medical treatment) [1992] 4 All ER 627

27 Alan Wolfe, *Moral Freedom: The Search for Virtue in a World of Choice* (Norton 2002).

28 Norrie is referring to instances of mistaken self-defence and how a particular, 'less inclusive' view of citizenship underlies their judicial interpretation. His suggestion is that a more 'honest' acknowledgement of these political and moral components of the defence's legal treatment might be 'meaner' (in that it would explicitly acknowledge the boundaries of socio-cultural membership) but less hypocritical. Determinations of consenting 'capacity' or 'validity' could arguably be put to the same task. See Alan Norrie, 'The Problem of Mistaken Self-Defense: Citizenship, Chiasmus, and Legal Form' (2010) 13 *NCLR* 357, 376.

29 Audre Lorde, 'Poetry is Not a Luxury' in *Sister Outsider: Essays and Speeches* (first published 1984, Crossing Press 2007) 38.

Secondary sources

Anderson MJ, 'From Chastity Requirement to Sexuality License: Sexual Consent and a New Rape Shield Law' (2002) 70(1) *Geo Wash L Rev* 51
Atwood M, *The Journals of Susanna Moodie* (OUP 1970)
Barnett RE, 'A Consent Theory of Contract' (1986) 86 *Colum L Rev* 269
Boissinot C, 'Fisticuffs: When Do We Say Enough's Enough' in Scott Irving, Normand Baillargeon, Christian Boissinot (eds), *Hockey and Philosophy* (University of Ottawa Press 2015)
Brown W, *Edgework: Critical Essays on Knowledge and Politics* (PUP 2005)
Butler J, 'Sexual Consent: Some Thoughts on Psychoanalysis and the Law' (2011) 21(2) *Colum J Gen & L* 3
Carr JL, 'The SlutWalk Movement: A Study in Transnational Feminist Activism' (2013) 4 *J Fem Sch* 24
Elliott J, *The Role of Consent in Human Trafficking* (Routledge 2014)
Englehardt HT, 'Allocating Scarce Medical Resources and the Availability of Organ Transplantation: Some Moral Presuppositions' (1984) 311 *NE J Med* 66
Fine M, 'Sexuality, Schooling, and Adolescent Females: The Missing Discourse of Desire' (1988) 58(1) *Harv Educ Rev* 29
Garland D, 'What is a "History of the Present"? On Foucault's Genealogies and their Critical Preconditions' (2014) 16(4) *Pun & Soc* 365
Gill M, *Already Doing It: Intellectual Disability and Sexual Agency* (University of Minnesota Press 2015)
Habiba M and others, 'Women's Accounts of Consenting to Surgery: Is Consent a Quality Problem' (2004) 13(6) *BMJ* 422
Hart HLA, 'Analytical Jurisprudence in Mid-Twentieth Century: A Reply to Professor Bodenheimer' (1957) 105 *U Pa L Rev* 953
Harvey D, *A Brief History of Neoliberalism* (OUP 2007)
Herzog D, *Happy Slaves: A Critique of Consent Theory* (UCHIP 1989)
Hurd H, 'The Moral Magic of Consent' (1992) 2(2) *LEG* 121
Katz J and Tirone V, 'Going Along With It: Sexually Coercive Partner Behavior Predicts Dating Women's Compliance with Unwanted Sex' (2010) 16(7) *VAW* 730
Lorde A, *Sister Outsider: Essays and Speeches* (first published 1984, Crossing Press 2007)
MacKinnon CA, 'Defining Rape Internationally: A Comment on *Akayesu*' (2006) 44(3) *Colum J Transnat'l L* 940
Norrie A, 'The Problem of Mistaken Self-Defense: Citizenship, Chiasmus, and Legal Form' (2010) 13 *NCLR* 357
O'Byrne K, 'Beyond Consent: Conceptualising Sexual Assault in International Criminal Law' (2011) 11(3) *Int CLR* 495
Remick LA, 'Read Her Lips: An Argument for a Verbal Consent Standard in Rape' (1993) 141(3) *U Pa L Rev* 1103
Rozovsky LE and Rozovsky FA, *The Canadian Law of Consent to Treatment* (3rd edn, Butterworths 2003)
Scott JW, 'Experience' in Judith Butler and Joan Wallach Scott (eds), *Feminists Theorize the Political* (Routledge 1992)
Simon JK, 'A Conversation with Michel Foucault' (1971) 38(2) *Partisan Review* 192
Thomas EJ, Stelzl M and LaFrance MN, 'Faking to Finish: Women's Accounts of Feigning Sexual Pleasure to End Unwanted Sex' (2017) 20(3) *Sexualities* 281

Valverde M, 'Police Science, British Style: Pub Licensing and Knowledges of Urban Disorder' (2003) 32(2) *Econ & Soc* 234

Wacquant L, 'Three Steps to a Historical Anthropology of Actually Existing Neoliberalism' (2012) 20 *Soc Anth* 66

Westen P, *The Logic of Consent: The Diversity and Deceptiveness of Consent as a Defense to Criminal Conduct* (Routledge 2004)

Wolfe A, *Moral Freedom: The Search for Virtue in a World of Choice* (Norton 2002)

Index

For Product Safety Concerns and Information please contact our EU representative GPSR@taylorandfrancis.com
Taylor & Francis Verlag GmbH, Kaufingerstraße 24, 80331 München, Germany

www.ingramcontent.com/pod-product-compliance
Ingram Content Group UK Ltd.
Pitfield, Milton Keynes, MK11 3LW, UK
UKHW011005180926
475701UK00004B/569
9780367785635